About the Companion CD

The CD that comes with this book contains tools to help you study for the CNA for NetWare 4 test:

- The CNA Study Guide for NetWare 4 Practice Test, which gives you 120 sample test questions to hone your test-taking abilities for the CNA text.

- The Micro House Technical Library Encyclopedia of I/O Cards (complete version), which allows you explore in depth how the MTL works.

- The Micro House Technical Library (demonstration version), which allows you to access the first few layers of every section of the MTL.

- The Novell Education Certification Sampler, the graphical, Windows-based testing program distributed by Novell Education.

- The Complete 801 Self Test from Big Red Self Test. This special version contains an expanded Service and Support section, providing you with extra study material for Novell Education's most practical exam.

- The CNE Test Master demo from PC Age, Inc., which provides 30 test questions for each of the six required CNE-4 tests and for the TCP/IP elective. Use the 4.1 Administration demo test to assess your knowledge for the CNA test and the other demo tests for CNE preparation.

Installing the CNA Practice Test

To install the CNA Study Guide for NetWare 4 Practice Test:

- Display the Run dialog box (in Windows 95, choose Start ➤ Run; in Windows 3.1*x*, choose File ➤ Run from Program Manager). Enter *cd_drive*:\cnatest\setup, where *cd_drive* is the drive letter assigned to your CD-ROM drive (for example, d:\cnatest\setup or e:\cnatest\setup), and choose OK.

- In Windows 95, open an Explorer or My Computer window for your CD-ROM drive, change to the CNATEST folder, and double-click on SETUP.EXE.

- In Windows 3.1*x* File Manager, display the contents of your CD-ROM drive, change to the CNATEST directory, and double-click on SETUP.EXE.

To run the CNA Study Guide for NetWare 4 Practice Test:

- in Windows 3.1*x*, double-click on its icon.

- in Windows 95, choose Start ➤ Programs ➤ CNA Study Guide for NetWare 4 ➤ CNA Practice Test.

(continued on the inside back cover)

The CNA^{CLM} Study Guide for NetWare® 4

The CNA^{CLM} Study Guide for NetWare® 4

Michael Moncur
James Chellis
with James Chavez

NETWORK PRESS®
SYBEX

San Francisco ■ Paris ■ Düsseldorf ■ Soest

Acquisitions Manager: Kristine Plachy
Associate Publisher: Steve Sayre
Developmental Editor: Guy Hart-Davis
Editor: June Waldman
Project Editor: Neil Edde
Technical Editor: Dave Kearns
Desktop Publisher: Susan Glinert
Production Coordinator: Kim Askew-Qasem
Technical Illustrator: Cuong Le
Indexer: Ted Laux
Cover Designer: Archer Design
Cover Photographer: Olynn Saville

SYBEX is a registered trademark of SYBEX Inc.

Network Press and the Network Press logo are trademarks of SYBEX Inc.

TRADEMARKS: SYBEX has attempted throughout this book to distinguish proprietary trademarks from descriptive terms by following the capitalization style used by the manufacturer.

This book is intended to provide accurate and authoritative information with regard to the subject matter covered. It is sold with the understanding that the publisher is not engaged in offering legal or other professional services. The publisher assumes no liability or responsibility for loss or damages arising from the information contained in this book or from the use of the disks and programs that accompany it. The publisher is not responsible for verifying current requirements for professional certification programs. It is the responsibility of the customer to consult with the appropriate program sponsor to verify actual course or professional program requirements.

Library of Congress Card Number: 96-67502
ISBN: 0-7821-1882-8

Manufactured in the United States of America

10 9 8 7 6 5 4 3

We dedicate this book to Laura, Sibylla, and our families and friends.

Acknowledgments

W E WOULD LIKE TO THANK the following people at Network Press, whose expertise and professionalism made the development of this book proceed with the utmost efficiency: Developmental Editor Guy Hart-Davis, Editor June Waldman, Project Editor Neil Edde, Technical Editor Dave Kearns, Desktop Publisher Susan Glinert, Production Coordinator Kim Askew-Qasem, Production Liaisons Elsie Yim and Scott McDonald, Veronica Eddy, and Kristine Plachy.

Michael Moncur: I would like to thank my wife, Laura, and my parents, Gary and Susan Moncur, for their support during this project. Thanks also go to the rest of my family and my friends, particularly Chuck Perkins, Cory Storm, Robert Parsons, Matthew Strebe, and Dylan Winslow.

James Chellis: Thanks to my family—Dad, Kiki, Mary Jo, Gayle, David, Paul, Aaron, Ray, and Bill—as well as my friends, especially Sibylla, Peter, Travis, John, Jairo, Bo, Heidi, Xtian, Sascha, Rune, Ishi, Oscar, Stuart, Baillee, Jim H., the Arica community, Kewei, Jin, Maia, and everyone working with EdgeTek.

Hardware Used for this Book

WE RELIED ON THE FOLLOWING equipment during our research for this book:

Centre Technologies

Pentium 100 Server

64 MB RAM

Four 4.3 GB drives duplexed and mirrored

2 Adaptec 2940 SCSI controller cards

3Com combo NIC

Toshiba Quad CD ROM

We were very fortunate that Centre Technologies allowed us to center our network around this powerhouse server. This machine is the same one chosen by Novell for its reseller communication system (minus the 64 modems Novell has on its unit). Needless to say, it performed flawlessly.

Gateway 2000 provided us with a Liberty notebook with which we experimented heavily. The fact that we had a portable computer with the power to act as both a remote client and server gave us the ability to test certain WAN capabilities of NetWare 4. The machine, which performed perfectly, was as follows:

Gateway 2000 Liberty

DX4-100 Notebook

24 MB RAM

720 MB HDD

EtherLink III 10Base-T PCMCIA adapter

We also relied upon several Pentium and 486 clone computers for our network. They were generally well-behaved, too. We'd like to thank Gateway 2000 and Centre Technologies for all of their help.

Contents at a Glance

Table of Contents

Introduction

SO YOU'VE DECIDED TO become a Certified Novell Administrator for NetWare! That's a smart career move—the demand for professionals who know how to work with Novell NetWare continues to climb impressively and Novell Education's CNA/CNE program is the most successful professional certification program in the computer industry today. The good news is that the CNA credential, which is widely respected in the networking industry, takes only a small fraction of the effort required for the CNE credential. With the right information (and preferably a little practice), you can quickly and easily pass the CNA exam and attain CNA certification.

In this book, we will show you the ins and outs of Novell's latest and greatest network operating system—NetWare 4.1. We'll show you what you need to know to manage a NetWare 4.1 network, and we'll give you the information you need to pass the CNA exam.

Should You Buy This Book?

You're standing in the bookstore with this book in your hand. Should you buy it?

YES—if you want to attain the latest CNA certification for NetWare 4. Whether you are seeking your first Novell credential or you simply want to upgrade your certification to the latest levels, this book is for you. This book gives you an affordable, efficient means of learning NetWare 4 and preparing for the CNA for NetWare 4 certification exam.

YES—if you want to learn about networking and about Novell NetWare 4. This book provides an introduction to computers and computer networking, as well as an in-depth exploration of Novell's latest version of its NetWare product—the most popular network operating system in the world. Whether you are a beginner trying to break into this complex but lucrative field or an accomplished network professional interested in expanding your understanding, this book will provide you with important and detailed information.

YES—if you are with a training company, since this book offers the best alternative to the expensive Novell Education NetWare 4.1 Administration training manual.

NO—if you are really interested in Windows NT and picked up this book by accident! (We do talk about NT, though, in case you're interested.)

What Does This Book Cover?

This book covers everything you need for the NetWare 4.1 CNA exam, and much more. To be more specific, the information presented in this book can help you in two distinct areas:

- The world of Novell Education, with its unique perspective on how things are and what you should know about networking

- The real world, where tough demands on your time and energy require you to focus on only the most important information

This book contains not only all the information you need to sail through the NetWare 4.1 CNA exam but also the information that will enable you to manage actual networks under real-world conditions. We know that you don't want exam-cram materials that will be of little use to you once you've taken the exam, so we've packed this book with information that will genuinely help you in your work with NetWare networks before and after you take the exam. We've presented everything you need to know in a logical and clearly accessible format, adding extra information and examples wherever they will help.

How Do You Become a CNA?

You need pass only one exam to become a CNA. Anyone can take the exam. The exam is a combination of multiple choice and interactive questions. The interactive questions give you a simulated NetWare 4.1 interface and require you to complete certain tasks (which we cover in this book). Novell's exams are administered by Drake Prometric testing centers and Sylvan Technology Centers. At the time of writing, the cost of the exam is $85. For more information on Drake testing, you can reach Drake at 1-800-RED-EXAM; you can reach Sylvan at 1-800-RED-TEST. Both offer the same exam and charge the same price. Choose the location nearest you.

How to Use This Book

This book is organized in four parts. If you want to make sure you have an in-depth understanding of NetWare 4.1 management, read all four sections. Part 2 covers what you need to understand for the CNA exam. The best way to prepare for the exam is as follows:

- Study each chapter of the second part carefully, making sure that you fully understand the information. If possible, practice using what you've learned on a network.

- Take the practice exam related to that chapter. (The answers to the practice exam questions are located in Appendix A.)

- Note which questions of the practice exam you did not answer correctly and study those sections of the book again.

- Take and pass the real CNA exam.

If you prefer to learn in a classroom setting, you have many options. Both Novell-authorized and independent training are widely available. A free training referral service, such as EdgeTek (1-800-800-1NET) can help you determine what resources are available in your area.

Having access to a NetWare 4.1 network on which to practice is definitely an advantage in the process of preparing for the exam. If you are practicing on a network used by others, be sure that you do not try anything that may affect their data in any way.

Consider setting up a practice network to help you prepare for the exam. You can obtain a two-user license for NetWare 4.1 inexpensively from various sources; some networking companies and associations even include them as special offers. A server and a single workstation will function well for most exercises. You may also want to consider running your practice network using OS/2, under which one computer can serve as a client and a server simultaneously.

The following pages contain a great deal of information. To learn all of this you will need to study regularly and with discipline. Try to set aside the same time every day to study and select a comfortable and quiet place in which to do it. If you work hard, you will be surprised at how quickly you can learn this material. Good luck!

Conventions Used in this Book

Where possible, we have tried to make the information clear and accessible by including Notes, Tips, and Warnings based on our personal experiences in the field of networking. Each has a special margin icon and is set off in special type.

Notes provide helpful asides, reminders, and bits of information that deserve special attention.

Tips provide information that will make the current task easier. Tips include shortcuts and alternative ways to perform a task.

Read any Warnings, so you can avert a possible disaster. The Warnings will help you avoid making mistakes that could require a tremendous effort to correct.

What's on the CD?

On the CD that comes with this book, you will find a Windows-based test-preparation program. It includes over 100 questions and answers to help you prepare for the NetWare 4.1 CNA exam.

Be sure that you really understand the questions and answers. If there is anything you don't understand, go back to the book and study the relevant chapters carefully. The testing program is an excellent way to help make sure that you have thoroughly assimilated the material in this book.

For your further reference, we have included a demonstration copy of the Micro House Technical Library, the authoritative guide to computer hardware specifications and configurations. This copy includes the entire I/O library.

If you are planning to pursue your CNE-4 certification after obtaining your CNA, you'll be happy to see that we've provided demo versions of two leading CNE testing programs—the Big Red Self Tests and PC Age's CNE

TestMaster. These testing programs also contain an additional 50 questions related to the CNA exam for NetWare 4.

How to Contact the Authors

Here's how to contact Michael Moncur and James Chellis:

- Michael Moncur

  Internet: mgm@xmission.com

  CompuServe: 102516,224

  World Wide Web: http://www.xmission.com/~mgm/

- James Chellis

  Internet: jchellis@well.com

  CompuServe: 76723,3471

Computer and Network Fundamentals

PART

I

An Introduction to Networking

THIS BOOK FOCUSES intensely upon one very important approach to computer networking: Novell's NetWare 4.1. But before we plunge into the world of NetWare 4.1, let's look at the basic components and the general types of networks.

What Is a Network?

IN ITS SIMPLEST FORM, a network is a group of computers that are connected together in some fashion. Wiring allows the separate computers to communicate with one another; share files, printers, and other resources; and communicate with mainframe computers and larger networks.

In order to manage communications over a network, several things are necessary:

- One or more *workstations*. The workstations are the computers where the users of the network do their work.

- A *network board* for each workstation. Since a typical PC doesn't have a built-in network connection, the network board acts as an interface between the PC and the network.

- *Peripherals*. These are the devices other than computers that are part of a network, such as printers, tape backup devices, and modems.

- A *communications medium* for network signals to travel across. This is a fancy term for the actual connections between the computers—the heart of the network itself—and can include cable as well as wireless media, such as radio or microwaves.

■ One or more *servers*. A server is a specialized machine that acts as a host for the other computers or workstations. (One type of network, called a peer-to-peer network, however, does not use specialized servers.)

A typical network including all of these components is shown in Figure 1.1. Not all networks look like this one, of course. Although the components are basically the same, an infinite number of combinations is possible. The components used in a network depend on the needs of the users of the network and the company's budget.

Because of the complexity of networks, one more component is necessary: a *network administrator,* or an expert who knows all of the details of the network—how it works, how to keep it running smoothly, and how to solve problems when they occur. By the time you make it to the end of this book, you'll be well on your way to becoming an expert.

Let's take a closer look at each of the network components.

FIGURE 1.1
A typical network includes a server, workstations, wiring, and peripherals.

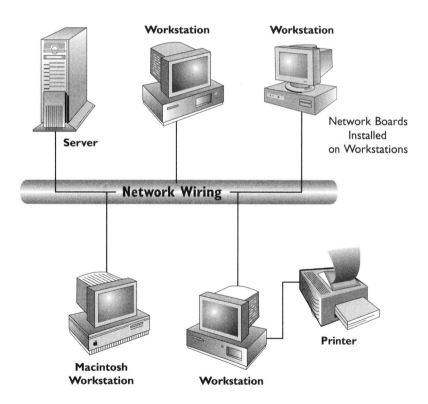

The Server

The network server acts as a host for the workstations. On the outside, the server often looks exactly like a workstation. In the case of a NetWare server, the server is an ordinary IBM-compatible PC with a 386, 486, Pentium, or better microprocessor. However, that's where the similarity ends.

The server runs a specialized piece of software called the *network operating system*, or NOS for short. The NOS is what makes a PC into a server. This software provides resources to the workstations. As you might have guessed, this book will focus on one particular NOS: NetWare 4.1. You'll learn more about the benefits of NetWare and other NOS choices, as well as the requirements for a NetWare 4.1 server, later in this chapter.

Because one of the main functions of a network server is to provide file-sharing services, the server is commonly referred to as a file server. *The keyboard and screen of the server PC are referred to as the* server console.

Workstations

A workstation is any computer that has a connection to the server. Workstations request resources from the server and exchange information with it. Workstations are also referred to as *clients*. Because the network revolves around the concept of clients communicating with servers, this type of network is called a *client-server* network.

The workstation is where users of the network do their work, using all types of software, including applications such as word processors, spreadsheets, and databases. The workstation runs *network client software,* which is the link between the workstation and the network and uses the network board installed in the workstation to communicate with the network.

The types of workstations supported depend on the NOS. NetWare 4.1 can support a wide variety of clients.

Although the server requires a 386 or higher processor, a wide range of IBM-compatible PCs can work as NetWare workstations—from the most powerful Pentium or Pentium Pro (aka P6) to the vintage-1975, 8088-based machine lurking in the corner of your basement. Of course, in order to enjoy the full benefits of NetWare 4.1, you should use one of the more recent machines. NetWare supports PCs running a variety of operating systems:

- Disk Operating System (DOS), including Microsoft MS-DOS, IBM's PC DOS, and Novell DOS.

- OS/2, IBM's graphical operating system, including version 3 (Warp) and older versions.

- Microsoft Windows 3.11 that runs under DOS and uses the DOS client software.

- Microsoft Windows 95 that uses a new 32-bit client. This software, called Client32, also supports older versions of Windows and DOS.

NetWare 4.1 provides the same support for Apple Macintosh and Macintosh-compatible machines as it does for PCs. Client software is available for older machines, but you will need Apple's System 7.0 or newer operating system in order to take full advantage of NetWare 4.1.

UNIX machines can also serve as NetWare 4.1 workstations.

Network Boards

The server and each workstation use a network board (also called a *network interface card* or NIC) to communicate with the network. In the case of a PC, the network card plugs into the ISA, VESA, EISA, or PCI slot. The back of the card has a connector that connects to the network cabling. Credit card-size PC-Card versions of network cards make it possible to connect notebook and hand-held machines to the network.

Network boards are not available from Novell, and they don't come with NetWare. You purchase them from a computer dealer. A wide variety of network boards are available from hundreds of manufacturers, including Intel, 3COM, and SMC. These days, it is becoming common to purchase PCs with network cards already installed.

In order to use the network card, you need a *network driver* (also called a *LAN driver*) for the workstation or server. The network driver is a specialized piece of software that works with the NetWare client or server software and knows how to communicate with that particular board. The network driver you need may not come with NetWare 4.1. Although NetWare's installation CD-ROM includes drivers for popular network cards, such as the Novell NE2000, you should use the most current driver provided by the manufacturer of the network card.

It's best to standardize on one type of network board for all of the computers within a company network. Standardization makes it easy to find the right drivers, and it also simplifies troubleshooting and support.

Peripherals

Peripherals provide extra functions to the network and its workstations. These are typically attached to a workstation, but they may also be connected directly to the network or to a server. Peripherals fall into several categories:

- *Output devices*, such as printers and plotters. These are used to provide printouts of network data, which you can then scatter around your office to look busy.

- *Storage devices*, including disk drives and tape drives. These are used to store information needed for network applications and backup data.

- *Communication devices*, such as modems. These are used to communicate either with computers that are not connected to the network or with other systems such as mainframes.

Communications Media

All of the components described so far won't do any good until they're hooked together. That's where the communications medium comes in. Many different types of wiring—referred to as *topologies*—are available. Different topologies use different systems and types of wiring to communicate. A few of the topologies supported by NetWare 4.1 include

- ARCnet (using coaxial cable)

- Ethernet 10Base2 (using thin coaxial cable)

- Ethernet 10BaseT (using twisted-pair cable)

- Token Ring (using coaxial or fiber-optic cable)

- FDDI (using high-speed, fiber-optic cable)

Different topologies don't just use different types of wire; the overall structure of the network is also different. The two most common structures are the bus and the star.

- A *bus* structure in which each workstation connects to the next workstation in the line is shown in Figure 1.2. In some ways, this method works like a cheap string of Christmas lights; if the cable to one workstation is disconnected, the entire network can go down. Ethernet 10Base2 networks use this system.

- A *star* structure in which each workstation connects to a central device called a network *hub,* also called a *concentrator* or MAU, is shown in Figure 1.3. A star keeps the network going even if a single workstation is disconnected and thus is much safer for your network than a bus structure.

FIGURE 1.2
A bus structure connects each workstation in the network to the next one in the line.

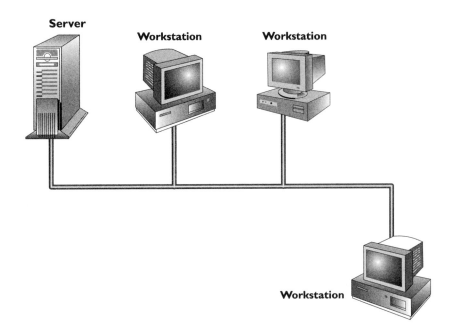

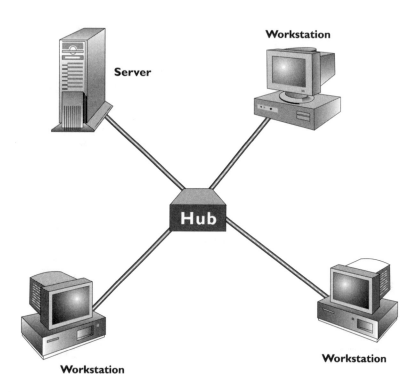

The Main Models of Networks

So far, when we have used the term *network* we have been using it in a limited
sense. There are actually several markedly different models of how computers
work together in a network. The three most important models are

- Centralized

- Distributed

- Collaborative

Centralized Computing

Centralized computing centers around large *host* computers. These monster
computers, which are often referred to as *mainframes,* handle all of the data

storage and processing. The *dumb terminals* connected to the mainframes normally serve as mere input/output devices, since they have little or no processing power.

The mainframes may be connected together in a type of network, but usually one mainframe is connected to weak-minded disciple computers, which can't think on their own. Some people argue that this is not a true "network" because no information is being shared. The disciple computers do not process or store any data; they just serve as input/output devices. Some mainframe systems may have "smart" terminals, which have some degree of independent computing power, but they typically have no disk storage. Figure 1.4 illustrates the centralized computing model.

True network or not, mainframe computers offered the first type of computer connectivity. They are expensive and hard to work with, but they have the advantage of allowing central management. (They also provided Hollywood with some fantastic imagery for sci-fi flicks: men wearing white suits in hermetically sealed rooms filled with blinking lights.)

When personal computers began to take over the corporate world in the mid-1980s, the decline of centralized computing and the rise of *distributed computing* began. Read on.

FIGURE 1.4
In the centralized computing model, a host computer handles all the data storage and processing.

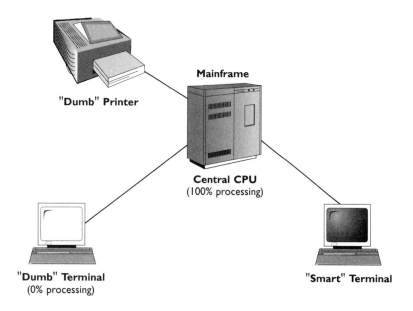

Distributed Computing

The *distributed* model of computing involves a network of *intelligent* computers, called *clients*, which is able to share the processing load. The advent of PCs, which offered low-cost processing power for individual users, made distributed computing possible.

In the distributed computing model, each client can process its own tasks. In a NetWare network, for example, a client (workstation) can execute an application entirely on its own. When the client requests an application from a file server, the application can be loaded into the client's memory and run from there without further resources from the network.

In the distributed model, some data are actually stored and processed on the clients, and services are requested from and provided by the server. The computers in the network are actually *sharing* capabilities and information. Figure 1.5 illustrates the distributed computing model.

FIGURE 1.5
The distributed computing model has clients that can share the processing tasks.

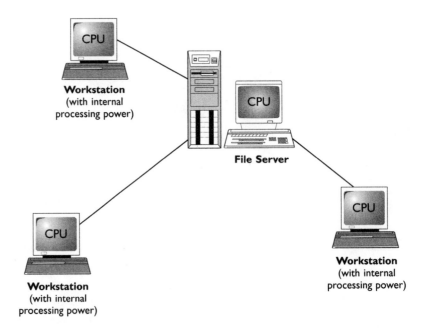

In a nutshell, two main features distinguish distributed computing from centralized computing:

- Clients with internal processing power

- True exchange of data and services

Collaborative Computing

The distinguishing feature of the *collaborative* computing model is the notion of computers working together to process the same task. In collaborative computing, also called *cooperative computing*, a computer might run part of a program on another computer in order to maximize processing power.

Collaborative computing is essentially an extension of the distributed computing model. Like distributed computing, it involves clients with internal processing power that can share data and services. But the collaborative model adds another vital factor: multiple computers cooperating to perform a task. A simple example of collaboration might be an e-mail system where the client creates a message and the server, or a separate e-mail server, sends the message to its destination.

Collaborative computing is becoming more and more important in the networking world, matching the growth in interest in maximizing network processing power, especially with today's powerful workstations. Figure 1.6 illustrates the collaborative computing model.

The proliferation of PCs created the rise in popularity of the second two models of networking (distributed and collaborative). Although the personal computer revolution brought PCs into homes, they were not well accepted in businesses because they couldn't work together. Each user worked with an independent set of data. At the time, mainframe computers provided an easy way for users to work on the same data (and as a bonus, they helped to heat the building).

The advent of networking brought the advantages of collaboration to the PC and the PC networking industry has blossomed. It's hard to find a company with more than 10 office employees that doesn't have a network of some sort. The use of mainframe computer systems, in the meantime, began a sharp decline, and millions of companies have had to turn back to conventional methods of heating.

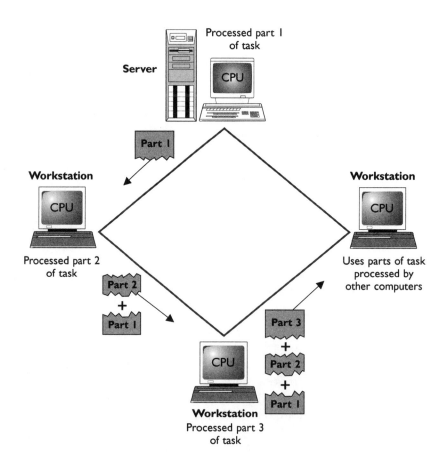

FIGURE 1.6
In the collaborative
computing model,
computers cooperate to
perform a task.

Sizes of Networks

Another way of categorizing networks is by size. The exact definitions of these categories generally depend on the person who is doing the explaining, but the size categories most often employed are local-area network (LAN), wide-area network (WAN), and metropolitan-area network (MAN). The following sections describe these categories of network sizes.

Local-Area Networks

LANs are the smallest of the three categories of networks. They tend to cover just a single building or college campus. If you have two PCs in your bedroom linked together with parallel-port cables, that's a LAN. The network a small business runs in the offices on the second floor is also a LAN. And what the local university has might well be a LAN, too, depending on how spread out it is. Typically, LANs use only one type of transmission medium (such as coaxial cable). Figure 1.7 illustrates a typical LAN.

Metropolitan-Area Networks

The name metropolitan-area network produces a snappier acronym than either local-area or wide-area network, but most people don't bother with this term. For a working definition, we can say that MANs are a bit bigger than LANs (up to the size of a metropolitan area) and usually require different hardware and transmission media (which are covered in detail in the next chapter) than LANs. Figure 1.8 shows an example of a MAN.

FIGURE 1.7
A local-area network (LAN) consists of computers located in a single location.

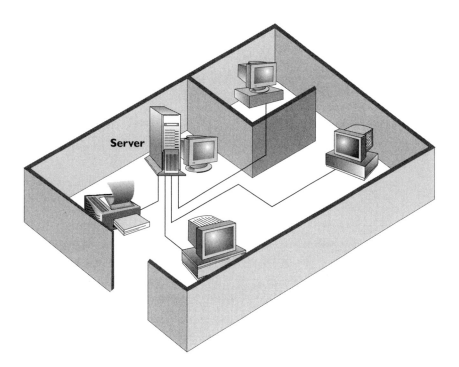

FIGURE 1.8

A metropolitan-area network (MAN) is similar to a LAN but covers a wider area—up to a good-size metropolis.

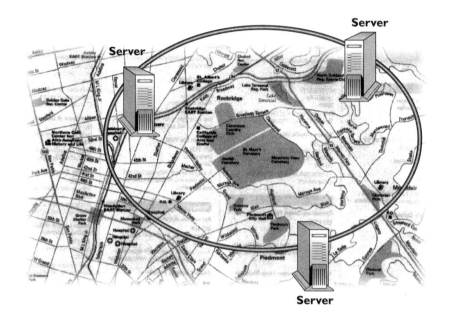

Wide-Area Networks

Any small business can have a LAN; and as we mentioned, few people use the term MAN these days. But no mom-and-pop shop will have a WAN. At their largest, WANs span the globe. At the very least, they cover multicity areas. Typically, WANs use telephone lines to provide the link between different network sites; and they can be relatively expensive, mainly because of the cost of leasing those long lines. Figure 1.9 shows an example of a heavy-duty WAN.

There are two subcategories of WANs:

- *Enterprise* networks connect the computers of a single organization. For example, MegaMoney Corporation may have sites on every continent in the world (with the possible exception of Antarctica), all connected together on one enterprise WAN. This enterprise WAN would be a private network used exclusively by a single organization, a single "enterprise."

- *Global* networks serve multiple organizations and cover multiple continents. The Internet, the "network of networks" serving thousands of different organizations and millions of individuals, is considered a global network because it is transcontinental and serves many separate organizations.

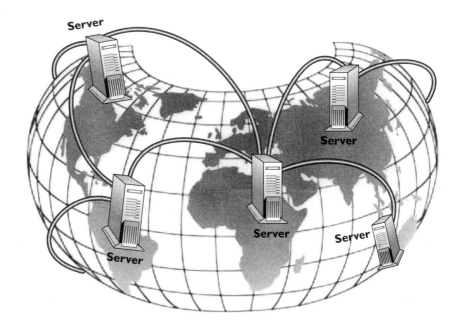

There is a reason for connecting all of these computers together. It is, in fact, so simple that we're almost embarrassed to bring it up in your company. But just to be clear, the reason for connecting computers is to share *services,* also called network resources.

Network Services

Network services are simply what computers have to offer on a network. For example, network services include print services, file services, e-mail, and database services. We'll cover some of these services in more detail later in this chapter.

When a computer is offering a service on a network, it is what Novell calls a *service provider.* A server is an example of a service provider. The list of resources that a service provider puts onto the network is what makes it possible for other computers to request services. A computer that requests services on the network is called a *service requester.*

NetWare version 3.12 (and earlier versions) focuses on the server as the logical center of network services and is termed a *server-centric* approach. In the traditional server-centric model of networking, servers usually function only as service providers and clients play the role of service requesters. This is in contrast to both the *peer-to-peer* approach, in which there is no dedicated server to center around, and the *network-centric* approach presented by NetWare 4.1, which focuses on a logical rather than physical network.

In the world of peer-to-peer networking, the line between those who give and those who receive is not so clear. A computer on a peer-to-peer network will often both request and provide services.

Now that we've identified the basic components and types of network, let's take a look at what NetWare 4.1 has to offer as a network operating system.

What Does NetWare Do for Networks?

F OR ABOUT 10 YEARS, Novell NetWare has been the world's most widely used NOS. NetWare has gone through many versions in that time, starting with 1.0. By version 2.2, NetWare networks had become commonplace. You can still see NetWare 2.2 in many companies. NetWare 3, originally introduced in 1989, was the first version to take advantage of the 386 processor. The most recent version of NetWare 3 is NetWare 3.12, released in 1993. At the time of this writing, NetWare 3.12 is the most popular NOS and is still available (although as you will learn in this chapter, there are many good reasons to choose NetWare 4.1 instead).

NetWare 4.0, also introduced in 1993, was originally intended as an enterprise networking system, which means that it was designed for large companies with multiple locations, and it had a price tag to match. This emphasis continued with the release of versions 4.01 and 4.02, which were still widely regarded as unstable compared to NetWare 3.12 and not worth the trouble unless you really needed the extra features.

With NetWare 4.1, Novell has produced a robust, easy-to-maintain NOS with many features that make it an ideal solution for a wide range of networks. In addition, the hefty price has been reduced. At the time of this writing, the retail price of NetWare 4.1 is the same as the price for 3.12. Since NetWare 4.1's licensing (explained in Chapter 2) is much more versatile, you may even save money by using NetWare 4.1. Novell is now marketing NetWare 4.1 to all companies, large and small, as a replacement for earlier versions. At this writing, NetWare 4.1 is the largest selling NOS worldwide.

NetWare 4.1 includes server software—the NOS itself—which you run on the server, as well as client software for a variety of clients. NetWare also includes a myriad of utilities, which are programs that you can use to manage the network and its resources. Although the server is the heart of the network, you run most of these utilities from a workstation. In addition, a few utilities run on the server console.

When you access the network, you use network services and resources:

- *Services* are the tasks that the network server performs, such as file and printer sharing.

- *Resources* are devices you can use through the network, such as disk drives and printers.

The following sections summarize the services and resources that NetWare 4.1 provides.

NetWare 4.1 Services

Although the definition of a network is simple, a modern server is expected to do much more than just connect computers. The NetWare 4.1 server offers many different services. Since the NetWare 4.1 server wears many hats, it can become overworked. In large networks, specialized servers, such as communications servers or printer servers, sometimes perform just one or two of these functions.

File Sharing

File sharing is the most basic service a network can provide, and it is the most important. File sharing simply means that users on different workstations can share files. Rather than store the files on their own disks, the users store the files on a *network drive*, typically a disk drive inside the NetWare server. Thanks to the NetWare client software, workstations can use this drive as if it were one of their own. For example, they can save files to it, copy files to and from it, and run applications from it.

With file sharing, you can access a file easily, no matter which workstation you are using, as long as you have access to the server. Users can literally share files—two or more users can access the same file at the same time. Network database applications take advantage of this power and allow many users to read, add, and change records in the same database at the same time.

Although the network server may be in another room (or another building), the network drive can be accessed quickly. In fact, you may find that the network drive is faster than the workstation's disk drive. This speed is due to features of NetWare, such as *file caching*, which keeps frequently used files in memory where they can be accessed instantly.

Printer Sharing

Another main service a network provides is printer sharing. You can attach a network printer to the NetWare server or to a workstation. In addition, you can attach many new printer models directly to the network cable. Regardless of how a printer is hooked up to the network, any user on the network can access it. The client software fools the workstation into thinking that the printer is local, so any application that can print to a local printer can be used with a network printer.

You may be wondering what happens if two users print to the printer at the same time. Users would be upset if their documents were actually printed at the same time—paper sharing is an idea that hasn't quite caught on. Fortunately, NetWare handles these situations very well. Rather than sending your document directly to the printer, NetWare uses a *print queue* to store the print jobs. The jobs wait in line in the print queue until it is their turn to print. Print queues allow even the busiest of printers to be managed efficiently.

Printing to a network and setting up network printers is actually much more involved than we've described here. Chapter 9 covers all the details.

Directory Services

A NetWare server on a large network can include hundreds or even thousands of users, printers, and other resources. NetWare keeps track of all of these in a database called the *Directory*. This system of organization is called *NetWare Directory Services*, or NDS. NDS is new to NetWare 4 and allows much better organization than previous versions. The Directory catalogs each user, server, printer, or other resource and makes it easy for users, workstations, and other servers to locate these resources.

The NDS database is called the Directory. *This is written with a capital D, to avoid confusion with disk directories.*

Since NDS is the most important new feature of NetWare 4.1, you will be reading a lot about it in this book. An in-depth examination of NDS begins in Chapter 5, which describes NetWare 4.1 fundamentals.

Security Features

Locks and alarm systems protect the resources of a company by preventing unauthorized access to them. The *security* features of NetWare 4.1 offer this same benefit for network resources. NetWare 4.1 provides security for all types of network resources. As a network administrator, you can control this security. You can specify the users who can access each resource.

NetWare provides many levels of security, from the most basic features that every network should use to advanced features that may be useful only for government organizations with abbreviations for names. By taking advantage of these features, you can be sure that unauthorized users don't access the network and that authorized users access only what they should.

The many components of network security include the following:

- **Login security:** Users must log in to the network by entering a username and password before they can access anything. As the network administrator, you will need to create usernames for each user. The system uses the username to identify files created by the user and to send messages to the user.

- **Console security:** If someone has access to the server console, that person can do all sorts of harm, including taking the server down, or worse, erasing data on the disks. To prevent this, you can require a password for access to the console.

- **Physical security:** Even a password can't protect the server from some types of attacks (such as turning it off, stealing it, or knocking it off the table). Most often, these events happen by accident. The solution is obvious, but often overlooked: place the server in a locked room and be sure only authorized individuals can get in.

- **File system security:** You can control access to each of the directories and files on the server's disk. This allows you to give users access to the data they need to view or update and keep them from viewing data they shouldn't see.

- **NDS security:** NDS security controls the management of NDS objects, including users, printers, and so on. You can keep tight control over who can create or delete objects.

- **Communication security:** The data in the network cables can sometimes be vulnerable to unauthorized snooping. NetWare features such as *encryption* and *packet signature* ensure that nobody can read your passwords or data in this manner.

- **Network auditing:** New to NetWare 4.1 is a versatile auditing system. The server can keep a log of files and NDS objects that are accessed, created, deleted, or changed. This log allows you to be sure there is no unauthorized access.

You'll learn more about security in Chapter 7, which covers both file system and NDS security.

Backup and Restore Capabilities

No matter how secure your server is, there is always a chance that you will lose data owing to hardware failure or software error. Keeping timely backups of the data can ensure that these failures will cause only small headaches, rather than larger ones.

Additional features, such as NetWare SFT III, allow data to be protected by redundancy—keeping multiple copies. Although these methods increase reliability, they should still be accompanied by a backup system.

NetWare includes built-in support for backups through the *Storage Management System*, or SMS. NetWare 4.1 also includes a backup utility called SBACKUP, which works with SMS to back up files on the network. SMS allows you to back up data on the server, and it also allows you to back up data on network workstations.

Backups are done to a *backup device*—usually a tape drive. These economical drives can hold anywhere from 80MB to 8GB (gigabytes) of data. When you plan a network server setup, always include a backup device. The first time a disk crashes on the server, you'll be glad you did.

NetWare's SBACKUP is a very basic backup application. Backup software from several third-party vendors provides additional features and may be more reliable than SBACKUP.

Messaging Services

Besides just sharing files, network users often wish to communicate with each other. In a small company, they can probably just shout, but in larger networks, particularly those that span multiple locations, *electronic mail* (usually abbreviated as *e-mail*) can be an important element of communication.

NetWare has built-in e-mail capabilities. The software that handles messaging is called the NetWare *Message Handling Service,* or MHS. MHS handles the basics of messaging. You need an e-mail application to provide an interface to MHS. NetWare includes a simple e-mail application, FirstMail. Like SBACKUP, FirstMail isn't the most sophisticated program, but it works and it's free.

Many commercial e-mail programs are available. These programs offer more features than FirstMail and can be used in larger applications. Novell produces one of these products, called GroupWise (formerly WordPerfect Office).

Communications Services

In a large network, things are a bit more complicated than a simple collection of workstations and a server. It may include multiple servers and more than one set of network cabling with different network topologies. You may even need to communicate with other network systems, such as AppleTalk, VINES, or IBM LAN Server.

NetWare 4.1 makes all of this possible through the NetWare *MultiProtocol Router,* or MPR. The MPR is a piece of software that runs on the NetWare server and allows it to act as a router. A *router* is simply a device that connects two different types of networks. Although any NetWare 4.1 server can act as a router, the MPR allows more sophisticated features.

Network Resources

The network's resources are devices that you can access and use through the network. These may be inside the server itself, such as disk drives, or attached to a server or workstation, such as a printer. As a network administrator, your main job is to manage these resources: install them, make them accessible, control access to them, and fix them when they're broken.

Each resource provides a different function to network clients. Resources offered by NetWare 4.1 include servers, volumes (disk drives in the NetWare server), printers, backup devices, routers, modems, and any other device users can access through the network system.

Choosing a Network Operating System

WHICH NOS IS RIGHT for your network? Usually, this is not an easy question. The answer depends on the needs of your users and on how much money you are willing to spend. You may also need to consider other factors, such as familiarity with a particular system, connectivity with mainframes or other systems, and the software that users will be running. We will now examine several of the alternatives, starting with the subject of this book: NetWare 4.1.

NetWare 4.1

NetWare 4.1 has many benefits compared to other NOSs. In fact, it has many benefits over NetWare 3.1x. These benefits are the subject of Chapter 2. Areas that used to be the most difficult in NetWare 3.1x, such as server installation, printing configuration, and changing SET parameters, have been greatly simplified in NetWare 4.1. Although many new features have been added, you should find NetWare 4.1 easy to learn.

NetWare 4.1 does have some new requirements, which are described in the following sections.

Cost Considerations

For new NetWare installations, the cost per user of NetWare 4.1 is similar to that of NetWare 3.*x*, so NetWare 4.1 is the obvious choice. When you are upgrading existing networks, however, the cost can be higher because the user license for your earlier version of NetWare (for example, 25 user or 50 user) does not carry over to NetWare 4.1.

In NetWare 3.*x*, licenses were issued for set amounts of users, and NetWare allows only that many users to access the network at any time. For example, if your company purchased a 25-user version of NetWare 3.*x* initially and later needed to add two or three more users, you would have no choice but to jump to the next level—in this case, 50 users. It's hard to justify the cost of 25 additional users when you only need a few.

The *additive licensing* feature of NetWare 4.1 provides a solution to this problem. This system lets you upgrade your network in increments of as few as 5 users. The license is provided on a *license diskette*, which is included with your copy of NetWare. If you have more than one copy of NetWare, you can add the license diskettes to the same server. For example, if you have a 5-user license and a 25-user license, you can install both licenses and make room for 30 users. This is where NetWare 4.1 can really save you money.

If you have several servers on your network, you can even remove a license from one server and install it on another so you can modify your network to accommodate changing user loads easily and without a great deal of expense. In a large corporate network, it may be useful to have a few extra 5-user licenses handy. Then you can add licenses to whichever servers need them as the company expands.

You can't install the same license diskette on more than one server. This action is illegal and not very nice. In addition, NetWare's copyright protection features make it impossible to use the same license on multiple servers in a network. Also, needless to say, you can't add the same license diskette to a server twice.

Hardware Considerations

As with most software, the latest version of NetWare 4.1 requires a slightly better computer system than any previous version of NetWare required to run efficiently. These requirements include a bit more disk space and 4MB to 8MB more RAM (random-access memory) than an equivalent NetWare 3.1*x* server requires. These requirements are explained in the next sections.

DISK STORAGE REQUIREMENTS   To run NetWare 4.1 on your server's disk drive, you need at least 50MB. However, if you plan on installing all of the NetWare files (including optional files such as client software, online documentation, and OS/2 utilities), you will need at least 100MB. An existing NetWare 3.1*x* server needs approximately 40MB free to perform the upgrade to NetWare 4.1.

These requirements are minimum *disk space requirements. You should always have at least 50MB more than you need; running out of disk space can cause your network to go down, and you might lose data.*

MEMORY REQUIREMENTS   Novell recommends 8MB as the minimum amount of RAM in a NetWare 4.1 server. However, the NetWare operating system itself uses about 7MB. This doesn't leave much room for applications or users. A NetWare 4.1 server with only 8MB will be painfully slow, unless your network is very small (5 users or less). A more comfortable minimum is 12MB. If your network has 20 or more users, you will probably need at least 16MB.

The amount of memory your server needs depends on the number of users, disk storage, and types of applications used. For information about calculating exact RAM requirements, see Chapter 15.

Compatibility Issues

NetWare 4.1 is *backward-compatible* with software and clients used in previous NetWare versions, which means that all of your software and hardware should work fine when you upgrade to NetWare 4.1. Complete backward compatibility is achievable only in an ideal world, however. In the real world, all sorts of applications are available, and it's impossible to know whether they will all work with NetWare 4.1. Some applications may be written to take advantage of features (or bugs) in the earlier versions.

When you are considering an upgrade, you should be sure that your hardware and software will work with the new NOS. Ideally, you should install NetWare 4.1 on an identical server as a test. Unfortunately, not everyone has a spare server handy. The best solution is to examine the documentation for each device to determine whether it is compatible. You should check drivers for network cards, disk and tape drives, software such as backup software, and any network-aware applications your users run. If you can't find compatibility information in the item's documentation, contact the vendor.

Network Support and Training

The advanced features of NetWare 4.1 can be a bit difficult to master, particularly if you are used to working with another version of NetWare. The users of the network should not notice a difference in the way they access the network, but they still may need training to take advantage of NetWare 4.1's new features. System administrators also need training. If you make it through this book, there will be one less network administrator who needs to learn NetWare 4.1.

Users and administrators who are not already familiar with another system will certainly need training. Since NetWare 3.1x may not be supported in the future, it's best to learn the newer version. Features of NetWare 4.1, such as graphical management of users and security, make 4.1 much easier for the beginning network administrator to learn than earlier versions of NetWare.

NetWare Server for OS/2

In early (2.x) versions of NetWare, you could run NetWare in a *nondedicated* configuration, which meant that the computer that NetWare was running on could also be used as a workstation. (You could even run both on a 286 machine.) In NetWare 3.1x, Novell no longer allows this setup. NetWare servers are *dedicated* machines; they can only run server software. In NetWare 4, you can once again run a nondedicated NetWare server. This is made possible by IBM's OS/2 operating system.

After you install NetWare Server for OS/2 on an OS/2 system, that server is able to function like any other NetWare 4.1 server. DOS and OS/2 clients running under OS/2 can share the network board used by the server. In this way, you can actually log in on the same machine that the server is running on. Thus, you can have a network inside your computer—what a way to impress your friends.

Although it sounds impressive, NetWare Server for OS/2 is not always practical. It may work for small networks in mom-and-pop companies (with up to five users), but this arrangement is probably not a good idea for anything larger. The disadvantages of this setup include the following:

- **Memory:** OS/2 requires 8MB of RAM to run, and NetWare 4.1 requires at least 8MB of RAM to run. This means that you'll need at least 16MB just to get NetWare Server for OS/2 to start. You may have a 16MB Pentium machine, which is a great workstation or NetWare server. But if you install NetWare Server for OS/2, you'll realize just how slow your machine can be. For practical use, you should have at least 20MB—and even more than that won't hurt.

- **Reliability and security:** Since NetWare Server for OS/2 runs on the same machine as a workstation, your entire network is at the mercy of the workstation's user. The user can access the console. If the user's software causes the machine to crash, the server can crash as well. And if that user is someone who just can't bear to leave his or her desk without turning off the computer, the network will go down whenever the user takes off.

- **Compatibility:** Since it tries to run NetWare and OS/2 at the same time, NetWare Server for OS/2 may not be compatible with all NetWare applications, device drivers, and utilities. Considering all of this, it is remarkably compatible. Most server software included with NetWare will run on an OS/2 server without a problem.

Although NetWare Server for OS/2 sounds like something of a novelty, it can be useful in many situations. For example, testing for this book and many of the screenshots were done on a machine running a server under OS/2 and logging in to a client window on the same machine. If you have a machine that can run it, you might find this type of server useful for practice in your CNA studies.

NetWare 3.12

Although this is a book about NetWare 4.1, NetWare 3.12 may actually be a better networking solution for certain situations. NetWare 3.12 does provide many of the same benefits as NetWare 4.1, including the enhanced client software and menu system described in this book. The main feature missing from NetWare 3.12 is NDS.

You might want to stick to NetWare 3.12 for your network in the following situations:

- If you, other administrators, or the users are well trained on NetWare 3.12, you may want to wait until NetWare 4.1 training is completed before moving on.

- If the budget is tight, NetWare 3.12 can usually handle more users on a server than NetWare 4.1 would on the same machine. Upgrading may require more disk storage or RAM.

- If you are using a third-party product, such as accounting software or for mainframe connectivity, these products may not yet support NetWare 4.1.

NetWare 4.1 includes support for full connectivity with clients and servers running older versions of NetWare, so you may want to make the move to NetWare 4.1 a gradual one, one server at a time. Servers that don't require the additional features of NetWare 4.1 may not ever need to be upgraded. If it works, why fix it?

Windows NT

A war is being waged right now between vendors of different NOSs, and the two biggest competitors are NetWare and Microsoft's Windows NT. NT (an acronym for *new technology*) was originally intended as an upgrade to the Microsoft Windows operating system, but it never caught on as a replacement for Windows. However, NT includes powerful networking features, and some companies have chosen Windows NT as an alternative to NetWare.

Versions of Windows NT

The latest release of Windows NT is available in two versions:

- Windows NT Workstation is a client workstation operating system similar to Microsoft Windows. It uses the same user interface as Windows and can run most Windows applications. The latest version of NT, 3.51, supports user interface elements similar to Windows 95 and can run most Windows 95 applications. Unlike Windows (or even Windows 95), Windows NT Workstation is a 32-bit, preemptive multitasking operating system.

- Windows NT Server is a dedicated server operating system, similar to NetWare 4.1. It also includes all of the features of Windows NT Workstation. Clients on a Windows NT network can include Windows NT, Windows, DOS, and OS/2.

You can manage Windows NT through utilities on the server or on a workstation. A system of *trusted domains* allows central management of the network, similar to what NDS provides for NetWare 4.1.

Why Choose Windows NT?

Windows NT has several advantages over NetWare 4.1:

- NT pricing is lower than NetWare 4.1 for small networks. Server licenses allow an unlimited number of users; however, client software must be licensed for each workstation. The latest version, 3.51, includes a "concurrent connection" licensing option, similar to that of NetWare 4.1.

- Windows NT provides greater integration with Microsoft Windows clients because Windows and Windows NT share some common components. In addition, because the server and clients can run the same operating system, there is less for the administrator to learn.

- Windows NT 3.51 supports PowerPC, DEC Alpha, and other high-powered RISC-based processors. It also supports Symmetric Multiprocessing (SMP) (NetWare recently introduced SMP support for NetWare 4.1).

On the other hand, Windows NT has a few disadvantages compared with NetWare 4.1:

- Although NT includes a domain system that is similar to NDS, it is not as versatile, as expandable, or as secure. Microsoft intends to remedy this with a future version of NT, code named Cairo, which is scheduled to ship in late 1996 or early 1997.

- Novell has a large number of training programs, including the CNE and CNA certification programs, so there are plenty of people around who know NetWare. Support for Windows NT is not quite as easy to find.

- Windows NT's security, although adequate for most companies, isn't as sophisticated as NetWare 4.1. If your network is in a top-secret organization that requires high security, NetWare is a better choice.

- Some of the features of NetWare 4.1, such as the MultiProtocol Router, are not included in Windows NT. Once again, Microsoft expects the release of Cairo to remedy this.

If you choose Windows NT, the decision doesn't need to apply to the whole network. NT has the capability to integrate with NetWare 4.1 and other network systems. Windows NT is gaining in popularity as an *application server*, which is a server that works in conjunction with the NetWare server and processes data for applications, reducing the workload of the workstations.

IBM LAN Server

IBM's LAN Server is a relatively low-cost system that provides basic networking services. It is based on IBM's OS/2 operating system. This allows the server to be run on the same machine as a workstation, similar to NetWare 4.1's NetWare Server for OS/2.

IBM also offers an Advanced Server option, which provides high-speed file and network access and enhanced security. LAN Server's principal advantage is that it allows easy integration with other IBM systems, including older mainframe and minicomputer systems, such as AIX and AS/400.

Although LAN Server has become less popular because of the explosive growth of NetWare and Microsoft's Windows NT, it is still used in many companies, particularly those who need strong connectivity with AS/400 systems.

Banyan VINES

VINES was introduced when NetWare 3.1 was still young. Although it has a catchier name than NetWare (it's actually an acronym for VIrtual NEtworking System), Banyan's product has always had a smaller market. It is most often used in larger networks that span multiple locations.

One benefit of VINES is that it provides a Directory Service, similar to NetWare 4's NDS. For this and other reasons, VINES was the preferred enterprise network system for many companies. This was, after all, before NetWare 4 became available.

The Directory Service provided by VINES is called StreetTalk. Now that NetWare 4.1 is becoming prevalent in large networks, Banyan has introduced methods of integrating StreetTalk with NetWare and other popular NOS software. Banyan's recent focus has been on integrating VINES and StreetTalk with the largest network of them all, the Internet.

Peer-to-Peer Networking

Some networks don't use a server at all. These *peer-to-peer* networks allow each workstation to share its own files or printers. In a sense, each workstation acts as a server to provide access to its own disk drives and printers. Peer-to-peer networks are easy to set up and usually easier to maintain than dedicated servers. In addition, there's no server to buy, so the price is lower.

Peer-to-peer networking isn't the answer for all networks, however. Since the file and printer sharing are done in the background on workstations, the system can't be as fast as a dedicated server and can't handle nearly as many users. In addition, peer-to-peer systems usually lack the more advanced network services, such as messaging and Directory Services. Thus, peer-to-peer networks are best suited for smaller networks (up to 20 users) or systems that require a minimum of resource sharing.

Peer-to-peer systems are available from many different companies. Here are a few:

- Novell Personal NetWare

- Microsoft Windows for Workgroups

- Microsoft Windows 95

- Artisoft LANtastic

- AppleTalk

- IBM OS/2 Warp Connect

Peer-to-peer systems can usually be used in combination with server-based networks such as NetWare. This combination allows the best of both worlds: Users can access files and printers on other users' workstations when needed, and they can enjoy the benefits of a full-scale network server.

Review

THE CONCEPT OF *networking* has revolutionized the use of PCs in businesses. A network is a system that connects multiple computers, allowing them to communicate with each other, share resources (files, printers, and so on), and communicate with mainframes and large networks.

Network Components

A typical network consists of several components. The *server* runs software called the *network operating system* (NOS), which allows it to provide services to the network.

Workstations are where the users of the network run applications. Workstations use the resources of the server. Each workstation has a *network board* (or card), which interfaces that computer to the network.

Peripherals, such as tape backup drives, modems, and printers, can be made available through the network and accessed by all users at workstations.

Finally, a *communications medium* connects the machines. This is the actual network wiring.

NetWare 4.1 includes *server software* (the NOS) that you run on the server. In addition, *client software* is provided for a variety of clients. NetWare also includes utilities that you can use to manage the network and its resources. Most of these utilities run from a workstation, but some run on the server console.

Network Models

Computer networks have developed from their origins in the *centralized* computing model of mainframe computers to the distributed processing model reflected in most current networks. In the *distributed* model of computing, *clients* are able to share the processing load. As they become more sophisticated, networks are beginning to integrate distributed computing capabilities.

Like distributed computing, the *collaborative* model involves clients that can do their own processing. The additional factor is that multiple computers can cooperate to perform a task.

Network Sizes

Networks are classified according to size:

- *Local-area networks* (LANs) usually reside in a single location and use only one type of transmission medium. Common types of LANs are ARCnet, Ethernet, FDDI, and Token Ring.

- *Metropolitan-area networks* (MANs) are somewhat bigger than LANs (up to the size of a metropolitan area) and usually require different hardware and transmission media.

- *Wide-area networks* (WANs) are the largest type. They can span the globe. WANs usually use telephone lines to provide the link between different network sites. The two subcategories of WANs are *enterprise networks*, which connect the computers of a single organization, and *global networks,* which serve multiple organizations and cover multiple continents.

Network Services

NetWare 4.1 is a NOS that provides the following services:

- *File sharing* allows users to access the same files, even at the same time.

- *Printer sharing* allows users to print to a network printer from anywhere on the network.

- *NetWare Directory Services* (NDS) provides an organization for network resources and keeps the information about each resource in a database.

- *Security* allows the administrator to control access to each network resource. There are several types of security: console, physical, file system, NDS, communication, and network auditing.

- *Backup and restore capabilities* let you keep a copy of network data on a tape or other media for safekeeping and restore it to the server if needed.

- *Messaging* lets users can send e-mail messages to one another.

- *Communications features* allow multiple networks, using different cable and different operating systems, to be connected together.

Network Operating Systems

The NOS that your network should use depends on the needs of your users, your company's budget, users' familiarity with a particular system, connectivity with mainframes or other systems, and the software that will be running. The alternatives include the following:

- NetWare 4.1

- NetWare Server for OS/2

- NetWare 3.12

- Microsoft Windows NT

- IBM LAN Server

- Banyan VINES

- Peer-to-peer networks (such as Novell Personal NetWare or Microsoft Windows for Workgroups)

NetWare 4.1 Compared with NetWare 3.1x

ACH VERSION OF NetWare is better than the one before, and Net-Ware 4.1 is no exception. The latest version of NetWare includes improvements in a wide variety of areas, which are explained in this chapter. If you are familiar with an earlier version of NetWare, this discussion should bring you up-to-date with the latest features. If you're new to NetWare, this chapter will introduce you to the many features of NetWare 4.1 and point out how they differ from the earlier versions. You can find in-depth information about these features in the following chapters.

NetWare Directory Services for Managing Network Objects

N ORDER TO MANAGE all of the users, groups, printers, and other network objects, NetWare uses a database. In NetWare 3.1*x* this database is called the *bindery*. The bindery is a simple, flat database—similar to a phone book, but not in alphabetical order. This arrangement is inefficient for networks with many objects. Imagine trying to find a particular name in a randomly ordered phone book, and you'll get the idea. Worse, some of the objects, such as printers, are stored in separate database files rather than integrated with the bindery.

In NetWare 4 the bindery has been replaced by *NetWare Directory Services* (NDS), which allows you to organize the objects in the network. The NDS database uses a tree structure—an upside-down tree to be exact. A typical NDS tree is shown in Figure 2.1. Even if you have more than one server, you can manage them all through the same NDS tree.

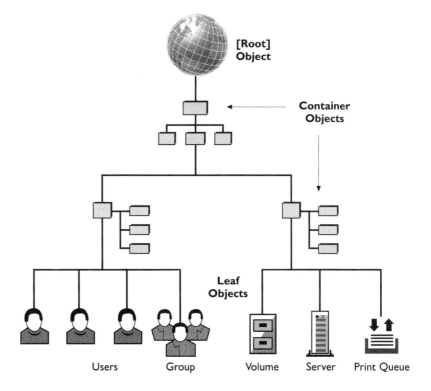

FIGURE 2.1
NDS uses a treelike
structure to organize
network resources.

In NDS every resource on the network is an *object*. You can organize objects in NDS by placing them inside *container objects*, which are special objects used to contain, or hold, other objects. The objects that represent actual resources— printers, users, and other objects—are called *leaf objects*. These form the leaves of the Directory tree, and they can't contain other objects.

To manage NDS objects, you use a utility called NetWare Administrator, or NWADMIN. NWADMIN runs from Microsoft Windows and provides a graphical look at the Directory tree. From this utility, you can manage every type of object and control security. A DOS utility, NETADMIN, allows you to perform most of the same functions, although it isn't nearly as good looking.

NDS is explained in detail in the next chapter. Managing NDS objects with NetWare Administrator is explained in Chapter 6.

Server Features

NETWARE 4.1 INCLUDES several improvements to the server software itself. These improvements include

- A simplified installation process

- The SERVMAN utility, for managing server settings

- Time synchronization, which allows multiple servers to keep the same time

- Support for new hardware, including optimization for the Pentium processor

- NetWare Server for OS/2, which allows you to run a server and workstation on a single computer

The Installation Process

Back in NetWare 2.2, installing a NetWare server was a complicated process. NetWare 3.11 was easier to install but still required you to perform many of the steps manually. NetWare 3.12 includes an INSTALL program that does most of the work for you, making it easy to install, even for people who are not network experts. NetWare 4.1's installation is even easier. In addition, it includes options that allow you to set up the new NetWare 4.1 features.

NetWare 3.12 has only one kind of installation. The installation program asks you questions about each phase of the installation. NetWare 4.1 has even more features and options, so it asks a lot more questions. To keep it easy for the nonexpert, Novell wisely chose to include a *Simple installation* option.

Even if you use Custom installation, the NetWare 4.1 installation process is quite simple once you understand it. A typical installation takes about 20 minutes.

If you choose Simple installation, NetWare answers many of the questions for you. If you are installing an "average" network, the default answers are probably correct. If not, you should use the other choice, *Custom installation*. This is the old-fashioned method, which asks every possible question.

You'll need to use the custom installation if you need to specify disk partition sizes, set up more than one volume, or install only certain features of NetWare 4.1. When in doubt, use the custom installation.

NetWare 4.1 has one more installation improvement: If you are upgrading the server from a previous version of NetWare, NetWare 4.1 is much more careful about replacing your files. NetWare checks before installing any file to make sure that the version to be installed is newer than the original version. If it is not, NetWare prompts you to decide whether to overwrite the file or leave the original version intact.

Manage the Server with SERVMAN

NetWare 3.1*x* has many parameters that you can adjust with the SET console command. This command allows you to fine-tune the network, improve compatibility with software and hardware, and mess things up horribly if you don't know what you're doing. Typically, you place SET commands in the AUTOEXEC.NCF file, which is a special file that contains commands to be executed when the server starts, similar to the AUTOEXEC.BAT file on a DOS workstation. Several SET commands are added to this file automatically when NetWare 4.1 is installed.

NetWare 4.1 includes a new server console utility, SERVMAN, which allows you to change these same parameters. However, SERVMAN is much politer than the SET command. SERVMAN is a menu-based utility from which you choose the type of parameter to adjust from a list of categories and adjust settings without needing to remember the SET command syntax. Almost any change that you can make with the SET command can be made from within SERVMAN. An example of a SERVMAN screen for changing Directory Services settings is shown in Figure 2.2.

When you exit SERVMAN, you have the choice of saving the changes in the AUTOEXEC.NCF or STARTUP.NCF files.

Synchronized Time

Workstation PCs have a built-in clock. NetWare uses this clock to mark the time that events occur, such as the creation of a file. This mark makes it easier

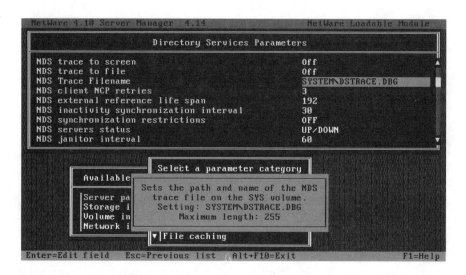

to determine which version of a file is the newest. In addition, the clock enables you to schedule events, such as backups, to occur at specific times.

As the saying goes, a man with one watch knows what time it is; a man with two watches is never sure. A network with 30 workstations has 30 different clocks. How's that for unsure? Fortunately, NetWare manages the clocks so that they all keep the same time.

In NetWare 3.1x, your workstation's time is set according to the server's time when you attach the workstation to the server. Thus all the workstations attached to a given server stay on the same time. If you have multiple servers, each server keeps its own time. As long as the times on the servers are reasonably close to each other, this system doesn't cause a problem, because each server has a separate bindery.

In NetWare 4.1, however, accurate time is even more important. NDS manages multiple servers, and time stamps keep track of changes to NDS objects. In order to work together, all of the servers must keep the same time. Fortunately, you don't need to monitor the times yourself. NetWare 4.1 handles this with *time synchronization*.

Time synchronization uses one or more *time servers* to maintain the time on the network. Each NetWare 4.1 server is a time server of one type or another.

Hardware Support

NetWare 4.1 supports a wider variety of hardware than previous versions. Here are the new features:

- NetWare 4.1 supports Intel's Pentium processor and takes advantage of its advanced features. These include a *paging* feature that allows memory to be moved in entire blocks, rather than one byte at a time.

- The PCI (*Peripheral Component Interconnect*) bus is the latest innovation in hardware interfaces for PCs. It is often seen in systems that include the Pentium processor. NetWare 4.1 now supports PCI communication as well as the older standards: ISA, EISA, and VESA local bus.

- PCMCIA (Personal Computer Memory Card International Association) is a standard for tiny, credit card-size peripherals, usually used with notebook computers. Network cards, modems, sound cards, and even hard disk drives are available. If you're wondering how you'll ever remember the abbreviation, you're in luck. The standard has recently been renamed and is now called PC Card. NetWare 4.1 supports network cards and disk drives that use this type of interface.

NetWare Server for OS/2

NetWare Server for OS/2 is included with NetWare 4.1. It allows you to run NetWare 4.1 as a nondedicated server so that a single machine can serve as both a workstation and a server.

NetWare Server for OS/2 requires a great deal of memory in order to run efficiently and is only practical for smaller networks. The specifics are covered in Chapter 1, in the discussion of NOS choices.

File System Improvements

THE NETWARE *file system* provides access to hard disks, organizes data on them into files, and manages their storage. NetWare 4.1 introduced some impressive improvements to the file system.

These improvements include the following:

- File compression

- Block suballocation

- Data migration

- NetWare Peripheral Architecture (NPA)

Although these features affect different areas of the file system, they serve a single purpose: to make access to disks more efficient. Files take less space and can be accessed faster. Let's take a closer look at each of these features.

File Compression

It seems that no matter how much disk storage your network has, it's never enough. NetWare 4.1 helps you save space with the *file compression* feature. File compression finds the files that you haven't used for a while and compresses them into a smaller amount of disk space. The compressed file is typically about 63 percent smaller than the original file.

How Does Compression Work?

You might expect that the only way to make a file smaller is to remove some of the data; fortunately, this is not how NetWare accomplishes compression. Netware uses several systems that allow a small amount of bytes to represent a larger amount. You may be familiar with compression software such as PKZIP and LHARC, which use similar techniques.

Let's consider a simple example. Imagine a file that contains the character *A* 400 times in a row. The normal file would store all 400 *A*'s, each in its own byte, for a total of 400 bytes. The compressed file would simply store a code that means "insert 400 *A*'s here." Thus, our 400-byte file would be reduced to 3 or 4 bytes, yet still retain all of its content.

In practice, few files compress quite that well. Different types of files will undergo different amounts of compression:

- Simple text files compress to about one-quarter of their original size. (Of course, files containing only a single character compress even better, but you probably don't have any of those.)

- Binary files (such as executable files or some word processor documents) compress a bit, but the benefit is not great.

- Some graphic files (such as uncompressed TIFF and Microsoft Power-Point) compress well—often to as little as one-tenth of their original size.

- Many graphic formats (including GIF and JPEG) include built-in compression, so they won't compress at all.

When Does Compression Happen?

You may have experience with on-the-fly file compression systems, such as Stac Electronics' Stacker and the DriveSpace program provided with some versions of MS-DOS. These compression programs usually have one thing in common: They slow down your system. As a file is written to the disk, it must be compressed, and compression takes a heavy toll on the CPU.

NetWare file compression works a little differently. Rather than compressing every file as it is written, NetWare scans the disk and looks for files that nobody has accessed for a while. By default, this time period is 7 days, but you can change it to anything from 1 day to 10,000 days. The server compresses the files that have been unused during the specified time period. This will still slow down the server, but NetWare is smart enough to wait until everyone has gone home to do its compression work. This time defaults to 6:00 a.m., but you can set it to a more convenient time for your company.

When a user tries to access one of these compressed files, the server uncompresses it and then allows it to be accessed as usual. The file remains uncompressed until it has not been touched for 7 days again.

Why Not Use Compression?

File compression is enabled on NetWare 4.1 servers by default. It usually works efficiently even with the default settings, and most users won't even know it's there. However, you may want to turn it off in certain situations. Here are some possible disadvantages of compression:

- When a user requests a file that has been compressed, there will be a delay as the server uncompresses the file. In most networks, this event won't happen very often. But if your users often need to access files that no one has used for more than seven days, the server may slow to a creeping halt. Depending on the file size and the server speed, decompression can take from 30 seconds to as long as 10 minutes.

- If you have a backup that was made from a compressed volume, you will need to restore it onto a volume that also has compression enabled to ensure that space is available. In addition, unless the backup system supports compression, files will be restored in an uncompressed state and NetWare will not compress them again for another seven days. Thus, if an entire volume is restored, the restored volume could require a much greater amount of disk space than the original (compressed) volume.

- Once you enable compression on a volume, you cannot turn it off and uncompress the files without re-creating the volume (which will erase all data on the volume!). You can, however, disable compression for individual files and directories.

As a network administrator, you have full control over the compression feature. You can choose which files and directories will be compressed and which should never be compressed. You can also set some directories or files to be compressed instantly when written.

Block Suballocation

When NetWare writes data to a disk, it uses increments called *blocks*. The disk drive is divided into blocks. These blocks are all the same size. NetWare 3.1x usually uses 4KB as the block size, but you can specify a different size during installation. NetWare 4.1 chooses an optimum block size based on the size of the drive and the server's RAM.

NetWare 3.1x and other operating systems use only entire blocks at a time. This means that a lot of space is wasted. For example, if the block size is 4KB, a 400-byte file will use an entire 4KB block. Similarly, a file 9KB in length will use three blocks, a total of 12KB. This use of blocks is illustrated in Figure 2.3.

NetWare 4.1's *block suballocation* feature allows the blocks to be used more efficiently. Instead of using entire blocks at a time, each block can be subdivided into 512-byte sections. A 400-byte file will use only one 512-byte section, or *suballocation unit*. This can save you a lot of disk space, especially if the block size is larger than 4KB. Block suballocation is illustrated in Figure 2.4.

FIGURE 2.3
Using entire disk blocks
can waste space.

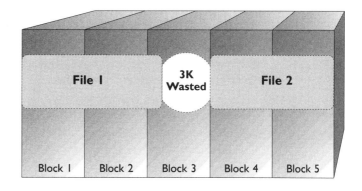

FIGURE 2.3
Using entire disk blocks
can waste space.

FIGURE 2.4
Files take less space with
block suballocation.

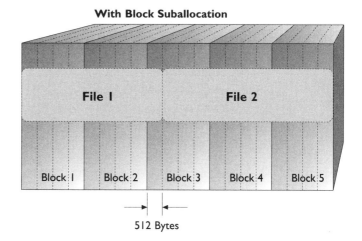

Block suballocation does have its disadvantages: It slows down disk access slightly and can cause disk errors to have more severe effects. For most networks, however, suballocation is a good idea. Suballocation is enabled by default on NetWare 4.1 volumes.

Data Migration

Many companies need extremely large amounts of disk storage. One application that requires a great deal of disk space is *imaging*. Imaging tries to replace filing cabinets full of paper by scanning documents and storing them as graphic files. These files are typically stored on an optical storage device, or *jukebox*. A jukebox has a very high storage capacity and stores data in a permanent form, which is less likely to be lost in the event of a device failure or system crash. These systems require time-consuming procedures to move old data onto the jukebox.

The name jukebox isn't a coincidence; these systems often work in the same way as the kind that plays music. A bank of optical disks is set up so that a mechanical arm can move the appropriate disk into the drive. A jukebox system is expensive, but at least you won't need to insert a quarter each time you want to use it.

NetWare 4.1's *data migration* features give you the best of both worlds: You can migrate data to the jukebox, yet still keep it accessible to your users. Files that are not in use can be moved to the jukebox automatically. These files still appear to be on the NetWare volume. When a user chooses to access one of these files, it is *demigrated*, or copied back to the NetWare volume. The only effect a user might notice when accessing a migrated file is a slight delay (typically less than a minute) while the file is retrieved from the jukebox.

Data migration is performed by a NetWare service called the *High-Capacity Storage System* (HCSS). You can enable or disable migration for each of the disk volumes on your server.

NetWare Peripheral Architecture (NPA)

NetWare uses *device drivers* to access storage devices on the NetWare server. The device driver provides an interface between the NetWare operating system and file storage devices, such as disk drives and tape drives. *NetWare Peripheral Architecture* (NPA) is a new standard for device drivers. In NPA, the disk driver is separated into two modules that work together to provide access to the disk or other device:

- The *Host Adapter Module* (HAM) provides the interface between NetWare and the *host adapter*, or drive controller card. This could be a SCSI, an IDE, or another type of controller.

- The *Custom Device Module* (CDM) provides the interface to the hardware devices (disk drives) attached to the host adapter. If several different types of disk drives are attached to the same host adapter, you can use a separate CDM for each one.

NPA provides two advantages to the traditional disk driver architecture: scalability and modularity. *Scalability* means that you can load only the particular modules that you need, saving memory and CPU resources. *Modularity* makes it easy to make hardware changes in the system. If you change the hardware configuration of the server, you need to replace only one driver (either the HAM or CDM).

Novell is making NPA the standard for disk drivers in all future versions of NetWare. At the moment, very few NPA drivers are available. Fortunately, the old style of disk drivers can still be used with NetWare 4.1.

New, Improved, and Combined Utilities

TO MANAGE THE NetWare server, you use NetWare *utilities*. These usually run from a workstation and serve a variety of functions to help you control the network and its resources. NetWare 3.12 includes lots of utilities—so many, in fact, that it's often difficult to remember which is which.

Novell must have realized this, because NetWare 4.1 actually includes *fewer* utilities. Fewer utilities doesn't mean fewer capabilities, however. You can still control everything that you could in NetWare 3.12 and much more. Many of the older utilities were simply combined into single, comprehensive NetWare 4.1 utilities. In addition, just about every utility has been improved in some way, and a few have been removed entirely and replaced by new utilities.

Printing Made Easy

Ask any NetWare administrator what causes the most problems in a network, and you will usually get the same answer: printing. The process of setting up network printers is a difficult one, and a print job must go through many links in the chain to reach the printer. When a printing problem occurs, identifying the link that failed can be difficult.

NetWare 4.1 doesn't solve all of these problems, but it takes a step in the right direction. For setting up network printing, the PCONSOLE printer utility includes a *Quick Setup* option. By using this option, you can create all the objects required to make printing work in a single step.

Like other NetWare 4.1 resources, printing is managed through NDS, which means that you can use the graphical NetWare Administrator utility to manage all aspects of printing. Using NetWare Administrator is much easier than working with the DOS-based utilities of NetWare 3.1x. A particularly handy feature in NetWare Administrator is the *Print Layout Page*. This option displays a picture of all of the objects involved in the printing process, complete with lines between them to show how they relate to each other. This pictorial representation makes it easy to spot a problem and determine its cause.

Online Documentation

As with previous versions of NetWare, NetWare 4.1 includes online documentation on CD-ROM. You can view the documentation directly from the CD-ROM on a workstation or install it on the server for viewing from any workstation attached to the server.

The online documentation in NetWare 3.1x was called *ElectroText*. In NetWare 4.1, the DynaText viewer replaces ElectroText. Although it has a different name and some new features, DynaText works in much the same way as its predecessor did.

NetWare 4.1 includes viewer programs for several operating systems, including Microsoft Windows, Macintosh, OS/2, and Novell UnixWare. (Since Novell no longer owns UnixWare, it may be discontinued.) A sample screen from the Windows DynaText viewer is shown in Figure 2.5.

All of the NetWare 4.1 manuals are included in the online version. DynaText uses a *hypertext* system, which means that you can click on highlighted words and instantly skip to the section they refer to. You are probably familiar with similar hypertext systems, such as the Help system in Microsoft Windows. You can view graphics, tables, and screenshots by clicking on their icons.

Novell's manuals are not known for being well organized; it can be difficult to find a particular item in a book, or even to figure out which book to look in. If you have access to the DynaText documentation, you can easily search for a word or phrase in all the books and skip directly to that section.

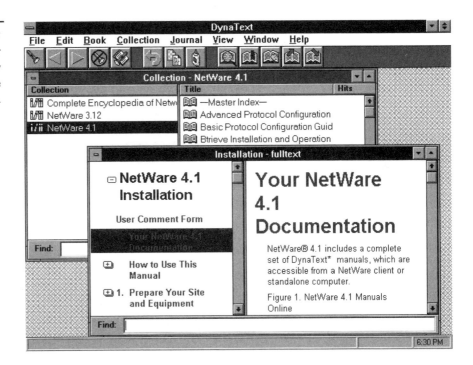

FIGURE 2.5
The DynaText viewer
allows you to view
NetWare 4.1 online
documentation.

Security Features

NETWARE HAS ALWAYS PROVIDED strong security features. Most companies don't need all of these features, but they can be useful for high-security situations. NetWare 4.1 adds even more security features—enough to make even the most paranoid network administrator happy.

Types of Security

Netware 4.1 has two main types of security:

- *NDS security* controls access to NDS objects.

- *File system security* controls access to files and directories.

For those companies that need high security, NetWare 4.1 provides extensive *auditing* features. An *auditor* is a special user who can monitor other users' actions on the network, including the actions of the network administrator. Even if you aren't interested in playing Big Brother, you may still find auditing useful to track usage of network resources and determine if adequate resources are available.

The details of NetWare 4.1's security, including auditing, are discussed in Chapter 7.

Memory Protection

The *memory protection* feature protects the server's memory from corruption. An NLM, or *NetWare Loadable Module*, is a program that is loaded on the file server. NetWare uses an *unprotected* memory management system to run NLMs. This means that every NLM has access to the server's entire memory. Therefore, a badly written or faulty NLM can write to memory belonging to other NLMs. Worse, it can write over the NetWare operating system itself. This causes corruption in the server's memory, usually resulting in a server crash or *abend* (abnormal end, NetWare's word for "crash and burn").

To pass Novell's NetWare Tested and Approved certification program, NLMs must prove that they do not cause these memory conflicts. Unfortunately, many NLMs are not Novell-certified, and even certified ones may not be perfect.

NetWare 4.1 allows you to play it safe with these suspect NLMs by using the memory protection feature. NetWare sets aside a *domain* (an area of memory) called the *protected domain* for unstable NLMs to run in. NLMs in this domain can access memory only in this domain, keeping them away from the memory used by the operating system and other modules. This scheme allows you to run otherwise unsafe NLMs (if you must) or to test new versions before allowing them full access to the server's memory.

This system is not usually needed and does have its disadvantages: Not all NLMs can be used in the protected domain. In addition, it is often necessary to keep NLMs in the unprotected areas so that they can communicate with each other.

Better Client Support

THE CLIENT SOFTWARE USED with NetWare 4.1 is also an improvement over older versions. The actual client software, called the *NetWare DOS Requester,* provides an improved way of accessing the network and its resources.

The DOS Requester (VLM.EXE) was introduced with NetWare 3.12, and an updated version is included with NetWare 4.1. The DOS Requester handles the connection between the network and the workstation. Previous versions of NetWare used the *DOS shell* (NETX.EXE). The DOS Requester provides more features, tighter integration with DOS, and support for NDS.

Clients running the DOS shell can still use the NetWare 4.1 network. However, you will need to use the DOS Requester to take full advantage of the features of NDS.

NetWare 4.1 supports a wider variety of clients, including PCs running DOS, Microsoft Windows, and OS/2; Apple Macintosh computers; and UNIX workstations. Non-PC workstations were not fully supported in older versions of NetWare. With NetWare 4.1, these machines get the respect they deserve: full support for NDS and most of the same features as the DOS Requester.

The DOS Requester also includes support for SNMP (Simple Network Management Protocol), which is an industry-standard network management protocol. Support for SNMP is now provided directly by the NetWare client software. Taking advantage of SNMP allows you to manage large networks efficiently.

Communication Improvements

ANOTHER SET OF IMPROVEMENTS in NetWare 4.1 involves the way that it sends data over the network. NetWare 4.1's installation program supports more protocols, or communication methods, than the previous versions. In addition, Netware 4.1 includes two features that streamline communication and improve speed: Packet Burst Protocol and Large Internet Packets.

More Protocol Support

Protocols are the languages that the server uses to communicate across the network. The most common network protocol is IPX, or *Internetwork Packet Exchange*. In NetWare 3.1*x*, IPX was the only protocol installed with a new server setup. If you required support for alternate protocols, such as AppleTalk, you needed to install them manually.

NetWare 4.1's installation program allows you to choose whether to install two additional protocols in addition to IPX:

- The AppleTalk protocol allows easy integration of NetWare with Apple Macintosh networks and peripherals.

- TCP/IP (*Transport Control Protocol/Internet Protocol*) is used to integrate NetWare with UNIX systems. In addition, TCP/IP is the standard protocol for communication over the Internet.

Packet Burst Protocol

The IPX protocol sends data across the network in units called *packets*. Packets are a specific size and contain a certain amount of information. The packets are sent using a *handshaking* process. In this process, after each packet is sent successfully, the receiving machine returns an acknowledgment. The sender waits until it receives this acknowledgment before sending the next packet. Although the term *packet burst* sounds slightly violent, it isn't what happens when a packet grows too large and explodes. The Packet Burst Protocol simply lets the server send groups of packets, or *bursts*, all at once. The burst is sent without handshaking, and the recipient sends an acknowledgment for the entire burst. If an error occurs, the sender needs to resend only the packet containing the error. Packet Burst Protocol is enabled by default in NetWare 4.1 and supported by both the server and workstation software. Figure 2.6 shows a comparison between Packet Burst Protocol and regular IPX communication.

Large Internet Packets

The packets transmitted over the network are usually a specific size, depending on the network protocol. When these packets are passed through a NetWare server acting as a router to another network, however, they are reduced to 512 bytes.

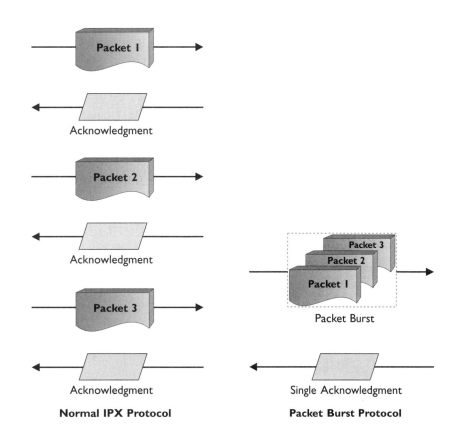

FIGURE 2.6
Packet Burst Protocol
allows large amounts of
data to be sent across the
network at once.

NetWare 4.1's *Large Internet Packet* (LIP) feature lets packets pass through the router without changing their size. This arrangement allows faster communication between networks. LIP can be combined with Packet Burst Protocol for efficient communication. NetWare 4.1 enables LIP by default.

International Features

NETWARE 4.1 GREATLY IMPROVES the international capabilities of NetWare with full support for multiple languages. Users can use NetWare utilities in their choice of language (English, French, Italian, German, or Spanish—the acronym FIGS might help you remember the non-English languages supported). You can choose a language for server and workstation utilities. Users at different workstations can even use the same utility in different languages. Future releases of NetWare 4 may include support for additional languages.

Other international features allow the server to use language-specific keyboards and to change the format of dates and numbers displayed by the system. NetWare 4.1 is sold in an English-only version and an international version. If you need support for a language other than English, make sure you purchase the international version.

Review

NETWARE 4.1 PROVIDES many new features that were not present in NetWare 3.1x. These include features that increase the speed of the network, improve communication, and provide additional services and resources.

The most important new feature of NetWare 4.1 is NDS, or NetWare Directory Services. NDS stores information about all of the users, printers, and other resources on the network in a database called the Directory. The Directory is organized into a treelike structure and consists of container and leaf objects.

Server Improvements

NetWare 4.1 introduced several improvements to the server software itself. These include

- A simplified installation process lets you use default settings.

- The SERVMAN utility makes it easy to manage server settings.

- Time synchronization allows multiple servers to keep the same time.

- Support for new hardware, including the Pentium processor.

- NetWare Server for OS/2 allows you to run a server and workstation on a single computer.

File System Improvements

The NetWare file system has also been improved with a number of enhancements that include the following features:

- *File compression* compresses data that is not in use, allowing more information to fit on the network disks.

- *Block suballocation* divides the disk into smaller units to allow more efficient storage.

- *Data migration* is provided by the *High-Capacity Storage System* (HCSS) and allows files that are not in use to be migrated to an optical storage device, or *jukebox*.

- *NetWare Peripheral Architecture* (NPA) provides a new method for vendors to write disk drivers.

Utility Improvements

NetWare utilities include the following improvements:

- Many of the utilities in NetWare 3.1*x* have been combined into single utilities for convenience.

- The PCONSOLE utility includes a Quick Setup option, which creates objects needed for printing in a single step.

- NetWare Administrator provides additional features for managing network objects.

As with previous versions of NetWare, NetWare 4.1 includes online documentation on CD-ROM. You can view the documentation directly from the CD-ROM on a workstation or install it on the server for viewing from any workstation attached to the server. The software used for this purpose is the DynaText viewer.

Security Improvements

NetWare has always provided strong security features. Improvements to security in NetWare 4.1 include

- Two types of security: file system security and NDS security to guard against disasters.

- Auditing features to monitor use of the network and its resources.

- The memory protection feature to protect the server's memory from corruption.

Other Improvements

Some of the other improvements in NetWare 4.1 are

- Improvements to the client software include the NetWare DOS Requester, support for additional clients (Macintosh, OS/2, and UNIX), and support for the Simple Network Management Protocol (SNMP).

- Communications improvements include support for additional protocols, Packet Burst Protocol, and Large Internet Packets (LIP).

- International features of NetWare 4.1 support multiple languages, including English, French, Italian, German, and Spanish.

PC Hardware

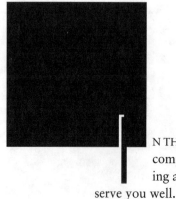

I N THIS CHAPTER we are going to take a look at the fundamental components of network hardware. As a network administrator, having a good understanding of the nuts and bolts of your network will serve you well.

Networks these days typically contain a variety of old and new technologies. Workstations may range from 12-year-old systems that boot from floppies (honestly!) to top-of-the-line Pentium multimedia workstations. As you might have guessed, not all companies have moved to the latest and greatest equipment. The next sections should give you an idea of what to expect.

This chapter and the next chapter are basic reviews of PC hardware and DOS. If you are an experienced computer professional, you may wish to skip these chapters; they are very basic and geared toward ensuring that everyone reading this book has an understanding of some fundamental concepts.

Understanding PC Technologies

P CS (PERSONAL COMPUTERS) are normally the most visible feature on Novell networks. So let's begin with an examination of what is under the cover of a PC.

A PC has the following basic components:

- **A motherboard,** which includes

    - The CPU (Central Processing Unit), also called the processor, the heart of the PC

    - The memory (RAM, or Random Access Memory)

    - The BIOS (Basic Input/Output Services)

- **A data bus and controller card,** which may include the following:

    - A *disk controller* that allows the PC to communicate with disk drives

    - An I/O (input/output) controller that provides one or more serial ports, used for communications, and parallel ports, usually used for printers

    - A NIC (Network Interface Card) that allows the PC to communicate with servers on the network

- **Storage devices,** including hard disk drives, floppy disk drives, and tape backup drives

- **A case** and **power supply** to hold the PC securely together and power the components

- **A monitor** to send output to the user

- **A keyboard** to receive input from the user

Now let's take a closer look at the components of a PC.

The Motherboard

The motherboard is the foundation upon which many of the most critical components of a PC rest. The large, printed circuit board, known as the motherboard, also serves as the backbone into which peripheral hardware is connected. Figure 3.1 shows a typical motherboard.

The most important pieces on the motherboard are the microprocessor; memory; interrupts, addresses, and ports; and the data bus.

The Microprocessor (CPU)

The CPU is commonly called the "brains" of a computer. Without the CPU, your computer would not be able to execute programs; it would be declared "dead."

In order to effectively execute programs, a CPU must be able to read and write information into the computer's memory, it must be able to recognize and carry out the series of commands or instructions supplied by the programs, and it must be able to direct the operation of the other parts of the computer. Furthermore, to survive in today's world, it must do all of this very quickly.

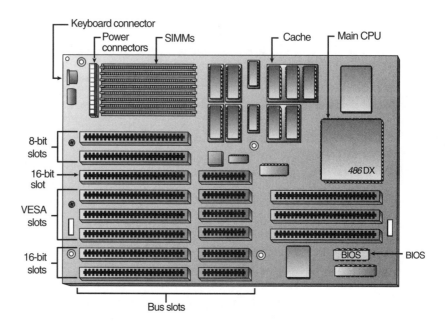

Intel is the manufacturer of the leading type of CPU. These processors range from the early 8086 and 8088 to the latest Pentium and Pentium Pro. Intel introduced its first CPU in June 1978, and since that time Intel chips have been the standard for PC processors.

Intel has built upon a successful design to create a series of CPUs, called the X86 family. Each new design has maintained 100 percent compatibility with previous versions, allowing every new design to execute software written for previous designs.

Although it is called the X86 family, the first Intel CPU to be widely accepted was called the 8088.

The speed of the CPU is measured in terms of megahertz (MHz). Since 1 MHz is equal to 1,000,000 cycles per second, we're talking about a lot of processing power in the CPU. Typical speeds range from 16 MHz for the older 386 computers to 133 MHz and beyond for the latest Pentiums.

These speeds are called *clock speeds* and are controlled by an internal timing source, or clock, on the CPU. However, some instructions—basic actions the CPU performs—can take more than one clock cycle to complete. Therefore, we measure the actual work that a processor can perform in MIPS—millions of instructions per second.

To the end user, the most noticeable difference among Intel CPUs is the speed. The chronological order of Intel CPUs, along with their processing speeds (measured in MIPS), follows:

8086	0.33 MIPS
8088	0.33 MIPS
80286	3 MIPS
80386	11 MIPS
80486	41 MIPS
Pentium (80586)	over 100 MIPS
Pentium Pro (80686)	over 300 MIPS

Other manufacturers, including AMD and Cyrix, sell Intel clone processors. They typically offer similar performance and a better price, but the clones may not be 100 percent compatible with all software and devices.

The 8088 was implemented with 29,000 transistors. Pentium-class processors have transistors numbering in the millions!

WHAT DO YOU REALLY NEED? Although Pentium processors and their successor, the new Pentium Pro or P6, are the most powerful processors, not everyone uses them—or needs them. Practically speaking, a 486 DX-33 or higher processor can be used for just about any application, and even a 386 is usable for DOS-based applications. Nevertheless, you'll find that many companies still try to do the nearly impossible—run Windows applications from the network using a 386, or even a 286. Even if the system does work, it will be very slow.

Statistically, 486 machines are the most popular workstations, but a great many 386 (and lower) machines are still out there. Some applications don't need anything better, and some companies aren't willing to spend the money to upgrade. Keep in mind, however, that NetWare's DOS Requester requires a 386 or better processor—so although a 286 can access the network, you won't be able to access NDS from that workstation.

BITS AND BYTES All of the information traveling across the motherboard of a computer is represented digitally as either the digit 1 or the digit 0. For example, the instruction that tells an Intel X86-family CPU to subtract is 0010110. This method of using 1s and 0s to represent information is called the *binary system*. The 1s and 0s are called binary digits, or more easily, *bits*. When a computer processes 1s and 0s, however, it does so in groups of 8, known as *bytes*.

Computer circuitry is capable of reacting to two states in the flow of the electric current that runs through it: high current and low current. These states of high and low current are what is represented by the 1s and 0s. One of the primary factors contributing to the development of computers as we know them is that it is relatively easy and inexpensive to create a circuit that can recognize the difference between high and low current (with an extremely low error ratio).

Since today's typical machine has over 8 million bytes of memory, we have adopted several metric terms to describe quantities of memory storage. Here are the most common terms:

- A byte is 8 bits.

- A kilobyte (K or KB) equals 1,024 bytes.

- A megabyte (M or MB) equals 1,048,576 bytes.

- A gigabyte (G or GB) equals 1,073,741,824 bytes.

Note that these terms aren't the nice round numbers that the metric system is famous for. This happens because of the binary system that computers use to address memory. Although 1,000 is a round number to you or me, it's not round to a computer—in binary 1,000 is expressed as 1111101000. Therefore, we measure memory in amounts convenient to the computer. Thus, a kilobyte is 1024 bytes— a nice round binary 10000000000. A megabyte is 1024 kilobytes, or 1024 × 1024 bytes, and so on.

Memory

Memory is crucial to the CPU's operation. It provides a quickly accessible storage place for all of the instructions that the CPU processes. Memory resides on the motherboard in close contact with the CPU.

The are two main types of memory:

- RAM (Random Access Memory)
- ROM (Read Only Memory)

RAM Because PC CPUs operate a such a high speed, they need quick access to the raw data, and they must be able to store the results of what has been processed quickly. The CPU itself can hold only a few bytes at a time, so memory must be able to hold enough bytes to support complex programs. Disks and tapes can store large quantities of information, but they are simply too slow for the CPU. The solution is RAM.

Random access memory has several characteristics that make it appropriate for working with the CPU. One of these characteristics is that the CPU can access programs and data that are stored in RAM directly, or "randomly." This access method is similar to the way you use a dictionary: You can open it directly to the entry you're looking for.

The terms memory and RAM are often used interchangeably.

The type of RAM most frequently used is *volatile*, which means that it requires a constant supply of electricity to maintain the data. If electricity is shut off, this RAM will lose its data. *Volatility* means that you can lose data that has not been saved to a disk or tape if the power to your PC goes down accidentally. Disks and tapes are examples of *nonvolatile* storage.

Newer PC motherboards often have two kinds of RAM:

- Dynamic RAM (DRAM)
- Static RAM (SRAM)

DRAM is typically found in the main memory. For example, a typical Pentium PC will have 8 or 16 megabytes of this type of RAM. DRAM is relatively inexpensive (single megabytes currently sell for about $40). It is, however, much slower than SRAM.

Although SRAM and DRAM are both volatile, SRAM is able to maintain the data as long as the power is on. DRAM, on the other hand, requires that each byte of memory be accessed several times per second in order to keep it. This constant cycle, called memory *refresh*, is the reason DRAM is slower.

SRAM often appears on a motherboard in small banks of chips that are used as data caches. Because SRAM is much faster than DRAM, it can help boost system performance.

Most PCs have another type of RAM called *complementary metal oxide semiconductor* (CMOS). CMOS is used to store system information about such things as the floppy and hard disk, the amount of installed memory, and the type of display. The CMOS memory is also volatile, but a small battery holds this information after you shut off your PC. Your system uses this information when it boots up again.

ROM Read only memory (ROM) is a type of permanent memory. It does not disappear when you shut off the PC and does not require a battery to keep it running. The data stored on ROM is usually stored on the chips by the manufacturer and cannot be changed. An important piece of ROM on a PC is called the *Basic Input/Output System* or BIOS.

The information stored in ROM is frequently called firmware.

The BIOS is responsible for some very fundamental functions in a PC, such as displaying text on a monitor and allowing keyboard input. When a PC boots up, the BIOS programs perform an elemental system test and then use information supplied by the CMOS to identify the disk drives attached to the system, which are then searched for the operating system.

Interrupts, Addresses, and Ports

Hardware devices installed in the PC, such as modems and network cards, use several methods to communicate with the computer. These methods are explained in the sections below.

INTERRUPTS (IRQS) The CPU in a PC has several inputs that allow devices to get its attention—to interrupt it—if it is performing another task. These inputs are called *interrupts*, or IRQs (for Interrupt Requests). Interrupts are numbered from 0 to 15. Some have specific purposes, while others are available for new devices you may install. The table below summarizes the IRQs and their typical uses.

Interrupt Number	Standard Use	Notes
0	System timer	Reserved by system
1	Keyboard	Standard for all machines

Interrupt Number	Standard Use	Notes
2	System I/O	Reserved by system
3	COM2/4 (serial port)	Standard for most machines
4	COM1/3 (serial port)	Standard for most machines
5	LPT2 (printer)	Available on most machines
6	Floppy disk	Standard for all machines
7	LPT1 (printer)	May be shared with some devices
8	Real-time clock	Reserved by system
9	Redirected IRQ2	Available in some cases
10	Unused	Available on most machines
11	Unused	Available on most machines
12	Unused	Available on some machines
13	Math coprocessor	Reserved by system if math coprocessor is installed
14	Hard Disk	Standard for most machines
15	Unused	Available on some machines; sometimes used for hard disks

An interrupt can typically be used by one device. When you install a new device such as a network card in the computer, you must choose an unused interrupt. You usually specify an interrupt by setting a jumper or switch on the device or by running a special configuration program.

The interrupts listed here are for 386 and newer CPUs. Although the list is similar for older systems, they did not allow the use of interrupt numbers above 9.

When two devices use the same interrupt, a conflict occurs. This conflict may cause the computer to *crash,* or refuse to function at all; or it may allow things to work normally and then crash when one or both of the devices are used. In any case, you should resolve the conflict quickly, since it can seriously affect the operation of your computer, and you may lose precious data.

PORTS (I/O ADDRESSES) Along with an interrupt, most devices use a small part of the upper memory area to send data back and forth to the CPU. This area is called a *port address*, or sometimes an *I/O address*. These addresses are used in small blocks—usually 16 bytes or less. Addresses are specified with a hexadecimal number and typically range from 300 to 360.

Like interrupts, multiple devices using the same address can cause a conflict. The use of addresses is not as standardized as interrupts, so you will often need to consult a device's manual to see which port address it is using.

MEMORY ADDRESSES Some devices, particularly video cards and high-speed network cards, use another area of memory as a larger buffer. These areas are specified with a hexadecimal number and usually range from C000 to E000.

DMA CHANNELS A final resource that a device may use is a DMA (direct memory access) channel. These are high-speed interfaces to the bus that allow a device to access memory directly. DMA channels are numbered from zero to two and are typically used only by time-critical devices, such as sound cards and high-speed disk controllers.

How a PC Uses Memory

Today's PC typically includes 4, 8, or 16MB of memory, well over 10 times the original 640KB. However, because of the limitations of the 8086 architecture—still present in today's Intel processors—memory must be accessed in several different ways. Here are the types of memory that can be accessed in a PC:

- **Conventional memory:** The 640KB area has been a standard for too long now. It is the same 640KB that the original IBM PC used when it first shipped. This area is used to store programs; many programs can still use only this area of memory.

- **Upper memory:** The memory just above the 640KB area, which includes a total of 384KB. Your video card, NIC, and other hardware components use a sizable amount of this space. Conventional 640KB and the upper 384KB add up to the first 1024KB—the first megabyte of RAM.

- **Expanded memory (XMS):** This memory uses a 64KB block of memory to access the higher areas of memory, swapping memory in and out of the block or *page frame*. This system is rarely used in today's PCs, but remains as a standard.

- **Extended memory:** The memory above 1MB. A computer that has 16MB of RAM has only 15MB of extended memory. Today's PCs can access this memory without swapping, but use of extended memory still requires a different method of access.

- **High memory:** This is a 64KB area that begins at the 1MB boundary. It is addressed by HIMEM.SYS, which ships with later versions of DOS or Windows. The most common use of high memory is for part of the COMMAND.COM file in DOS 5 and 6.*x* products from Microsoft. This allocation scheme allows DOS to take a much smaller portion of the precious 640KB area.

The IBM XT's 8086 could address a maximum of 1MB of RAM. The 286 addressed 16MB RAM. The 80386 and later processors can address as much as 4GB of RAM. However, a computer that has an 80386 processor will not always address more than 16MB of RAM. The computer's motherboard must also support the addressing. For example, the IBM PS/2 Model 80 is an 80386 machine that was commonly used as a file server. System administrators who installed more RAM were disappointed to find that the IBM PS/2 Model 80 supported a maximum of 16MB of RAM, even though the Intel 80386 processor in the IBM is capable of addressing up to 4GB.

A PC operates in two modes when accessing memory: *real mode* and *protected mode*. Real mode is a backward-compatible technology developed for *x*86 processors. When a 286, 386, 486, or 586 is running in real mode, it is running like an 8086 processor. This feature means that programs created for the original IBM XT will still run on your Pentium Pro chip (although just a bit faster).

Protected mode was developed for 286 chips or later. Many programmers writing for the original 8086 chip's memory would walk over each other's memory, causing conflicts and instability. Protected mode helps solve this conflict by making programs request memory from the operating system.

The theory is that memory used by a program is protected by the operating system. Another program running on the PC is required to request memory from the operating system. The operating system will give access only to memory that is not used.

Optimizing Memory

When Intel designed the 8088 CPU for IBM to use in the original IBM PC, it could address only 1MB of memory and programs were able to use only the 640KB base memory. Later Intel CPUs kept this memory design to maintain backward-compatibility and to ensure programmers that new Intel hardware would not make their programs obsolete. This guarantee eventually created an enormous base of prospective software buyers, since all existing computers could run the software. Consequently, Intel-based computers have the largest commercial software selection in the world.

Lotus, Intel, and Microsoft joined forces at the 286 introduction to create the LIM (Lotus/Intel/Microsoft) memory standard, which was a method for programs to access more than 640KB of memory. The LIM standard has given way to *extended memory,* now widely implemented through Microsoft's HIMEM.SYS files and EMM386.EXE drivers for Windows and DOS.

Although the use of extended memory has overcome the 640KB barrier, the limit still applies to many programs, which use only conventional memory. Thus, you may even get out-of-memory errors when you have 8 or 16MB of RAM. Most likely, it's the 640KB conventional memory that is running out.

In its DOS 6.*x* versions, Microsoft ships two handy utilities to optimize memory: MEM.EXE and MEMMAKER.EXE. MEM.EXE shows current memory usage file by file, and MEMMAKER.EXE optimizes the memory settings. You can also purchase third-party memory optimization programs, such as Quarterdeck's QEMM Optimize program. IBM DOS and Novell DOS also sell memory optimization utilities.

Although MEMMAKER will almost always give you an automated configuration that is superior to manual optimization, you can sometimes outdo it. If MEMMAKER doesn't give you the results you need, try loading programs in a different order as a last resort. Since memory is filled on a first-come first-served basis, this sequence may allow for a more efficient arrangement.

The Data Bus

A CPU is useless by itself. It can process data, but it can't read data from a disk or display it on your screen. In order for the CPU to communicate with the memory and output devices, there must be a medium through which data is transmitted. On a PC motherboard, this medium is known as the *bus.*

The bus that connects the CPU to the memory on a motherboard is known as the *data bus.* This bus is made of printed-circuit wiring on the motherboard. This bus also connects to the *expansion bus,* which carries data to and from the bus slots. The slots accept the adapters that allow you to add capabilities to your computer—video cards and network cards, for example.

A PC motherboard normally has several *bus slots*; refer to Figure 3.1 to see the bus and the slots. These slots are attached to the expansion bus and are used to connect *adapter cards* to the motherboard. Adapter cards give a computer the ability to have serial, parallel, and game ports; to communicate across modems; to produce video output on a monitor and audio output to external speakers; and to connect to a network. Typical adapter cards include network interface cards, video cards, disk controller cards, input/output (I/O) cards, sound cards, and modems.

The standard bus, developed with the advent of the PC, is the ISA (Industry Standard Architecture) bus. Newer standards that allow faster communication include the following:

- EISA is an enhanced version of ISA and is often used for network servers.

- VESA local bus is a popular high-performance bus standard. It became very popular as the first high-speed bus available at a reasonable price. Inexplicably, it is not well supported by NetWare or by network cards. PCI is rapidly replacing VESA in most new PCs.

- PCI is the latest bus innovation and is well supported by NetWare and by network cards. The PCI bus is much faster than VESA and allows full 32-bit communication between I/O cards and the motherboard. Since the PCI specification is still in a state of flux, be sure you purchase cards that are guaranteed to be compatible with your system.

- PCMCIA, or PC Card, is a standard for credit card–size adapters. These are traditionally used to connect network cards and other peripherals to portable notebook computers. In addition, some new models of desktop PCs include slots for PC cards.

Within the circuitry of the CPU there is another bus called the internal data bus. This bus carries data among the different parts of the CPU itself. A bus is measured in terms of how many bits it can carry at one time. Internal data buses of the first popular Intel CPU, the 8088, carried 8 bits at a time. Pentium 586s have 64-bit internal data buses. Apple Macintosh machines are also popular in many companies, particularly those involved with graphic design or art. The Macintosh architecture uses a 68000-series CPU developed by Motorola and an operating system created by Apple. The latest Mac operating system is System 7.5, and System 8 is in the works. New Macintosh machines called Power Macs use the PowerPC processor, a new processor line from Motorola and IBM. The PowerPC is as fast as a Pentium, and in some cases it is faster. The PowerPC can also run Windows NT, and a version of NetWare for the PowerPC is in development.

Review

N THIS CHAPTER we have examined the fundamental components of network hardware. Networks typically contain a variety of old and new technologies. We have explored the components of a PC; the most common network client and server; and how the CPU, memory, and external devices interact.

PC Components

The basic components of a PC include the following:

- **A motherboard,** which includes

    - The CPU (Central Processing Unit), also called the processor

    - The memory (RAM, or Random Access Memory)

    - The BIOS (Basic Input/Output Services)

- **A data bus and controller card,** which may include the following:

    - A *disk controller* that allows the PC to communicate with disk drives

    - An I/O (input/output) controller that provides one or more serial ports, used for communications, and parallel ports, usually used for printers

    - A NIC (Network Interface Card) that allows the PC to communicate with servers on the network

- **Storage devices,** including hard disk drives, floppy disk drives, and tape backup drives

- **A case** and **power supply** to hold the PC securely together and power the components

- **A monitor** to send output to the user

- **A keyboard** to receive input from the user

PCs and Memory

All of the information traveling across the motherboard of a computer is represented digitally as either the digit 1 or the digit 0. This is called the *binary system*. The 1s and 0s are called binary digits, or, more easily, *bits*. The following other measures are used:

- A byte is 8 bits.

- A kilobyte (K or KB) equals 1,024 bytes.

- A megabyte (M or MB) equals 1,048,576 bytes.

- A gigabyte (G or GB) equals 1,073,741,824 bytes.

There are two main types of memory:

- RAM (Random-Access Memory)

- ROM (Read-Only Memory)

Hardware Communication

Hardware devices installed in the PC, such as modems and network cards, use several methods to communicate with the computer:

- Interrupts (IRQs)

- Ports (I/O addresses)

- Memory addresses

- DMA channels

PC Memory

Five types of memory can be accessed in a PC:

- Conventional memory is the 640KB area that the original IBM PC used.

- Upper memory is just above the 640KB area and includes a total of 384KB. Your video card, NIC, and other hardware components use this area.

- Expanded memory (XMS) uses the top 64KB of upper memory as a swap area for system programs.

- Extended memory is the memory above 1MB.

- High memory is a 64KB area that begins at the 1MB boundary. It is addressed by HIMEM.SYS, which ships with later versions of DOS or Windows.

DOS and Windows

NTIL THE DAY many network administrators dream of, when everything on computer networks will be handled with ultra-friendly graphical user interfaces, a basic understanding of DOS is an unavoidable necessity. In this chapter, we are going take a whirlwind tour through the world of DOS. First we will define what it is. Then we will explain some handy DOS features, and we'll provide a few tips for improving PC performance using DOS. Finally, we will look at the most popular attempt at a friendly graphical user interface, Windows, and its newest incarnation, Windows 95.

The Basics of DOS

OS STANDS FOR Disk Operating System. DOS is a type of software that resides on a computer and provides very fundamental functionality. It has two main roles:

- DOS manages computer resources, such as memory and hard drives, acting as an intermediary between applications and system hardware. When an application requires access to the hardware on a system, it uses DOS.

- DOS provides an interface with which you can manage system resources.

Because DOS is able to communicate directly with a computer's BIOS, it is able to manage hardware for an application. An application can simply make a request for hardware access to DOS, which in turn communicates the request to the BIOS, which directly accesses the hardware. DOS is helpful because it speaks BIOS's language.

Many of the functions DOS provides are so basic that it is easy to take them for granted. DOS handles input with a keyboard and output to a monitor as well as communication between computer components. DOS also provides the files in which you can store information and the directories that you can use to organize files.

Microsoft's MS-DOS, the most popular type of DOS, is found on about 90 percent of all of the microcomputers on NetWare networks.

DOS includes commands that allow you to do things like copy disks, read and write to files, and check your disk for errors—very basic stuff. These commands are the part of DOS that network administrators use daily. Because these commands are of great practical use, we'll look carefully at them later in this chapter, but first you need to understand how DOS actually gets started on your computer.

In this chapter, when you see the word DOS, we mean MS-DOS. IBM and Novell both have versions of DOS, PC-DOS and DR-DOS, respectively. They are actually very similar to MS-DOS. Because MS-DOS is so prevalent, however, we will focus upon it.

How DOS Gets Started on a Computer

As we saw in the last chapter, the BIOS performs some very basic checks when a computer is first turned on (or warm booted). After the start-up checks, the BIOS searches the A drive (normally a floppy disk drive), the B drive, and the C drive (normally a hard drive) for an operating system. DOS may reside on either a floppy disk or a hard drive, depending on whether you have loaded it onto the hard drive or booted it from a floppy.

When the BIOS finds DOS, it loads the most important DOS files into memory. Among these files are two of special concern to a network administrator: AUTOEXEC.BAT and CONFIG.SYS. Network administrators often edit these two files for workstation-specific purposes. We'll look at these files a bit further along in this chapter.

After the important files have been loaded into memory and the necessary program lines have been executed, the *DOS prompt* appears on the screen. The DOS prompt often appears as the letter A or C, representing one of the drives on your computer. It is typically followed by a colon, a greater than sign, and a blinking line, called a *cursor*, and looks like this:

```
C:>_
```

The DOS prompt can be customized using the PROMPT command. You can enhance the drive designation with your own text and information supplied by your computer, such as the time, date, or current directory.

The DOS prompt is your doorway into the inner workings of DOS. After DOS has been loaded into memory, it takes control of your machine, except for the input that you enter through the DOS prompt. By typing a recognized command, you can set DOS into motion—creating directories, copying files, or doing whatever it is that you have instructed it to do.

In order to convince DOS to carry out a command, you must be very careful to follow the correct syntax. You must type each command precisely with no extra spaces or spelling errors. (You can, however, use either upper or lower case.) For example, to find out what version of DOS you are using, type the command **VER** at the DOS prompt and press enter. DOS will show you what version is running on your machine. If, however, you try to spell the command phonetically and type "VURRR," DOS will quickly alert you to the error of your ways by displaying this message:

```
Bad command or file name
```

Even seasoned DOS users don't always remember the correct syntax for DOS commands. Fortunately, DOS provides online help. If, in the midst of your trials and tribulations, you can remember how to spell *help* correctly, simply type it at the DOS prompt and you will have access to DOS Help and detailed descriptions of correct DOS usage.

DOS Help contains a selection of commands on which you can get help, as shown in Figure 4.1. If you select a command, you will see the correct syntax for that command. You will see that some commands permit more than one way to spell their names. For example, to change the current directory, you can type either **CD** or **CHDIR**.

In DOS Help, you may also see references to something called a *switch*. A switch is a brief command that you can use to override the normal execution of many other commands. For example, the command ERASE can be switched so that it prompts you for approval before erasing a file. The switch for this is /P. To have a prompt appear before erasing, you would use the ERASE command as usual, but type **/P** at the end of your command.

FIGURE 4.1
The main screen
of DOS Help.

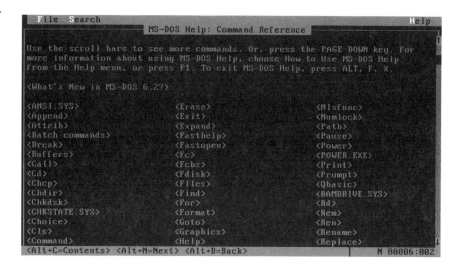

*A switch is always indicated by a forward slash (/), not to be confused with a backslash (\),
which is used to designate a directory or to separate file and directory names.*

You can also get immediate help on any DOS command by typing its name
followed by the /? switch. This command displays that command's available
options. For example, the command below returns the list of options for the
FORMAT command:

```
FORMAT /?
```

DOS versions 4 and higher offer a type of graphical interface that is one
step up from the command line approach. Rather than requiring you to type in
each command, you can simply make selections using a mouse or arrow keys.
The interface, called the DOS Shell, is nothing to get too excited about. It is
about as rudimentary as graphical interfaces get, but it does offer an alternative
way of using DOS. Most professional DOS users, however, find it easier to
simply memorize the commands and type them at the prompt.

DOS Files and Directories

The basic building blocks of DOS are files and directories. Anytime you enter a
command, you are working with programs that are stored in files, which are

organized under directories. Everything you (or an application you use) adds to DOS is stored in a file that resides in a directory, so it's pretty safe to say that files and directories form the basis for DOS.

Files are simply organizational structures in which data is stored. A file can contain a letter, a spreadsheet, a program, or other types of data. Each file has a name that is unique in its directory. A directory is like a folder that you use to organize paper files in a filing cabinet, providing larger units of order.

When you view a directory, as in Figure 4.2, you see that file entries include the following information about each file:

- File name

- Extension

- File size

- Date last modified

- Time last modified

There is one special directory that has a unique role in DOS. This is known as the root *directory. This directory is installed by DOS when the disk is prepared. Other directories are organized under the one and only root directory. For this reason, some people call other directories* subdirectories, *since they are really branches of the root directory.*

FIGURE 4.2
A typical DOS directory.

```
D:\>dir

 Volume in drive D is BS
 Volume Serial Number is 195D-08FA
 Directory of D:\

NWSERVER     <DIR>         01-01-96  12:55p
WINDOWS      <DIR>         01-16-96  11:01p
WP61         <DIR>         01-16-96  11:01p
PARADOX      <DIR>         01-16-96  11:02p
QEADM        <DIR>         01-16-96  11:02p
TILLMAN      <DIR>         01-16-96  11:02p
FNORD        <DIR>         01-16-96  11:02p
NEWAUTO  BAT           553 06-18-95  10:04p
AUTOEXEC BAT           311 01-13-96   5:53p
SCANDISK LOG         1,915 12-13-95  11:06p
CONFIG   SYS           403 01-13-96   5:53p
COPYOFLO SYS       129,078 07-14-95  12:00a
        12 file(s)         132,260 bytes
                        17,950,720 bytes free

D:\>
```

Each directory is organized under the root directory and referenced using its *path name*. Any time you want to find a directory other than the current directory, you must use its path name. The following is an example of a path name for a directory called EDGETEK:

```
C:\COMPANY\TRAINING\EDGETEK
```

In this example, EDGETEK is a directory appearing under the directory TRAINING, which is under a directory called COMPANY, which is under the ROOT directory (C:\). A path is the route from the root directory to a particular directory or file.

To access a directory or file from a drive other than the one on which the directory or file resides, you must use the full path name, such as in the example above. If you are on the same drive, you can start the path at the current directory. For example, to get to EDGETEK from the COMPANY directory, you could simply use the following path:

```
TRAINING\EDGETEK
```

File Names

DOS has rigid rules about how you can name files. Some of them, such as the eight-character limit on file names, are pretty unpopular. Nevertheless, we're stuck with them. The rules you'll want to keep in mind when creating file names are as follows:

- File names consist of a name that is no longer than eight characters, a period (.), and an extension of up to three letters.

- File names cannot have any spaces.

- DOS reserves the following file names: AUX, CLOCK$, COM1 through COM4, CON, LPT1 through LPT3, NUL, and PRN.

- File names can include any letter, number, or symbol on the keyboard except the following:

  *

  ?

  [

  ]

  <

  >

  ,

  "

  ;

  :

  /

  \

  +

  =

Extensions are often used to identify file types. For example, Microsoft Word uses the extension DOC to identify the files it creates. DOS reserves several types of file name extensions for special functions. They are as follows:

- EXE—Executable files containing programs.

- COM—Another type of executable program file, called a command file.

- BIN—Another type of executable program file.

- BAT—A batch file containing programs composed of DOS commands. Batch files allow you to execute multiple commands automatically or by entering a single command.

- SYS—System driver files that allow DOS and computer hardware to interface.

Some examples of valid DOS file names are the following:

- AUTOEXEC.BAT

- COMMAND.COM

- CONFIG.SYS

- SALES.DOC

- MISC.XXX

- 123.ABC

- MGM@XM.9_9

When you create a file with a valid file name, DOS registers it in the File Allocation Table (FAT). The FAT is where DOS keeps track of file statistics, such as name and extension, size, and location on the disk.

File Attributes

Another feature of the file system is file attributes. These are characteristics that a file can have. Attributes are often called flags, since they indicate a certain characteristic of a file. DOS includes the following file attributes:

- H (Hidden):

- S (System):

- R (Read only):

- A (Archive):

To change attributes, you use the ATTRIB command described later in this chapter.

CONFIG.SYS and AUTOEXEC.BAT

As we mentioned earlier, AUTOEXEC.BAT and CONFIG.SYS are two DOS files of special importance.

CONFIG.SYS

During the boot process, DOS automatically reads and processes a file called CONFIG.SYS. The contents of this file help determine how your PC is configured; it includes options for how your PC runs and commands that load programs that allow DOS to communicate with computer hardware. These programs, called *device drivers*, support devices that the BIOS does not support directly. Here is an example of a CONFIG.SYS file:

```
DEVICE=C:\DOS\HIMEM.SYS
DEVICE=C:\DOS\EMM386.EXE NOEMS
DOS=HIGH,UMB
LASTDRIVE=Z
FILES=40
BUFFERS=25
```

Let's take a closer look at each command:

- HIMEM.SYS is a driver that allows the high memory area to be used.

- EMM386.EXE is the expanded memory manager. In this case, the NOEMS switch is used. This means that no expanded memory will be allocated, but the upper-memory area is made available.

- DOS=HIGH,UMB specifies that DOS will be loaded into high memory. This is a feature of MS-DOS 5.0 and higher. The UMB switch provides upper-memory blocks for application use.

- LASTDRIVE=Z specifies the last drive letter used for DOS drives. If the DOS Requester is being used for network connectivity, this line also includes network drives.

- FILES=40 specifies the number of DOS file handles that are available. Effectively, this controls how many files DOS can have open at one time.

- BUFFERS=25 specifies the number of buffers available for file reads and writes. A low number can cause a decrease in speed.

CONFIG.SYS commands are completely separate from DOS commands. One good way to recognize them is that the CONFIG.SYS commands always include an equals sign (=).

AUTOEXEC.BAT

Next in the boot process, DOS executes commands from another file: AUTOEXEC.BAT. These commands are actual DOS commands, as described in the next section.

Commands in AUTOEXEC.BAT are typically used to load TSR (terminate and stay resident) programs. These are programs that run in the background and provide an extra function. The network drivers that allow access to NetWare 4.1 are examples of TSR programs. Here is an example of an AUTOEXEC.BAT file, including the network drivers. Detailed explanations of each of these commands are given under the appropriate command name in the next section.

```
C:\DOS\SMARTDRV.EXE
PROMPT $P$G
PATH C:\DOS;C:\WINDOWS;C:\
CD\NWCLIENT
LH LSL
LH 3C5X9
LH IPXODI
VLM
F:
LOGIN MAIN\BOB
```

Understanding DOS Commands

DOS COMMANDS ARE EASY TO USE—after you've played with them a few times. All you need is to understand the syntax and spelling and to press enter after you type the full command. As you go through this section, you may wish to practice and experiment with the commands.

After you've used these basic commands for a while in your work on computers, spend some time looking through DOS Help to discover the subtleties of the DOS commands you use most. Sometimes adding one little switch to your repertoire can really speed up your routine work.

You can place most of these commands in the AUTOEXEC.BAT file to execute when the computer boots and to avoid having to type them routinely. Of course, some are more useful than others.

CD (CHDIR)

If you type **CD** at the prompt, you will see the name of the current directory. This may seem odd, since CD stands for Change Directory; if you type **CD** followed by the name of a directory, DOS will move you to that directory. Hence, the name CD.

There are a few different ways you can use CD:

- CD\ takes you to the root.

- CD\ followed by the name of a directory takes you to that directory if it is under the root. For example, CD\DOS will take you to the DOS directory. Note that there is no space between CD\ and DOS.

- CD followed by the name of a directory takes you to that directory if it is under the current directory. For example, if you type **CD TEMP** while in the DOS directory, you will be taken to the C:\DOS\TEMP directory.

- CD .. moves you to the parent directory of the current directory. Note that there *is* a space between CD and "..". For example, if you are in the C:\DOS\TEMP directory, typing **CD ..** will take you to the DOS directory.

CHKDSK

DOS version 6.2 introduced a command called SCANDISK, which you should use instead of CHKDSK if you have it. Otherwise, you may want to use CHKDSK on occasion to recover lost disk space. DOS loses disk space when it fails to keep its file tracking system in order. The CHKDSK command produces a hard disk status report that can alert you to errors in DOS's filing system. It also has a limited ability to fix disk errors.

To check a hard disk and attempt to resolve disk errors, type **CHKDSK** followed by the drive letter and the switch /F, as in the following example:

```
CHKDSK C: /F
```

CLS

Anytime you have too much useless stuff printed on your screen, type the clear screen command, CLS, to wipe it away. This command clears the screen and returns you to a DOS prompt at the top of the screen.

COPY

This command makes a duplicate of one or more files. For example, if you want to make a backup of your CONFIG.SYS file, you can go to the directory in which it is stored and make a copy using the copy command as follows:

```
COPY CONFIG.SYS CONFIG.BAK
```

You can also make copies to save in other locations. For example, if you want to copy your CONFIG.SYS file to a floppy on the A: drive, type the following:

```
COPY C:\CONFIG.SYS A:
```

COPY also allows you to duplicate a file to other directories on the same drive. For example, the following command makes a duplicate of the CONFIG.SYS file in a directory called BACKUP under the OTHERS directory:

```
COPY C:\CONFIG.SYS C:\OTHERS\BACKUP
```

If you want to copy multiple files at the same time, you may find that a wildcard is helpful. For example, to copy all of the files on a floppy in the A: drive that end with EXE to a directory on the C: drive called MISC, you could type the following:

```
COPY A:*.EXE C:\MISC
```

Two of the most useful DOS tools are the wildcard characters: the question mark (?) and the asterisk (*). These can be used in place of any group of characters when you want to work with groups of files or when you're just not sure of an exact file name. The wildcard characters can be used in the file name and/or the extension. The question mark can match any single character except a blank. The asterisk can match any number of characters, blanks included.

If you COPY a file to a destination directory with a file that has the same name, the new file will overwrite the existing file in the destination directory. Even worse, you cannot undelete the file using UNDELETE!

The syntax for the COPY command is as follows:

```
COPY [source drive and file name][target drive and
    file name]
```

If you are copying to and from the same directory, you do not need to specify the drive.

DEL

When you want to delete one or more files, you can use DEL (or ERASE). The following, for example, deletes the document NONEED:

```
DEL NONEED.DOC
```

DEL can also be used with wildcards. To delete all files ending with DOC in a directory, for example, you could type the following:

```
DEL *.DOC
```

Using wildcards can be dangerous. When using them, be sure that you don't accidentally erase a needed file. DOS versions 4 and later allow you to add the /P switch at the end of a DEL command. This switch instructs DOS to prompt you before deleting a file.

DELTREE

This command was introduced with DOS 6. It allows you to delete a directory and all the file and subdirectories contained within it (i.e., a "tree") in one fell swoop. Normally, you will be prompted to confirm the deletion, but if you are feeling especially bold, you can add the switch /Y to skip the prompt. To delete a directory called EXTRA, along with all subdirectories and files, the following would suffice:

```
DELTREE C:\EXTRA
```

If you delete a file's directory, you cannot undelete it.

DIR

When you want to know what files and directories are in the current directory, type **DIR.** This command produces a listing that includes the file names, extensions, size, and last update time/date.

If you are ever bored, go to a Windows directory and type **DIR.** Try to read the files as they fly by. Once you are thoroughly frustrated, type **DIR /P.** This switch allows you to move down the list one screen at a time. The command DIR /W lists files in five columns across the screen, but the only information listed will be file names and extensions.

DISKCOPY

You use this command to copy diskettes. The diskettes must be the same size and density (e.g., 3.5" high-density floppies). To make a copy using this command, type **DISKCOPY** followed by the location of the original diskette and the location of the target diskette. For example, the following command copies a floppy in drive A: to a similar floppy in drive B:

```
DISKCOPY A: B:
```

If you have only one floppy drive, you will need to do the floppy swap to get the job done.

DISKCOPY will automatically format and unformat disks for you.

DOSSHELL

Although, on first glance, this command may look like a terrible place to go, DOSSHELL really takes you to a relatively pleasant graphical interface called the DOS Shell. The DOS Shell allows you to use DOS by selecting graphics, rather than typing commands. The shell is fairly useful for beginners, but you'll probably find that typing command lines is actually much quicker. The DOS Shell is not included with DOS 6.2.

EDIT

To make changes to your AUTOEXEC.BAT or CONFIG.SYS files, you can use the EDIT command. For example, the following command opens the editor using the CONFIG.SYS file:

```
EDIT C:\CONFIG.SYS
```

The editor is a full-screen interface that allows you to save, load, and search and replace within the file. You can type in the editor window directly to change the file. Use ALT+F to access the file menu and save your file. You can also press F1 while in EDIT for a useful help system.

Edit first appears in DOS 5. If you have an earlier version, you can use the command EDLIN.

FORMAT

The FORMAT command prepares a disk for its first use. (Your hard disk was probably formatted when it was installed.) The formatting process creates the FAT and divides the disk so that it is ready to store files.

The most common use for FORMAT is for formatting floppy disks (although many of these now come preformatted). Here is the command to format a disk in the A: drive:

```
FORMAT A:
```

Note that formatting permanently erases all data on the disk. There is one exception to this rule: In DOS 5.0 and later, the UNFORMAT command can recover a disk you just formatted. However, if you've used the disk after the format, there's nothing you can do to recover lost files.

If you *want* to erase a disk and ensure that it cannot be unformatted, add the /U switch. This command prevents any data from being saved on the disk in the A: drive:

```
FORMAT A: /U
```

FORMAT is one of the few commands that can really damage something if you're not careful with it. Do not format a disk unless it's blank or unless you are certain there is no useful data on it. FORMAT can be used on hard drives, such as C:, so be especially careful.

MD (MKDIR)

MD stands for Make Directory. To create a subdirectory called Sales in your current directory simply type

```
MD SALES
```

If you want to create a directory somewhere other than in the current directory, specify the path. For example, if you are in another directory but want to make a Sales subdirectory under a directory called BIZNIZ, you could type the following:

```
MD C:\BIZNIZ\SALES
```

MEM

DOS versions 5 and later have this memory status command. By typing **MEM** at the DOS prompt, you can see what portion of the total RAM on your computer is available. If you add the switch /C, you can see how much memory is being used by the programs that are currently loaded. If a long list is whizzing by, you can use the /P switch to view single pages at a time.

MOVE

DOS 6 and later include the MOVE command. It is used to move files from one location to another. For example, to move the file MAACK from the directory C:\WORK\ALLDAY to a new directory called C:\PLAY\BOY, you could type the following

```
MOVE C:\WORK\ALLDAY\MAACK C:\PLAY\BOY
```

You can also use the MOVE command to rename a directory. The following command renames a directory called ANCIENT:

```
MOVE C:\ANCIENT C:\MODERN
```

PATH

If you want DOS to be able to find a DOS program file that is not in your current directory, you can use the PATH command to expand the DOS search range.

By default, DOS searches only the current directory. DOS will then proclaim "Bad Command or Filename" if you attempt to execute a program file (such as a file ending with .COM, .EXE, or .BAT) that is not in your current directory.

When you put a PATH command in your AUTOEXEC.BAT, for example, you can set DOS to search in additional directories. To have DOS search your DOS directory, your LOTUS directory, and your root directory, in that particular order, use the following command:

```
PATH C:\DOS;C:\LOTUS;C:\
```

Notice that directories are separated by semicolons.

PRINT

If you type **PRINT,** followed by the name of a text file, DOS will print that file to the default printer. If you want to print multiple files, simply list them. For example, use the following command to print the text files DOG and BARK:

```
PRINT DOG.TXT BARK.TXT
```

RD (RMDIR)

If you have an empty directory just hanging around, you can delete it using the remove directory command. Simply type **RD** followed by the name of the directory.

REN

The rename command allows you to rename files. Type **REN** followed by the name of the file and the desired new name, and REN changes the file's name. The file will no longer exist under the original name.

SCANDISK

As we mentioned earlier, SCANDISK is the preferred method of analyzing and repairing hard disks. After you type SCANDISK, the program checks the current drive for errors. If SCANDISK finds an error, a dialog that explains the problem will appear, as shown in Figure 4.3.

SCANDISK is very easy to understand and use; it works on both compressed and uncompressed drives.

FIGURE 4.3
A Problem Found dialog
in SCANDISK.

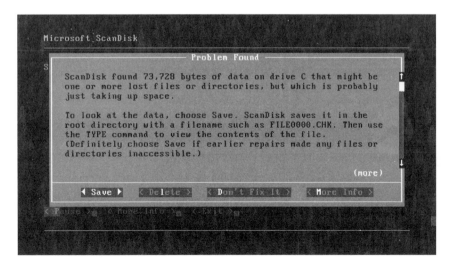

TYPE

If you want to view the contents of a text or batch file, use the TYPE command. In order to prevent the contents of the file from whizzing by as you try to view them on your screen, type |**MORE** at the end of the command. The contents will appear one screen at a time. The following command displays your CONFIG.SYS file:

```
TYPE C:|CONFIG.SYS |MORE
```

If you use this command on a program file (such as one that ends with an .exe or .com) you will see a jumble of binary characters that won't make any sense—even if you are a programmer.

UNDELETE

Suppose that you have somehow accidentally deleted a very important file. What do you do? If you have DOS 5 or later, try UNDELETE! It's surprising more children have not been named Undelete out of gratitude for the files this little command has saved.

To attempt to undelete a file, type **UNDELETE** followed by the name of the file ASAP. Do it before the file is written over! Here is an example:

```
UNDELETE C:\WORD\YURJOB
```

Note that UNDELETE can't work if the file has already been overwritten. Any data that is written to the disk will overwrite the deleted file. For this reason, the safest time to run UNDELETE—and the only time you can be absolutely sure it will work—is immediately after you have deleted the file.

XCOPY

XCOPY is COPY on steroids. If you have a large group of files and DOS 5 or higher, XCOPY is probably the way to go. This command allows you to copy files and subdirectories all in one shot. The following switches give XCOPY its extra power:

- /S extends the copying to include an entire directory, subdirectories included.

- /E copies empty subdirectories when it is typed after /S.

- /V verifies data integrity by employing read-after-write verification.

- /P means XCOPY will prompt you for permission before copying.

If you XCOPY a file to a destination directory with a file that has the same name, the new file will overwrite the destination directory file! Even worse, you cannot undelete the file using UNDELETE!

Using DOS Batch Files

A *BATCH FILE* IS a special type of file that contains a list of DOS commands. These files can be very useful to simplify the operation of your PC. If you execute any commands frequently, you can simply place them in a batch file.

Batch files have the extension .BAT and are considered executable files by DOS. We've already introduced one batch file: AUTOEXEC.BAT. DOS executes this file's commands automatically when the machine boots. Although other batch files aren't executed automatically, they can be very useful.

For example, let's look at the following commands, which are required to attach and log into a NetWare 4.1 network:

```
SET NWLANGUAGE=ENGLISH
CD\NWCLIENT
LSL
3C5X9
IPXODI
VLM
F:
LOGIN FRED
```

Each time this user logs into the network after rebooting, all of these commands must be executed. This can be a lot of typing! The solution is to place all of the commands into a batch file. You can create a batch file with any text editor; EDIT, provided with DOS 5.0 and above, is a good choice.

Once these commands are in a batch file, say STARTNET.BAT, the user can type the following single command to load all of the network drivers and log in:

STARTNET

As a matter of fact, the NetWare client installation program does create a STARTNET.BAT file with the required commands. This file is called from the AUTOEXEC.BAT file by default.

Versions of DOS

MS-DOS (MICROSOFT DISK OPERATING SYSTEM) was the first operating system for IBM PCs. At the time of this writing, the current version is 6.22. This is probably the last version, as Microsoft is focusing development on Windows 95 and other graphical systems that do not require DOS. (Technically, a version of DOS, which identifies itself as DOS 7.0, is hidden inside Windows 95.) However, this version of DOS is not currently available by itself.

Because DOS has had many upgrades and at least three different manufacturers in the past five years, it's rare to find a network where all the DOS machines are running the same DOS version. Each manufacturer's versions operate a little differently than the others, and not all software will run on all DOS versions.

You will still see DOS 5.0 on many network workstations, and DOS 3.3 is not uncommon. There are even a few machines still running DOS 1.0. Most of these machines could benefit from a DOS upgrade. The latest versions are more versatile, include more commands, and can support higher levels of hardware. DOS versions below 4.0, for example, can't access more than 32MB per disk partition.

Other DOS Versions

Other companies have also produced disk operating systems:

- IBM's PC-DOS was originally a licensed version of MS-DOS, so there are many similarities. The latest version, PC-DOS 7, is newer than any version of MS-DOS and has a variety of new features, including better memory management and a sophisticated text editor.

- Digital Research Corporation produced DR-DOS. Novell bought DR-DOS 6.0 from Digital and later upgraded it and marketed it as Novell DOS 7.0. Novell has recently announced that it is no longer in the DOS market. Because Novell DOS is often discussed in NetWare courses and tests, we've included a further description of it in the next section.

DR DOS and Novell DOS

DR-DOS was originally developed by Digital Research Corporation. Novell purchased DR-DOS when it was at version 6.0 and continued to develop it. The final version was called Novell DOS 7.0. Novell left the DOS market recently, and Novell DOS is no longer available. However, you will still run into Novell DOS and DR-DOS in the real world (as well as on the current version of Novell's Service and Support CNE test).

Novell went to great lengths to maintain compatibility with Microsoft DOS and to surpass it in features and ease of use. Two of this operating system's alluring features are its excellent memory management and disk compression programs. Novell DOS 7.0 was the first operating system to ship with its own disk defragmenting utilities, disk caching, and task switching so you could run more than one DOS program simultaneously without Microsoft Windows.

One downfall of DR-DOS and Novell DOS was that administrators who were familiar with MS-DOS could not switch over to this version of DOS painlessly. Its memory management programs and commands, although good, are quite different in their use and settings. Switching from Microsoft DOS to Novell DOS required a considerable amount of time to come up to speed—a luxury that most network administrators cannot afford.

These are a few of the enhancements you'll find on Novell DOS:

- **DiskMax:** A disk management utility with considerable power. Disk compression, optimization, caching, and undelete capabilities are a few of its features.

- **DOSBook:** An online documentation program for this version of DOS.

- **TaskMax:** The task-switching utility. It allows multiple DOS programs to run simultaneously in expanded, extended, and conventional memory;

the user can switch between them with a keystroke. It also supports cut-and-paste operations between applications.

- **Lock:** Allows users to lock their keyboards. Unlocking requires a password.

- **Setup:** A comprehensive, full-screen setup utility for many of the DOS features, including Memo, DiskMax, TaskMax, and security.

- **HIDOS.SYS:** A memory configuration driver for this DOS.

The command

```
HIDOS=ON, HIBUFFERS=xx
```

is the equivalent to Microsoft's DOS=HIGH command, which allows high memory and upper memory use. It also supports the transfer of COMMAND.COM out of conventional memory to the high memory area.

Novell DOS, in the most recent version (7.0), also includes a peer-to-peer networking system based on Personal NetWare. This enhancement made version 7.0 an excellent value, but the networking system is very difficult to configure and use.

Just like MS-DOS 6.x, Novell DOS and DR-DOS will display help information for any DOS command if you execute the command with a /? switch.

Novell DOS and DR-DOS also included improved versions of the following DOS commands:

- CHKDSK

- HELP

- MEM

- REPLACE

- TREE

- XCOPY

- UNDELETE

- TREE

- DISKCOPY

The Graphical Alternative: Windows

THE LAST GREAT COMPUTER REVOLUTION came when Microsoft introduced Windows 3.0 and the world became interested in GUI (Graphical User Interface) computing. (Of course, the Macintosh had been available with a powerful GUI—comparable to Windows 95—for years, but Apple simply didn't have the marketing budget that Microsoft had.) Microsoft quickly followed Windows 3.0 with Windows 3.1, which fixed the bugs in 3.0 and became a fixture in most workplaces. At least half of the computers in use in businesses today are running Windows.

Alternate versions of Windows include Windows for Workgroups, which includes peer-to-peer networking features, and Windows 3.11, a minor upgrade to 3.1 that fixed a few bugs.

Technically, Windows isn't an operating system. It actually runs on top of DOS. The latest version of Windows, known as Windows 95, is an entirely self-contained OS (although it does include a DOS command-line interpreter, which identifies itself as DOS 7.0).

Windows 95

At this writing the public fascination with Windows 95, Microsoft's latest OS, is in full swing. Windows 95 is a true 32-bit, multitasking OS that includes many features not found in Windows 3.1. (Although DOS is still hidden inside it, DOS and Windows are now integrated into a single system.) To take full advantage of Windows 95, you'll need to run 32-bit applications whenever possible.

Windows 95 includes most of the functions of Windows 3.1 and many enhancements and additions. It includes a better user interface, many more networking features, and improved multitasking (the ability to run multiple programs at once).

All of the power of Windows 95 doesn't come without a price, however. It requires a much more powerful system to run. Windows 95 requires a minimum of 12MB of RAM to run efficiently; in addition, the system takes about 60MB of hard disk space—not to mention the space you'll need for 32-bit applications. Windows 95 can be slower than Windows 3.1 unless you have a fast machine; we recommend a minimum of a 486/66.

Windows 95 will run most of your Windows 3.1 applications at about the same speed. To really benefit from Windows 95, you need 32-bit applications.

Most software vendors are now rushing to get 32-bit versions of their products out the door, and many are already available.

If you're rich, you may be tempted to purchase a machine that uses Intel's latest processor: the Pentium Pro (P6). Be warned, however: Since Windows 95 still contains quite a bit of 16-bit code, it may actually run *slower* on a P6 than on a Pentium. The P6 is optimized for 32-bit software. A future release of Windows (Windows 97, perhaps?) should remedy this situation. If you really can't wait, you may want to look into an OS that does run faster on the P6: Windows NT or OS/2.

Other Operating System Choices

WHILE DOS AND WINDOWS ARE RUNNING on 90 percent of the computers in most businesses today, there are a few alternatives. These may be useful in specialized situations or even as an alternative to Windows. We'll give you a basic introduction to each of them.

Windows NT Workstation

Microsoft's Windows NT Workstation is a client workstation operating system similar to Microsoft Windows. It uses the same user interface as Windows 3.*x* and can run most Windows applications. A module available for the latest version of NT, 3.51, provides user interface elements similar to Windows 95 and can run most Windows 95 applications. Future versions of Windows NT Workstation will have the Windows 95 user interface. Unlike Windows (or even Windows 95), Windows NT Workstation is a fully 32-bit, preemptive multitasking operating system. Thus, it can run quickly and communicate with hardware at optimum speeds over high-speed buses, such as PCI, and can run just about any application in the background.

Windows NT doesn't offer much of an advantage as a NetWare client. However, Microsoft is working on NetWare support for future versions, which would allow a tight integration between Windows NT (workstation or server) and NetWare 4.1. Novell has already released a Windows NT requester, which allows full client access to NDS.

OS/2 Warp and Warp Connect

IBM's OS/2 was originally Microsoft's attempt to create a new, 32-bit OS in the late 80s. Microsoft decided to abandon the project, and IBM took over. OS/2 is a very robust system. The latest version, OS/2 Warp 3.0, runs Windows applications almost as quickly as Windows itself and performs extremely well with OS/2 applications. It includes many of the features found in Windows 95 and was available a full year earlier than the Microsoft product. Unfortunately, because of the stranglehold Microsoft has on the market, OS/2 applications are scarce. Nevertheless, it's worth a try.

OS/2 does have some advantages over Windows—and even over Windows 95. It is a more solid OS with many years of development. It multitasks better, particularly when you are running several DOS applications at once. It is also fully 32 bit, so it can take advantage of the speed of the P6 processor.

OS/2 Warp Connect is the latest package from IBM. Although it is more expensive, it includes a full array of network support. It can easily connect with NetWare, Windows NT, and even Windows 95 and also includes tools for Internet support.

Macintosh System 7

One company, Apple, produced an OS with many of the features of Windows 95 way back in 1984. This OS, built into Apple's Macintosh line of computers, introduced the world to graphical user interfaces. The latest version of the Mac OS, System 7.5, provides many improvements, and many users (notably Macintosh users) believe it to be better than Windows 95.

The Macintosh is a non-PC-compatible system. It runs on the Motorola 68000 series of processors (68040 being the most recent). The new Macintosh machines, called PowerMacs, use the PowerPC processor, a fast RISC processor that rivals the speed of the Pentium Pro.

Probably the main reason that Macintosh and its OS don't do as well in the market as PCs, DOS, and Windows is that the Macintosh was a proprietary system. While thousands of companies entered the PC-clone market and provided cheap alternatives to the original IBM PC, Apple kept strict control over its architecture; the only Macintosh machines were made by Apple.

Apple has finally realized the error of its ways, and several companies are now producing lower priced Macintosh-compatible machines. Although it will probably never overtake Windows, the Macintosh is still popular in specialized markets, such as scientific research and graphics production.

Review

N THIS CHAPTER we've looked at DOS—the most commonly used operating system for clients on NetWare networks. We've looked at the commands and features that DOS provides. In addition, we've taken a look at the new trend in operating systems: graphical interfaces such as Windows and Windows 95. Finally, we've introduced a few OS alternatives.

DOS

DOS stands for Disk Operating System. DOS is a type of software that resides on a computer, providing very fundamental functionality. It has two main roles:

- It manages computer resources, such as memory and hard drives, acting as an intermediary between applications and system hardware.

- It provides an interface with which you can manage system resources.

After the important files have been loaded into memory and the necessary program lines have been executed, the *DOS prompt* appears on the screen. The DOS prompt often appears as a letter A or C, representing one of the drives on your computer.

The basic building blocks of DOS are files and directories. Anytime you enter a command, you are working with programs that are stored in files, which are organized under directories. Everything you (or an application you use) adds to DOS is stored in a file that resides in a directory.

DOS provides a wide variety of commands, which allow you to manage files, directories, and disks on your system.

DOS Batch Files

A *batch file* is a special type of file that contains a list of DOS commands. These files can simplify the operation of your PC. If you execute certain commands frequently, you can simply place them in a batch file.

Batch files have the extension .BAT and are considered executable files by DOS. One example is AUTOEXEC.BAT, which executes automatically when the machine starts.

DOS Versions

MS-DOS (Microsoft Disk Operating System) was the first operating system for IBM PCs. At the time of this writing, the current version is 6.22. Other companies have also produced disk operating systems:

- IBM's PC-DOS was originally a licensed version of MS-DOS, so there are many similarities. The latest version, PC-DOS 7, is newer than any version of MS-DOS and includes a variety of new features.

- Digital Research Corporation produced DR-DOS. Novell bought DR-DOS 6.0 from Digital and later upgraded it and marketed it as Novell DOS 7.0. Novell has recently announced that it is no longer in the DOS market.

Windows and Windows 95

The last great computer revolution began when Microsoft introduced Windows 3.0. Microsoft quickly followed up with Windows 3.1, which fixed the bugs in 3.0 and became a fixture in most workplaces. At least half of the computers in use in businesses today are running Windows.

Technically, Windows isn't an operating system. It actually runs on top of DOS. The latest version of Windows, known as Windows 95, is an entirely self-contained OS (although it does include a DOS command-line interpreter, which identifies itself as DOS 7.0).

Windows 95 includes most of the functions of Windows and many additional capabilities. It includes a better user interface, many more networking features, and much improved multitasking (the ability to run multiple programs at once); however, it requires more powerful (and expensive) hardware than Windows and may require a fast processor to achieve the same speeds.

Other Operating Systems

Although DOS and Windows are running on 90 percent of the computers in most businesses today, there are a few alternatives.

Microsoft's Windows NT Workstation is a client workstation operating system similar to Microsoft Windows—it uses the same user interface as Windows 3.*x* and can run most Windows applications. A module available for the latest version of NT, 3.51, provides user-interface elements similar to Windows 95 and can run most Windows 95 applications. Windows NT Workstation is a fully 32-bit, preemptive multitasking operating system. Thus, it can run quickly and communicate with hardware at optimum speeds over high-speed buses such as PCI. It can run just about any application in the background.

OS/2 is IBM's alternative to Windows. It has some advantages over Windows—and even over Windows 95. It is a more solid OS with many years of development. It multitasks better, particularly when you are running several DOS applications at once. It is also fully 32 bit, so it can take advantage of the speed of the P6 processor.

The Macintosh is a non-PC-compatible system. It runs on the Motorola 68000 series of processors (68040 being the most recent). The new Macintosh machines, called PowerMacs, use the PowerPC processor, a fast RISC processor that rivals the speed of the Pentium Pro. The Macintosh OS provides most of the same benefits as Windows 95.

What You Need to Understand for the CNA-4 Exam

PART

2

NetWare 4.1
Networking
Fundamentals

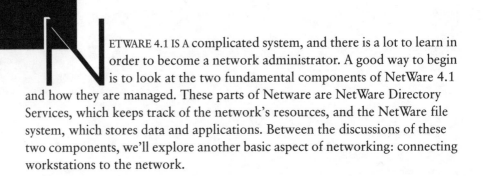

ETWARE 4.1 IS A complicated system, and there is a lot to learn in order to become a network administrator. A good way to begin is to look at the two fundamental components of NetWare 4.1 and how they are managed. These parts of Netware are NetWare Directory Services, which keeps track of the network's resources, and the NetWare file system, which stores data and applications. Between the discussions of these two components, we'll explore another basic aspect of networking: connecting workstations to the network.

How NDS *Organizes the Network*

ETWARE 4.1 MANAGES the network's resources through NetWare Directory Services, or NDS. Information about each of these resources—users, groups, printers, servers, and other items—is organized into a single database: the NetWare *Directory*. This database works for the entire network, rather than for just one particular server.

We spend a lot of time talking about NDS in this chapter because NDS is at the heart of the NetWare 4.1 network. Once you understand NDS, you will have no trouble understanding other aspects of the network and servers.

To distinguish it from a disk directory, the NetWare Directory is written with a capital D.

What NDS Does for the Network

NDS provides many benefits to your network, which include the following:

- **Ease of administration:** Users and other NDS objects can be managed from NetWare Administrator, a friendly Microsoft Windows program. Network management can be done by a central administrator or divided among several administrators.

- **Organization:** You can bring order to the chaos of network administration by dividing the objects in the Directory into manageable groups.

- **Increased security:** Security can be applied to any NDS object.

- **Scalability and interoperability:** These fancy words mean that NDS can work with networks of any size and can interface with other types of networks.

- **Fault tolerance:** The Directory can be stored on multiple servers. Thus, if an accident should befall one of the servers, the data is intact on the others.

Let's take a closer look at each of these benefits.

Ease of Administration

NetWare 3.1*x* uses the bindery to keep track of the network's resources. The bindery is a simple, flat database—a simple list of resources, similar to a phone book. When you attempt to access a resource, the server must read entries from the bindery until it stumbles upon the one you need.

Each server keeps its own bindery, and there is no connection between the binderies on the servers. If you want to access a resource, you need to log in to the server where it's located. If you need resources on two servers, you need to log in to each one. Worse, an account must be set up for you on each server—with the appropriate rights to each resource you want to access. (The need to set up and manage all these user accounts may explain the sour mood exhibited by many NetWare 3.1*x* network administrators.)

Because NetWare 3.1*x* and earlier versions keep a separate list of resources for each server, their organization is called *server centric*. This description means that each server is the center of its own little world. It may be connected to other servers, but it doesn't cooperate with them very well. A server-centric organization is illustrated in Figure 5.1.

NetWare 4.1, on the other hand, uses a *network-centric* system. Each server on the network is part of a single, unified network. The network has only one list of resources. These resources may be on different servers, but the Directory lists them all, and you can access them all. This network-centric organization is shown in Figure 5.2.

In a network-centric system, you can access any resource just by knowing its name and where it fits into the Directory tree. If someone moves it to a different server, you shouldn't even notice the difference. Best of all, you need to create

FIGURE 5.1

A server-centric organization keeps a separate list of resources at each server.

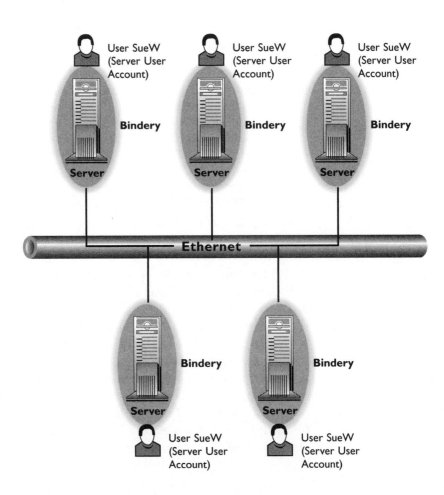

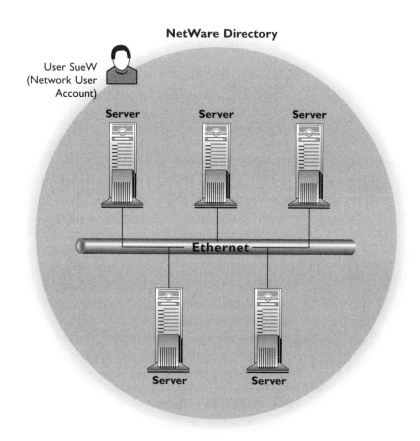

only one account for each user. You can then give the user access to whichever resources he or she needs, no matter where that user is in the network.

A precursor to NDS, NetWare Naming Service, allows similar features in NetWare 3.1x. Novell no longer supports this product.

NDS allows very versatile methods of administration. You can give a single, all-powerful administrator access to manage all of the objects in the network, or you can divide the Directory tree and assign an administrator for each branch. You can even create very specific administrators, who might have exciting titles such as "phone number correctness verifier" or "terminated employee account remover."

Organization

NDS stores information about each object in the Directory tree. The Directory tree is organized like an inverted tree. You can create separate limbs of the tree for each department, location, or workgroup within the company. This structure makes it easy to organize users and other objects into logical groups, rather than stuffing everything into one big, messy bindery.

Increased Security

NDS offers improved security by providing encrypted, single-login authentication. All this means is that the user logs in once for the entire network. The authentication, or password-checking, process uses *encrypted* versions of passwords, so it is impossible to "snoop" on people's passwords by detecting the data on the network cable.

The treelike structure of NDS allows you to manage sophisticated security features using a simple graphical interface. Because you can control the entire network from a single workstation, you can monitor the network and make sure everything is secure without flying to other locations or taking someone else's word for it.

Scalability and Interoperability

Although they're buzzwords in the computer industry and are thrown around constantly by computer magazines, *scalability* and *interoperability* do have meanings and they do benefit your network.

Scalability means that NDS is constructed in a *modular* fashion (another buzzword). You can easily expand the network to include more resources and services. You can add users more easily with additive licensing (discussed in Chapter 2). Novell's Application Program Interface (API) allows programmers to make their own improvements and to add specialized objects to NDS.

Interoperability means that NDS is backward-compatible with previous Novell products, such as the bindery of NetWare 2 and NetWare 3. You can even manage these objects from within NDS. The NetWare Directory is also compatible with other Directory Services, particularly the X.500 standard, an international specification for network directories. NDS borrows much of its structure from the X.500 specification, although it is not 100 percent compatible.

Fault Tolerance

NDS is a *distributed database,* which means that copies of the database, or portions of it, are stored on several servers throughout the network. Thus, the safety of your data doesn't depend on one particular server. If a server goes down, a replica (another copy) of the database on another server can take over. When the server is restored, the Directory information can once again be copied to that server.

Fault tolerance applies to NDS data; it doesn't protect the data on your servers. Be sure to make regular backups. Many backup packages allow you to back up NDS data, which is also a good idea. Redundant storage solutions, such as NetWare SFT III, can provide another layer of protection. You can never be too safe.

How the Directory Is Organized

In NDS, every resource on a network is represented by a record in the Directory database. This record is called an *object.* Objects exist for each type of resource, such as User objects, Printer objects, and Server objects.

There are three basic types of objects in the Directory database:

- The [Root] object

- Container objects

- Leaf objects

A sampling of these objects is illustrated in Figure 5.3, and each of them is explained in the following sections.

The [Root] Object

As you might guess from its name, the *[Root] object* is at the top of the Directory's upside-down tree structure. There is only one [Root] object in the Directory. It is created when NDS is installed on the first server. You can't delete, rename, or move this object. The [Root] object is always referred to with brackets around its name (presumably so you won't confuse it with the root of the kind of tree that grows outdoors).

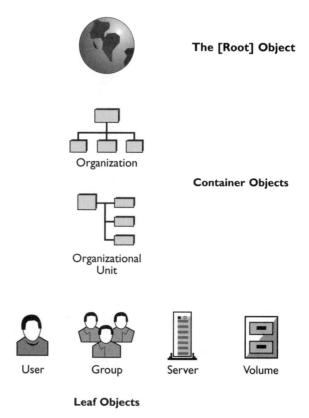

FIGURE 5.3
NDS is organized into a [Root] object, container objects, and leaf objects.

The [Root] Object

Organization

Container Objects

Organizational Unit

User   Group   Server   Volume

Leaf Objects

Container Objects

A container object doesn't represent a network resource directly. Instead, it's used to organize other objects. Container objects can hold leaf objects (users and printers, for example). In addition, they can hold other container objects. This nesting quality allows you to create resources in a very organized fashion. The [Root] object is the ultimate container object; it contains every single object in the Directory tree. The other kinds of container objects are Country, Organization, and Organizational Unit objects.

COUNTRY If you use them, Country objects go directly under the [Root] object. Country objects let you divide a multinational corporation into sections for each country. The name of the Country object must be a valid two-character abbreviation for a country.

The Country object is included as part of the X.500 standard, and that's where the two-letter abbreviations come from. For example, US represents the United States, FR is France, DE is Germany, and CH is Switzerland. Some of these abbreviations may seem odd, but they would be obvious if you happened to speak the various languages. Of course, if you are multilingual, you could probably find a more profitable career than network administrator.

Although the Country object is available in NDS, Novell doesn't recommend its use in most situations. It was included just because the X.500 standard needed it. X.500 actually includes another container object, the Locality object. NDS doesn't support this one at all, although it is included in the NetWare manuals. Locality objects may show up in a future version of NetWare.

ORGANIZATION The Organization object is used to divide the network into big pieces, such as a company, a university, or a department. The Directory tree must have at least one Organization object. Since most networks do not need to use Country objects, the Organization object is usually the first object beneath the [Root] object.

Some large corporations and governments might require multiple Organization objects, but the vast majority of companies use a single Organization object to hold the entire Directory tree. You can subdivide the Organization object with Organizational Units or create leaf objects directly under the Organization if you wish.

ORGANIZATIONAL UNIT The Organizational Unit object is where the network really gets organized. You can use several levels of Organizational Units to further divide the tree into categories. For example, one company could have Organizational Units to represent its accounting, research, marketing, and customer service departments, as illustrated in Figure 5.4.

Leaf Objects

Leaf objects are the leaves of the Directory tree. They can't contain other objects. Leaf objects represent the network resources. They must be placed within either Organization or Organizational Unit objects. About 20 leaf objects are available. Here are the common ones:

- **User:** The User object represents a user on the network.

- **Group:** You can organize users into logical groups, called Group objects, so that they share the same rights.

FIGURE 5.4
Organizational Unit
objects can be used to
further divide the
network's resources.

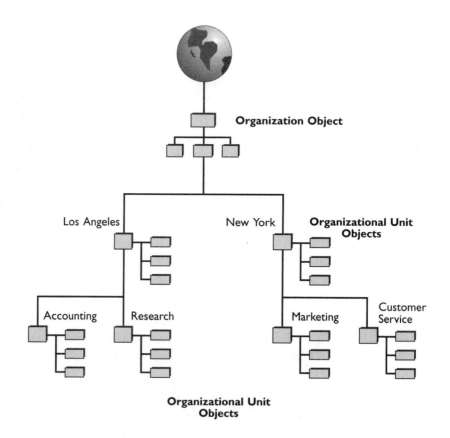

- **Organizational Role:** This is an assignment that is given to a user. For example, an Organizational Role called "backup administrator" might be used for the person who runs a tape backup. You would assign the user who currently does the job to the Organizational Role to give that user whatever rights are needed to back up the server. If a different user was assigned to the task, you would simply switch that user to the Organizational Role. Organizational Roles are explained in Chapter 6.

- **NetWare Server:** This object represents a NetWare 4 server.

- **Volume:** A Volume object represents a disk volume on a server. By browsing through objects under a Volume object, you can look at the files and directories on the volume.

- **Profile**: You can use a Profile object to group users who require a similar login script. Login scripts are explained in Chapter 8.

- **Printer, Print Queue, Print Server**: These are used for network printing. Network printing is explained in Chapter 9.

Properties and Values

Each type of object in NDS has a list of *properties*. These are pieces of information that can be stored about that type of object. For example, a User object has properties such as Login Name, Full Name, Title, and Telephone Number. The information stored in a property is called the *value* of the property. For example, the value of the Title property might be "Vice President."

Not all properties make sense for all objects. It's unlikely that a Printer object will have a Telephone Number, for instance. Therefore, NDS has a different list of properties for each of the types of objects. However, the same types of objects have the same properties available. For example, all User objects have the same list of properties, and all Printer objects have the same list of properties.

Some properties are *required*. For example, a User object must have a Login Name property. Other properties, such as the User's Telephone Number and Title properties, are optional. It can be useful to fill these out in order to identify and catalog the objects in your network, but it is not a requirement.

Some properties can hold more than one value. For example, the Telephone Number property for a User object can hold multiple numbers for each user. This type of property is called a *multivalue* property. The majority of properties are the opposite; they are *single-value* properties, which can have only one value.

NetWare 4.1 includes utilities that let you work with properties and their values. The NLIST utility, for example, allows you to search for objects with a certain property value or to list certain properties, such as all users and their telephone numbers.

It will be easier to search for resources on your network if you keep property values consistent. In planning your network, you should decide which properties you will use for objects and how to format their values. This part of the NDS planning procedure is covered in The CNE-4 Study Guide, *also published by SYBEX.*

The type of objects you can create and the list of properties for each one of them are defined in the *NDS schema*. This schema defines the basic structure of NDS and is installed on the server with NDS. The NetWare API allows programmers to *extend* the NDS schema so that it is possible to add specialized types of objects or new properties for existing objects.

Referring to NDS Objects

You can access any object in the Directory if you know its name and its location in the tree. The next sections describe the different types of syntax you can use to refer to NDS objects and how to determine the name for each object.

Object Names

Each object in a Directory tree has an *object name*. NetWare 4.1 has a specific terminology for object naming. The object name is usually the most obvious name for the object; a user's object name is the login name, and a server's object name is the server name. The object name is also referred to as the object's *common name*.

The common name isn't enough to identify an object uniquely. NDS allows you to create Users or other objects with identical object names, as long as they are in different container objects. To completely identify the object, you also need to know where it is in the tree.

Understanding Context

An object's *context* is a description of the object's location in the tree. The context is the name of the object's parent object, which is the container object that it resides in. A context is described with a list of container objects, beginning with the object that is the most distant from [Root]. For example, if the Organizational Unit IDAHO is under the Organization WESTERN in the Country US, the context for any leaf object under IDAHO is

```
.IDAHO.WESTERN.US
```

NDS keeps track of your *current context*, or default context. This is usually the context that contains your User object. When you access a resource without specifying its full location, NetWare looks for it in the current context.

Full Distinguished Names

By combining an object's common name with its context, you can determine its *full distinguished name*. Since this name includes the name and location of the object, it is a unique name for the object. Although two objects can have the same common name, each has a unique distinguished name.

Distinguished names begin with a period and also use a period between each object's name. For example, if the User object JOHN is in the Organizational Unit MARKETING, which is in the Organization ABC, John's full distinguished name is

```
.JOHN.MARKETING.ABC
```

Relative Distinguished Names

To avoid needing to specify all of the container objects over an object, you can use a *relative distinguished name,* or RDN. The RDN relies on your current context and starts there, instead of at [Root], to look for the object.

Remember the period that begins a full distinguished name? If you leave it out, the name is considered to be an RDN. The simplest example of using an RDN is when you access an object that is in your current context. For example, if your current context is .ACCT.PHILCO (the ACCT Organizational Unit under the PHILCO Organization) and you want to access a printer called PRINTER1 in the same context, you can simply specify its name as

```
PRINTER1
```

When an object is outside your current context, you can still use an RDN. Enter a period at the end of the RDN to move up a level in the Directory tree. For example, if you are in the .ACCT.PHILCO context and you wish to access a printer called PRINTER2 in the MKTG.PHILCO context, the RDN is

```
PRINTER2.MKTG.PHILCO.
```

Typeless Names and Typeful Names

So far, we've been using *typeless* names. They include the names of objects but not the types of objects. For instance, in the distinguished name .SUE.PR.ACCT.WNC, we know that SUE is a common name, but we don't say whether PR, ACCT, and WNC are Organizations or Organizational Units. We can make an educated guess, and NetWare can too. These typeless names can be used in almost any situation where NetWare asks for an object's name.

Nevertheless, a more formal method of naming is possible: *typeful* naming. As the name implies, this kind of name includes the type for each object. The object types can include the following:

C	Country
O	Organization
OU	Organizational Unit
CN	Common Name

To make the typeful name, add the object type and an equal sign to each object. The typeful name for the user SUE mentioned above would be

```
.CN=SUE.OU=PR.OU=ACCT.O=WNC
```

You should understand typeful names because you will need to use them occasionally. For the vast majority of NDS tasks, however, the typeless name works fine, and it is much easier to type.

Connecting to the Network

O ACCESS THE NETWORK, you will need to establish a connection to a server. This is accomplished by running *client software* at the workstation. Because DOS workstations are the most common clients, we refer to this type in the following discussion. Similar client software is used with OS/2 and Macintosh workstations.

A DOS workstation normally works as a stand-alone machine. The operating system provides access to the workstation's own resources, such as disk drives and printers. DOS is still based on software that was introduced before networks existed; because of this, there is no built-in way for the workstation to attach to the network.

This is where the network client software comes in. The client software allows DOS to access NetWare volumes and printers. Once the client software is running, network drives can act just like local drives and network printers can act just like local printers. Client software allows any software—even applications that were never intended to run on a network—to be used with network resources.

The client software for DOS is called the NetWare DOS Requester. The DOS Requester replaces the NetWare shell used by previous versions of NetWare. The NetWare DOS Requester provides the following benefits:

- Support for NDS

- Background authentication through NDS

- Modularity, which means that portions of the DOS Requester can be loaded and unloaded as needed

- Support for Packet Burst Protocol and Large Internet Packets (LIP)

- *Auto-reconnect* to restore your connection to the network after a disconnection without requiring you to log in again

Network Protocols

Your workstation communicates with the NetWare server through the use of *communications protocols*. A protocol is a set of rules for moving data across the network. In a sense, the protocol is the "language" used for communication on the network, and it is important that the client and the server speak the same language. The principal protocol used for NetWare workstation connections is IPX. Your network may support additional protocols, such as TCP/IP and AppleTalk.

The IPX Protocol

The IPX (Internetwork Packet Exchange) protocol is the standard protocol for NetWare networks. IPX divides data into *packets*. These packets contain the data that are to be transmitted along with the addressing information that determines the workstation or server that the packet should be sent to. NetWare networks use three main addresses:

- The *IPX external network number* is set for all servers that share a common network wire, or *segment*. Multiple servers in the same network segment use the same number. This number is used to transmit data across multiple networks.

- The *IPX internal network number* is set at each server. This number is used to locate the server on the network, and it must be unique.

- Each workstation has a *network address* that is used to locate a specific workstation on the network. Network addresses are usually set in hardware in the network card and usually cannot be changed. Each network card in a server also has a unique network address.

The ODI Specification

ODI (Open Data-Link Interface) is a specification used with the IPX protocol for DOS workstations on the network. ODI allows workstations or servers to use multiple protocols on the same network. Each workstation can use a combination of protocols on the same network card. This specification allows your workstation to communicate with the NetWare 4.1 network and other systems, such as mainframe computers, concurrently.

In addition, the ODI specification provides a modular way of installing network drivers. When a network adapter is replaced, only one file—the network driver—needs to be replaced.

Client Software Components

The NetWare 4.1 client software is actually four separate programs. The most important is the NetWare DOS Requester, mentioned earlier.

These client software programs are TSR (terminate-and-stay-resident) programs, which stay in memory and operate in the background while the workstation performs other tasks. You must load the client software in the following order:

- LSL.COM

- LAN board driver (MLID)

- IPXODI.COM

- VLM.EXE

To keep you on your toes, the order for loading client software is different from the order in which these programs are used to transport data. When transporting data, the sequence is the network card driver, LSL, IPXODI, and finally the DOS Requester (which is loaded by the VLM.EXE program), as illustrated in Figure 5.5. The following sections describe these important client software programs.

Network Card Driver [MLID]

The LAN driver is the software that communicates with the network card. After the data is sent across the network and received by the network card, this program converts it into a standard format that the NetWare client software understands. The type of LAN driver used for NetWare 4.1 is called an MLID, or Multiple Link Interface Driver. This is a term for any driver that supports the ODI specification.

As mentioned in Chapter 1, the LAN driver is the only part of the client software that is not guaranteed to come with NetWare 4.1. Although NetWare provides drivers for common network cards, you should use the most current driver provided by the manufacturer of your network card. That driver should be included on a disk that came with the card.

FIGURE 5.5

Data pass through several components between the workstation and the server.

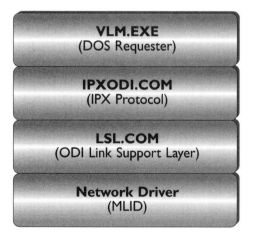

LSL (Link Support Layer)

The LSL handles the ODI specification. This program communicates with the protocols, such as IPX, and makes the connection between these protocols and the network card. The TSR program used for LSL is LSL.COM.

IPXODI (IPX Protocol for ODI)

The IPXODI.COM program handles the IPX protocol. Packets are created and passed on to the LSL for processing by the network card. If you use other protocols, such as TCP/IP or AppleTalk, you load them along with (or instead of) IPXODI.

The NetWare DOS Requester

The final layer of communication is provided by the NetWare DOS Requester. The DOS Requester is responsible for communications with DOS and the application software on the workstation. The DOS Requester allows DOS applications to use network resources, such as files and printers, as if they were local to the workstation.

The DOS Requester program is called VLM.EXE. This program is actually a shell that loads subprograms, called Virtual Loadable Modules (VLMs). Each of the VLMs provides a specific service. VLMs are modular, so they can be loaded and unloaded as needed. You can conserve memory by loading only the components you need.

Login and Logout

Once the client software is loaded, you can log in to the network by using the LOGIN command followed by your username. You must first switch to a network drive. For example, to switch to network drive F: and log in as user SUE, use these commands:

```
F:
LOGIN SUE
```

The LOGIN program is called LOGIN.EXE, which is located in the LOGIN directory on the server. This directory is the only one you can access when you are not logged in. Once you type the LOGIN command, you will be asked to enter your password. If you type the password correctly, you will be allowed access to the network.

Before you can log in, you will need an account on the network, which means that a User object must be created in NDS. This process is explained in Chapter 6.

The opposite of LOGIN is LOGOUT. The LOGOUT command ends your access to the network. The client software keeps the connection to the network so you (or another user) can access the LOGIN directory and log back in.

The NetWare File System

NETWARE'S *FILE SYSTEM* is the system that manages disk storage on the network. NetWare uses files and directories, similar to those used by DOS. In fact, the NetWare file system is specifically designed to be compatible with DOS clients.

Components of the File System

The NetWare file system organizes disk access into several components. These include volumes, directories and subdirectories, and files. The next sections describe each of the components.

Volumes

A *volume* is the major unit of storage in a NetWare server and is similar to a disk drive under DOS. However, a NetWare volume isn't necessarily a single disk drive. There is a sophisticated relationship between disks and volumes. A single disk drive can be divided into multiple volumes. In addition, a volume can span more than one disk drive.

A volume is located on a NetWare server. Each server can have many separate volumes. NDS uses a Volume object to represent the volume. Volume objects are automatically given a name that combines the name of the server and the name of the volume. For example, the VOL1 volume on file server CENTRAL has the NDS common name of CENTRAL_VOL1. This naming system allows several servers to have volumes with the same name even if they reside in the same NDS container.

When you install NetWare 4.1, at least one volume must be created: the SYS volume. This volume contains the NetWare operating system files for the server's use. Each server must have a SYS volume. If you delete or rename the SYS volume, the server will become confused and refuse to start properly.

Directories and Subdirectories

A volume is divided into directories that allow you to organize the file system in the same way that container objects organize the NDS tree. The structure of file system directories is similar to the NDS Directory. But don't let that fool you; they are two very different things.

Each file system directory can contain other directories, or subdirectories. When you install a NetWare server, several directories are created automatically on the SYS volume:

- SYSTEM contains NetWare server utilities, configuration files, and NLMs. Most tasks performed on the file server use the SYSTEM directory.

- PUBLIC contains utilities that run from a workstation. By default, all users on the network have access to PUBLIC.

- MAIL stores configuration files for each user. This directory is used mainly for access by bindery-based clients.

- ETC contains sample files for the TCP/IP protocol. TCP/IP is an optional protocol that can be used to integrate NetWare with UNIX systems and the Internet.

A subdirectory is simply a directory inside another directory. The terms directory and subdirectory are often used interchangeably.

When you refer to a directory on a NetWare volume, the standard syntax is to use a colon between the volume name and the directory and to use a backslash (\) between directory and subdirectory names. For example, the SYSTEM directory on the SYS volume is referred to as SYS:SYSTEM. To refer to the

DATA subdirectory under the PUBLIC directory on the VOL1 volume, use this syntax:

```
VOL1:PUBLIC\DATA
```

Since you can access multiple servers at the same time, you can specify the server name as well. Include the server name before the volume name and use a backslash between the server name and the volume. As a final example, the CHECKS subdirectory under the AP subdirectory under the DATA directory on the VOL5 volume on the QED server (did you get all that?) is called

```
QED\VOL5:DATA\AP\CHECKS
```

Files

At last we come to the really useful item. The whole point of the file system is to store and manage files. A file can contain an application program, a word processor or spreadsheet document, a database, a graphic image—any item that can be stored on a disk.

NetWare 4.1 uses the DOS file name format to store files. Each file has an eight-character name and a three-character *extension*. The extension is usually used to specify the type of file, such as TXT for a text file or EXE for a DOS program. File names are usually written in all uppercase letters, but the file system is not case sensitive; you can type names in either case.

NetWare allows an alternate format for file names: the NetWare file name format. You can choose this format instead of the DOS format when you install the server. Among other things, it allows both lower- and uppercase characters in file names. This format can cause compatibility problems with DOS programs, though, and Novell does not recommend its use.

Using Command-Line Utilities

NetWare includes a wide variety of utilities, which are programs that you can use to manage the server and network resources.

Some of the utilities that you can use to manage the file system are *command-line* utilities. Command-line utilities don't present you with a menu or ask you questions. You must specify all of the parameters for the command after the name of the command itself. You can run these utilities on any DOS workstation attached to the network.

Since the NetWare file system acts just like a DOS file system, you can also use most DOS or Windows file utilities to manage files on the server. However, most of these utilities don't support the additional features of NetWare's file system, such as security and file attributes.

*You can display a list of available options for just about any NetWare utility by typing the name of the utility followed by /?. For example, type **NDIR /?** to see a list of the options for the NDIR utility.*

You might find the following command-line utilities useful for managing your network file system:

- **NDIR:** You are probably familiar with the DIR command in DOS. This is probably the most commonly used command. Its function is to list all of the files in a directory. The NDIR command is a special NetWare version. In addition to the list of files, the NDIR listing includes NetWare-specific information, such as the owner of the file. Typing NDIR by itself lists all the files in the current directory. Advanced options allow you to view only certain files or to search an entire volume for a file.

- **NLIST:** When you need to see a list of items, you can use this utility. NLIST is a general-purpose utility for listing NDS objects. The NLIST VOLUME command lists Volume objects that are available in the Directory tree. You can also use the /D option to display additional information about a specific volume.

The SYS:PUBLIC directory contains NetWare utilities that run from a workstation. By default, all users on the network have access to this directory.

Mapping Network Drives

As we mentioned before, DOS doesn't really understand networks. The network client software adds networking capabilities to DOS, but it still isn't tightly integrated with NetWare. Most DOS applications don't allow you to refer to NetWare volumes by their volume names. This is where *mapped drives* come in.

The universal naming convention (UNC) notation enables you to use NetWare names directly in most Windows programs. This notation uses backslash characters to specify the server, volume, and directory: \\server\volume\directory\filename.

DOS uses drive letters to refer to the drives on the workstation. Typically, drives A: and B: are floppy drives, and the workstation hard drive is usually the C: drive. If your workstation has several drives, they will use additional letters.

When you map a network drive, you basically assign a drive letter, or *drive pointer*, to a certain volume and directory. Unless you change the defaults, drives A: through E: will be reserved for local drives and the first available network drive will be F:.

The LASTDRIVE statement in CONFIG.SYS determines which drive letters may be used. Using the old NetWare shell, the typical setting is LASTDRIVE=E, which allows drives beyond E: to be network drives. With the DOS Requester, all drives are considered DOS drives, so LASTDRIVE=Z is the usual setting.

You use the MAP command to map network drives. The MAP command line includes the drive letter to be used, an equal sign, and the network volume and directory to map the drive to. For example, the following command maps drive G: to the PUBLIC directory on the SYS: volume:

```
MAP G:=SYS:PUBLIC
```

By default, NetWare maps the next available drive (usually F:) to the SYS: volume. Before you log in, the LOGIN directory will be the only accessible directory on that drive. You can specify an alternate drive letter for the first network drive by adding a command like the following to the workstation's NET.CFG file:

```
FIRST NETWORK DRIVE = L:
```

Mapping Search Drives

NetWare uses a second kind of drive mapping called a *search drive*. Search drives point to directory paths that will be searched when you type a command name or request a file. For example, the MAP command itself is in the SYS:PUBLIC directory. A search drive that points to this directory allows MAP to be found when you type the command, no matter which directory you are in at the time.

Search drives are assigned both a number and a letter. The map command refers to them by number. You can map up to 16 search drives, numbered S1 through S16. When you type a command, NetWare looks for the command file in each of the search drives, beginning with S1. The first one that it finds is executed.

For example, the command to map the S1: search drive to the SYS:PUBLIC directory is

```
MAP S1:=SYS:PUBLIC
```

Review

THIS CHAPTER PRESENTED an overview of two fundamental areas of NetWare 4.1:

- NetWare Directory Services (NDS)

- The NetWare file system

NetWare Directory Services

NetWare 4.1 manages the network's resources through NetWare Directory Services, or NDS. Information about each of these resources is organized into a single database: the NetWare *Directory*. This database works for the entire network, rather than for one particular server.

NDS offers many benefits, including ease of administration, a more manageable organization, increased security, scalability and interoperability, and fault tolerance.

In NDS, every resource on a network is represented by a record in the Directory database. This record is called an *object*. Objects exist for each type of resource. There are three basic types of objects in the Directory database:

- The [Root] object

- Container objects (Country, Organization, Organizational Unit)

- Leaf objects (User, Printer, and so on)

Each type of object in NDS has a list of *properties*. These are pieces of information that can be stored about that type of object. The information stored in a property is called the *value* of the property. Each type of NDS object has a separate list of properties.

NDS Object Naming

The following guidelines are used in naming NDS objects:

- Each object in a NDS tree has an *object name*. The object name is also referred to as the object's *common name*.

- An object's *context* is a description of the object's location in the tree.

- An object's *full distinguished name* is its common name and context. This type of name begins with a period and includes all objects up to [Root].

- A *relative distinguished name* (RDN) provides a path to the object from the current context. The RDN does not begin with a period. One or more periods can be used at the end of the RDN to move up the Directory tree.

Client Connections

The client software runs on the workstation and establishes a connection to a server. The client software for DOS is called the NetWare DOS Requester, which replaces the NetWare shell used by previous versions of NetWare.

The workstation communicates with the server through the use of *communications protocols*. The principal protocol used for NetWare workstation connections is IPX (Internetwork Packet Exchange).

ODI (Open Data-Link Interface) is a specification used with the IPX protocol for DOS workstations on the network. ODI allows workstations or servers to use multiple protocols on the same network. It also provides a modular way of installing network drivers.

The NetWare 4.1 client software consists of four separate TSR (terminate-and-stay-resident) programs. You must load the client software in a certain order: LSL.COM, LAN board driver (MLID), IPXODI.COM, and then VLM.EXE. However, the loading order is different from the order in which the programs are used to transport data. The latter order is as follows:

- **LAN driver:** This is the software that communicates with the network card. After the data is sent across the network and received by the network card, this program converts it into a standard format that the NetWare client software understands. The type of LAN driver used for NetWare 4.1 is called an MLID (Multiple Link Interface Driver).

- **LSL (Link Support Layer).** This program (LSL.COM) handles the ODI protocol. It communicates with the protocols, such as IPX, and makes the connection between these protocols and the network card.

- **IPXODI.COM:** This program handles the IPX protocol. You can load other protocols, such as TCP/IP or AppleTalk, along with (or instead of) IPXODI.

- **NetWare DOS Requester:** This program, VLM.EXE, is responsible for communications with DOS and the application software on the workstation. It is actually a shell that loads Virtual Loadable Modules (VLMs), each of which provides a specific service.

From the workstation that has the client software loaded, you can log in to the network by using the LOGIN command followed by your username (after you switch to a network drive). The LOGIN program (LOGIN.EXE) is located in the LOGIN directory on the server. This directory is the only one you can access when you are not logged in. To disconnect from the network, use the LOGOUT command.

The File System

NetWare's *file system* manages disk storage on the network. NetWare uses files and directories, similar to those used by DOS. Components of the file system include the following:

- *Volumes* are the major unit of NetWare disk storage.

- *Directories* and *subdirectories* divide the volume.

- *Files* store data or applications within a directory.

In order to access a NetWare volume from DOS, you map a drive. Mapped drives include the following:

- *Network drives* are used to access volumes and directories.

- *Search drives* provide a list of possible locations for executable commands.

CNA *Practice Test Questions*

1. NetWare Directory Services (NDS)

   A. Stores information for each network resource

   B. Uses a treelike structure

   C. Refers to each resource as an object

   D. All of the above

2. Which of the following is *not* a benefit of NDS?

   A. Better organization of resources

   B. Fault tolerance

   C. An efficient file system

   D. Increased security

3. The type of organization NDS uses is

   A. Server-centric

   B. Network-centric

   C. Noncentralized

   D. Resource-centric

4. The three basic types of NDS objects are

   A. Container, Leaf, [Root]

   B. Properties, Values, Objects

   C. Organization, Organizational Unit, Country

   D. Typeless, typeful, distinguished

5. The [Root] object

   A. Can be located anywhere in the Directory

   B. Contains all objects in the Directory

   C. Can be deleted when it is no longer needed

   D. All of the above

6. Container objects include

   A. Country, Group, Organization

   B. Organization, [Root], Group

   C. Country, Organization, Organizational Unit

   D. Organization and Group

7. Leaf objects include

   A. User, Group, Organization

   B. User, Printer, Resource

   C. User, Group, Printer

   D. All container objects plus User

8. NDS properties

   A. Are the same for all objects

   B. Are used by container objects only

   C. Are all optional

   D. Can be assigned values

9. An object's name in its context is

   A. Its distinguished name

   B. The relative distinguished name

   C. Its common name

   D. Its context name

10. An object's context is

   A. Any object in the same container

   B. The container object it resides in

   C. Its common name

   D. The name of the Directory tree

11. A relative distinguished name (RDN)

   A. Begins at the [Root] object

   B. Begins at the current context

   C. Begins with the first Organization object

   D. Uses the default system context (DSC)

12. Which is an example of a *typeless* name?

   A. .CN=FRED.OU=ACCT.O=ORION

   B. CN=FRED

   C. .FRED.ACCT.ORION

   D. .CN=FRED.ACCT.O=ORION

13. The protocol usually used with NetWare is

   A. VLM

   B. IPXODI

   C. IPX

   D. TCP/IP

14. Which is the correct order for loading network drivers?

   A. LSL, LAN driver, IPXODI, VLM.

   B. IPXODI, LAN driver, VLM, LSL

   C. IPX, ODI, LAN driver, VLM

   D. LSL, LAN driver, IPXODI, VLM

15. Which program represents the NetWare DOS Requester?

   A. LOGIN.EXE

   B. VLM.EXE

   C. IPXODI.COM

   D. NETX.COM

16. Until you log in, the only files you can access are

A. LOGIN.EXE and client software

B. All files in the PUBLIC directory

C. All files in the LOGIN directory

D. All files on the SYS: volume

17. Which is the correct order of NetWare file system organization?

A. Directory, file, volume

B. Volume, directory, file

C. File, volume, directory

D. File, directory, NDS

18. The NDIR utility

A. Must be used in place of the DOS DIR command

B. Lists files in the current directory

C. Lists information about NDS objects

D. All of the above

19. The NLIST utility

A. Can be used to list volumes or other NDS objects

B. Displays a list of files in the current directory

C. Is another name for NDIR

D. Was used in NetWare 3.1x

20. Which is the correct syntax to map drive F: to the SYS:PUBLIC directory?

A. MAP F: SYS\PUBLIC

B. MAP SYS:PUBLIC /D=F

C. MAP SYS:PUBLIC=F:

D. MAP F:=SYS:PUBLIC

How to Manage Container and Leaf Objects

CHAPTER

6

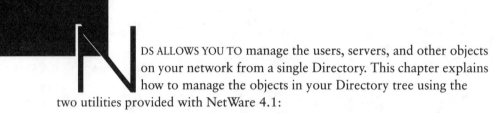

DS ALLOWS YOU TO manage the users, servers, and other objects on your network from a single Directory. This chapter explains how to manage the objects in your Directory tree using the two utilities provided with NetWare 4.1:

- NWADMIN (NetWare Administrator) is a Windows-based utility. With NWADMIN you can browse through the objects in the tree and create, modify, and delete them. This utility also includes features to manage the file system and its security and to control partitioning and replicating.

- NETADMIN is a DOS-based alternative, similar to the SYSCON utility in NetWare 3.1x. You can manage the Directory and its objects with NETADMIN, but it doesn't include file system or partitioning features. For those features, you can use the FILER and PARTMGR utilities.

You should become familiar with both utilities, because you will use them in your career as a network administrator and because you'll need a basic knowledge of them for the CNE tests.

This chapter provides an overview of each utility and how to use them to create and manage NDS objects. The final section describes the NDS objects you will use most often.

Using NetWare Administrator

ETWARE ADMINISTRATOR, also known as NWADMIN, is probably the most important utility in NetWare 4.1. You can use NWADMIN to manage all aspects of the network, including users, security, printing, and even the file system. As a network administrator, you'll spend a lot of time using NWADMIN.

Since NWADMIN is a Microsoft Windows-based utility, you need a version of Windows to run it. Here are your options:

- Windows 3.1, 3.11, or Windows for Workgroups will run NWADMIN just fine. In order to access NDS, you need to be running the latest version of the DOS and Windows client software and be logged in to the NDS tree you wish to manage.

- OS/2 2.1 or OS/2 Warp can run NWADMIN in a Windows session. However, the OS/2 Requester software doesn't give NDS access to Windows applications. A special option in the NetWare client software, VLMBOOT, provides a way around this.

- Windows 95, using either Microsoft's NDS client or Novell's new client software, Client32, can run NWADMIN. Although NWADMIN is still a 16-bit Windows program, it will work under Windows 95.

The NetWare client software that is included with Windows 95 does not support NDS. In order to run NWADMIN, you'll need to obtain the updated Microsoft client from Microsoft or the latest NetWare client from NetWire or Novell's World Wide Web site.

Running NetWare Administrator

Here are the steps to get started with NetWare Administrator:

1. Load the DOS client software and log in to the network. If you have more than one Directory tree, log in to the one you want to manage. If you are running Windows 95, the DOS client is not necessary.

2. Start Windows. If you are using Windows 95, you need to log in at this point.

3. Choose Run from the Program Manager's File menu or from the Windows 95 Start button menu.

4. Type **NWADMIN** as the name of the program to run. You should not need to specify a path.

Creating a NWADMIN Icon

Since you'll be using NWADMIN quite regularly, you should create a Program Manager icon for it. Follow these steps for Windows 3.1:

1. Choose File and then choose New from Program Manager.

If you already have a NetWare Tools program group, or another group you would like to use, you can open it and skip steps 1 through 3.

2. Choose Group as the type of new object to create.

3. Type **NetWare Tools** as the name of the group. A window for the new group will be displayed.

4. Choose File and then New again.

5. Select Icon as the type of new object to create.

6. Type **NetWare Administrator** as the name and **NWADMIN** as the command. You should not need to fill in any other information.

Now you can start NWADMIN by double-clicking on its icon in the Program Manager window.

For Windows 95, follow these steps to create a shortcut—that is, an icon—to NWADMIN on the desktop:

1. Right click on a blank area of the desktop.

2. Select New and then select Shortcut.

3. Type **NWADMIN** as the command line and click the Next button.

4. Type **NetWare Administrator** as the name of the shortcut and press Next.

5. Add NWADMIN to the Start menu (optional) by dragging the icon and dropping it on the Start button.

When NWADMIN starts, you will see a picture of the Directory tree and a standard Windows menu bar, as shown in the example in Figure 6.1.

We will now take a guided tour of the options that NetWare Administrator makes available. If you have access to a NetWare 4.1 server, you might find it useful to try things out on your own Directory tree as you read.

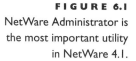

FIGURE 6.1
NetWare Administrator is the most important utility in NetWare 4.1.

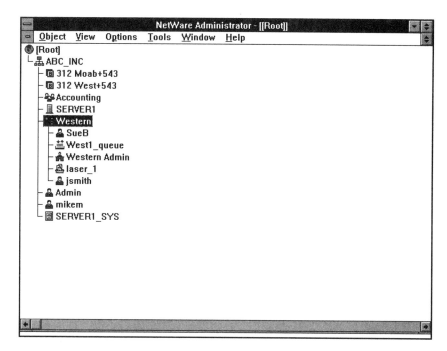

The Object Menu

The Object menu, shown in Figure 6.2, allows you to create, rename, or delete an object; modify properties; and control object rights. Before you select an option from this menu, highlight the object you want to affect.

Instead of using the Object menu, you can click the right mouse button ("right-click") after highlighting the object. You will see a pop-up menu with common commands that can be performed on that type of object.

Creating an Object

The Create option allows you to create a new NDS object. Before selecting this option, highlight the container object that will hold the new object. The new object will be created in this container. After you select the Create option, NWADMIN presents a list of object types, as shown in Figure 6.3. Choose the type of object that you wish to create and click on OK.

FIGURE 6.2
The Object menu allows
you to perform functions
related to objects.

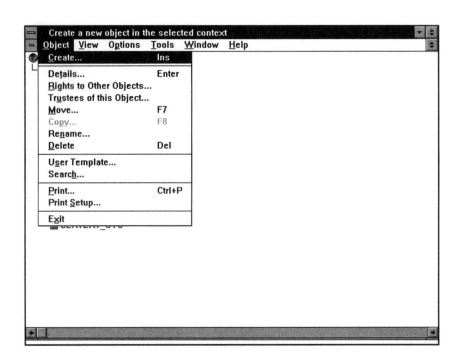

FIGURE 6.2
The Object menu allows
you to perform functions
related to objects.

FIGURE 6.3
Select the type of object
you wish to create.

The next dialog box presents some properties of the object for you to fill in. The properties list depends on the type of object. For example, when you are creating a User object, the Create User dialog box asks you to specify the Login Name and Last Name properties, as shown in Figure 6.4. These are the properties that are required to create the object.

You can use the four checkboxes in the Create User dialog box to set additional options:

- **Use User Template:** Copies the default settings for a new User object from a user template. User templates are explained later in this chapter.

- **Define Additional Properties:** Brings up the Details dialog box to allow you to set values for the other properties of the object.

- **Create Another User:** Returns you to the Create User dialog box after creating the user so that you can create another user immediately.

- **Create Home Directory:** Sets up a home directory for the user and allows you to specify its location (the server, volume, and directory).

FIGURE 6.4

You are required to enter certain properties to create an object.

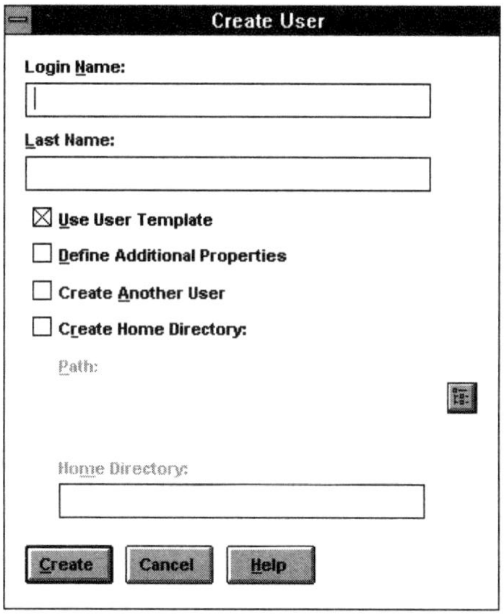

Create User

Login Name:

Last Name:

☒ Use User Template
☐ Define Additional Properties
☐ Create Another User
☐ Create Home Directory:

Path:

Home Directory:

[Create] [Cancel] [Help]

Viewing Property Values

The Details option on the Object menu allows you to view all of the properties of an object and specify or change their values. For example, when you highlight a User object and select Details, you will see the dialog box shown in Figure 6.5.

Properties are divided into categories. The categories and properties displayed depend on the type of object that is being modified. Use the buttons along the right side of the dialog box to select a category. You can then fill in the values of properties to change existing values.

FIGURE 6.5
The Details option allows
you to change properties
of an object.

User : cjensen	
Identification	
Login Name: cjensen.Western.ABC_INC	Identification
Given Name:	Environment
Last Name: jensen	Login Restrictions
Full Name:	Password Restrictions
Generational Qualifier: Middle Initial:	Login Time Restrictions
Other Name:	Network Address Restriction
Title:	Mailbox
Description:	Foreign EMail Address
Location:	Print Job Configuration
Department:	Login Script
Telephone:	
Fax Number:	

OK   Cancel   Help

Moving a Leaf Object

The Move option on the Object menu allows you to move a leaf object from one container to another. This option can be useful if you are reorganizing the Directory tree or if a user changes departments within the organization. Select the leaf object that you wish to move and then select the Move option. Next, you will see the Move dialog box, shown in Figure 6.6. Browse the Directory to find the destination container object and then select OK.

Although you can select the Move option for a container object, you won't be allowed to move the container objects using this menu option. You must use NWADMIN's Partition Manager, described in Chapter 11 of this book, to move container objects.

FIGURE 6.6

Select the container
object to move the leaf
object into.

Deleting an Object

The Delete option of the Object menu allows you to delete an object. You can use this option to remove any leaf object or empty container object (you cannot delete a container object unless you first delete all of the objects within the container). After selecting Delete, you are prompted to confirm that you wish to delete the object.

Renaming an Object

The Rename option of the Object menu allows you to change an object's common name. After selecting Rename, type the new name for the object. The Rename dialog box also contains two options that you can control with checkboxes:

- **Save Old Name:** Adds the object's old name to the object's Other Names property. This option allows you to track an object after renaming it.

- **Create Alias in Place of Renamed Container:** For container objects, check this box to create an Alias object with the old name of the container. This option allows users to continue using the old name to refer to the object. Alias objects are discussed later in this chapter.

Creating a User Template

The User Template option on the Object menu allows you to create or modify a *user template*. This is a special type of User object that does not represent an actual user; instead, it is used to assign default properties for new users that you create.

Each container object (context) can have a separate user template, which controls the defaults for users created in that container. The first time you select the User Template option, a User object is created in the highlighted container. The User object's name is USER_TEMPLATE. Next, you will see the Details dialog box for the template, as shown in Figure 6.7. The property values that you assign to this User object will be copied when a new user is created in the container.

If you wish to create a user without using the default values in the user template, you can uncheck the Use User Template box in the Create User dialog box. This will create a user without any of the property values already filled in.

User templates do not have any effect on existing users. These defaults are used only for new users created after the template is created.

FIGURE 6.7
Property values entered for the user template will be copied to new User objects in the same container.

User : USER_TEMPLATE

Identification

Login Name:	USER_TEMPLATE.Western.ABC_INC
Given Name:	user template
Last Name:	template
Full Name:	
Generational Qualifier:	**Middle Initial:**
Other Name:	
Title:	
Description:	
Location:	
Department:	
Telephone:	
Fax Number:	

Identification
Environment
Login Restrictions
Password Restrictions
Login Time Restrictions
Network Address Restriction
Mailbox
Foreign EMail Address
Print Job Configuration
Login Script

OK   Cancel   Help

Searching for an Object

The Search command on the Object menu allows you to search the Directory tree for objects with certain property values. The options in the Search dialog box, shown in Figure 6.8, allow you to set specific parameters for the search. These options work as follows:

- **Start From:** Allows you to specify a container object where the search will begin. If the Search Entire Subtree box is checked, NWADMIN will search all the objects in child containers of the container; otherwise, the search will be confined to a single container. The Browse button to the right of the Start From value allows you to select a container from a graphic display of your Directory tree.

- **Search For:** Allows you to specify the type of object that will be searched for, such as User, Printer, or Server.

- **Property:** Specifies the property that you want to find. The list of properties here depends on the type of object you have selected.

The two boxes beneath the Property option allow you to specify a condition for the search. In the box on the left, you can choose whether to find properties that are Equal To or Not Equal To a value or Present or Not Present. Enter the value to search for to the right of the condition. This will be used with the Equal To or Not Equal To option to match objects. For example, the options in Figure 6.8 search for User objects with the value of Accounting in the Department property.

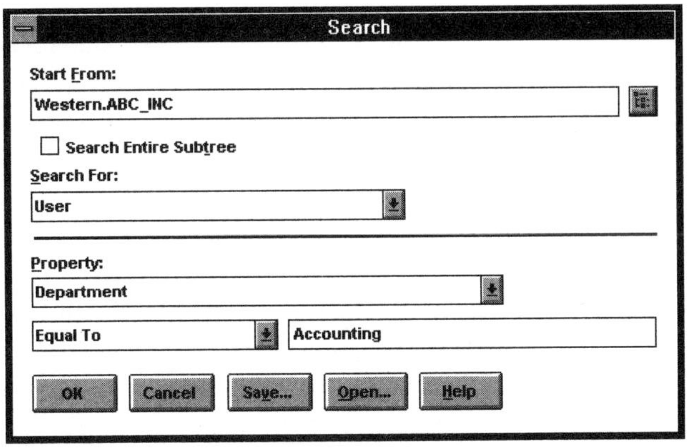

FIGURE 6.8
The Search command allows you to find objects with certain property values.

The Save button allows you to save the search parameters to a file. You can use the Open button in the Search dialog box to load these saved search parameters later. In this way, you can keep a library of frequently used search criteria and perform specific searches quickly. For example, you could set up a search to quickly list all of the Printer objects in the Directory tree.

After the search is completed, you are presented with a list of objects that meet the criteria you selected. You can then perform any of the operations described in this chapter on those objects.

Printing the Directory Tree

The Print option on the Object menu allows you to print the listing of objects in the current context. You can use the Print Setup option on the Object menu to change options related to printing or to change the printer to be used.

The View Menu

NetWare Administrator's View menu, shown in Figure 6.9, provides several options that allow you to control the way in which NDS objects are displayed. These include setting the current context, choosing objects to include, sorting objects, and expanding or collapsing the display.

Choosing a Context

The Set Context command on the View menu allows you to change the current context. You can select any container object. This object will be the shown first in the NWADMIN window, and it will be the default context for further operations. The Set Current Context dialog box is shown in Figure 6.10.

You can type the name of a container object in the New Context area or click the button to the right of this space to browse the Directory tree and select a container object as the context.

Choosing Objects to Display

The Include option on the View menu allows you to specify which types of NDS objects are displayed in the NWADMIN window. The Include dialog box, shown in Figure 6.11, lists all of the possible object types. You can highlight the ones you wish to include in the display. By default, all types are highlighted.

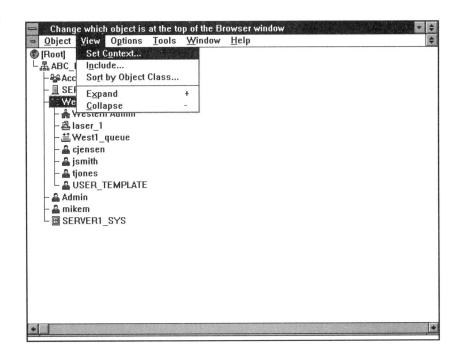

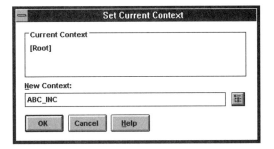

The Include dialog also includes the following options:

- **Directory Service Object Name Filter:** Allows you to enter a partial object name. Objects that include the partial name will be the only ones displayed. You can use wildcards, similar to in a DOS file name. For example, entering WEST* for the object name filter displays only objects whose names begin with *WEST*.

FIGURE 6.11
The Include option allows you to display only certain types of objects.

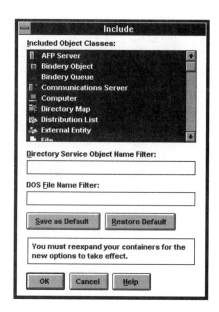

- **DOS File Name Filter:** Allows you to enter a partial file name for files in the file system. Enter a file name using wildcards to display only the files that match the pattern.

- **Save as Default:** Allows you to save the Include options as the default settings for your workstation.

- **Restore Default:** Restores the previously saved defaults.

Sorting the Display

The Sort by Object Class option on the View menu allows you to specify the order in which different types of NDS objects are displayed. For example, you could have Organizational Units displayed first, then Groups, then Users. The Sort by Object Class dialog box is shown in Figure 6.12.

Object types are listed in the order in which they will be displayed. To change this order, highlight an object type and use the up- and down-arrow buttons on the right side of the dialog box to move the object up and down in the list.

FIGURE 6.12
The Sort by Object Class
option allows you to
specify the order in
which NDS objects are
displayed.

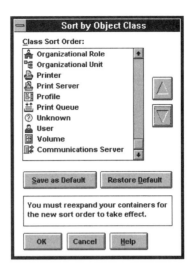

FIGURE 6.12
The Sort by Object Class
option allows you to
specify the order in
which NDS objects are
displayed.

After making changes, you can use the Save as Default button to save the order as the default sort order for your workstation. The Restore Default button restores the default order that was saved previously.

The sort options change only the order in which you view NDS objects. They don't affect the NDS database itself.

Expanding and Collapsing Container Objects

The Expand and Collapse options on the View menu allow you to control whether objects under a container object are displayed. Highlight a container object before selecting these commands. The Expand command displays all objects under the container. The Collapse command displays only the container object.

If you make changes to the Include or Sort settings, you must re-expand the containers in the display before the settings will take effect. A quick way to do this is to highlight the object at the top of the display (usually [Root]), select Collapse, and then select Expand.

You can also double-click on a container object to expand it. Double-click again to collapse the display.

The Options Menu

NetWare Administrator's Options menu, shown in Figure 6.13, allows you to set several options related to the behavior of the program. Selecting each of the options toggles the option's status. A checkmark is displayed to the left of each activated option.

- **Save Settings on Exit:** Controls whether settings, including window sizes, current context, and view settings, are saved as the default when you exit the program.

- **Show Hints:** Controls the display of hints. These are displayed in the title bar of the NWADMIN window as you select different options. For example, if you select Create from the Object menu, you will see the hint "Creates a new object in the selected context."

- **Confirm on Delete:** Controls whether the confirmation dialog box is displayed when you delete an object. If this option is turned off, the object will be deleted immediately when you select Delete.

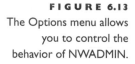

FIGURE 6.13
The Options menu allows you to control the behavior of NWADMIN.

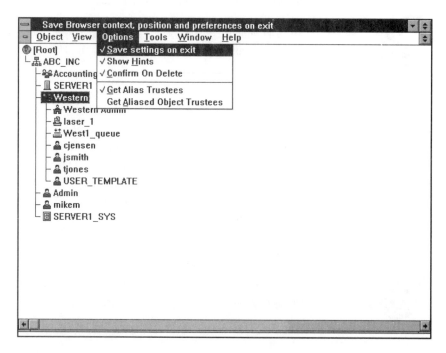

- **Get Alias Trustees** and **Get Aliased Object's Trustees:** Control how the Trustees of This Object command works with Alias objects (described later in this chapter). You can choose to see the trustee list of either the original object or the Alias object itself. Only one of these options can be selected.

The Tools Menu

NetWare Administrator's Tools menu provides options to open new NWADMIN windows and start other programs:

- **Partition Manager:** Opens the Partition Manager utility, which is built into NWADMIN. This utility is used to control NDS partitioning and replicating (explained in Chapter 11 of this book).

- **Browse:** Opens a new NWADMIN window with the selected container object at the top. This allows you to examine objects within the container in a separate window.

- **Salvage:** Provides a method of restoring deleted files. The Salvage window, shown in Figure 6.14, lists the deleted files and allows you to salvage (restore) or purge (permanently remove) them.

FIGURE 6.14
The SALVAGE option allows you to restore deleted files.

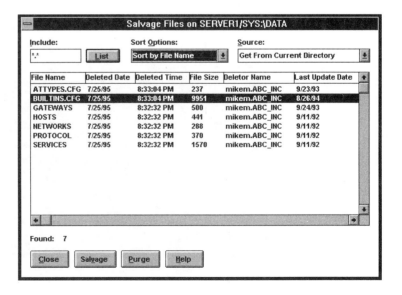

■ **Remote Console:** Runs the Remote Console (RCONSOLE) utility in a window. (The first screen you see will remind you that RCONSOLE is not always reliable when it's run under Windows.)

NETADMIN: *The DOS Alternative*

NETADMIN IS NETWARE'S DOS-based utility for managing network objects. This program provides most of the same features as NetWare Administrator (NWADMIN). NETADMIN can be useful on DOS-only machines or for users who prefer to use DOS utilities. It is in the SYS:PUBLIC directory on the file server.

You run NETADMIN by typing **NETADMIN** at the DOS prompt. NETADMIN's main screen is shown in Figure 6.15.

The following sections explain how to manage objects with NETADMIN. You will find that most of the options are similar to their counterparts in NetWare Administrator.

FIGURE 6.15
NETADMIN is a DOS-based utility that provides most of the same features as NetWare Administrator (NWADMIN).

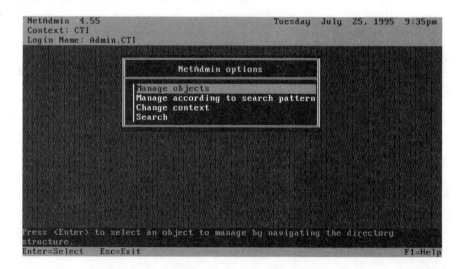

```
NetAdmin  4.55                              Tuesday  July  25, 1995  9:35pm
Context: CTI
Login Name: Admin.CTI

                         ┌──────────── NetAdmin options ────────────┐
                         │ Manage objects                           │
                         │ Manage according to search pattern       │
                         │ Change context                           │
                         │ Search                                   │
                         └──────────────────────────────────────────┘




Press <Enter> to select an object to manage by navigating the directory
structure.
Enter=Select   Esc=Exit                                          F1=Help
```

NETADMIN should run on just about any version of DOS, but you need the latest DOS client software, the DOS Requester, to provide access to NDS. Novell's new Client32 software also provides this access.

The Main Menu

The main NETADMIN menu offers the following options:

- **Manage Objects:** Lists objects in the Directory tree and allows you to modify, delete, rename, and move them.

- **Manage According to Search Pattern:** Allows you to enter a pattern to search for and then lists only objects that match the pattern.

- **Change Context:** Changes your current context.

- **Search:** Allows you to search for a specific type of object or for objects with certain property values.

The Manage Objects option takes you to a Directory tree display, the Object, Class screen, as shown in the example in Figure 6.16. From this screen, you can browse the tree. Press Enter on a container object to see the objects in

FIGURE 6.16
The Manage Objects function of NETADMIN allows you to browse the Directory tree.

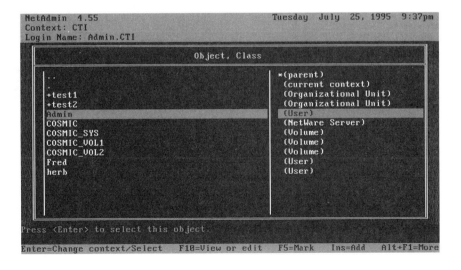

the container. When you find the object you want to manage, select it. Then you can perform any of the actions described in the next sections.

Creating an Object

You can create a new NDS object from NETADMIN's Directory tree display. Follow these steps:

1. Type **NETADMIN** at the DOS prompt.

2. Choose Manage Objects from the main menu.

3. Highlight the parent object for the new object on the Object, Class screen and press Insert. Then choose the type of object to create, as shown in Figure 6.17.

FIGURE 6.17
Select the type of object
to create.

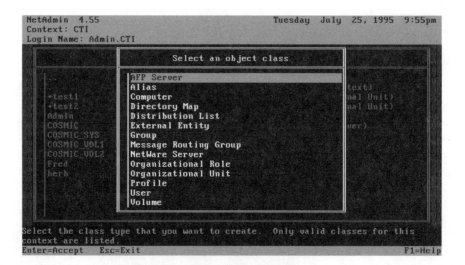

```
NetAdmin 4.55                                     Tuesday  July  25, 1995  9:55pm
Context: CTI
Login Name: Admin.CTI
┌─────────────────────────────────────────────────────────────────────────┐
│                          Select an object class                           │
│             ┌─────────────────────────────────────────┐                   │
│             │ AFP Server                               │             text) │
│  +test1     │ Alias                                    │         nal Unit) │
│  +test2     │ Computer                                 │         nal Unit) │
│  Admin      │ Directory Map                            │                   │
│  COSMIC     │ Distribution List                        │                   │
│  COSMIC_SYS │ External Entity                          │         ver)      │
│  COSMIC_VOL1│ Group                                    │                   │
│  COSMIC_VOL2│ Message Routing Group                    │                   │
│  Fred       │ NetWare Server                           │                   │
│  herb       │ Organizational Role                      │                   │
│             │ Organizational Unit                      │                   │
│             │ Profile                                  │                   │
│             │ User                                     │                   │
│             │ Volume                                   │                   │
│             └─────────────────────────────────────────┘                   │
└─────────────────────────────────────────────────────────────────────────┘
Select the class type that you want to create.  Only valid classes for this
context are listed.
Enter=Accept   Esc=Exit                                              F1=Help
```

4. Press Enter. The next screen allows you to enter the required properties for the object. The properties that are required depend on the type of object being created. For example, for a new User object, you must enter the Login Name and Last Name properties, as shown in Figure 6.18.

5. Press F10 to create the object.

FIGURE 6.18

Enter the user's login name and other information to create a User object.

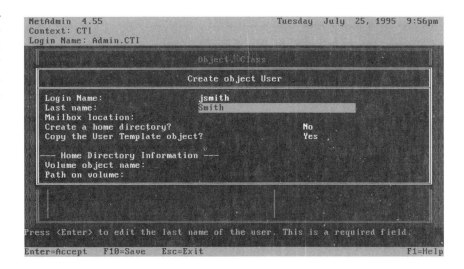

Managing an Object

You can press F10 on any object in the Directory tree display to manage the object from the Actions menu, shown in Figure 6.19. The Actions menu allows you to change the object's properties; delete, rename or move the object; and control NDS security for the object. These actions are described in the following sections.

FIGURE 6.19

The Actions menu allows you to manage an object or its properties.

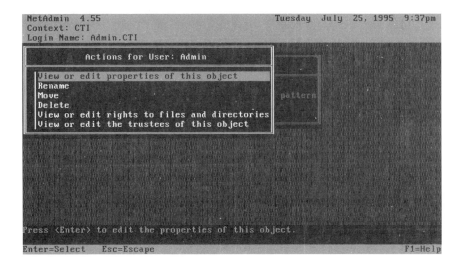

Modifying Property Values

To modify an object's properties, select View or Edit Properties of This Object from the Actions menu. The next menu lists property categories for the type of object you selected. The property categories for a User object are shown in Figure 6.20.

Press Enter on the category of properties you wish to modify. NETADMIN displays a list of properties in the category and their current values. You can change any of these values by typing a new value and pressing Enter. After you have made your changes, press F10 and then press Esc to save the changes and exit.

FIGURE 6.20
To change object properties, select the category of properties to manage.

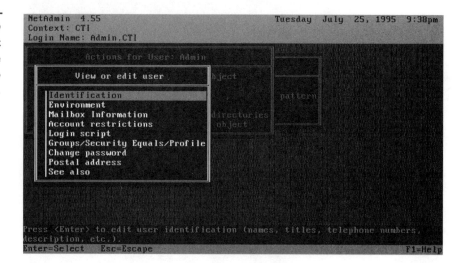

Renaming an Object

Select Rename from the Actions menu to rename the object. You will see the screen shown in Figure 6.21.

Enter the new name for the object in the first blank. Answer Yes or No to save the old name. If you select Yes, NETADMIN stores the object's old name in the object's Other Names property.

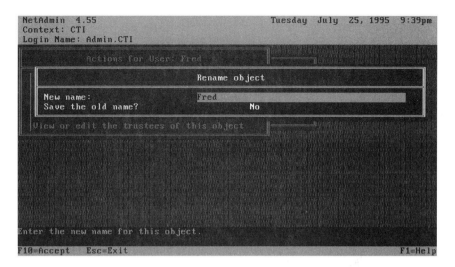

Deleting an Object

Select Delete from the Actions menu to delete the object and confirm the action by selecting Yes or No. After you select Yes and press Enter, the object is deleted from the Directory.

Moving a Leaf Object

You can move a leaf object to a new context by selecting Move from the Actions menu. You will see the screen shown in Figure 6.22.

The object's current context is shown on the first line. Enter the new context for the object on the second line. This option does not work with container objects; it moves leaf objects only.

Creating a User Template

As explained earlier in the chapter, a user template is a special type of User object that you can use to assign default properties for new users that you create. Although NETADMIN does not have a specific option to create a user template, you can set one up by creating this special user account yourself.

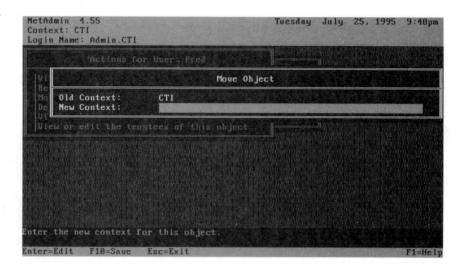

```
NetAdmin  4.55                                    Tuesday  July  25, 1995  9:48pm
Context: CTI
Login Name: Admin.CTI
┌──────────────────────────────────────────────────────────────────────┐
│        Actions for User: Fred                                          │
│  ┌──────────────────────────────────────────────────────────────┐     │
│ Vi│                      Move Object                              │     │
│ Re│                                                               │     │
│ Mo│  Old Context:      CTI                                        │     │
│ De│  New Context:      [                                    ]     │     │
│ Vi│                                                               │     │
│ View or edit the trustees of this object                          │     │
│                                                                        │
│                                                                        │
│                                                                        │
│ Enter the new context for this object.                                 │
│ Enter=Edit    F10=Save    Esc=Exit                            F1=Help  │
└──────────────────────────────────────────────────────────────────────┘
```

Start NETADMIN and choose Manage Objects from the menu. Switch to the container in which you wish to create the user template, press Insert, and choose to create a new User object. For the Login Name property, type **USER_TEMPLATE** (in all uppercase letters separated by an underscore). Type the last name as **template** (all lowercase letters). Then fill in the property values that you want to use as defaults for the new users you create.

After setting up your user template, when you create a new user in NETADMIN, leave the Copy the User Template Object set to Yes to use those defaults. Change it to No if you don't want the new user to have those property values.

Using Leaf Objects

NOW THAT YOU KNOW how to manage the objects in the Directory, we'll take a look at the types of leaf objects available for your Directory tree. There are actually about 25 leaf objects available in

NDS. The following are the ones you'll need to understand for the Basic Administration test:

User	Represents a user on the network.
Group	Represents a set of users who share the same rights.
Organizational Role	Represents a role, or job, assigned to one or more users.
NetWare Server	Represents a NetWare 4.1 server.
Volume	Represents a volume (disk area) on a server.
Alias	Serves as a pointer to another object in the Directory.
Profile	Provides a way to group users who require a similar login script.
Directory Map	Points to a directory in the file system.
Printer	Represents a network printer.
Print Queue	Represents a network print queue.
Print Server	Represents a network print server.

You can create some of these objects with NWADMIN or NETADMIN. Others are created automatically and can't be changed, but you can examine and modify their properties.

In the next sections, we'll take a closer look at most of these objects and how to manage them. The exceptions are the Printer, Print Queue, and Print Server objects, which are used for network printing, the subject of Chapter 9.

The NDS container objects (Country, Organization, and Organizational Unit) are described in Chapter 5.

User Objects

Each user who needs to access the network must have a User object. When you create the User object, you specify the login name and last name for the user.

After that, the user is ready to log in to the network. If necessary, you can give the user rights to files, directories, or other NDS objects.

As explained earlier in the chapter, if you create a user template, each new User object you create will automatically receive the properties you specified for that template. You can have a separate user template for each container object, which will affect objects in that container.

Group Objects

When you create multiple users in a container object, they form a *natural group*—they are automatically given rights based on the container object. The Group object lets you do the same thing for a list of User objects, whether they're in the same container or not. This presents two possibilities:

- You can choose only some of the users in a container.

- You can choose users from multiple containers.

You can create a Group object in any container. After you create it, you can add users to it by using a special property of the Group object: the Member List. You can choose User objects in the current container or in other containers. These users are called the *members* of the group. A User object can be a member of more than one group.

The Group object is used for security and also is useful in login scripts (to assign drive mappings, printer queues, and so on). Any member of a group will receive the same rights that the Group object has. We'll talk more about security in Chapter 7.

Organizational Role Objects

The Organizational Role object is similar to a Group. It is usually used to assign a role, or job, to a particular user. This user is called the *occupant* of the Organizational Role. An Organizational Role can have more than one occupant.

Using Organizational Roles makes it easier to manage a network in a changing company. If you assign rights to users individually, you will need to do so any time a new person takes a job. Thanks to the Organizational Role object, the process is simple. You can just add a new occupant and remove the old one.

An important use of Organizational Roles is in assigning administrators—users who have the right to manage an area of the Directory tree or file system. The various types of administrators you can set up for your network are explained in Chapter 7.

The NetWare Server Object

The Server object is used to represent a server on the network. You cannot create this type of object; it is created automatically when a server is installed. You should not need to change the properties of the Server object.

Be careful, you *can* delete the Server object. Although this won't destroy the server or the data on it, it will make it inaccessible through NDS. You should do this only if you want to remove the server from the network.

The Volume Object

When you install the server, a Volume object is created for each disk volume on the server. You cannot normally create a Volume object yourself. Like the Server object, the Volume object should not be deleted unless the volume is no longer in use.

Although the Volume object is not a container object, you can "expand" it like a container object in NWADMIN. Under the Volume object you will find a list of directories on the volume. You can browse through the directories of the file system in the same way that you can view NDS objects. This is how you control security in the file system. You can also do routine file management tasks, such as creating new directories and deleting and renaming files.

NETADMIN doesn't allow you to browse the file system, but another DOS utility—FILER—allows you to manage files under DOS.

Alias Objects

You've seen the word *alias* on wanted posters, and the Alias NDS object serves the same purpose: It's another name for an object. However, a criminal uses an alias to avoid being found; NDS aliases are usually used to help users find the object.

You can create an Alias object yourself. The main use for this is to make a resource, such as a printer, in one container available to users in another container. For example, users in the ACCT Organizational Unit might need to access a printer in the MKTG Organizational Unit. You can create an Alias object for the printer in the ACCT container. To the users, it's just another available printer. They can access it without specifying a different container.

In addition, NWADMIN automatically creates Alias objects to help users find an object that has been moved or renamed. When you move or rename an object, you can check the Create Alias in Place checkbox to create a pointer from the old object to the new object.

Profile Objects

Each user in NDS has a login script, which is a series of commands that are executed each time the user logs in. The Profile object has its own login script. Assigning users to a Profile object provides an easy way to give them all the same login script.

Profile objects and their use with login scripts are discussed in Chapter 8.

Directory Map Objects

The Directory Map object is a special object that points to a directory in the file system. This object allows you to simplify MAP commands and makes it easier to maintain the system when an application or data directory is moved.

When you create a Directory Map object, you set the Directory Path property to the path that the Directory Map object will point to. You will first need to find the Volume object in the NDS tree.

As an example, suppose you created a Directory Map called WP to point to the directory that you used for word processing files, SYS:APPS\WP. Users who wish to map a drive to that directory could simply type a MAP command like this:

```
MAP F:=WP
```

A more important benefit of using a Directory Map object is the work it can save you when you reorganize your directories. For example, suppose that you moved word processing files to a different volume to make more space available on the SYS: volume. The new location is VOL2:APPS\WP. Rather than changing all the login scripts to point to the new directory and telling everyone about the change, you can simply point the Directory Map to the new location. Then users could use the same MAP command to reach the new directory.

Review

NDS ALLOWS YOU TO manage all of the users, servers, and other objects on your network from a single Directory tree. In this chapter, you learned the details of managing objects using two utilities: NWADMIN (a Microsoft Windows-based utility) and NETADMIN (a DOS-based utility). This chapter also describes the commonly used NDS objects.

NWADMIN

With NWADMIN you can browse through the objects in the tree and manage them. You can run NWADMIN by choosing Run from the Windows Program Manager's File menu or from the Windows 95 Start button. NWADMIN's menus offer options for managing and viewing information about your network:

- The Object menu allows you to create, rename, or delete an object; modify properties; and control object rights.

- The View menu allows you to control the way in which NDS objects are displayed, including setting the current context, choosing objects to include, sorting objects, and expanding or collapsing the display.

- The Options menu allows you to set several options related to the behavior of the NWADMIN program.

- The Tools menu provides options to open new NWADMIN windows and start other programs.

NETADMIN

The NETADMIN program provides most of the same features as NetWare Administrator (NWADMIN). To run this utility, type **NETADMIN** at the DOS prompt.

To create a new object, choose Manage Objects from the main menu. On the Object, Class screen, highlight the container object in which you want to create the new object and press Insert. Choose the type of object to create and fill in the necessary properties.

To manage an existing object, press F10 on the object in the Object, Class screen. This brings up the Actions menu. From this menu, you can change the object's properties; delete, rename, or move the object; and control NDS security for the object.

Commonly Used Leaf Objects

The leaf objects you will use most often include the following:

- User object, which represents a user on the network. You must create a User object for anyone who needs to log in to the network.

- Group object, which allows you to organize users into logical groups that share the same rights.

- Organizational Role object, which is an assignment or "job" given to a user. You can change the occupant of the Organizational Role to give the rights to a new user.

- NetWare Server object, which represents a NetWare 4.1 server, is created automatically when the server is installed.

- Volume object, which represents a volume (disk area) on a server. This object is created automatically when the server containing the volume is installed.

- Alias object, which is a pointer to another object in the Directory. This object is used to make a resource accessible to users in a different container and as a pointer from the old name or location of an object to the new one.

- Profile object, which you can use to group users who require a similar login script.

- Directory Map object, which points to a directory in the file system. This object allows MAP commands to be simplified and makes it easy to move directories without updating MAP commands in login scripts.

- Printer, Print Queue, and Print Server objects, which are used for network printing.

CNA Practice Test Questions

1. The two utilities used to manage NDS objects are

   A. NetWare Administrator and NWADMIN

   B. NETADMIN and NetWare Administrator

   C. SYSCON and NETADMIN

   D. NDSADMIN and NWMANAGE

2. The Create function in NWADMIN is found under

   A. The File menu

   B. The Function menu

   C. The Actions menu

   D. The Object menu

3. The required properties when creating a User object are

   A. Login name and address

   B. First name and last name

   C. Login name and last name

   D. Network address and first name

4. A user template

   A. Is created for each user

   B. Specifies defaults for new User objects

   C. Lets you change all User objects at once

   D. Lets you control access rights

5. The menu item used to display property values is

   A. Properties

   B. Values

C. Attributes

D. Details

6. The Move option can move which types of objects?

    A. User, Server, and Printer

    B. Container objects only

    C. Leaf objects only

    D. User objects only

7. NETADMIN can be used to manage

    A. User objects only

    B. Only the basic NDS objects

    C. All NDS objects

    D. Bindery objects

8. The Group object can group users

    A. In the same container only

    B. In different containers only

    C. In the same or different containers

    D. In the [Root] container only

9. To assign a user to an Organizational Role, you use the

    A. User's Role property

    B. Organizational Role's Member property

    C. User's Profile property

    D. Organizational Role's Occupant property

10. The NetWare Server object

    A. Can be created when you wish to install a new server

    B. Is created automatically when the server is installed

    C. Is deleted automatically when the server is removed

    D. Can be used to add logins to the server

11. The Alias object

    A. Represents, or points to, another object

    B. Is created whenever an object is deleted

    C. Can be used instead of the User object

    D. All of the above

12. Which is the correct MAP command for the Directory Map DATA?

    A. MAP F:=DATA:

    B. MAP F:=DATA.MAP

    C. MAP F:=DATA

    D. MAP F: DATA /DM

How to Use NetWare Security

7

I N MODERN TIMES, we can't have enough security—we have locks, car alarms, home alarms, personal alarms. Sadly, these measures are also necessary in networking. The security features of NetWare 4.1 allow you to control who can access what on the network. You can make the network as secure—or insecure—as you need it to be.

NetWare 4.1 provides two kinds of security:

- *File system security* controls access to the file system.

- *NDS security* controls access to NDS objects.

Both types of security have their uses, although you will use file system security more often than NDS security. The two types of security are very similar. We'll discuss some of their common features next and then delve into each type of security.

Trustees

M UCH OF NETWARE 4.1 security centers around *trustees*. A trustee is, simply, anyone who has rights to a file, directory, or NDS object. Well, anyone or *anything*, to be precise. With NDS security, any object can be a trustee—in other words, any object can be given rights to any other object.

The following types of objects are often used as trustees in the file system or in NDS:

- The [Root] object

- Organization objects

- Organizational Unit objects

- Organizational Role and Group objects

- User objects

- The [Public] trustee

These objects are explained in the sections that follow.

The [Root] Object

Rights can be assigned to the [Root] object, but this practice can be dangerous because all users in the Directory tree are given these rights. For small networks, assigning rights to the [Root] object can be an easy way to assign rights to publicly available files, such as those in the PUBLIC subdirectory.

Organization Objects

Since an Organization object is usually a major division of the Directory tree, the same warning given about the [Root] object applies here. Assigning rights to an Organization object should be used only for files that need to be made available to the entire organization.

Organizational Unit Objects

The Organizational Unit object is the most common and convenient place to assign file system rights. Since these containers are usually specific to a particular department or class of users, rights assigned here can be given to logical groups of users. The advantages of a well-designed directory tree become obvious when you are assigning rights to these containers.

Organizational Role and Group Objects

Organizational Role objects or Group objects can be used when files are not needed by all members of a container object. These types of objects allow you to keep tight control of who can access these files and may be useful for applications that you want to restrict to a specific set of users. When using this method, be sure to add the users to the Group or Organizational Role object.

User Objects

Finally, rights can be assigned to a User object. In a well-designed network, you should rarely have to use user rights because assigning rights to the previously discussed objects allows easy maintenance without having to assign rights to each user. Assigning rights to a User object can be useful, however, when only a certain user should have access to a file or directory.

The [Public] Trustee

The [Public] trustee object does not represent an actual object in the Directory tree. Instead, it provides a method of assigning rights to all users attached to the network—*even those who are not logged in*. Obviously, it would be very dangerous to assign rights to this trustee. You should use this method only for special cases. NetWare 4.1 assigns a minimal set of rights to this trustee to enable users to log in.

Using File System Security

F IRST, WE'LL LOOK AT file system security, which is the most common kind of security used in NetWare 4.1. By controlling access to the file system, you can protect data from users who should not access it. In addition, you can give users access to the directories and files they need while keeping those files safe.

File System Rights

A trustee can have several different types of rights to a file or directory. These rights specify which actions the trustee can perform in that file or directory.

If you are assigned rights in a directory, these rights are called *explicit rights* or *trustee rights*. You can also receive *group rights* from a group that you belong to. Here are the available file system rights:

Right	Description
Read [R]	Read data from an existing file.
Write [W]	Write data to an existing file.
Create [C]	Create a new file or subdirectory.
Erase [E]	Delete existing files or directories.
Modify [M]	Rename and change attributes of files.
File Scan [F]	List the contents of a directory.
Access Control [A]	Control the rights of other users to access files or directories.
Supervisor [S]	Users with the Supervisor right are automatically granted all other rights.

Inherited Rights

If a user is a trustee of a directory, the rights are *inherited* into subdirectories of that directory. The *Inherited Rights Filter* (IRF) controls which rights can be inherited. The IRF cannot be used to grant rights; it can only block or allow rights that were given in a parent directory.

The IRF is simply a list of the rights that a user or other trustee can inherit for that directory or file. If a right is included in the IRF, it can be inherited. If you leave a right out of the IRF, then no user can inherit that right for that directory.

Effective Rights

Your rights in a directory begin with the rights granted explicitly to you or your group or inherited from a parent directory. The IRF then filters these rights, and the end result is called your *effective rights* in the directory. Effective rights are what NetWare actually looks at when controlling user access.

(Remember that only the NDS database Directory is written with a capital D.)

For example, in Figure 7.1 user RALPH has been given the rights RWMF in the DATA directory. He inherits the same rights in the AP directory because the IRF allows all rights [RWCEMF]. In the AR directory, however, his rights are limited to R and F by the IRF. Although the C right is included in the IRF, user RALPH does not receive this right because he did not have it in the DATA directory.

File Attributes

Another layer of file system security is *attribute security*. Attributes are options that can be applied to a file or directory to give it certain behaviors. An example is the Hidden attribute, which hides a file from the directory listing. Some attributes are set by the user or system administrator; others are set automatically by NetWare to indicate a condition. For example, the Archive Needed attribute indicates that the file has changed since the last backup.

FIGURE 7.1
Effective rights are the actions a trustee can perform in a file or directory.

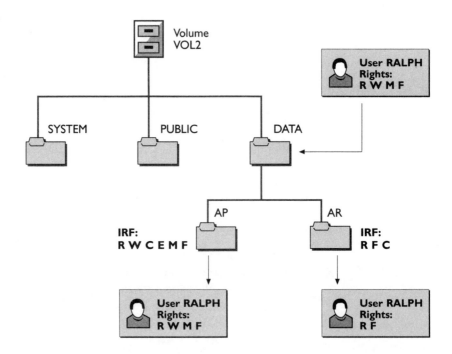

The table below lists the possible file attributes. Many of these attributes concern NetWare 4.1 features such as file compression and disk suballocation; these will be discussed in Chapter 15.

Attribute Name	Description
A (Archive Needed)	NetWare sets this attribute automatically when a file is changed. Backup programs use this to indicate which files need to be backed up.
Ci (Copy Inhibit)	Stops users from copying the file (Macintosh files only).
Cc (Can't Compress)	This attribute is set by NetWare to indicate that no significant amount of space would be saved by compression.
Dc (Don't Compress)	Prevents a file or directory contents from being compressed.
Di (Delete Inhibit)	Prevents a file or directory from being deleted.
Dm (Don't Migrate)	Prevents file or directory contents from being migrated to an optical jukebox, tape, or other high-capacity storage device.
Ds (Don't Suballocate)	Causes the file to be written in whole blocks, regardless of whether block suballocation is enabled.
Ic (Immediate Compress)	Causes the file, or all files in the directory, to be compressed immediately when written.
M (Migrated)	Indicates files that have been migrated to high-capacity storage.
H (Hidden)	Prevents a file or directory from being shown in the directory listing. This attribute affects DOS programs only; the NDIR utility shows hidden files if the user has the File Scan right.
I (Indexed)	Activates the turbo FAT indexing feature on the file.

N (Normal)	Normal is not an actual file attribute but is used by the FLAG command to assign a default set of attributes. (Shareable, Read/Write).
P (Purge)	Causes the file to be purged (erased) immediately when deleted. The file cannot be recovered using the SALVAGE utility.
Ri (Rename Inhibit)	Prevents the user from renaming the file or directory.
Ro (Read Only)	Prevents users from writing to, renaming, or erasing the file. Ro automatically sets the Ri (Rename Inhibit) and Di (Delete Inhibit) attributes.
Rw (Read/Write)	Allows both reading and writing to the file. This attribute is set when the Ro (Read Only) attribute is cleared.
S (Shareable)	Allows multiple users to access the file at the same time.
Sy (System)	Indicates files used by the system. A combination of the Read Only and Hidden attributes.
T (Transactional)	Indicates that the file is a TTS file and is protected by the Transaction Tracking System. This feature can be used only with applications that support TTS.
X (Execute Only)	Prevents the file from being modified, renamed, or copied. Once set, this attribute cannot be removed except by deleting the file.

Managing File System Security

To run the NetWare Administrator utility, make sure you are logged in to the NetWare 4.1 network, start Windows, and choose Run from the Program Manager menu. In the dialog box, type **NWADMIN** and press Enter. NetWare Administrator should start.

Note that you cannot make changes to security unless you have the correct rights. If possible, log in as the user ADMIN or an equivalent to follow along with the examples in this chapter.

Browsing the File System

Using the NetWare Administrator program, you can view the directory structure of your NetWare volumes. The capabilities of this program are similar to those of the FILER utility in earlier versions of NetWare. You can copy, move, rename, and delete files through NetWare Administrator. In addition, you can set NetWare attributes for files and directories and assign trustees.

You can browse a volume in two ways:

- Double-click on the name of a volume to expand the listing with the names of files and directories under the root directory of the volume, as shown in Figure 7.2.

FIGURE 7.2

Double-click on a volume name to view the contents of the volume in the main NDS window.

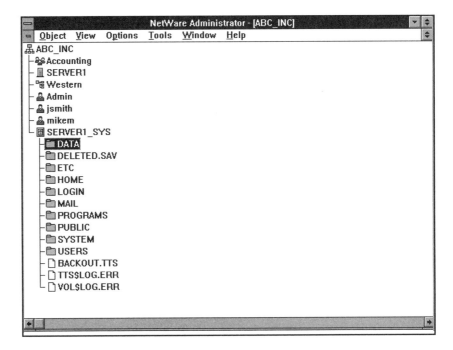

■ Click on the volume name once to highlight it. Select Tools from the menu bar and then select Browse to open a new window that shows only the volume, as you can see in Figure 7.3.

After you open the volume for display, you can navigate through the directories. Double-clicking on a directory opens that directory. If you select a file or directory, the Object menu includes options that allow you to perform file operations, such as copy, move, rename, and delete. In addition, the Details option on the Object menu allows you to view the attributes and trustees of the file or directory and to make changes.

You can also manage files using the drag-and-drop feature of Microsoft Windows. If you drag a file into a directory with the mouse pointer, you can move or copy the file. This feature is similar to dragging and dropping in the Windows File Manager.

F I G U R E 7.3
The Browse option on the Tools menu allows you to open a new window for viewing the directory.

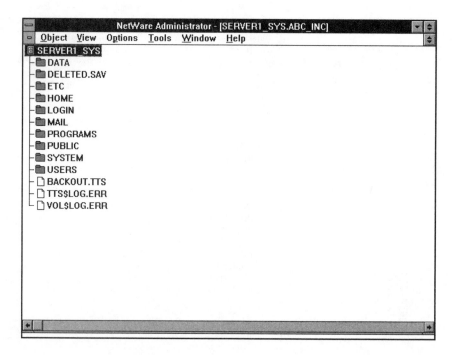

Assigning Trustee Rights

You can assign trustees in several ways:

- Add users as trustees to a file using NETADMIN, the NetWare Administrator utility (NWADMIN), or the FILER utility.

- Add file and directory trustee rights to a user using the NetWare Administrator or NETADMIN utility.

Assigning Trustees to a File or Directory

In the NetWare Administrator utility, you can assign trustees to a file or directory by following these steps:

1. Click on the file or directory with the mouse pointer to highlight it.

2. Select the Object menu and then select Details. The Details screen for the file appears.

3. Click on the Trustees of this Directory button, located along the right side of the Details screen, to display the trustees information for a directory, as shown in Figure 7.4.

4. Select a trustee (if trustees are already assigned to the directory) to see the rights for that user in the directory.

5. Add or remove rights by clicking on the checkboxes next to their names.

6. Add a new trustee by clicking on the Add Trustee button. This presents the Select Object dialog box that allows you to select a user, group, or another object, as shown in Figure 7.5.

7. Assign rights to the new trustee by clicking on the checkboxes. The Read and File Scan rights are granted by default.

8. Click on the OK button to save your changes.

NetWare Administrator provides a shortcut to accessing the Details option. After selecting the file or directory, click the right button on your mouse to display a pop-up menu. The Details option is listed first. The other options that can be accessed from this menu depend on the type of object selected.

FIGURE 7.4
Click the Trustees of this
Directory button to
display the current
trustees of the directory.

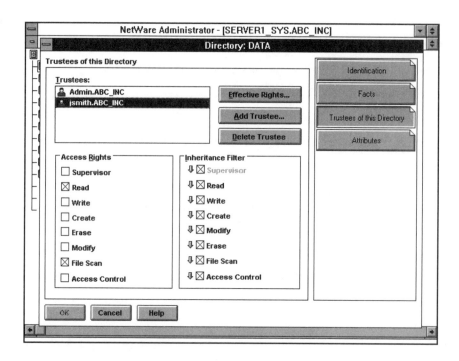

FIGURE 7.5
After choosing the Add
Trustee button, use the
Select Object dialog box
to find the user or other
object to be added.

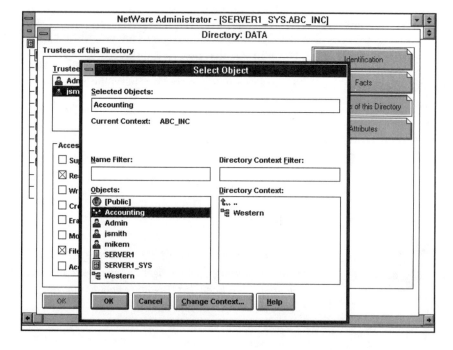

Assigning File System Rights to a User

An alternate method of assigning file system rights is to start with the user. This method also works with other objects, such as groups or containers. Follow these steps:

1. Navigate through the NDS tree and highlight the user (or other object) whom you want to add as a trustee.

2. Select the Object menu and then select Details. The Details screen for the user (or other object) appears.

3. Select the Rights to Files and Directories button.

4. Select the volumes to be displayed. The simplest way is to use the Find button, which allows you to find all volumes in the current directory quickly. All directories and files that the user has rights to are displayed, as shown in Figure 7.6.

FIGURE 7.6
The current trustee rights given to a user are displayed when you choose the Rights to Files and Directories button.

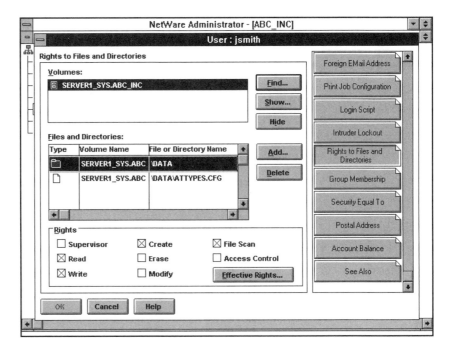

5. Click on the Add button to add the user as a trustee to another directory or file. You'll see the Select Object dialog box, which allows you to select files. (Refer to Figure 7.5.)

6. Highlight a file or directory after it has been added to the list. NetWare Administrator displays the rights that the trustee has. By default, these are Read and File Scan.

7. Click on the checkboxes to add or remove rights.

8. Select the OK button to save your changes.

Modifying the Inherited Rights Filter (IRF)

You can view and modify an IRF for a directory by using the Details screen, which is the same screen that displays the trustees for that directory. To display this screen, select the directory, choose the Details option (from the Object menu or the pop-up menu that appears when you click with the right mouse button), and then click on the Trustees button.

In the Inheritance Filter list, you can change the inheritance status for each right by clicking on its checkbox. An arrow icon to the left of the checkbox indicates whether the right is allowed or blocked.

Displaying Effective Rights

An Effective Rights button appears in both the User object's Rights to Files and Directories screen and the directory's Trustees screen. Click on this button to view the current effective rights for the user in that directory. Rights that the user has been granted are displayed in black. Those that the user does not have are grayed. Figure 7.7 shows the Effective Rights dialog box.

The effective rights in this dialog box are updated whenever you view them; the user doesn't have to log in or out to display the current effective rights. However, when you make a change to a user's rights, you must save the changes with the OK button before the Effective Rights dialog box can reflect those changes.

By viewing the Effective Rights dialog box, you can easily determine whether you have assigned rights correctly. It is a good idea to check the effective rights whenever you have made changes, because of the interaction between explicit, inherited, and group rights.

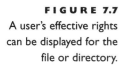

FIGURE 7.7

A user's effective rights can be displayed for the file or directory.

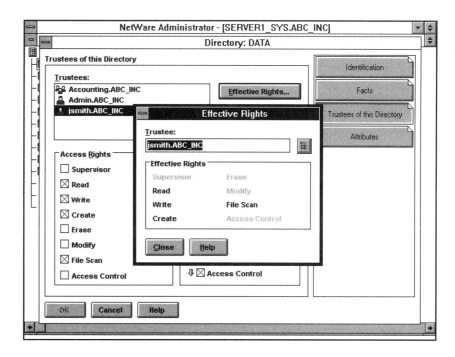

Modifying File Attributes

You can also modify file attributes using the NetWare Administrator program. Follow these steps:

1. Click on the file or directory to highlight it.

2. Select the Object menu and then select Details.

3. Click on the Attributes button on the right side of the screen to see the current attributes for the file, as shown in Figure 7.8.

4. Add or remove attributes by clicking on the checkboxes next to the attribute names.

5. Select the OK button to save your changes.

The list of attributes is dynamic. If an option is not available for the current file or directory, the item is grayed on the menu and you cannot select it. Also, some selections are made automatically. For example, selecting the Read Only attribute automatically selects the Delete Inhibit and Rename Inhibit attributes.

FIGURE 7.8
File and directory attributes can be modified from within the NetWare Administrator utility.

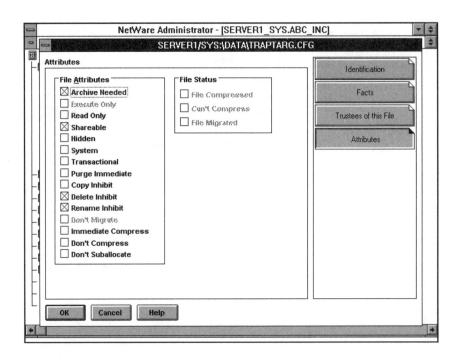

Using NDS Security

WHILE FILE SYSTEM SECURITY allows you to control access to volumes, files, and directories on a server, NDS security is used to control access to objects in the Directory—users, groups, printers, and entire organizations. You can control the ability of the users to modify and add objects and to view or modify their properties. With an understanding of NDS security, you can assign users the rights they need in the Directory while maintaining a secure network.

Login Security

NDS provides *login security* for the network. This security was also provided by the bindery in NetWare 3.1*x*. Login security is handled by a password for each user object. The workstation software sends this password to NDS in an encrypted form, so there is no way of reading these passwords from elsewhere in the network.

Although NDS provides incredibly sophisticated levels of security, none of them will be effective if your users use simple passwords or no password at all. You should require passwords on the network and advise users not to use common words or names. (You would be amazed how many users on the average network use their children's names for passwords.) This policy ensures that there are no weaknesses in network security.

Trustee Rights

Like the file system, NDS security assigns rights through the use of trustees. The trustees of an object are called *object trustees*. An object trustee is any user (or other object) who has been given rights to the object. The list of trustees for an object is called the *Access Control List*, or ACL. Each object has a property containing the ACL.

While the file system has a set list of rights that a trustee can receive, NDS security provides two categories of rights: object rights and property rights.

Object Rights

Object rights are the tasks that a trustee can perform on an object. There are five types of object rights:

Right	Description
Supervisor	The trustee is granted all of the rights listed below. Unlike the Supervisor right in the file system, the NDS Supervisor right can be blocked by the IRF.
Browse	The trustee can see the object in the Directory tree. If the Browse right is not granted, the object is not shown in the list.
Create	The trustee can create child objects under the object. This right is available only for container objects.
Delete	The trustee can delete the object from the Directory. In order to delete an object, you must also have the Write right for All Properties of the object.
Rename	The trustee can change the name of the object.

Property Rights

Property rights are the tasks that a trustee can perform on the object's properties and allow the trustee to read or modify the property values. There are five types of property rights, which are not the same as the types of object rights:

Right	Description
Supervisor	The trustee is given all of the property rights listed below. Once again, this right can be blocked by the IRF. Trustees with the Supervisor object right are automatically given supervisory rights to all properties of the object.
Compare	The trustee is allowed to compare the property's values to a given value. The trustee can search for a certain value but not look at the value itself.
Read	The trustee can read the values of the property. The Compare right is automatically granted.
Write	The trustee can modify, add, or remove values of the property.
Add Self	The trustee is allowed to add or remove itself as a value of the property. For example, a user who is granted the Add Self right for a group can add him/herself to the group. The Write right automatically grants the Add Self property.

Property rights can be granted in two ways: All Properties or Selected Properties. If All Properties is selected, the same list of rights is granted to each of the properties of the object.

You should think twice before assigning rights to All Properties of an object. This action can be a security risk. It is usually better to assign rights to only the properties that the trustee needs to access.

When granting Selected Properties, you are allowed to activate or deactivate each of the property rights for each property of the object. This option allows you to fine-tune the security and allow access only to what is needed. Because of the security risks involved in using the All Properties option, you should use Selected Properties for all users except administrators.

An object trustee can have both All Properties rights and Selected Properties rights for the same object. Selected Properties rights override the All

Properties rights for that property. For example, you could grant the Supervisor right to All Properties for an object trustee and then use Selected Properties to limit rights to certain properties. Rights without a Selected Properties assignment follow the All Properties assignment.

One of the object properties that can be selected is the Object Trustees property. This property contains the trustee list, the ACL, itself. If a user is given Supervisor or Write rights to this property, the user can add and delete trustees from the object. To avoid this security risk, don't assign the Write or Supervisor rights to the Object Trustees property or to All Properties.

Inherited Rights in NDS

Like the file system, NDS uses a system of *inherited rights*. When an object trustee is given rights to a container object, the trustee also receives the same rights for all children of the object. Inheritance affects both object rights and property rights.

Object Rights Inheritance

Object rights are inherited in the same fashion as file system rights. When a trustee is given object rights for an object, the rights are inherited by child objects—the trustee receives rights for these objects also unless the rights are blocked.

Property Rights Inheritance

Property rights can be inherited in the same manner as object rights with one exception—only rights given with the All Properties option can be inherited. If a trustee is given rights to Selected Properties of an object, those rights cannot be inherited by child objects. This happens because each type of object, such as users and organizational units, has a different list of properties.

Blocking Inherited Rights

When a trustee is given rights to a container object, the rights flow down the Directory tree until they are blocked. You can block inherited rights in two ways: with a new trustee assignment or with the IRF.

EXPLICIT ASSIGNMENTS You can block the rights a trustee can inherit for a particular object by giving the trustee a new *explicit assignment* to the object. For example, in Figure 7.9 user RON is given full rights [SBCDR] to the entire NHA_CO Organization. However, RON has been given a new explicit assignment of Browse and Rename only [BR] for the ORLANDO Organizational Unit. While RON receives full rights in the TAMPA Organizational Unit, his rights in ORLANDO are limited to [BR] by the new trustee assignment.

FIGURE 7.9
Inherited rights can be
blocked with a new
explicit assignment.

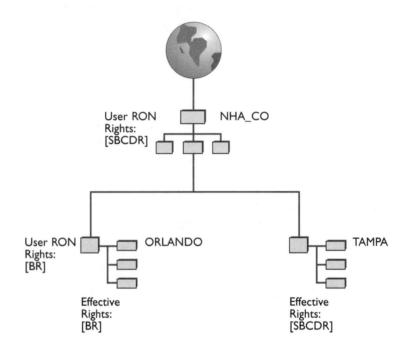

A new trustee assignment can be used to block rights, as in the example, or to add additional rights. The new trustee assignment replaces the rights that would have been inherited. Because an explicit assignment blocks inherited rights, you do not need to consider inherited rights if an explicit assignment has been granted.

The Inherited Rights Filter (IRF)

Each NDS object has an IRF for object rights. The IRF is a list of the rights that a User can inherit for the object. For example, in Figure 7.10 User JANS has been given the [BCDR] rights to the ACCTG Organizational Unit. She inherits these

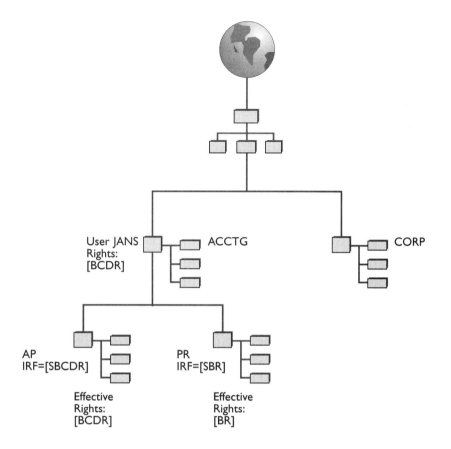

FIGURE 7.10
The Inherited Rights Filter
can be used to block
inherited rights.

same rights in the AP Organizational Unit, which has the default IRF. The IRF for the PR Organizational Unit has been set to [SBR], so JAN's rights in PR are limited to [BR].

Each object also has an IRF for property rights. Like the rights themselves, the IRF can be set for All Properties or Selected Properties. You can also set an IRF for All Properties and set different IRFs for certain Selected Properties. Remember, the rights are inherited only if they were assigned to All Properties for the parent object.

Remember, the IRF cannot give a user additional rights; it can be used only to filter (block) rights that a user would otherwise inherit. Also, the IRF affects only inherited rights—it doesn't block security equivalence, which is described in the next section.

Security Equivalence in NDS

In several situations in NDS, a trustee automatically receives all of the rights given to another trustee. This event is referred to as *security equivalence*. By understanding these equivalences, you can easily grant rights to users and make sure that unnecessary rights are not granted. There are two types of security equivalence: implied and explicit.

Implied Security Equivalence

When rights are given to a container object, all objects within the container receive the same rights through security equivalence. If one of these objects is a container object, the objects underneath it also receive the rights. This is referred to as *implied security equivalence* or *container security equivalence*.

For example, in Figure 7.11, giving a trustee assignment to the ACCTG Organization would give the same rights to the PAYABLES and BILLING Organizational Units and all leaf objects under them. Giving a trustee assignment to the [Root] object would give the same rights to all objects in the entire tree.

Because rights flow from container objects to their children, you may be tempted to describe this process as "inheritance." However, this is not inheritance in the NetWare definition. Inheritance means that rights given to a trustee for a container object are given to the same trustee for the object's children.

It is important to understand the difference between inheritance and implied security equivalence because the IRF *does not affect* security equivalences. This distinction can be one of the most difficult concepts to master in NDS security. You can avoid confusion by remembering the following statements:

- An object *inherits* the trustees assigned to its parent objects. These rights can be blocked by the IRF.

- A trustee is *security equivalent to* its parent objects. These rights cannot be blocked by the IRF.

These concepts are further illustrated in Figure 7.12. Look at this Directory tree carefully and read the following statements about the objects in the Directory.

FIGURE 7.11
In implied security
equivalence, rights given
to a container are passed
on to objects within the
container.

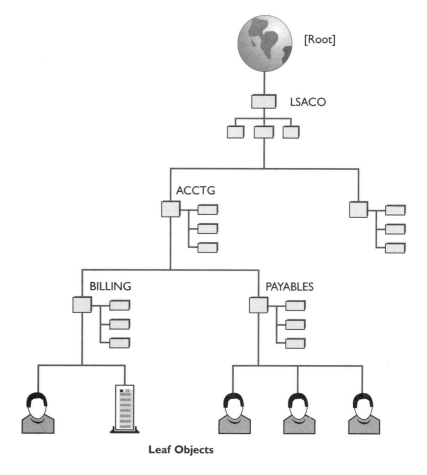

Leaf Objects

- The CORP Organizational Unit has been given full rights to the ACCTG Organizational Unit. (CORP is a trustee of ACCTG.)

- The ADMIN and PAYROLL Organizational Units both have an IRF of [BR] (Browse and Rename only).

- Jane receives full rights [SBCDR] to objects in the ACCTG Organizational Unit. This is because Jane has an implied security equivalence to the CORP container object. The IRF given to the ADMIN Organizational Unit does not affect Jane's rights.

FIGURE 7.12
This Directory tree shows examples of both inherited rights and implied security equivalence.

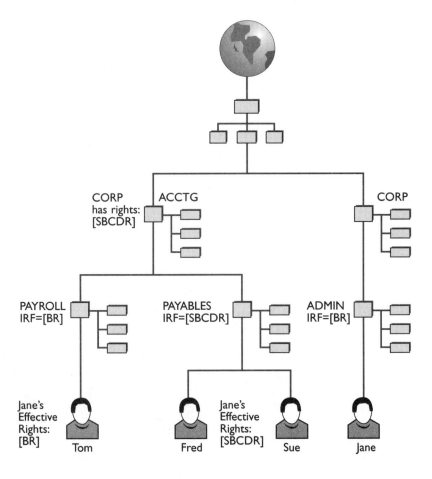

- Jane inherits full rights to all objects in the PAYABLES organizational unit, including the User objects Fred and Sue.

- Jane's rights to the User object Tom are limited to Browse and Rename only [BR] by the IRF of the PAYROLL Organizational Unit.

Explicit Security Equivalence

A second, much simpler type of security equivalence is also available: *explicit security equivalence*. This is a security equivalence that is specifically given to a user. You can assign explicit security equivalences in three ways:

- Each user has a Security Equal To property. You can add users or other objects to this list, and the user receives the rights given to those objects.

- If a user is assigned to the membership list of a Group object, the user becomes security equivalent to the Group object.

- If a user is an occupant of an Organizational Role object, the user becomes security equivalent to the Organizational Role object.

All explicit security equivalences are listed in the user's Security Equal To property. Security equivalences that the user receives through an organizational role or group membership are automatically added to this list.

Security equivalences cannot be combined or "nested." For example, if the user John is made security equivalent to another user, Wendy, and Wendy is made security equivalent to the ADMIN user, John does not become security equivalent to ADMIN and does not receive administrative rights. He receives only those rights given to (or inherited by) Wendy's User object.

Calculating Effective Rights

A user's *effective rights* are the tasks the user can actually perform on the object. As you have learned, many factors affect a user's rights to an object in the Directory:

- Rights given directly to the user (explicit trustee assignments)

- Inherited rights from rights the user has been given to objects higher in the Directory tree

- The IRF or an explicit assignment that can block inherited rights

- Rights received from containers the user resides in through implied security equivalence

- Security equivalences to Group or Organizational Role objects

Luckily, the NetWare Administrator utility provides a simple method of displaying a user's effective rights to an object. If you find it necessary to calculate effective rights manually, you can do so by following these steps:

1. Start with any explicit rights given to the user for the object.

2. If there are no explicit rights, calculate the inherited rights—any rights given to the user for parent objects minus those blocked by the IRF.

3. Add any rights given to the user's security equivalents for the object. These include group memberships, organizational roles, or members of the user's Security Equivalent To property.

The process of calculating effective rights is illustrated by the flowchart in Figure 7.13.

FIGURE 7.13
A flowchart for calculating effective rights.

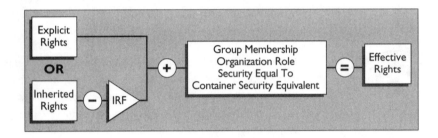

Using NetWare Administrator to Control NDS Security

You can use the NetWare Administrator utility to manage the following aspects of NDS security:

- Viewing trustee rights

- Adding a trustee

- Changing object and property rights

- Modifying the IRF

- Displaying effective rights

These topics will be discussed in the following sections.

Viewing Trustee Rights

NetWare Administrator provides two ways to view trustee rights. Both of these options are accessed from the Object menu:

- The Trustees of This Object option allows you to view a list of trustees for the object you have selected, as shown in Figure 7.14. You can then select a trustee to view detailed information.

FIGURE 7.14
The Trustees of This
Object option allows you
to view an object's
trustee list.

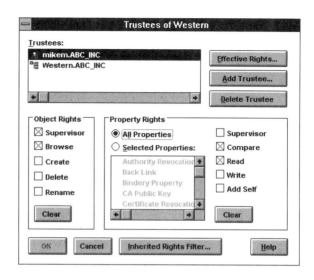

■ The Rights to Other Objects option allows you to view a list of objects
that the selected object is a trustee of. First, enter a context to search in.
You can then select an object from the list to view the trustee's rights to
the object, as shown in Figure 7.15.

FIGURE 7.15
The Rights to Other
Objects option allows you
to list a trustee's rights.

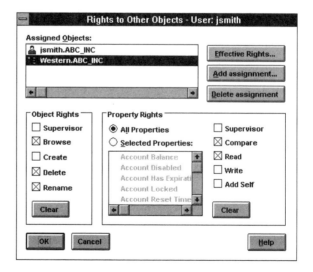

Each of these screens includes all of the possible rights for the object. A checkbox next to the option displays whether the right is granted and allows you to grant or revoke the right.

These techniques allow you to view and change explicit rights only. To view a user's effective rights, see the Displaying Effective Rights section later in this chapter.

Adding a Trustee

Similarly, you can add a trustee in two ways. The first is to add trustees to an object:

1. Browse the Directory tree to find the object and highlight it.

2. Select Trustees of This Object from the Object menu.

3. Click the Add Trustee button to access the Select Object dialog box, shown in Figure 7.16.

4. Find the object that will become a trustee in the Select Object dialog box and press the OK button.

FIGURE 7.16
To add a trustee, select the object from the Directory tree.

The trustee is added to the list. (To change the trustee's rights, see the next section, Changing Object and Property Rights.)

A second way to add a trustee is to add objects to a trustee:

1. Browse the Directory tree to find the object that will become a trustee and highlight it.

2. Select Rights to Other Objects from the Object menu.

3. Click the Add Assignment button to access the Select Object dialog box.

4. Select the object that the trustee will have rights to and press OK.

The object is added to the list of objects the trustee has rights to.

Changing Object and Property Rights

While either the Rights to Other Objects or Trustees of This Object dialog boxes are displayed, you can change the object rights given to the trustee. Simply highlight the trustee or object and click the checkbox next to each type of right to grant (check) or revoke (uncheck) it.

You can also change property rights from either of these dialog boxes. You can assign rights for All Properties by selecting All Properties and then by checking or unchecking the box next to each property right.

To assign rights to selected rights, click the Selected Properties button. You are presented with a list of properties that depends on the type of object. Select the property to change rights for and check or uncheck the boxes as appropriate.

A checkmark is displayed to the left of each property that you have changed the rights for. Properties without a checkmark have not been changed in Selected Properties and will default to the setting for All Properties.

Modifying the IRF

The IRF can be changed from the Trustees of This Object dialog box. Follow these steps to change the IRF for an object:

1. Browse the Directory tree to find the object and highlight it.

2. Select Trustees of This Object from the Object menu.

3. Click the Inherited Rights Filter button. The dialog box shown in Figure 7.17 is displayed.

4. To change the IRF for object rights, use the checkboxes on the left. A checked box means that the right is allowed for inheritance, and an unchecked box means that the right is blocked. An arrow or blocked arrow to the left of the checkbox indicates your selection.

5. To change the IRF for All Properties, click the All Properties button and then check or uncheck the boxes for each possible property right.

6. To change the IRF for Selected Properties, click the Selected Properties button and then select the property to be changed. Check or uncheck the appropriate boxes. A checkmark to the left of the property name indicates that the All Properties IRF is overridden for this property.

Displaying Effective Rights

An Effective Rights button appears in both the Trustees of This Object and the Rights to Other Objects dialog boxes. Click on this button to view the current effective rights for the user for the object. Rights that the user has been granted are displayed in black. Those that the user does not have are grayed. Figure 7.18 shows an example of the Effective Rights display.

If you have made changes to a trustee's rights, you must save the changes with the OK button before the Effective Rights display can reflect those changes.

FIGURE 7.17
You can change a user's inherited rights by clicking the checkbox for each type of right.

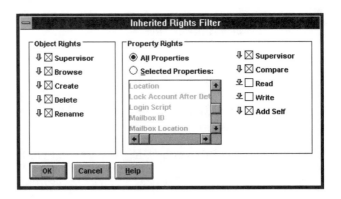

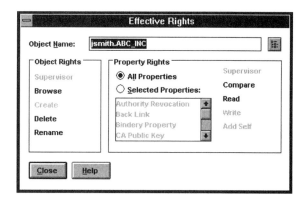

By viewing the Effective Rights display, you can easily check whether you have assigned rights correctly. It is a good idea to check the effective rights whenever you have made changes because of the interaction between explicit, inherited, and group rights.

Review

THE SECURITY FEATURES of NetWare 4.1 are used to control which users and other NDS objects have access to files, directories, and objects. NetWare 4.1 has two kinds of security:

- *File system security* controls access to the file system.

- *NDS security* controls access to NDS objects.

Much of NetWare 4.1 security centers around *trustees*. A trustee is anyone—or anything—who has rights to a file, directory, or NDS object. With NDS security, any object can be a trustee—in other words, any object can be given rights to any other object.

The following types of objects can be made trustees in the file system or in NDS:

- The [Root] object

- Organization objects

- Organizational Unit objects

- Organizational Role and Group objects

- User objects

- The [Public] trustee

File System Security

The available file system rights are as follows:

Right	Description
Read [R]	Read data from an existing file.
Write [W]	Write data to an existing file.
Create [C]	Create a new file or subdirectory.
Erase [E]	Delete existing files or directories.
Modify [M]	Rename and change attributes of files.
File Scan [F]	List the contents of a directory.
Access Control [A]	Control the rights of other users to access files or directories.
Supervisor [S]	Users with the Supervisor right are automatically granted all other rights.

If a user is a trustee of a directory, the rights are *inherited* into subdirectories of that directory. The *Inherited Rights Filter* (IRF) controls which rights can be inherited. The IRF cannot be used to grant rights; it can only block or allow rights that were given for a parent directory.

Your rights in a directory begin with the rights granted explicitly to you or your group or inherited from a parent directory. The IRF then filters these rights, and the end result is called your *effective rights* in the directory. Effective rights are what NetWare actually looks at when controlling user access.

Another layer of file system security is *attribute security*. Attributes are options that can be applied to a file or directory to give it certain behaviors.

NDS Security

While file system security allows you to control access to volumes, files, and directories on a server, NDS security is used to control access to objects in the Directory—users, groups, printers, and entire organizations. You can control the ability of users to modify and add objects and to view or modify their properties. With an understanding of NDS security, you can assign users the rights they need in the Directory while maintaining a secure network.

Like the file system, NDS security assigns rights through the use of trustees. The trustees of an object are called *object trustees*. An object trustee is any user (or other object) who has been given rights to the object. The list of trustees for an object is called the *Access Control List*, or ACL. Each object has a property containing the ACL.

While the file system has a set list of rights that a trustee can receive, NDS security provides two categories of rights: object rights and property rights.

Object rights are the tasks that a trustee can perform on an object. Here are the five types of object rights:

Right	Description
Supervisor	The trustee is granted all of the rights listed below. Unlike the Supervisor right in the file system, the NDS Supervisor right can be blocked by the IRF.
Browse	The trustee can see the object in the Directory tree. If the Browse right is not granted, the object is not shown in the list.
Create	The trustee can create child objects under the object. This right is available only for container objects.
Delete	The trustee can delete the object from the Directory. In order to delete an object, you must also have the Write right for All Properties of the object.
Rename	The trustee can change the name of the object.

Property rights are the tasks that a trustee can perform on the object's properties and allow the trustee to read or modify the property values. There are five types of property rights, which are not the same as the types of object rights:

Right	Description
Supervisor	The trustee is given all of the property rights listed below. Once again, this right can be blocked by the IRF. Trustees with the Supervisor object right are automatically given supervisory rights to all properties of the object.
Compare	The trustee is allowed to compare the property's values to a given value. The trustee can search for a certain value but not look at the value itself.
Read	The trustee can read the values of the property. The Compare right is automatically granted.
Write	The trustee can modify, add, or remove values of the property.
Add Self	The trustee is allowed to add or remove itself as a value of the property. For example, a user who is granted the Add Self right for a group can add him/herself to the group. The Write right automatically grants the Add Self property.

Property rights can be granted in two ways: All Properties or Selected Properties. If All Properties is selected, the same list of rights is granted to each of the properties of the object.

Inherited Rights in NDS

Like the file system, NDS uses a system of *inherited rights*. When an object trustee is given rights to a container object, the trustee also receives the same rights for all children of the object. Inheritance affects both object rights and property rights.

Object rights are inherited in the same fashion as file system rights. When a trustee is given object rights for an object, the rights are inherited by child objects—the trustee receives rights for these objects also unless the rights are blocked.

Property rights can be inherited in the same manner as object rights, with one exception—only rights given with the All Properties option can be inherited. If a trustee is given rights to Selected Properties of an object, those rights cannot be inherited by child objects. This happens because each type of object, such as User or Organizational Unit, has a different list of properties.

When a trustee is given rights to a container object, the rights flow down the Directory tree until they are blocked. You can block inherited rights in two ways: with a new trustee assignment or with the Inherited Rights Filter (IRF).

Security Equivalence in NDS

There are several situations in NDS in which a trustee automatically receives all of the rights given to another trustee, which is referred to as *security equivalence*. There are two types of security equivalence:

- *Implied security equivalence* means that an object receives rights given to its parent containers.

- *Explicit security equivalence* is given with the Security Equal To property, group membership, or Organizational Role occupancy.

Effective Rights in NDS

A user's *effective rights* are the tasks the user can actually perform on the object. If you find it necessary to calculate effective rights manually, you can do so by following these steps:

1. Start with any explicit rights given to the user for the object.

2. If there are no explicit rights, calculate the inherited rights—any rights given to the user for parent objects minus those blocked by the IRF.

3. Add any rights given to the user's security equivalents for the object. These include group memberships, organizational roles, or members of the user's Security Equivalent To property.

CNA Practice Test Questions

1. The two types of NetWare 4.1 security are

    A. File system security and NDS security

    B. File system security and object rights

    C. Trustee rights and object rights

    D. All properties and selected properties

2. Which of the following can NOT be a trustee?

    A. Organization

    B. User

    C. Organizational Role

    D. File

3. The File Scan right

    A. Allows you to copy files

    B. Allows you to list files in a directory

    C. Allows you to read the contents of files

    D. Allows you to search for a file

4. The IRF affects

    A. Security equivalence

    B. Inherited rights

    C. Explicit assignments

    D. All of the above

5. File attributes

    A. Are always set by NetWare itself

    B. Are always set by the user

   C. Cannot be changed

   D. Give a file certain behaviors

6. You can manage file system security with

   A. NetWare Administrator

   B. NETADMIN

   C. SYSCON

   D. SECURE

7. The IRF lists

   A. Rights to be blocked

   B. Rights to be granted

   C. Rights allowed to be inherited

   D. Rights that cannot be inherited

8. The list of trustees for an object is stored in

   A. The Trustees property

   B. The ACL

   C. The Trustee database

   D. The Trustee file

9. The two types of rights in NDS are

   A. Object rights and file rights

   B. Object rights and property rights

   C. All Properties and Selected Properties

   D. Object rights and the IRF

10. Inherited rights can be blocked with

   A. The IRF

   B. An explicit assignment

C. Both A and B

D. None of the above

11. Explicit security equivalences can be granted with

   A. Container occupancy

   B. Group, Organizational Role, Security Equal

   C. Group, container

   D. All of the above

12. Which of the following does NOT affect effective NDS rights?

   A. Explicit rights

   B. Inherited rights

   C. Rights given to child objects

   D. Rights given to parent objects

13. The [Public] Trustee

   A. Assigns rights to all users when logged in

   B. Assigns rights to anyone attached to the network

   C. Assigns rights to ADMIN only

   D. Assigns rights to the file system only

How to Use
Login Scripts
and Menus

CHAPTER

8

S A NETWORK ADMINISTRATOR you should remember the maxim The easier things are for the users, the fewer questions you'll have to answer. In this chapter you will learn two ways to make life easier for users in this chapter:

- *Login scripts* can set up drive mappings and other defaults for the user so that he or she doesn't have to type DOS commands to set up drives or printers.

- The *menu system* lets you define lists of applications a user can run and gives the user a simple way of accessing them.

If you're careful about setting up these options, you can make the network friendly and accessible to the users—even those who fear computers. In addition, even the most computer-literate users appreciate not having to type the same complicated commands each time they log in or access an application.

Using Login Scripts

LOGIN SCRIPT IS A LIST of commands that NetWare executes each time the user logs in. You can use login scripts to set defaults, such as drive mappings, search drive mappings, printer configurations, and variable settings, and to execute commands, such as starting a menu.

You can create and edit login scripts using the NetWare Administrator or NWADMIN utility. Each of the objects we'll talk about below—User, container, and Profile—has a Login Script property, which you use to enter login script commands.

Login Script Types

There are four types of login scripts: user, container, profile, and default. When a user logs in, NetWare checks for each of these and executes them. Login scripts are always executed in the same order:

1. **Container login script** for the user's parent container (if found)

2. **Profile login script** (if assigned)

3. **User login script** (if defined)

4. **Default login script** (If NetWare doesn't find a user login script, it executes the commands in the default login script instead.)

Each type of login script has its own purpose. You can provide a complete configuration for your users with a minimum of maintenance for yourself by taking advantage of each type of script. The sections below explain each of the login script types.

NetWare 3.1*x* has a *system login script,* which is executed for any user on the server. There is no system login script in NetWare 4.1, but you can use container login scripts for the same purpose. However, if the users are divided into several different containers, you will need to provide a container login script for each one.

Container Login Scripts

You can create a *container login script* for any Organization or Organizational Unit object. This script is the first script executed for users in the container. You can use this login script for drive mappings, printer settings, and other options that all users in the container need.

NetWare executes only one container login script—for the user's parent container. For example, in Figure 8.1 user JOHNM has the distinguished name JOHNM.AP.ACCT.AQP_CO. Although JOHNM is in the containers AP,

FIGURE 8.1
Only one container
login script is executed
for each user.

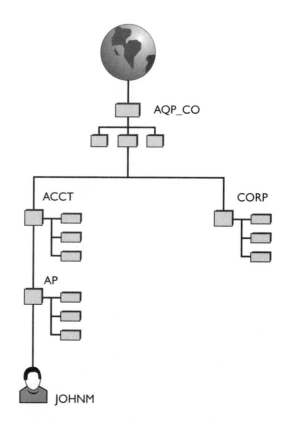

ACCT, and AQP_CO, only the login script for AP is executed because AP is JOHNM's parent container. If the AP Organizational Unit has no login script, no container login script is executed.

To edit the container login script, you can use NetWare Administrator or NETADMIN. The login script is stored in the container object's Login Script property. The container script must be edited by a user with rights to this property, usually the ADMIN user or container administrator.

Profile Login Scripts

The Profile object, introduced in the previous chapter, is a special NDS object that you can use to assign the same login script to several users. You can use a *profile login script* to execute a certain set of drive mappings or other commands for certain users in the directory, even if they are in different containers.

Follow the steps below to set up a profile login script. This can be done from NetWare Administrator or NETADMIN.

1. Create a Profile object. You can place this object in any container, but the logical place for it is in the same container as the users who need it.

2. Edit the Profile object's Login Script property and insert the desired commands.

3. Make the User object for each user who will execute the profile login script a trustee of the Profile object. Give the User object the Read [R] right for the Profile object's Login Script property.

4. Each User object has a Profile property. Edit each User object's Profile property and select the Profile object you have created. You can select only one Profile object per user.

User Login Scripts

The final login script to execute is the *user login script*. You can use a user login script to execute specific commands for a particular user. One important use for the user login script is to override certain commands in the container login script.

Each user has a Login Script property. You can edit this property using NetWare Administrator or NETADMIN to create or modify the user's login script. Advanced users may wish to modify their own login script; they have the right to do so by default.

The Default Login Script

The *default login script* is built in to the LOGIN utility. You cannot edit it. The default script is executed when a user has no user login script. The default login script provides a basic set of search and drive mappings—for example, a search mapping for the PUBLIC directory.

The default login script allows users to log in to a new system without having to create a login script. If you are using container or profile login scripts, the default login script may cause conflicts. You can prevent conflicts with a special login script command: NO_DEFAULT. If you include this command in the container or profile login script, it prevents the execution of the default login script, even if the user has no user login script.

The default login script executes the following commands. You will learn what each command means later in this chapter.

```
MAP DISPLAY OFF
MAP ERRORS OFF
MAP *1=SYS:
MAP *1=SYS:%LOGIN_NAME
IF "%1"="ADMIN" THEN MAP *1:=SYS:SYSTEM
MAP INS S1:=SYS:PUBLIC
MAP INS S2:=SYS:PUBLIC\%MACHINE\%OS\%OS_VERSION
```

Login Script Variables

Login script variables let you include changing information in a login script. You can use login script variables anywhere in the login script; NetWare substitutes the current value of that item. Use the percent (%) sign at the beginning of each variable name to indicate that it is a variable. Variables may be uppercase or lowercase, but since some commands require them to be uppercase, it's best to use uppercase all of the time.

The table below lists the most common login script variables. The full list of variables can be found in the NetWare manuals.

Variable name	Purpose
MACHINE	Specifies the type of computer being used, typically IBM_PC.
OS	Specifies the type of DOS, usually MS_DOS.
OS_VERSION	Specifies the DOS version, such as 6.22.
STATION	Represents the connection number (network address) of the workstation.
LOGIN_NAME	Gives the login name of the user.
GREETING_TIME	Specifies a time of day—MORNING, AFTERNOON, or EVENING.

Login Script Commands

Each login script is a sequence of *login script commands*. Each type of login script uses the same set of commands. Although some of these commands are the same as NetWare commands, most are specific to login scripts. The sections that follow explain the most important login script commands, including the commands that are new to NetWare 4.1. For a complete list of commands, refer to the NetWare manuals or the online documentation.

MAP

MAP is probably the most commonly used login script command. You can use this command to assign drive letters as network drives and search drives, just like the MAP command-line utility, with one exception: The MAP NEXT command, which is used to map the next available drive letter to a directory, cannot be used in login scripts.

In addition to the usual MAP commands, you can use two other commands in login scripts: MAP DISPLAY and MAP ERRORS. Both of these have a single parameter, ON or OFF.

- MAP DISPLAY controls whether NetWare displays drive mappings as the MAP commands are executed.

- MAP ERRORS controls whether NetWare displays map error messages as it executes the login script. These errors are usually caused by an invalid path or by a MAP command for a path the user does not have rights to.

IF, THEN, and ELSE

You can use the IF command to execute a command or set of commands *conditionally.* The IF command is followed by a condition, the keyword THEN, and a command or list of commands to be executed. Here is a simple IF command:

```
IF MEMBER OF "PAYABLES" THEN MAP F:=SYS:DATA\AP
```

In this example, the MAP command for drive F: will be executed only if the user is a member of the PAYABLES group.

You can use two keywords for more sophisticated conditions:

- The ELSE keyword specifies commands to be executed when the condition is not met.

- The END keyword ends a complex IF statement. It must be used if the IF statement uses more than one line.

Here is a more complicated example of an IF command:

```
IF %LOGIN_NAME = "ADMIN" THEN
   MAP F:=SYS:SYSTEM
   MAP J:=VOL1:TOOLS\ADMIN
  ELSE
   MAP F:=SYS:HOME\%LOGIN_NAME
   MAP J:=VOL1:TOOLS\PUBLIC
END
```

In this example, drives F: and J: are mapped to certain directories for the ADMIN user and to different directories for all other users.

The condition in the IF statement uses login script variables. NetWare sets these variables when running the login script. You can use them to test individual information for the user or workstation. You can also use these variables with the WRITE command, described later in this section.

You can use another keyword, IF MEMBER OF, to perform actions based on group membership. The first example uses this method. You can use IF NOT MEMBER OF to perform actions if the user is not a member of the specified group.

INCLUDE

The INCLUDE command allows you to include another login script within the current script. The other script can be the script belonging to another container or profile or a DOS text file containing login script commands. Here are some examples:

- **INCLUDE .OU=VIP** runs the login script for the VIP Organizational Unit.

- **INCLUDE SYS:PUBLIC\LOGIN1.TXT** executes commands from a text file.

NetWare executes the commands in the other login script or file as if they were included in the current login script. If the login script or file ends with the EXIT command, the current login script ends; otherwise, the current script continues with the commands after the INCLUDE command.

CONTEXT

You can use the CONTEXT command to set the current Directory context for the user. For example, the following command sets the context to the AP Organizational Unit under the main ZYX_CO Organization:

```
CONTEXT .AP.ZYX_CO
```

WRITE

You can use the WRITE command to display a message to the user. You can use login script variables to display specific information for the user. For example, the following WRITE command displays a greeting message such as "Good Morning, Bob Smith.":

```
WRITE "Good %GREETING_TIME, %FULL_NAME."
```

Another WRITE command displays a message with the current time for example, "The time is 11:30:23 AM.":

```
WRITE "The time is %HOUR:%MINUTE:%SECOND %AM_PM."
```

By taking advantage of the WRITE command, you can advise users of conditions that may affect their use of the network.

DISPLAY and FDISPLAY

You can use these commands to display the contents of a text file when the user logs in. FDISPLAY uses a *filtered* format to display the file, removing printer codes and unprintable characters; DISPLAY writes the file to the screen in raw format. Here is an example of the FDISPLAY command that simply displays the NEWS.TXT file to the user during the login process:

```
FDISPLAY SYS:PUBLIC\NEWS.TXT
```

You can use the display commands to display information, such as system news or warnings about system problems. You can also combine display commands with the IF command to display detailed error messages. For example, you might use the FDISPLAY command below to explain a printer error to the user:

```
#CAPTURE L=1 Q=LASER1_QUEUE
IF ERROR_LEVEL > 0 THEN FDISPLAY
   SYS:PUBLIC\PRTERROR.TXT
```

In this example, if the CAPTURE command fails, the PRTERROR.TXT file is displayed. This file could give instructions on correcting the problem or let users know who to call for help.

REM or REMARK

These commands allow you to insert a comment in the login script. A semicolon (;) or asterisk (*) can also be used to indicate a comment. The following are all comments:

```
REM The following commands set up drive mappings
***Be sure to include the user's mappings here***
;Don't try this at home
Remarkably enough, this line won't execute.
```

COMSPEC

You can use the COMSPEC command to specify the location of the COMMAND.COM file. DOS uses this file to run the command interpreter. Some DOS programs unload COMMAND.COM and reload it when they finish. If this is not specified correctly, the workstation reports the error message "Unable to Load COMMAND" and requires rebooting.

You must use COMSPEC if your users are using DOS commands from a directory on the network. If they run DOS commands from their individual workstations only, this command is not needed.

PAUSE

The PAUSE command simply stops the login script until you press a key. This command can be useful in debugging login scripts; by including PAUSE in strategic places you can view messages that would normally have scrolled off the screen. PAUSE is also useful to give the user a chance to read a message you display with the DISPLAY command.

DOS Commands

You can also use any DOS command or NetWare command-line utility in your login scripts. Precede each command with the number sign (#). This feature is most commonly used with the CAPTURE command to control network printing. You can use any DOS or NetWare command, with the following restrictions:

- You should execute only DOS commands that return immediately, such as CAPTURE. If you wish to execute a menu or other program and end the login script, you should use the EXIT command.

- Don't use the pound sign with the MAP command. Instead, use the login script version of MAP.

- You can't use the SET command to set DOS variables in a login script. You should use the DOS SET login script command instead.

- The DOS commands here are *external* commands, meaning that they are contained in a separate program. *Internal* DOS commands, such as DIR, cannot be used unless you execute a copy of COMMAND.COM. (Execute COMMAND.COM with command /c *commandname*.)

Using EXIT with Login Scripts

You can use the EXIT command to end the current login script. You can also include a command that executes at the DOS prompt after the user logs in. One use for EXIT is to run a menu, as described in the next section.

Because the EXIT command ends the login script, it should be the last command in the script. In addition, the EXIT command prevents any further scripts from executing. Thus, if the EXIT command is included in the container login script, it prevents the profile and user login scripts from executing. If you include EXIT in the profile login script, it prevents the user login script from executing.

You can use the EXIT command by itself or follow it with a command in quotation marks, such as in the next example that automatically starts a menu at the end of the login script:

```
EXIT "NMENU ACCT"
```

DOS executes the command after the login script has finished. NetWare actually places the command in the keyboard buffer, so DOS believes the user typed it. The size of the keyboard buffer limits the command to 14 characters. This trick works only under DOS; you can't use EXIT to execute a command in other operating systems.

If you are executing a DOS program that will stay running, such as NMENU, you should run it with the EXIT command. Although you can execute DOS commands anywhere in the script with the # prefix, the LOGIN.EXE program remains in memory while the DOS program executes. By passing commands to DOS through the keyboard buffer, EXIT executes the command after the LOGIN program has finished.

By default, users have the rights to edit their own user login scripts. You can add the EXIT command at the end of the container or profile login script if you wish to prevent user login scripts from executing.

Using the Menu System

NETWARE PROVIDES A *MENU SYSTEM*—a convenient way for users to execute a set list of applications. Figure 8.2 shows an example of a user menu. By using menus, you can provide a specific list of applications that each user can access and keep the system secure by restricting access to the DOS prompt.

The NetWare menu system runs under DOS and is strictly for DOS applications. If your organization uses a lot of Windows applications, you will have little use for this system. However, for users who require DOS applications, the NetWare menu system is simple and versatile. In addition, you can use a menu to provide a friendly interface for NetWare and DOS utilities, including command-line utilities.

Planning User Menus

Before you begin the process of creating a menu for a user or a group, you should list all of the applications that the user or group needs to access. Since menus can be divided into submenus, it is useful to divide applications into categories. Figure 8.3 shows an example of a menu plan including several submenus.

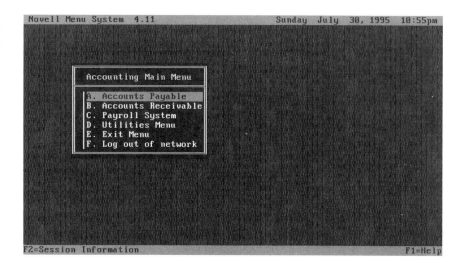

FIGURE 8.2
The NetWare 4.1 menu system allows users to run applications from a list.

You should also know the exact path for each of the applications you wish to include in the menu. In addition, be sure that you have given the user or group the rights he or she needs to execute the applications.

Using Menu Commands

You create a menu by placing menu commands in a menu *source file*. This file usually has the extension SRC. Here is an example of a simple menu source file:

```
MENU 01, Tom's Menu
   ITEM DOS Prompt
      EXEC DOS
   ITEM File Management
      EXEC FILER
   ITEM Word Processing
      EXEC F:\APPS\WP\WP.EXE
   ITEM Exit this Menu
      EXEC EXIT
   ITEM Log out of the Network
      EXEC LOGOUT
```

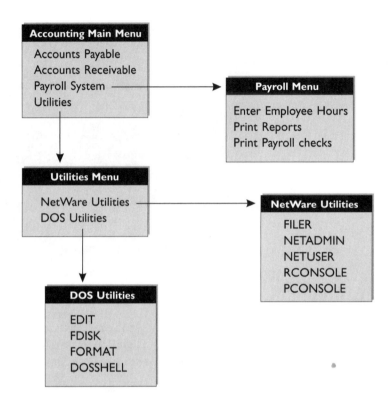

Figure 8.4 shows the menu that would result from this source file.

As you can see, the menu source file is composed of *menu commands*. These commands are specific to the menu system. For example, the MENU command begins the menu and specifies the title, and the ITEM command lists each option in the menu. There are actually quite a few menu commands, each with its own purpose. The next sections explain each of these in detail.

MENU

You begin each menu file with the MENU command. Each submenu within the file also has a MENU command. Here is an example:

```
MENU 01, Applications Menu
```

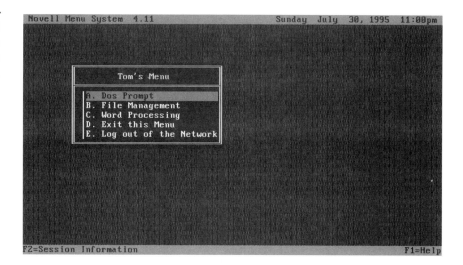

After the MENU command, specify a number for the menu. This number identifies the menu, and it can range from 1 to 255. In addition, the numbers don't have to be in order. You can use any unique number, but you must use a different number for each MENU command within the file.

Place a comma after the menu number and then include a name for the menu. Names can be up to 40 characters long and can be used to identify the type of functions included in the menu.

ITEM

The MENU command is followed by ITEM commands. Each ITEM command defines an item to be included in the menu. You should indent the ITEM commands by a few spaces to set them off from the MENU command. Here is a typical ITEM command:

```
ITEM File Management
```

A description of the menu item follows the ITEM command. This command can also include several options. To use one of these options, place the option name in braces after the item description. The available options are

- {BATCH}: The menu program is unloaded from memory before executing the item. This technique can be useful for programs that require large amounts of memory. If the BATCH option is not used, a portion of the menu program is kept in memory, using about 32KB. In some cases, using the BATCH option may prevent the menu from returning after the selected program executes.

- {CHDIR}: The current directory is saved, and after the item executes, the original directory becomes the current directory again. You can use this option to avoid incompatibilities with applications that change to their own directories. Using the BATCH option automatically sets the CHDIR option.

- {PAUSE}: After the item is executed, the menu program displays a "press any key" message and waits for you to respond before returning to the menu. You can use this option to make sure the output of the item is visible. For example, if you place the NDIR command in a menu item, you should include the {PAUSE} option so that you can see the directory listing before returning to the menu.

- {SHOW}: Displays the name of the command being executed in the upper-left corner of the screen. This is useful for DOS commands or for NetWare command utilities that don't display their own titles.

The menu lists each item with a letter next to it. You can type the letter to execute the item. NetWare usually assigns these letters; however, you can use a final ITEM option to specify the letter for a menu option by using the caret (^) character and the desired letter as the first two characters of the item description. The following ITEM command specifies the letter *L*:

```
ITEM ^LLog out of the network
```

If you assign a letter to any item, you should assign letters to other items in the menu. If you don't, NetWare may choose the same letter for another option.

EXEC

Here's the command that actually does the work in a menu. You can use EXEC to run a program or command. Follow the EXEC command with the name of a DOS or NetWare command or utility or the name of another executable program. If the program is not in a path referenced by a search drive or PATH entry, you need to specify the full path. Here is an example of the EXEC command:

```
EXEC FILER
```

In addition to specifying the name of a program, you can use special keywords with EXEC to perform specific functions. These include the following:

- **EXEC EXIT:** Allows the user to exit the menu system and return to the DOS prompt.

- **EXEC LOGOUT:** Exits the menu and logs the user out of the network. The user is returned to the DOS prompt but needs to log in again before using any network resources.

- **EXEC CALL:** Executes a DOS batch file. After the batch file is completed, the user is returned to the menu.

- **EXEC DOS:** Allows the user to run a DOS shell from within the menu. The DOS prompt is displayed. After executing DOS commands, the user can type **EXIT** at the DOS prompt to return to the menu.

SHOW

The SHOW command can be used in a menu item to execute a submenu. The number assigned in the MENU command for the submenu is used in the SHOW command to refer to it. For example, the following menu source file includes a submenu accessed with the SHOW command:

```
MENU 01, Main Menu
    ITEM NetWare Utilities
        SHOW 05
    ITEM Word Processing
        EXEC WP
    ITEM Log out
        EXEC LOGOUT

MENU 05, NetWare Utilities Menu
    ITEM File Management
```

```
            EXEC FILER
        ITEM NDS Management
            EXEC NETADMIN
        ITEM Remote Console
            EXEC RCONSOLE
```

The SHOW 05 command in the first ITEM command executes the submenu numbered 05. You must include this submenu in the same menu source file. The first menu in a file is the main menu and is executed when the menu starts. Other menus in the file are submenus and must be called by number with SHOW commands to execute. Submenus can also use the SHOW command to execute another menu. Submenus are opened in a window on top of the main menu, as shown in Figure 8.5.

LOAD

The LOAD command is similar to the SHOW command in that it also executes a different menu. However, the LOAD command allows you to execute a menu in a different file. Here is an example of a menu item that uses LOAD:

```
        ITEM Accounting Menu
            LOAD ACCT
```

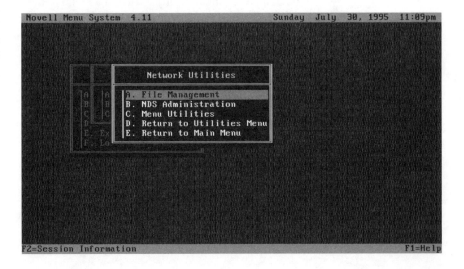

FIGURE 8.5
Submenus allow you to organize categories of options.

The file that the LOAD command refers to must be in the current directory or in a path assigned to a search drive. This file is not a menu source file but a *menu data file*, described later in this chapter.

GET

The GET commands can be used to get input from the user before the EXEC command executes the program. This input can be used to pass information to an application program or to provide a friendly interface to DOS or NetWare command-line utilities. Three GET commands are available:

- **GETO** gets *optional* input from the user. The user can press Enter and leave the input blank.

- **GETR** specifies *required* input. The user cannot execute the program without entering a value.

- **GETP** assigns the input value to a variable (%1, %2, etc.), which allows you to specify commands to the program using these variables. The values of the variables can also be used for later commands.

The GET commands require a specific format, which is the same for all three commands. Here is an example:

```
GETR Enter User Name: { } 10,GUEST,{ }
```

The following components make up a GET command:

- The GET command itself: GETO, GETR, or GETP.

- The values in braces are the *prepend* and *append* values. The braces indicate the beginning and end of the value on the command line. These values can be left blank, but the braces must be included.

- The number (10 in this example) that follows the prepend value is the maximum number of characters the user may enter.

- The default value follows the length and is placed between commas. This value is displayed as the default when the user is prompted, and if the user presses Enter, this value is used. If you do not wish to use a default value, your GET command must still include two commas with nothing between them.

The main purpose of GET commands is to make command-line utilities more friendly. For example, the following menu item is used to provide an interface to the NCOPY command-line utility:

```
ITEM Copy Files {PAUSE}
    GETR Source File: { } 15,,{ }
    GETR Destination: { } 15,,{ }
    EXEC NCOPY
```

When the user selects the Copy Files option in the menu, the following actions are performed:

1. The user is prompted for the source file and allowed to enter up to 15 characters. This dialog is shown in Figure 8.6.

2. The user is prompted for the destination file and allowed to enter up to 15 characters. Both the source file and the destination file are required.

3. The NCOPY command is executed with the two GETR values as parameters. This command copies the source file to the destination file.

4. The system pauses after the NCOPY command finishes because we used the {PAUSE} option. After checking to see whether the command is successful, the user can press any key to return to the menu.

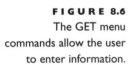

FIGURE 8.6
The GET menu commands allow the user to enter information.

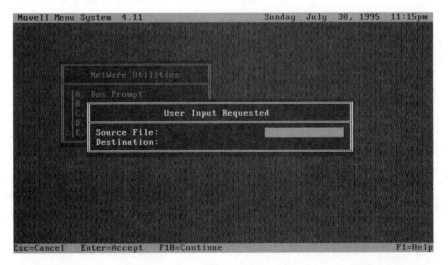

Compiling Menus with MENUMAKE

After you have created the menu source file, you must *compile* it before you can use it. You compile a menu source file with the MENUMAKE utility. This utility reads the file and creates a *menu data file*, which has the same name as your source file with a DAT extension. The menu data file is the file that you use to execute the menu.

To compile your menu, you should be in the directory that contains the menu source file. Simply type **MENUMAKE** followed by the name of the source file. You do not need to include the SRC extension. Here's an example of a MENUMAKE command that reads the file MYMENU.SRC and compiles it into a data file called MYMENU.DAT:

```
MENUMAKE MYMENU
```

If MENUMAKE finds any errors in the source file, it stops without creating the menu data file. If this happens, read the error message carefully. You must then edit the source file to eliminate the error and use the MENUMAKE command to restart the compile process. Some tips for troubleshooting menus are given in the Testing and Troubleshooting Menus section later in this chapter.

Once MENUMAKE has compiled your menu, the menu data (DAT) file is used to execute the menu; the source file is no longer needed. However, since the DAT file cannot be changed, you should save the source file so that you can make changes to the menu later.

Running Menus

Once you have successfully compiled your menu with the MENUMAKE utility, you can run the menu. The NMENU command (provided by a batch file called NMENU.BAT in the SYS:PUBLIC directory) is used to execute a menu. To run a menu, simply type **NMENU** *filename*, where *filename* is the DAT file created by the MENUMAKE utility. This file must be in your current directory or search path. You do not need to specify the DAT extension.

Although you should run the menu from the DOS prompt to test it, you will probably want to run it automatically from the user's login script by using the EXIT login script command. Here's a typical command to start a menu from a login script:

```
EXIT "NMENU TOM"
```

Because the EXIT command uses the workstation's keyboard buffer to pass information, the command in the quotation marks is limited to 14 characters. This should be sufficient for any NMENU command, but there is not room to specify a full path. Be sure that the DAT file for the menu is located in the user's default directory (usually the user's home directory) or in the search path.

Testing and Troubleshooting Menus

After you have compiled a new menu, you should run it as described above and test all of the options. You will probably find a few items that don't execute correctly because of an incorrect spelling of a command, an incorrect path name, or improper menu syntax. Some errors may prevent the menu from compiling at all. Here are some troubleshooting hints to help you cope with common menu problems:

- Be sure that you have a MENU command at the beginning of each menu with a unique menu number.

- Make sure that each menu item has an ITEM command followed by an EXEC, SHOW, or LOAD command.

- Check the SHOW commands for correct menu numbers.

- Check the syntax of menu commands. The GET commands are especially easy to mistype.

- Be sure that the correct paths are specified for commands or that the commands are in a search path. You should also be sure that the user has the correct rights to the application directories.

- Check the amount of available memory. If an application crashes or complains of insufficient memory, you may want to use the {BATCH} option in the menu item. This option adds 32KB of available memory.

- Check to make sure the application is being run from the correct directory. Some applications need to be run from a certain directory. The menu system has no way to do this. One solution is to create a batch file that changes directories and then runs the application. You can use the batch file with the EXEC CALL option in the menu item.

Even if you don't intend to allow the user to exit to the DOS prompt, add the EXEC EXIT command as a helpful menu option until the menu is completely tested. This way you can repeatedly test the menu after making changes without having to log out or reboot the workstation.

Securing the Menu System

One benefit of the menu system is that it can be used to increase security on your network. By allowing users to run the applications they need from a menu, you can avoid giving them access to the DOS prompt. This security measure ensures that users can execute only commands to which you have given them access. To create a secure menu system, follow these instructions:

1. Add the NMENU command to the user's login script, as described in the previous section.

2. Be sure the EXEC EXIT command is not present in any of the menus. Use the EXEC LOGOUT command instead. Therefore, the only way that the user can exit the menu is to disconnect from the network.

3. Add the LOGIN command to the workstation's AUTOEXEC.BAT file to encourage users to log in immediately. LOGIN should be the last command in the file; otherwise, the remaining commands won't execute until the user exits the menu.

Although these features allow you to make the menu system reasonably secure, they are no substitute for network security. Be sure the files and NDS objects on your network are secured properly. NetWare security is discussed in Chapter 7.

Converting Older NetWare Menus

NetWare versions prior to 3.12 used menu files with the MNU extension; these files were not compiled but were run directly by the menu program, MENU.EXE. You cannot use MNU files with NetWare 4.1's MENUMAKE utility; however, the MENUCNVT utility provides a way to convert the old files to ones you can use in the MENUMAKE utility.

To use this command, type **MENUCNVT** *filename* at the DOS prompt, where *filename* is the name of the old menu file (do not include the MNU extension). This creates a NetWare 4.1 menu source file with the same name and the SRC extension. After this process is complete, use the MENUMAKE utility, described above, to compile the menu into a data file that can be used with NMENU.

The menu conversion process is not perfect, and some features of the old system may not be converted properly. After you have converted a menu, be sure to test it thoroughly. Follow the instructions in the Testing and Troubleshooting Menus section if you encounter any problems.

Review

THIS CHAPTER DISCUSSED two systems that affect the user's environment:

- *Login scripts* can set up drive mappings and other defaults for the user so that he or she doesn't have to type DOS commands to set up drives or printers.

- The *menu system* lets you define lists of applications a user can run and gives the user a simple way of accessing them.

Login Scripts

There are four types of login scripts: user, container, profile, and default. Login scripts are always executed in the same order:

1. **Container login script** for the user's parent container (if found)

2. **Profile login script** (if assigned)

3. **User login script** (if defined)

4. **Default login script** (if no user script is found)

Each of these scripts has a specific purpose:

- You can create a *container login script* for any Organization or Organizational Unit object. This script is the first script executed for users in the container. You can use this login script for drive mappings, printer settings, and other options that all users in the container need.

- You can use a *profile login script* to execute a certain set of drive mappings or other commands for certain users in the directory, even if they are in different containers.

- You can use user login scripts to execute specific commands for a particular user. One important use for the user login script is to override certain commands in the container login script.

- The *default login script* is built in to the LOGIN utility. You cannot edit it. The default script is executed when a user has no user login script. The default login script provides a basic set of search and drive mappings.

The login script is composed of login script commands:

- MAP for mapping network drives and search drives

- IF, THEN, and ELSE for conditional actions

- INCLUDE to include other files or scripts

- CONTEXT to set the current context

- WRITE to display a message to the user

- DISPLAY and FDISPLAY to display an entire file

- EXIT to end a script

- Any external DOS command or program preceded with the # sign

The Menu System

The menu system allows you to list applications a user can execute. The NetWare menu system runs under DOS and is strictly for DOS applications. If your organization uses a lot of Windows applications, you will have little use for this system.

However, for users who require DOS applications, the NetWare menu system is simple and versatile. In addition, you can use a menu to provide a friendly interface for NetWare and DOS utilities, including command-line utilities.

The menu is composed of *menu commands*:

- MENU begins each menu screen.

- ITEM precedes each menu item's description.

- EXEC specifies the program to run.

- SHOW executes a submenu.

- LOAD executes a submenu from a different file.

- GETO gets optional input from the user.

- GETR gets required input.

- GETP assigns GET values to variables.

After you have created the menu source file, you must *compile* it before you can use it. You compile a menu source file with the MENUMAKE utility, which reads the file and creates a *menu data file*. This file has the same name as your source file with a DAT extension. The menu data file is the file that you use to execute the menu.

The NMENU command is used to execute a menu. To run a menu, type **NMENU** *filename*, where *filename* is the DAT file created by the MENUMAKE utility. This file must be in your current directory or search path.

You can also use the MENUCNVT to convert menus that were created for earlier versions of NetWare. After converting a menu, you must compile it with MENUMAKE.

CNA Practice Test Questions

1. Which is the correct order for login script execution?

   A. User, container, default, profile

   B. Container, user, profile, default

   C. Container, profile, user, default

   D. Container, default, user, profile

2. The container login script is executed

   A. For each container the user is in

   B. For the user's parent container

   C. For the profile container only

   D. For the [Root] container only

3. Which is a correct MAP command in a login script?

   A. MAP F:=SYS:APPS

   B. #MAP F:=SYS:APPS

   C. MAP NEXT SYS:APPS

   D. MAP F:=SYS

4. The INCLUDE command

   A. Exits the login script and starts another

   B. Executes another script, and then returns

   C. Adds commands to a login script

   D. Adds a login script to the Profile object

5. Which of the following is NOT a valid comment?

   A. REM Do not change this script

   B. ***Do not change this script***

    C. # Do not change this script

    D. ;Do not change this script

6. To use a DOS command in a login script

    A. Include the name of the command only

    B. Include # and the name of the command

    C. Include ; and the name of the command

    D. Place the command in an INCLUDE file

7. Which is a valid EXIT command?

    A. EXIT "NMENU MYMENU.DAT"

    B. EXIT NMENU /N=MYMENU

    C. EXIT "NMENU MYMENU"

    D. EXIT TO MENU MYMENU.DAT

8. Which is a valid MENU command?

    A. MENU #1: The Main Menu

    B. MENU Main Menu, 01

    C. MENU "The Main Menu"

    D. MENU 01, The Main Menu

9. Which is the correct menu command to exit the menu?

    A. EXIT

    B. EXIT "MENU.DAT"

    C. EXEC EXIT

    D. EXEC "EXIT"

10. The LOAD menu command

    A. Runs a submenu from the same file

    B. Runs a submenu from a different file

C. Includes a menu within the current menu

D. Exits to a different menu

11. Menus are compiled with the _____ command.

    A. MENUCON

    B. COMPILE

    C. MENUCNVT

    D. MENUMAKE

12. Which of the following MENU commands is optional?

    A. MENU

    B. ITEM

    C. EXEC

    D. GETR

How Printing Works

9

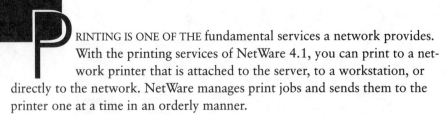

RINTING IS ONE OF THE fundamental services a network provides. With the printing services of NetWare 4.1, you can print to a network printer that is attached to the server, to a workstation, or directly to the network. NetWare manages print jobs and sends them to the printer one at a time in an orderly manner.

There's more to printing than just you and a printer. The next section introduces the components of the NetWare 4.1 printing services.

Components of NetWare 4.1 Printing

EVERAL COMPONENTS INTERACT to provide NetWare 4.1 printing services: print servers, print queues, and printers. You can create these objects under NDS and maintain them from within the NetWare Administrator utility. Additional components include the CAPTURE utility and the port driver (NPRINTER.EXE or NPRINTER.NLM), which complete the interface between the workstation and the printer. The components of NetWare 4.1 printing are shown in Figure 9.1 and described in the next sections.

FIGURE 9.1
Several components interact to provide network printing services.

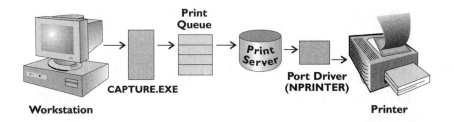

Print Queues

In order to print to a printer on the network, you must first send the data to a *print queue*. The print queue stores each set of data, or *print job*, that it receives. The jobs are then sent, one at a time, to the print server (described next). Print queues serve two main purposes:

- To allow you to continue working while the printer prints. Your workstation quickly sends the job to the print queue, and printing is performed by NetWare without using your workstation.

- To allow multiuser printing. Many users can add jobs to the queue, and they are printed in the order received. A complete job is always printed before another job starts.

NetWare 4.1 stores all print queue information in properties of the Print Queue object. This includes identification information for the print queue and information for each of the print jobs. The print jobs themselves are stored on a file server volume. The process of selecting a volume is described later in this chapter.

Print Servers

The *print server* accepts print jobs from print queues and sends them to the appropriate printer. In NetWare 3.1*x*, print servers were limited to 16 printers; in NetWare 4.1 this limit has been increased to 256 printers. Thus you can easily use a single print server for the entire network.

You create the Print Server object in NDS. The properties of the Print Server object provide identification information and define the list of printers the server can send jobs to.

Along with the NDS object, you must run the print server software (PSERVER.NLM) on a server. This is the program that actually controls the printing process.

Although PSERVER.NLM is referred to throughout this chapter (and on the CNA test), it isn't the only choice. Many printers and network connection products can act as print servers themselves. NetWare 3.1*x* includes PSERVER.EXE, which allows a workstation to act as a print server. Although NetWare 4.1 doesn't support this feature, you can still use it if you have both NetWare 3.1*x* and NetWare 4.1 on your network.

Printers

You must create a Printer object to represent each network printer. The properties of the printer object identify the printer and list the print queues that the printer accepts jobs from. Other properties define the type of printer and how it is accessed. Printers can be attached to a server, to a workstation, or directly to the network. Printer types are described in the following sections.

Printers Attached to the Server

Printers can be connected directly to a printer port on a server, which is the simplest method to connect printers to a network and is easy to configure and use. Before you configure a printer in this way, note the following:

- You must have an available port (serial or parallel) on the server for each printer. A typical machine has one to three parallel ports and two serial ports.

- The printer usually needs to be located near the server. The limit for a parallel printer cable is 15 feet. Serial devices have a longer range.

- Unlike NetWare 3.1x, in NetWare 4.1 you do not need to load PSERVER.NLM on the same server the printer is attached to. However, you must run NPRINTER.NLM to drive the printer. NPRINTER.NLM is described later in this section.

Remote (Workstation) Printers

Printers can also be attached to workstations. These printers are referred to as workstation printers or *remote printers*. The print server sends each job to the workstation, and the workstation sends it to the printer.

In order to use a workstation printer, you run the NPRINTER.EXE program on the workstation. NPRINTER replaces the RPRINTER program used in NetWare 3.1x and is faster and much more reliable than RPRINTER. You can run up to seven copies of NPRINTER on your workstation to drive multiple printers. A workstation can have a maximum of three parallel and four serial printers.

Since NPRINTER is a TSR (terminate-and-stay resident) program, you can continue to use the workstation while the network printers are being used. You must leave the workstation turned on in order to make the printer available to network users. Remote printing has the following disadvantages:

- The workstation can be slowed down if a printer is used heavily or if multiple printers are supported.

- If the workstation crashes or is turned off, the printer is unavailable to network users.

- Each remote printer on the workstation uses a small amount of memory (approximately 10KB).

You can run Windows on a workstation that supports remote printers, but in order to do so, you must run NPRINTER for each printer before starting Windows. NPRINTER is more reliable than RPRINTER under Windows, but some Windows applications can cause instability even with NPRINTER.

To use NPRINTER, specify the printer name on the command line. For example, the following command might be used to remotely attach the Check_Printer Printer object:

```
NPRINTER .Check_Printer.ABC_INC
```

If you use a workstation printer as a network printer, be sure to use the CAPTURE command on the workstation to send jobs to the queue. If the user prints to the printer locally, network print jobs can be interrupted and the workstation may crash.

Directly Connected Network Printers

A final type of printer is attached directly to the network. This capability is built into many high-end printers, and many others can be attached to the network with an add-on card. Hardware devices are also available to interface the network to one or more printers. Directly connected printers are a very efficient way to manage printing.

Directly connected printers can be configured in one of two modes:

- In *remote mode,* the printer acts as a remote (workstation) printer. Instead of running NPRINTER.EXE on a workstation, the hardware device handles these functions. This configuration is better than a workstation printer because no workstation is slowed by printing.

- In *queue server mode,* the printer acts as a separate print server. Jobs are sent directly from the print queue to the printer. This can be the best arrangement because the load on the server is insignificant.

Many printers are not yet NDS aware; however, network printers developed for NetWare 3.1*x* can be used on NetWare 4.1 networks with no problems. You need to enable Bindery Services (discussed in Chapter 13) to use printers or hardware print servers without NDS support.

To determine which mode to use, consult the documentation for your printer or network interface. Most network printers also include an installation program that can create the needed bindery or NDS objects and configure the printer.

Redirecting Printers with CAPTURE

Some applications (such as WordPerfect) support network printing directly. You can select a network queue to print to rather than a local printer. However, many applications do not provide this support. You can use the CAPTURE command-line utility to print to network printers from these applications.

CAPTURE is a TSR program that allows you to *redirect* printing to a network printer. You specify a local printer port (usually LPT1, LPT2, or LPT3) with the CAPTURE command. After the CAPTURE command is executed, any printing that your workstation sends to this port is redirected to the network queue you specified.

Most Windows applications don't require CAPTURE to print to network printers. In addition, the Windows client software allows you to redirect ports to printers using a graphical interface as an alternative to CAPTURE.

A basic CAPTURE command specifies which local port to redirect from and which network queue to redirect to. The following command redirects the workstation's LPT1 port to a print queue called WEST41_Q:

CAPTURE /L=1 /Q=WEST41_Q

A new feature of NetWare 4.1 allows you to specify a printer name without knowing which queue it is attached to. This command captures the LPT2 port to a printer called PRINTER5:

CAPTURE /L=2 /P=PRINTER5

Even if you specify a printer to capture to, a print queue is used. NetWare finds the first available print queue serviced by the printer you specify. Since NetWare must search for a queue, you can improve performance by specifying the queue name rather than the printer name.

You can use other CAPTURE options to control the printing process. Use forward slashes (/) or spaces to separate the parameters. A summary of the CAPTURE options follows:

- **AU (Autoendcap) or NA (No Autoendcap):** Allows jobs to be sent to the printer as soon as the application is finished sending the job to the queue. Not all applications support this option. Autoendcap is enabled by default. You can use the NA option to deactivate it.

- **B=*text* (Banner) or NB (No Banner):** Specifies whether a *banner* is printed before the job. The banner is a page that describes the job and the user that sent it and can be used to send printouts to the appropriate person. If you specify the B option, follow it with text to be included at the bottom of the banner, such as **B=ACCOUNTING**.

- **C=*number* (Copies):** Specifies the number of copies to be printed.

- **CR=*filename* (Create file):** Allows you to redirect printing to a file instead of a printer. The file can later be sent to a printer.

- **D (Details):** Displays details about a captured port. Use the L option (described below) to specify the port.

- **EC (End Capture):** Ends capturing to the port. This option replaces the ENDCAP command in NetWare 3.1*x*. Any job that is currently being sent is completed. There are three options for EC:

  - **EC L=*port*:** Ends capturing for the specified port. If no port is specified, LPT1 is assumed.

  - **EC ALL:** Ends capturing for all ports.

  - **EC CA:** Ends capturing and cancels the current job. Nothing is sent to the print queue.

- **F=*number or name* (Form):** Allows you to specify a form to be used with print jobs. Forms are defined with the PRINTDEF utility or in NetWare Administrator and are described later in this chapter.

- **FF (Form Feed) or NFF (No Form Feed):** Specifies whether a *form feed* character is sent to the printer after the print job is completed. This option ensures that printing for the next job starts at the top of a page. Most applications send a form feed by default. Using the FF option unnecessarily results in blank pages being printed between jobs.

- **/? or /H (Help):** Displays a list of options for the CAPTURE command.

- **HOLD (Hold job):** Specifies that print jobs are to be *held* in the print queue and not printed. You can later release the jobs using PCONSOLE or NWADMIN.

- **J=*name* (Specify job):** Selects a *print job configuration* to be used. A print job configuration contains options similar to CAPTURE options, and its name can be used with no other options. You can create print job configurations using the NWADMIN or PRINTCON utilities.

- **K (Keep):** Tells CAPTURE to keep your print job even if the capture has not ended correctly. A capture may not end correctly if your workstation is disconnected or turned off while a job is being sent to the queue. Without the Keep option, the job is discarded when either of those events occur. With the Keep option, the job is sent to the queue.

- **L=*number* or LPT*n* (Local port):** Specifies the logical port number to redirect to the queue. You can use numbers from one to nine, as described below. The options **L=2** and **LPT2** both select the LPT2 port for redirection.

- **NAM=*name* (Banner name):** Specifies a name to be included at the top of the banner. This defaults to your login name. This option also activates the Banner option.

- **NOTI (Notify) or NNOTI (No Notify):** Specifies whether you are notified when the print job has finished printing. If notify is enabled, you receive a message on your screen or in a pop-up window (under Windows) when the job has completed.

- **P=*name* (Printer)** or **Q=*name* (Queue):** Specifies a printer or queue for the port to be redirected to. Only one of these options can be used.

- **S=*name* (Server):** Specifies a server name for the queue. This option is used for bindery-based queues only.

- **SH (Show):** Displays the current CAPTURE parameters for each port when used by itself. You can also specify a port number to show status for with the **L** or **LPT** option.

- **T=*number* (Tab spacing)** or **NT (No tab conversion):** Specifies the number of spaces to use in place of tab characters in the document. Use the NT option if your print job does not require conversion.

- **TI=*number* (Timeout):** Specifies a timeout in seconds to be used to end a print job. If the specified number of seconds elapses with no data having been sent to the printer, the job is considered finished and sent to the print queue.

When you use CAPTURE, data is sent to a print job in the specified queue. The following three events can end the job and send it to the printer:

- You can end capture with the EC option. This sends the job to the printer and discontinues CAPTURE.

- You can set a timeout with the TI option. If the specified number of seconds elapses with no printing having occurred, NetWare assumes that the job is finished and sends it to the printer. The port remains captured for future jobs.

- You can set the AU (Autoendcap) option. AU allows applications to tell NetWare when they are finished with the printer. If the application supports AU, this option is the fastest method to send the document to the printer. If you set both the AU and timeout options, the timeout covers the applications that don't support the AU option.

In NetWare 4.1, redirection is no longer limited to LPT1, LPT2, and LPT3. You can use port numbers up to nine. In order to do so, you must add a line to the workstation's NET.CFG file in the NetWare DOS Requester section to specify the number of allowed ports:

NETWORK PRINTERS = 9

Note that the port numbers used in the CAPTURE command are *logical ports*. These have no relation to *physical ports*, the actual ports used to connect printers. Your workstation does not need to have a physical port available in order to capture a logical port.

The logical ports used by CAPTURE are strictly parallel, or LPT, ports. Serial ports (such as COM1) cannot be redirected.

If your workstation does have a physical port with the specified number, the CAPTURE command overrides the printer and sends data to a print queue instead. In order to print to a local printer (a printer hooked to a physical port on your workstation), you must either use the EC option to end capturing to that port or not capture the port. You can also define your workstation's printer as a network printer, which was described earlier in this chapter.

When you define a Printer object, you specify the LPT port it is hooked to. This is a physical port number and has no relation to the logical port numbers used in the CAPTURE command.

The Port Driver (NPRINTER)

Before data is sent to the printer, it is sent to the *port driver*. The port driver receives data from the print server and transmits it to the printer. NPRINTER can be run in one of three ways:

- For a printer connected to a server, load NPRINTER.NLM on the server. If the printer is attached to the same server that the print server (PSERVER.NLM) is running on, NPRINTER is loaded automatically for the printer. You can also attach the printer to a different server and load NPRINTER.NLM manually on that server.

- For remote (workstation) printers, run the NPRINTER.EXE program, described in the Remote (Workstation) Printers section earlier in this chapter.

- For directly connected network printers, you do not need to run NPRINTER. The NPRINTER software is built into the printer or interface.

Managing Printing with NetWare Administrator

BECAUSE PRINTING SERVICES HAVE BEEN integrated into NDS, you can use the NetWare Administrator utility to manage all aspects of printing, which includes creating the objects required for printing, configuring them, and managing print jobs in print queues.

Creating Objects

You can use NetWare Administrator to create the objects required for printing. The properties of these objects control how they interact and define the devices used for printing. In order to enable printing with NDS, you must create a Print Server object and at least one Printer and Print Queue object.

These objects can be created anywhere in the Directory tree. However, in order to provide easy access, it is best to create all of the objects in the context where the users who use the printers are located, or as close to it as possible. You can create the objects in any order.

Creating the Print Server

You must create a Print Server object for each server that runs PSERVER.NLM and for directly connected network printers that use queue server mode. Since each print server can provide access to up to 256 printers, you typically need only one Print Server object for the entire network.

To create the Print Server object, follow these steps:

1. Highlight the context to create the Print Server object in.

2. Select Create from the Object menu.

3. Select Print Server as the type of object.

4. Enter the Print Server name in the Create Print Server dialog box, which is shown in Figure 9.2.

After the Print Server object is created, you can change its properties by selecting Details from the Object menu. The properties of the Print Server object are used to identify the print server and to specify parameters. Several

FIGURE 9.2

Enter the print server name to create a new print server.

pages (categories) of properties are available. These categories are described in the sections that follow.

IDENTIFICATION This page specifies information about the Print Server object. The Identification information includes the name, network address, status, and other information. You enter this information in the Identification properties page, which is shown in Figure 9.3. Most of these properties are optional; only the name is required in most cases. You can use the Change Password button to choose a password for the print server; this password will be required when PSERVER.NLM is loaded at the server. The status of the print server is also shown in the Identification properties page. If the print server is running, you can disable it with the Unload button.

FIGURE 9.3

The Identification properties page specifies information about the Print Server object.

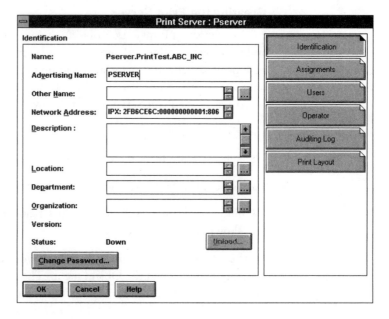

ASSIGNMENTS This page lists the printers that have been assigned to the server. After you create the Printer object, you can use the Add button to add the printer to the list. Only printers in this list can receive jobs from the print server. The Assignments properties page is shown in Figure 9.4.

USERS You can use this page to specify which users can send jobs to printers in the print server. You can add specific users to this list or use groups or container objects to provide access to multiple users.

OPERATOR You can use this page to specify one or more users who have Operator privileges on the print server. These users can unload the print server and perform other control functions. This list can include individual users; you can also use an Organizational Role object here to assign a print server operator.

AUDITING LOG This page, shown in Figure 9.5, provides a powerful *auditing* feature for printing. If this feature is enabled, a log of the print server's activities is maintained. Each print job is added to the log, and the information in the log specifies whether printing was successful, which printer the print job went to, and how long it took to print the job. To activate the auditing feature, use the Enable Auditing button. The text on this button then changes to read Disable Auditing and can be used to stop the auditing process.

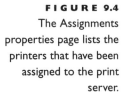

FIGURE 9.4
The Assignments properties page lists the printers that have been assigned to the print server.

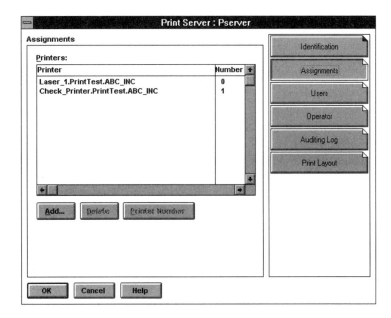

FIGURE 9.5
The Auditing Log page
allows you to audit
printing.

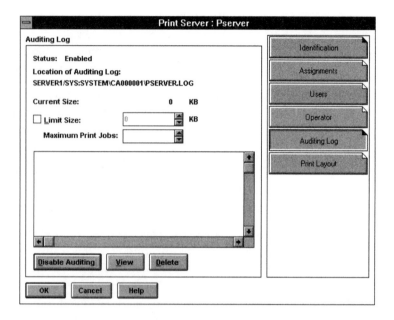

FIGURE 9.5
The Auditing Log page
allows you to audit
printing.

PRINT LAYOUT The Print Layout page allows you to view the configuration of the print server graphically. This is a powerful feature that you can use to determine how printing has been configured and to troubleshoot printing problems. The Print Layout properties page is shown in Figure 9.6.

The print server, print queues, and printers are shown with lines between them to define their relationship. You can watch for two indicators of printer problems:

- An icon with a red exclamation mark is displayed to the left of objects that are not functioning. This icon means that the print server is not running, the printer is not connected, or the print queue is not accepting jobs.

- A dashed line is displayed instead of a solid line if the connection is a temporary one and will not be reestablished the next time the print server is loaded.

Creating Print Queues

You must create at least one print queue for each printer on the network. Print queues can also be serviced by multiple printers, and multiple queues can be

FIGURE 9.6
The Print Layout
properties page provides
an illustration of how the
components of printing
interact.

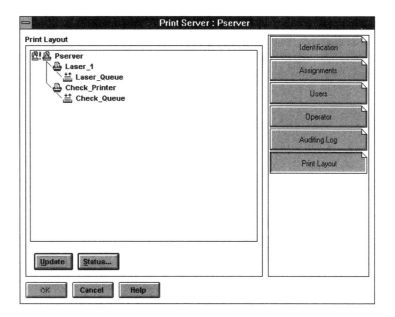

routed to a single printer. In addition to NetWare 4.1 print queues, you can define a Print Queue object that sends print jobs to a queue on a bindery-based server. This object makes it easy to integrate bindery and NDS printing.

To create the Print Queue object, follow these steps:

1. Highlight the context to create the print queue in. For easiest access, it should be located in the same context as users who use this queue.

2. Select Create from the Object menu.

3. Select Print Queue as the type of object to create. You will be presented with the Create Print Queue dialog box, shown in Figure 9.7.

4. Select whether this print queue is an NDS queue or will reference a bindery queue.

5. Select a name for the print queue. For bindery queues, enter the name as it appears on the bindery server.

FIGURE 9.7
Enter the required
information to create a
new Print Queue object.

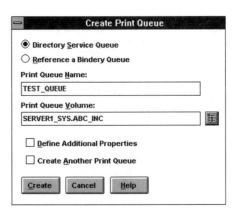

6. Select a volume to store print queue entries on. For NDS queues, you can use any volume; for bindery queues, use the SYS volume on the bindery server.

7. Click the Create button to create the Print Queue object.

After the Print Queue object is created, highlight it and select Details from the Object menu to define its properties. The properties are discussed in the following sections.

IDENTIFYING THE PRINT QUEUE The Identification properties page, shown in Figure 9.8, allows you to view and change identifying information for the print queue. In addition, three checkboxes in the Operator Flags section of the page allow you to control the print queue's behavior:

- **Allow Users To Submit Print Jobs** controls whether users can add jobs to the print queue. If you turn off this option, users receive an error message when they attempt to print to a port that has been redirected to the queue.

- **Allow Service By Current Print Servers** controls whether entries in the queue are printed by the print servers. If you turn off this option, entries are added to the queue but are not printed until it is turned back on.

- **Allow New Print Servers To Attach** controls whether new print servers can be attached to the print queue. If you turn off this option, all current print servers continue to print, but new ones are not able to attach.

FIGURE 9.8
The Identification
properties page shows
information about the
print queue and allows
you to control it.

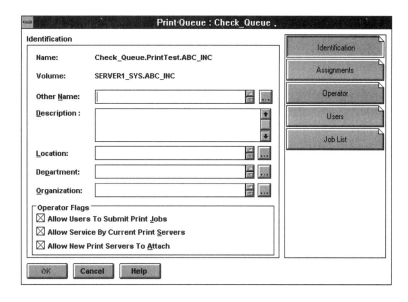

FIGURE 9.8
The Identification properties page shows information about the print queue and allows you to control it.

VIEWING QUEUE ASSIGNMENTS The Assignments properties page allows you to view the objects that have been assigned to this print queue. These objects include print servers that are authorized to obtain entries from the queue and printers that are set up to print jobs from the queue.

The properties on the Print Queue object's Assignments page are for your information only and cannot be changed from this page. Changes to the assignments are made from the Assignments properties of the Print Server and Printer object dialog boxes.

QUEUE USERS AND OPERATORS The Users properties page allows you to specify a list of users who can submit jobs to the print queue. Use the Add button to add to this list. You can add individual users, but it is more common to add multiple users by using Group objects or container objects.

The Operator properties page allows you to specify users who can control print jobs in the queue, as described in the next section. You can include individual users in the list or use an Organizational Role object to assign a print queue operator.

MANAGING PRINT JOBS The final page of properties for the Print Queue object is the Job List properties page. This lists each of the print jobs that have been submitted to the queue and describes their status. This screen is shown in Figure 9.9.

You can use the Job List properties page to view the jobs that have been sent to the printer. In addition, you can manage the jobs with the following functions:

- **Job Details** displays complete information about the highlighted job. This screen is shown in Figure 9.10. You can modify certain information, such as the job description, and place the job on hold if desired.

- **Hold Job** allows you to place a job on hold; the job is not printed until released.

- **Resume** allows a held job to be printed.

- **Delete** removes an entry from the queue.

Creating Printer Objects

The Printer object is the final object required for network printing. You must create a Printer object to represent each printer on the network. You can create a Printer object by following these steps:

1. Highlight the context to place the Printer object in.

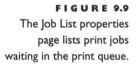

FIGURE 9.9
The Job List properties page lists print jobs waiting in the print queue.

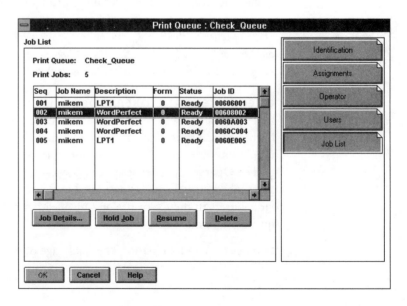

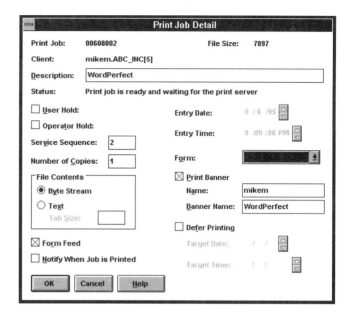

2. Select Create from the Object menu.

3. Select Printer as the type of object to create.

4. Enter a name for the printer and press the Create button to create the object.

After the Printer object is created, you can modify its properties by using the Details option from the Object menu. The properties of the Printer object allow you to identify the printer, specify how it is connected to the network, and specify print queues to print from. These properties are described in the sections below.

SELECTING PRINTER ASSIGNMENTS The Assignments properties page, shown in Figure 9.11, allows you to assign Print Queue objects to be serviced by the printer. You can use the Add button to add additional queues. The Priority arrows allow you to change a queue's priority, and the Delete button allows you to remove a print queue from the list.

FIGURE 9.11
The Printer object's
Assignments properties
page lists queues serviced
by the printer.

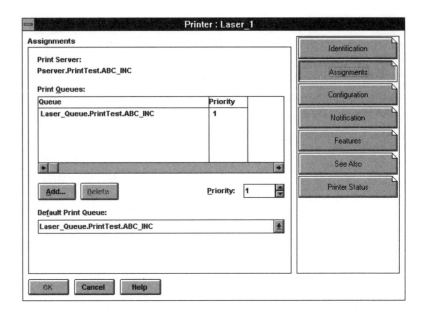

The Default Print Queue option allows you to choose the print queue to be captured to when a user uses the P option in the CAPTURE command to specify the printer's name (rather than identifying a print queue).

CONFIGURING PRINTERS   The Configuration properties page, shown in Figure 9.12, allows you to configure the printer. This page controls the type of port the printer is connected to, the communication parameters, and other settings.

Available options on this screen include:

- **Printer Type** allows you to specify the type of printer. This specifies the type of port, parallel or serial, the printer is attached to. You can also specify UNIX or AppleTalk printers.

- **The Communication button** allows you to view parameters specific to the type of port used. The Parallel Communication screen for a parallel printer is shown in Figure 9.13. You use this screen to specify the physical port the printer is attached to, speed of communication, and other settings.

FIGURE 9.12
The Printer object's
Configuration properties
define the type of printer
and its connection.

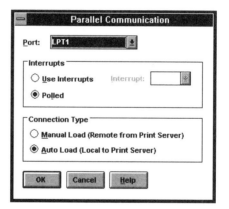

FIGURE 9.13
The Parallel
Communication screen
allows you to define
specific communication
parameters for the
printer.

- **Banner Type** specifies whether the banner used for the printer is in text (ASCII) or PostScript format. The PostScript format can be used on compatible printers only.

- **Service Interval** controls how often the printer checks for new jobs in the print queue. The default is five seconds.

- **Buffer Size in KB** controls the size of the buffer used to store data before it is sent to the printer. The buffer size can range from 3KB to 20KB. The buffer is stored in the RAM of the server or workstation that runs NPRINTER. Increasing this number may improve performance but will require additional memory.

- **Starting Form** selects the default type of form for the printer.

- **Network Address Restriction** allows you to select a certain list of network addresses that the printer can attach to.

- **Service Mode for Forms** specifies how form changes are managed.

OTHER PRINTER PROPERTIES The remaining pages of printer properties allow you to identify the printer, provide notification for printer errors, and display printer status:

- **Identification** allows you to define a name and other information for the printer. Most of this information is optional but can be useful to catalog network resources.

- **Notification** allows you to list users who are notified when an error occurs at the printer.

- **See Also** allows you to reference other objects that are related to the Printer object. This is for your information only and is not used by NetWare. You may want to use this property to indicate printers that are in the same area or used for the same type of form.

- **Printer Status** displays the current printer status and information about the job that is currently printing.

Managing Printing with PCONSOLE

YOU MAY BE FAMILIAR WITH the PCONSOLE menu utility used to manage most aspects of printing in NetWare 3.1x. This DOS-based utility has been improved in NetWare 4.1.

If you prefer PCONSOLE to NetWare Administrator, you can use PCONSOLE to perform most of the printing management tasks described in this chapter. In addition, PCONSOLE offers a Quick Setup feature that allows you to create all of the objects needed for printing in one step. The main PCONSOLE menu is shown in Figure 9.14.

The following sections describe how to use PCONSOLE to set up and manage network printing. See the preceding section, Managing Printing with NetWare Administrator, for details on the properties of the print objects.

FIGURE 9.14
PCONSOLE is a DOS menu utility that allows you to control network printing.

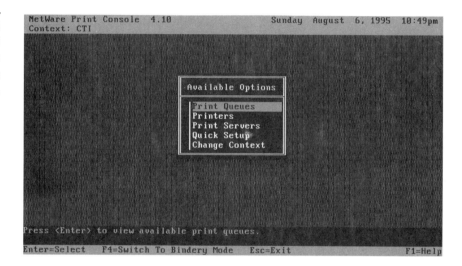

Using Quick Setup

The Quick Setup option on PCONSOLE's main menu provides the easiest way to set up network printing without requiring you to know about the interaction between the print objects. Quick Setup creates each of the required print objects and assigns the correct properties for them to work together. You can use this option to create a working setup quickly and then examine and modify the objects if necessary.

After you select Quick Setup, you see the screen in Figure 9.15. You can specify a printer name, queue name, and print server name or use the default names. If the print server you specify does not exist, it is created automatically.

FIGURE 9.15
Print Services Quick
Setup creates all the
objects required for
network printing.

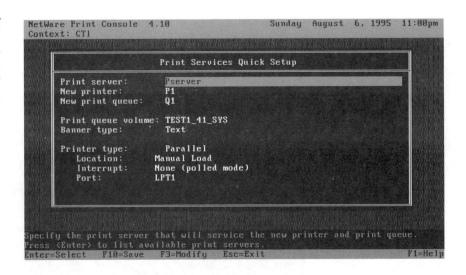

```
NetWare Print Console  4.10                Sunday  August  6, 1995  11:00pm
Context: CTI

                        Print Services Quick Setup

          Print server:      Pserver
          New printer:       P1
          New print queue:   Q1

          Print queue volume: TEST1_41_SYS
          Banner type:        Text

          Printer type:       Parallel
            Location:         Manual Load
            Interrupt:        None (polled mode)
            Port:             LPT1




Specify the print server that will service the new printer and print queue.
Press <Enter> to list available print servers.
Enter=Select   F10=Save   F3=Modify   Esc=Exit                      F1=Help
```

Managing Printer Objects

PCONSOLE also allows you to control the three types of objects required for
printing: print queues, printers, and print servers. You can create new objects
and specify all of their properties from within this utility. Most of the options
are similar to the ones in the PCONSOLE utility in NetWare 3.1x.

*You can perform many tasks in more than one way from PCONSOLE, which makes it easy
to find the option you need. For example, you can create Printer objects from the
Print Server option.*

Print Queues

PCONSOLE's Print Queues option allows you to create and modify
Print Queue objects and their settings. When you select this option, you
will see a list of currently defined print queues. Press Insert to create a
new print queue or press Enter to view information for a print queue. From the
Print Queue Information menu, shown in Figure 9.16, you can control the properties of the print queue and manage print jobs.

FIGURE 9.16
The Print Queue
Information menu allows
you to monitor and
control the print queue.

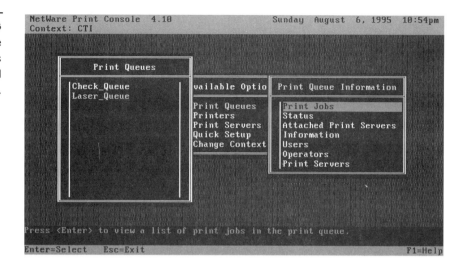

Printers

PCONSOLE's Printers option displays a list of currently defined printers. You can create a new Printer object by pressing the Insert key from this screen. Press Enter when the name of a printer is highlighted to display the Printer Configuration screen, shown in Figure 9.17. This screen allows you to set options for the printer type, configuration options, and other properties of the Printer object.

Print Servers

Press Enter on PCONSOLE's Print Servers option to view a list of currently defined print servers. You can press Insert to create a new Print Server object or press Delete to delete a server. Press Enter when the name of a print server is highlighted to view the Print Server Information menu, shown in Figure 9.18. This menu allows you to define the properties of the print server.

FIGURE 9.17
The Printer
Configuration screen
allows you to control the
Printer object's
properties.

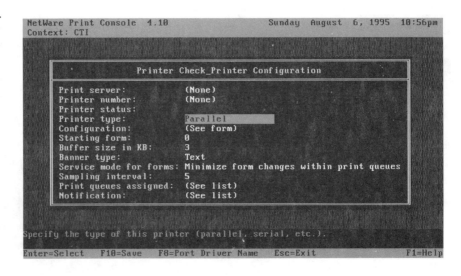

FIGURE 9.18
The Print Server
Information menu allows
you to define the print
server's properties.

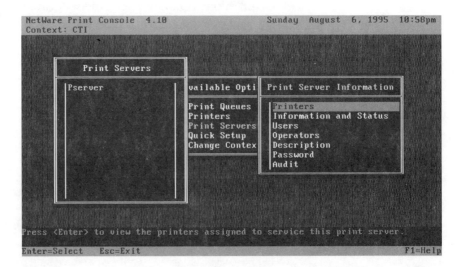

Creating Custom Print Configurations and Forms with NetWare Utilities

THE PRINTCON AND PRINTDEF utilities, also available with NetWare 3.1*x*, have been improved in NetWare 4.1. You can use these utilities, or the NetWare Administrator utility, to create custom print configurations and to print forms.

In NetWare 3.1*x* the print configuration and form definition databases are stored as files on the server. In NetWare 4.1 they are properties of User or container objects in NDS.

Using **PRINTDEF** to Create Printer Forms

The PRINTDEF utility allows you to create printer *forms*. These forms can be used to specify commands to be sent to the printer at the beginning of a print job. You can also use different form types for different types of paper loaded into the printer. In this way forms allow you to control printer output, even when using software that doesn't support your specific printer. If you specify a certain form type when you submit a job, NetWare does not allow it to be printed until that form is mounted. Figure 9.19 shows the main menu of the PRINTDEF utility.

By defining forms, you can control the printer's formatting functions for applications that do not support the printer directly. Most applications, and all Microsoft Windows applications, provide printer support that makes PRINTDEF configurations unnecessary. Nevertheless, PRINTDEF is very useful for older software and for many custom-written business applications.

Using **PRINTCON** to Configure Print Jobs

The PRINTCON utility allows you to create custom print job configurations. The configurations consist of a list of options, similar to the options for the CAPTURE command. Figure 9.20 shows the main menu of the PRINTCON utility.

FIGURE 9.19
The PRINTDEF utility allows you to create printer forms.

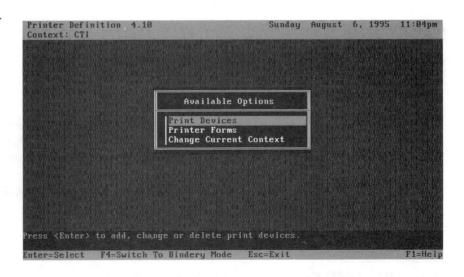

FIGURE 9.20
The PRINTCON utility allows you to create custom print job configurations.

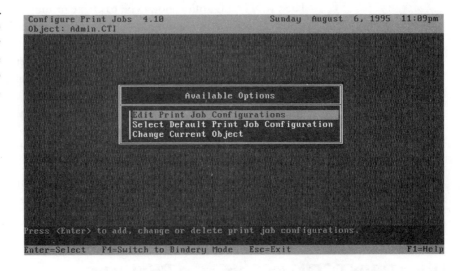

If you specify a print job configuration, you can omit all other CAPTURE options. For example, the following CAPTURE command specifies a print job configuration called TEST:

```
CAPTURE /j=TEST
```

Using NetWare Administrator to Create Forms and Configure Print Jobs

You can also control form definitions and print job configurations using the NetWare Administrator utility. The printer form information is stored as an attribute of each container object, and that information affects leaf objects in that container.

You can create print job configurations using the NetWare Administrator utility as follows:

- Each user has a Print Job Configurations property that can be used to define configurations specific to the user.

- Each Organization or Organizational Unit object also has a Print Job Configurations property. This allows you to define job configurations that can be used by any user in the container.

Review

PRINTING IS A FUNDAMENTAL SERVICE of NetWare 4.1. Printing is handled by several components:

- In order to print to a printer on the network, you must first send the data to a *print queue*. The print queue stores each set of data, or *print job*, that it receives. The jobs are then sent, one at a time, to the print server.

- The *print server* accepts print jobs from print queues and sends them to the appropriate printer. In NetWare 3.1x, print servers were limited to 16 printers; in NetWare 4.1 this limit has been increased to 256, which allows you to easily use a single print server for the entire network. You create the Print Server object in NDS. The properties of the Print Server object provide identification information and define the list of printers the server can send jobs to.

- You must create a *Printer object* to represent each network printer. The properties of the printer object identify the printer and list the print queues that the printer can accept jobs from. Other properties define the type of printer and how it is accessed. Printers can be attached to a server, to a workstation, or directly to the network.

- CAPTURE is a TSR (terminate-and-stay resident) program that allows you to *redirect* printing to a network printer. You specify a local printer port (usually LPT1, LPT2, or LPT3) with the CAPTURE command. After the CAPTURE command is executed, any printing that your workstation sends to this port is redirected to the network queue you specified.

- Before data is sent to the printer, it is sent to the *port driver*. The port driver receives data from the print server and transmits it to the printer. The port driver is also called NPRINTER and is run by NPRINTER.EXE or NPRINTER.NLM.

To manage printing, use NetWare Administrator. The print server, print queue, and Printer objects can be controlled from within this utility.

CNA Practice Test Questions

1. The NDS objects used for printing are

    A. Print server, print queue, port driver

    B. Print server, print queue, printer

    C. Printer, print server, port driver

    D. CAPTURE, printer, print server

2. The number of printers controlled by a NetWare 4.1 print server

    A. Is limited only by the server's memory

    B. Is limited to 16 printers

    C. Is limited to 256 printers

    D. Is limited to three parallel printers and two serial printers

3. The three basic types of network printers are

    A. Workstation, server, queue

    B. Workstation, server, directly connected

    C. NDS, bindery, workstation

    D. Dot matrix, laser, daisy wheel

4. Which is the correct CAPTURE command to capture the LPT2 port to the CHECKS queue?

    A. CAPTURE J=2 P=CHECKS

    B. CAPTURE L=1 B=2 Q=CHECKS

    C. CAPTURE LPT2 P=CHECK_PRINTER

    D. CAPTURE LPT2 Q=CHECKS

5. The Print Server object

    A. Is not used in NetWare 4.1

    B. Moves jobs from the print queue to the printer

    C. Moves jobs from the print queue to the port driver

    D. Stores a list of jobs to be printed

6. To configure a workstation printer, you use the _____ program.

    A. RPRINTER

    B. REMOTE

    C. WPRINTER

    D. NPRINTER

7. Which is the correct order of components when a print job is processed?

    A. CAPTURE, print queue, printer

    B. CAPTURE, print queue, print server, port driver, printer

    C. CAPTURE, port driver, print server, print queue, printer

    D. port driver, CAPTURE, print queue, print server, printer

8. CAPTURE can use which LPT ports?

    A. LPT1-3

    B. LPT1-5

    C. Only those you have the hardware for

    D. LPT1-9

9. The Print Server object

    A. Is created automatically when the printer is installed

    B. Needs to be created for each printer

    C. Can handle up to 256 printers

    D. Is not needed for most printers

10. You can stop and continue a print job with which NWADMIN functions?

    A. Pause and play

    B. Pause and resume

    C. Hold and resume

    D. Hold and unhold

11. The number of printers on the network is limited by

    A. The print server

    B. The number of ports on the server

    C. The number of queues

    D. Disk storage available

12. You can CAPTURE to

    A. A printer or a print server

    B. A printer only

    C. A printer or a queue

    D. A printer or NPRINTER

Administering
the File Server

CHAPTER

10

THE NETWARE 4.1 SERVER doesn't work like a regular PC. None of the DOS commands you might be familiar with work on the server. There are special commands that do, however.

In this chapter we'll take a look at the components of a NetWare 4.1 server and the types of commands and utilities that you can use at the server. In addition, you will learn how to access the server from a workstation on the network and how to prevent unauthorized access to the server.

What's in a NetWare 4.1 Server?

A NETWARE SERVER IS any computer that runs the NetWare operating system. NetWare can run on any PC-compatible computer with a 386 or better processor. You should also have sufficient RAM and disk storage space—those requirements were discussed in Chapter 2.

The software that runs on the NetWare 4.1 server includes the operating system—NetWare itself—and loadable modules. Let's take a look at each of these in detail.

Operating System

The NetWare operating system provides the basic services of a network. The basic part of the operating system is called the *core* operating system. The services provided by the core OS were introduced in Chapter 1 and include

- File sharing

- Printer sharing

- Security

- Routing

- NDS

All of the other services that NetWare 4.1 provides are actually provided by additional programs called *NetWare Loadable Modules* (NLMs), which are described next.

NetWare Loadable Modules (NLMs)

Along with the core OS, the server can run NetWare Loadable Modules, or NLMs. NLMs are programs that run on the NetWare server. The NetWare operating system allows NLMs to integrate fully with the system, that is, NLMs and the OS share the same memory and can perform some of the same functions.

Because NLMs provide some of the services of NetWare, Netware 4 is called a *modular* network operating system. Modularity has some advantages over a fixed system:

- NLMs can be loaded and unloaded. You can load only the modules you need, which allows you to save memory for needed services.

- Third parties can also develop NLMs. You can find NLM virus software, backup software, and many other applications.

Netware 4.1 comes with many NLMs; these modules fit into four categories, described in the following sections.

Disk Drivers

Disk drivers provide an interface to the disk controller hardware on the server. In order to access the disk, the NetWare core operating system sends messages to the disk driver. Disk drivers usually have a .DSK file extension. The new disk driver standard is called NPA *(NetWare Peripheral Architecture)*. Drivers that use this standard actually consist of two files with two different extensions:

- A Host Adapter Module, or HAM, communicates with the host adapter, or disk controller card.

- A Custom Device Module, or CDM, provides an interface to each device (disk drives, tape drives, etc.) that can be attached to the adapter.

LAN Drivers

Just as disk drivers interface NetWare with the disk drives in the server, LAN drivers interface Netware with LAN cards in the server. You can load a module for each card in the server and unload it if you stop using that card. LAN driver modules have the .LAN extension; NetWare 4.1 also supports modular LAN drivers.

Name Space Modules

NetWare 4.1 provides a full set of features that allow access from non-DOS operating systems, including the Macintosh and OS/2. Both of these operating systems allow long file names instead of the typical DOS eight-character name. In order to fully support long file names, NetWare uses *name space modules*. These modules have the extension .NAM.

If you are using a system that allows extended file names, you should always load the name space module for that OS when you start the server. OS2.NAM is used for OS/2 support, and MAC.NAM is used for Macintosh support.

The OS/2 name space module (OS2.NAM) can also be used to support long file names in Windows 95, since there is not yet a specific name space module for Windows 95.

Utility NLMs

The final category of NLMs includes utilities that perform a wide variety of functions. These utilities all have the extension .NLM. NLMs that come with NetWare or are available separately from Novell or other companies provide the following functions:

- Network printing and management
- Backup and restore
- Remote console access
- Server monitoring
- Power supply monitoring
- Network management
- Communications

- Media management
- Data migration

NetWare 4.1 Console Commands

YOU'RE PROBABLY FAMILIAR WITH the DOS prompt—the prompt where you enter a command on a DOS workstation. The NetWare file server console has a similar prompt where you can enter NetWare *console commands*. You can use these commands to perform a wide variety of functions, maintain the server, and load and unload NLMs.

The file server prompt is referred to as the *colon prompt* because it always ends with a colon. The prompt is usually the name of the file server. For example, if you accessed the console of a server called TRIFFID, the prompt would appear as

```
TRIFFID:
```

If you're running additional NLMs on the server, they may have their own screen displays. You can switch between these screens and the colon prompt by pressing the ALT+ESC key. The next sections explain each console command. You'll need to understand these in order to manage the server.

BROADCAST

The BROADCAST command allows you to send a message to users on the network. To use this command, specify a message to be sent and a user to send it to. You can send the message to all users who are currently attached to the network by leaving off the username.

The main purpose of BROADCAST is to let users know about conditions that might affect their use of the network. The following command sends a message to all users:

```
BROADCAST "The system will be going down at 9:00"
```

Another NetWare 4.1 console command, SEND, is identical to BROADCAST.

CLEAR STATION

Use this command as a last resort to force a user off the network. CLEAR STATION is not commonly used because the powerful MONITOR utility allows you to do the same. This command can be used to free a workstation that is hung; however, it doesn't finish any disk writes that may be in progress, so data may be lost. MONITOR's clear feature shares this limitation but also offers an easy way to tell whether any important files are open

CLS

This command simply clears the screen on the file server—useful if you wish to hide the commands you've typed from prying eyes or if you just like to be tidy.

CONFIG

CONFIG displays a summary of how the server is configured. This command can be useful in determining which version of NetWare is running and how many licenses your server has. It also lists LAN drivers in use. The output of the CONFIG command is shown in Figure 10.1.

FIGURE 10.1
The CONFIG command displays a summary of the server's configuration.

```
IPX internal network number: 2FB6CE6C
     Node address: 000000000001
     Frame type: VIRTUAL_LAN
     LAN protocol: IPX network 2FB6CE6C
Server Up Time:  55 Minutes 21 Seconds

Novell NE2000
     Version 3.29    November 1, 1994
     Hardware setting: I/O ports 300h to 31Fh, Interrupt Ah
     Node address: 080000292329
     Frame type: ETHERNET_802.3
     Board name: NE2000_1_E83
     LAN protocol: IPX network 6231CA67

Novell NE2000
     Version 3.29    November 1, 1994
     Hardware setting: I/O ports 300h to 31Fh, Interrupt Ah
     Node address: 080000292329
     Frame type: ETHERNET_802.2
     Board name: NE2000_1_E82
     LAN protocol: IPX network CC662033

Tree Name: MGM
Bindery Context(s):
<Press ESC to terminate or any other key to continue>
```

DISABLE LOGIN

The DISABLE LOGIN command prevents users from logging in. It does not affect users who are already logged in, only those who try to log in after you type the command. If you're feeling mischievous, you might enjoy doing this every now and then just to cause a stir; otherwise, the best use for this command is when the server is having a problem and you need to take it down.

DISMOUNT

This command dismounts a volume, making it inaccessible to users. This is the opposite of the MOUNT command. A volume must be mounted before it can be accessed.

DISPLAY NETWORKS

This command displays a list of internal network numbers that NetWare can detect on the server and other servers it is communicating with. DISLAY NETWORK can be useful for configuring communication between servers.

DISPLAY SERVERS

This command displays a list of servers that can be seen across the network from the current server. If you are on a multiserver network, this command is a way to verify that the network connection is still intact and communication is working. An example of the list of servers is shown in Figure 10.2.

You may be surprised by the length of the DISPLAY SERVERS list. Since certain services, such as NDS and printing, use their own server names, each server in your network may be listed several times.

DOWN

This is probably the most drastic server command—but you'll use it more often than most others. The DOWN command is used to take the server down. If any users are on the network, they receive a message saying that the server is

FIGURE 10.2

The DISPLAY SERVERS
command lists
accessible servers.

```
SERVER1:display servers
   MGM_____    0    MGM_____    0    SERVER1    0    SERVER1    0
There are 4 known servers
SERVER1:
```

going down. NetWare then checks for open files; if any files are open, it asks you to type **Y** before bringing the server down. It then closes all files and dismounts all volumes.

After the DOWN command finishes taking the server down, you are returned to the colon prompt. At this point only two commands can work: EXIT or RESTART SERVER.

EXIT

The EXIT command is the second half of the server-down process. If you wish to return to DOS after taking the server down, you can use this command. An alternative is the RESTART SERVER command, which brings the server back up.

HELP

HELP may be the most useful command of all. It allows you to display instructions for any server command. For example, the following command displays a list of options for the BROADCAST command:

    HELP BROADCAST

The output of this HELP command is shown in Figure 10.3.

FIGURE 10.3
The HELP command
displays instructions for a
console command.

```
SERVER1:help broadcast
BROADCAST "message" [[TO] username:connection_number] [[and:,] username:
        connection_number...]
 Send a message to all users logged in or attached to a file server or to a
list of users or connection numbers.
 Example:  broadcast "Please delete unneeded files to free disk space"

SERVER1:
```

LOAD

LOAD is a commonly used command. It allows you to load an NLM. After the NLM loads, you may see a screen provided by that utility. NLMs are discussed later in this chapter.

A complimentary command, UNLOAD, allows you to remove an NLM from memory.

MOUNT

The MOUNT command is used to mount a disk volume. MOUNT is not really necessary in most circumstances—NetWare automatically mounts all available volumes when the disk drivers are loaded. You may need to use this command, or its complement DISMOUNT, if you wish to mount or remove a disk volume while the server is up.

MODULES

MODULES is another command that applies to NLMs. This command lists all of the NLMs that are currently in the server's memory. You may find this command useful to determine which modules are running or whether a particular module, such as a LAN driver, was loaded correctly. Each module's name is listed, along with a brief description. An example of the output of this command is shown in Figure 10.4.

RESTART SERVER

When you've typed DOWN to bring the server down, you can use the RESTART SERVER command instead of EXIT to bring the server back up. This sequence of commands is useful when you need to bring the server down and back up quickly—for example, when you install new software or make a change to the server configuration files.

SET

SET allows you to modify parameters that affect the server's performance. For example, the following command controls whether file compression will be performed:

```
SET File Compression = OFF
```

FIGURE 10.4
The MODULES command displays a list of NLMs that are currently in memory.

```
SERVER1:modules
IDE.DSK
   NetWare 4.01/4.02/4.10 IDE Device Driver
   Version 5.00    September 30, 1994
   Copyright 1994 Novell, Inc.  All rights reserved.
UNICODE.NLM
   NetWare Unicode Library NLM
   Version 4.10    November 8, 1994
   Copyright 1994 Novell, Inc.  All rights reserved.
DSLOADER.NLM
   NetWare 4.1 Directory Services Loader
   Version 1.25    October 22, 1994
   Copyright 1993-1994 Novell, Inc.  All rights reserved.
TIMESYNC.NLM
   Netware Time Synchronization Services
   Version 4.13    October 14, 1994
   (C) Copyright 1991-94, Novell, Inc.  All rights reserved.
MSM.NLM
   Novell Generic Media Support Module
   Version 2.32    August 23, 1994
   Copyright 1994 Novell, Inc.  All rights reserved.
<Press ESC to terminate or any other key to continue>
```

There are literally hundreds of SET commands for different purposes—worse, you have to spell them correctly. Luckily, NetWare 4.1 comes with SERVMAN. SERVMAN is an NLM that lets you change just about every SET parameter from a convenient menu. SERVMAN is discussed later in this chapter.

TIME

The TIME command gives you the time; in addition, it tells you the time synchronization status of the server. The output of the TIME command is shown in Figure 10.5.

UNLOAD

UNLOAD lets you remove an NLM from memory; execution of the NLM stops immediately. Since a poorly written NLM may crash when you unload it, be careful using this command.

FIGURE 10.5

The TIME command displays the server's time and synchronization information.

```
SERVER1:time
  Time zone string: "MST7MDT"
  DST status:  ON
  DST start:    Sunday, April 7, 1996    2:00:00 am MST
  DST end:      Sunday, October 29, 1995    2:00:00 am MDT
  Time synchronization is active.
  Time is synchronized to the network.
Monday, September 11, 1995    2:17:02 pm UTC
Monday, September 11, 1995    8:17:02 am MDT
SERVER1:
```

NetWare 4.1 NLM Utilities

NEXT WE'LL TAKE A LOOK AT the most important NLMs. These utilities provide a variety of services for managing the server, installing software, and setting parameters.

INSTALL

The INSTALL loadable module is used to install NetWare 4.1, to change installation parameters, and to upgrade or install additional software. You can access this module at any time by typing **LOAD INSTALL** at the server console. The main INSTALL menu is shown in Figure 10.6.

INSTALL includes the following options:

- **Driver options** allow you to load and unload network and disk drivers.

- **Disk options** allow you to set up partitions on a disk and use the mirroring features.

- **Volume options** allow you to set up volumes on a disk partition and mount and dismount them.

FIGURE 10.6
The INSTALL NLM allows you to install and configure the server and other products.

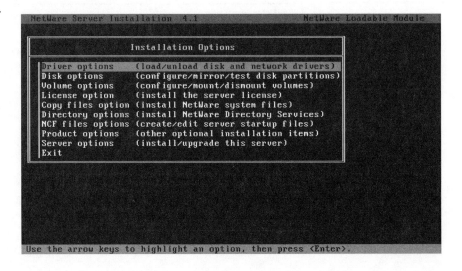

```
NetWare Server Installation 4.1                NetWare Loadable Module

                       Installation Options
     ┌──────────────────────────────────────────────────────────────┐
     │Driver options     (load/unload disk and network drivers)       │
     │Disk options       (configure/mirror/test disk partitions)      │
     │Volume options     (configure/mount/dismount volumes)           │
     │License option     (install the server license)                 │
     │Copy files option  (install NetWare system files)               │
     │Directory options  (install NetWare Directory Services)         │
     │NCF files options  (create/edit server startup files)           │
     │Product options    (other optional installation items)          │
     │Server options     (install/upgrade this server)                │
     │Exit                                                            │
     └──────────────────────────────────────────────────────────────┘



 Use the arrow keys to highlight an option, then press <Enter>.
```

- **License option** adds or changes server licenses. The licenses are kept on a license diskette provided with NetWare. You can add additional licenses in any combination or delete installed licenses.

- **Copy files option** copies files into the SYSTEM and PUBLIC directories on a new server.

- **Directory options** allow you to install or remove NDS.

- **NCF files options** allow you to create or edit the AUTOEXEC.NCF and STARTUP.NCF files.

- **Product options** add or remove optional products.

- **Server options** install a new server or upgrade an existing server.

MONITOR

The MONITOR NLM is probably the most widely used NetWare utility. It is loaded on the server, usually in the AUTOEXEC.NCF file. The MONITOR screen, shown in Figure 10.7, provides a dynamic display of information about the server. If you watch these numbers carefully, you can be sure your server is running smoothly.

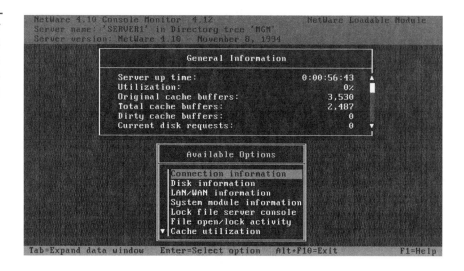

FIGURE 10.7
MONITOR provides statistics that let you know how the server is running.

Along with the information displayed at the top of the screen, MONITOR has a menu that you can use to display specific categories of information. Most of these include running statistics that are updated as server conditions change. MONITOR offers these options:

- **Connection information** lets you see who is logged into the server. You can view specific information about a user, such as files they have open, by pressing Enter on their login name. Pressing the Delete key when a user's name is highlighted logs the user out forcefully. This is similar to the CLEAR STATION command. Before you issue the MONITOR command, be sure the user does not have any data files open; data may be lost if a file is being written to when you disconnect the user.

- **Disk information** displays information about disks on the server and the volumes on them.

- **LAN/WAN information** displays network numbers, LAN driver information, and statistics for each LAN or WAN network.

- **System module information** lists the NLMs loaded on the server.

- **Lock file server console** allows you to enter a password to lock the console. Users won't be able to access the console without this password (or the ADMIN password).

- **File open/lock activity** displays information about open files on a volume.

- **Cache utilization** displays statistics about cache buffers and lets you determine which applications are using them.

- **Processor utilization** displays statistics about processor cycles used by each module.

- **Resource utilization** displays statistics about resources used by each module.

- **Memory utilization** displays the types and quantities of memory used by each module.

- **Scheduling information** shows what percentage of the server's time is spent with each module. You can easily determine if a particular module is slowing down the server. (See Figure 10.8.)

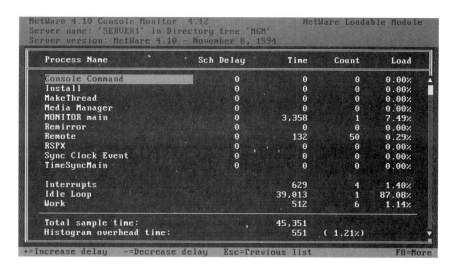

SERVMAN

SERVMAN (Server Manager) is an NLM that allows you to view server information and control server settings. Rather than use the SET command to set parameters, you can browse through available parameters with SERVMAN, select one to change, and assign a new value. Changes you make with SERVMAN take effect immediately. You also have the option of saving changes to the AUTOEXEC.NCF or TIMESYNC.CFG files.

To change settings, select Server Parameters from the main SERVMAN screen. The next screen, shown in Figure 10.9, lists several categories of options that you can set. After selecting a category, you can review the list of possible settings for the category and their current values. For example, Figure 10.10 shows Directory Services Parameters. Select a setting and press Enter to change its value.

After you change one or more settings with SERVMAN, you are asked whether to save the changes in AUTOEXEC.NCF or TIMESYNC.CFG, whichever is appropriate. If you answer Yes, NetWare sets that option each time the server starts. If you do not wish to save the changes, select No. Although changes are not written to the file, the setting is in effect until the server is restarted or until you change it again.

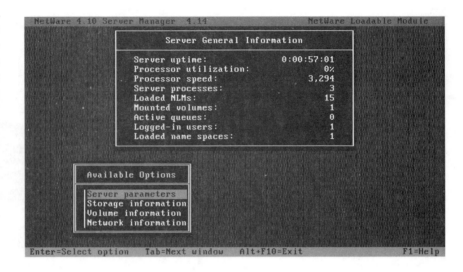

FIGURE 10.9
The SERVMAN utility
allows you to browse
server settings by
category.

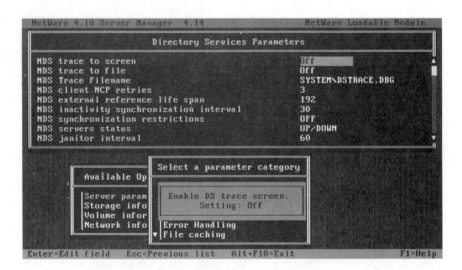

FIGURE 10.10
SERVMAN lists specific
settings in each category,
such as these for
Directory Services.

Remote Access to the Server

MOST OF THE UTILITIES you use to manage NetWare 4.1 are run from the workstation, but the utilities introduced in this chapter have to be run at the server. Since it's possible that your server is in another room, another office, or another country, NetWare provides another way to access the console. The *remote console* utility—RCONSOLE—runs at a workstation and allows you to take over the server's keyboard and screen, as if you were there. When you're online with RCONSOLE, you can do anything you would do at the actual console.

Before you can use RCONSOLE, you need to load two NLMs at the server. These NLMs handle the server's end of the communication. The following commands load the needed NLMs:

```
LOAD REMOTE password
LOAD RSPX
```

The password specified in the command line above is a password that is required for users to access the remote console. If you do not specify this password, the ADMIN password is used.

To start the remote console, type **RCONSOLE** at the workstation. Then choose the connection type:

- SPX is used for typical connections across a network.

- Asynchronous is used for modem connections.

Next you'll see a list of servers that are available—those that are running RSPX and REMOTE. Select a server and press Enter. Type in the remote console password (described above). After you enter the correct password, you hear a beep and the server's screen is displayed on your screen.

You can now perform regular server functions. However, you can't use the ALT+ESC key to navigate screens from RCONSOLE. Instead, use ALT+F3 and ALT+F4 to move back and forth through the different screens.

Securing the Server Console

I F YOU READ THE PREVIOUS DESCRIPTION of the DOWN command, you probably realize that you shouldn't let anyone access the server console unless authorized. You can take several precautions to be sure that the server console is safe and secure:

- To ensure *physical security*, place the server in a locked room if at all possible. If the computer has a keyboard lock switch that uses a key, keep it locked.

- The Lock Server Console option in the MONITOR utility lets you lock the server console. You are asked for a password; after you enter it, the server is not accessible to anyone who does not know that password.

- Be sure that you use a password for RCONSOLE. As with all passwords, do not share this password.

- The SECURE CONSOLE command can be used at the colon prompt to remove the remains of DOS from memory and prevent anyone from using the EXIT command to reach the DOS prompt. A user at this prompt could easily erase data on the server.

Physical security is, by far, the most important. If someone is allowed to walk up and access your file server without being watched, he or she can do damage no matter how secure your network is. These security considerations should be part of a complete security plan. You can find the details about NetWare 4.1's security features in Chapter 7.

Review

T HE NETWARE 4.1 SERVER doesn't work like a regular PC. A NetWare server is any computer that runs the NetWare operating system. NetWare can run on any PC-compatible computer with a 386 or better processor. You should also have sufficient RAM and disk storage space.

The software that runs on the NetWare 4.1 server includes the operating system—NetWare itself—and loadable modules. The following services are provided by the operating system itself, the core operating system:

- File sharing

- Printer sharing

- Security

- Routing

- NDS

Along with the core OS, the server can run NetWare Loadable Modules, or NLMs. NLMs are programs that run on the NetWare server. The NetWare operating system allows NLMs to integrate fully with the system, that is, NLMs and the OS share the same memory and can perform some of the same functions.

NLMs include

- **Disk drivers** to interface with disk controller hardware

- **LAN drivers** to interface with LAN cards

- **Name space modules** to provide extended file naming services

- **Utilities** to perform server management functions

The NetWare file server console has a prompt where you can enter NetWare *console commands*. These can be used to perform a wide variety of functions, maintain the server, and load and unload NLMs. The file server prompt is referred to as the *colon prompt*, because it always ends with a colon. If a screen that doesn't display the colon prompt is visible, you can use the ALT+ESC key to switch screens until you see the colon prompt.

Console commands include

- BROADCAST to send messages to users

- CLEAR STATION to disconnect a user

- CLS to clear the server's screen

- CONFIG to display configuration information

- DISABLE LOGIN to prevent user logins

- DISMOUNT and MOUNT to control disk volumes

- DISPLAY NETWORKS to display available networks

- DISPLAY SERVERS to display available servers

- DOWN and EXIT to bring the server down

- HELP to display instructions

- LOAD and UNLOAD to control NLMs

- MODULES to display module information

- RESTART SERVER to bring the server back up

- SET to change server parameters

- TIME to display time and synchronization information

The final category of server utilities are NLMs. The following NLMs were introduced in this chapter:

- INSTALL for installing NetWare and other services

- MONITOR for watching file system statistics

- SERVMAN for changing SET parameters easily

CNA *Practice Test Questions*

1. Commands that you can use at the server console include

    A. DOS commands

    B. NLMs and console commands

    C. NLMs only

    D. DOS or NLM commands

2. The NetWare core operating system does NOT include

    A. File sharing

    B. NDS security

    C. Network management

    D. NDS

3. NLMs come from

    A. Novell

    B. Third parties

    C. Both of the above

    D. None of the above

4. The two parts of a NPA disk driver are

    A. NPA and CDA

    B. HAM and CAM

    C. HAM and CDM

    D. NPA and HDM

5. LAN Driver modules have the extension

    A. NLM

    B. DRV

    C. LAN

    D. MOD

6. The command to display configuration information is

   A. DISPLAY CONFIG

   B. MODULES

   C. CONFIG

   D. VERSION

7. The command to prevent logins is

   A. SET LOGIN = NO

   B. DISABLE LOGIN

   C. LOGIN OFF

   D. SECURE CONSOLE

8. The two commands needed to bring down the server and exit to DOS are

   A. DOWN and QUIT

   B. DOWN and RESET

   C. DOWN and CLS

   D. DOWN and EXIT

9. The key(s) used to switch screens in RCONSOLE is

   A. F3 or F4

   B. ALT+ESC

   C. CTRL+ESC

   D. ALT+F3 and ALT+F4

10. The two modules you must load to enable remote access are

   A. REMOTE and MONITOR

   B. REMOTE and ACCESS

   C. RSPX and REMOTE

   D. RSPX and RCONSOLE

Advanced
Netware 4.1
Management

PART

3

Advanced
NetWare
Directory
Services

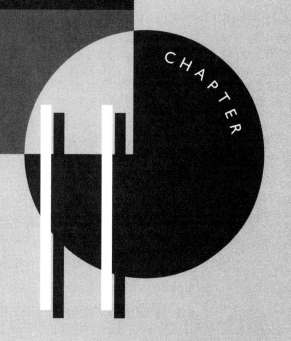

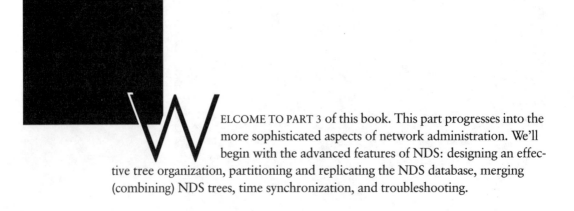

ELCOME TO PART 3 of this book. This part progresses into the more sophisticated aspects of network administration. We'll begin with the advanced features of NDS: designing an effective tree organization, partitioning and replicating the NDS database, merging (combining) NDS trees, time synchronization, and troubleshooting.

Designing the NDS Tree

S YOU LEARNED in the previous chapters, NDS provides you with the ability to manage your network and its resources in simpler ways than were possible in previous versions of NetWare. However, to take advantage of these features, you must plan the structure of your Directory tree so that it suits the needs of your network.

A carefully planned and organized Directory tree has the following benefits:

- **Simplified administration:** By organizing users and resources into containers and groups, you simplify the job of the administrator.

- **Ease of access:** Users can quickly find the network resources that they need to access.

- **Improved security:** Whether it will be managed by one administrator or several, your network can take advantage of NetWare 4.1's many security features.

- **Fault tolerance:** By placing replicas and partitions strategically, you can eliminate the risk of data loss in the event of a server crash.

- **Optimized network traffic:** By using partitions and replicas and by managing time synchronization, you can minimize the traffic over wide-area network (WAN) links.

- **Transparent upgrade:** A well-planned NDS upgrade strategy allows you to perform the upgrade piece by piece, with minimal impact on the users.

Tree Design Considerations

In order to receive the benefits listed above, you'll need to consider several items in your design:

- **Administration:** If the company has separate administrators for each location, it may be best to organize by location. This arrangement makes it easy to give each administrator the correct rights.

- **Network topology:** If WAN links are used, it may be wise to separate the locations as much as possible to minimize traffic. You can still use an integrated organization if you place partitions and replicas appropriately, as discussed later in this chapter.

- **Bindery Services:** If you use NetWare 4.1's Bindery Services feature, you must consider where to place the bindery contexts. Up to 16 of these can be assigned.

- **Tree depth:** Although the NDS tree can be as complicated as you need it to be, effective trees usually have between three and eight layers. Trees with too many layers can be difficult to work with.

Although there is no limit to the depth of the NDS tree, there is a limit to the length of an object's distinguished name. Object names are limited to 256 characters. To avoid running into this limit, make sure you do not use too many layers and that your Organization and Organizational Unit objects have short, concise names.

Choosing a Tree Structure

The most visible aspect of your NDS plan will be the structure, or organization, of the Directory tree itself. There are several possible strategies for organizing your NDS tree. Most networks are based on one of these strategies or a combination of them. The following sections discuss each of the tree-structure strategies.

The Default Organization

When you install NetWare 4.1 and accept the defaults, a simple Directory tree structure is created for you. This tree consists of a single Organization object under the [Root]. All leaf objects (resources) on the network are created within this container. An example of this organization is shown in Figure 11.1.

The default organization places all objects in a single, flat database, organized no better than the bindery used in previous versions of NetWare. This structure may be adequate for small networks (with 10 to 20 users), but it offers few of the benefits of NDS. For most networks, you will want to find a more appropriate way to organize the Directory tree.

FIGURE 11.1
The default Directory tree structure places all objects under a single Organization object.

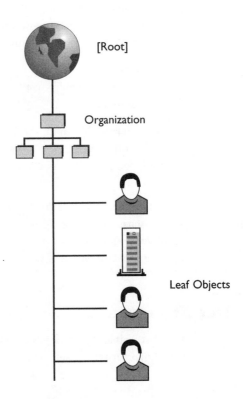

If you've already installed NetWare 4.1 and used the default organization, don't worry—it's not too late. Read on to determine a more appropriate organization and then modify your organization using the NDS utilities.

Organizing by Division

A common Directory tree organization uses the *divisional* approach, which divides the tree into Organizational Unit objects based on divisions or departments of the company, such as Sales, Accounting, Research, Production, and so on. The structure of NDS will resemble the company's organization chart. Figure 11.2 illustrates a simple divisional organization.

This is a good strategy to use when there are clear divisions within the company, as with most medium-size or large companies. Since users within a division often require access to the same data and applications, the divisional approach simplifies network administration.

FIGURE 11.2

The *divisional* Directory tree organization divides the company according to functional divisions.

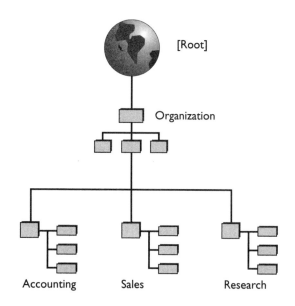

Organizing by Location

In companies with multiple locations, the *locational* strategy is often used. In this approach, you create Organizational Unit objects for each of the physical locations of the company, as shown in Figure 11.3.

This strategy provides a simple organization and makes it easy to create partitions. A large company might choose to have a different LAN administrator at each of the locations. This type of network management is easy to implement if the locational strategy is used.

You can also organize locations using the Country object, which is placed directly under the [Root], above the Organization objects. Country objects should only be used in large, multinational corporations or for compatibility with larger directories, such as the Internet's DNS (Domain Name Service). If you use a Country object, its name must be a valid two-character country abbreviation (determined by the X.500 standard), as explained in Chapter 5.

The locational structure works well when the locations of a company are managed separately. However, if employees in various locations work closely together on projects, a workgroup or hybrid organization, described in the next sections, may be more practical.

FIGURE 11.3

The *locational* organization includes separate Organizational Unit objects for each physical location.

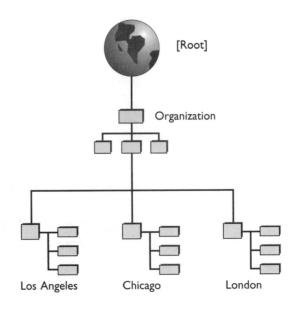

[Root]

Organization

Los Angeles   Chicago   London

Organizing by Workgroup

The organization of modern companies often includes *workgroups*—groups of users who perform similar tasks, usually on the same project. You could organize your Directory tree according to these workgroups, as shown in the example in Figure 11.4.

Since workgroups can be flexible and a user may belong to more than one group, you may find it useful to use Group objects instead of a container object to arrange some workgroups. The workgroup organization may be combined with other strategies, as described in the next section.

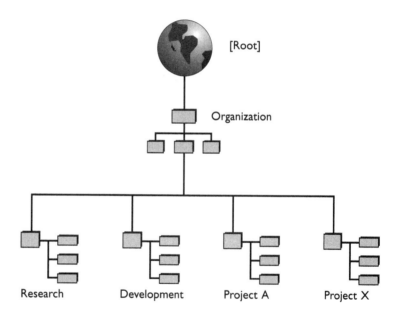

[Root]

Organization

Research   Development   Project A   Project X

Using a Hybrid Organization

For many companies, particularly large ones, you will find that none of the above strategies is ideal. A *hybrid*, or combination, approach based on the organization of your company may be the solution. The hybrid approach combines the strengths of two or more types of NDS organization.

Figure 11.5 shows one example of a hybrid organization. In this example, the company's Directory tree is organized at the top level by location—Los Angeles, Chicago, and London. Each location is then organized by

FIGURE 11.5

An example of a hybrid organization. This tree is divided by location and then by department.

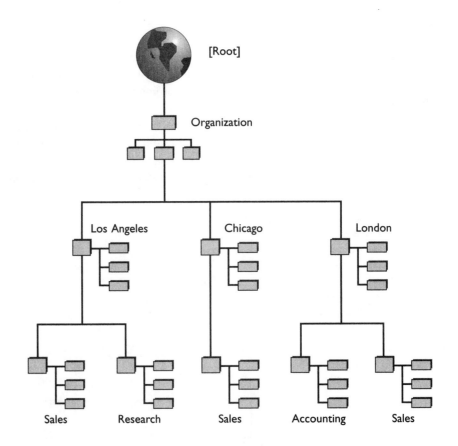

departments. Each location has its own Sales department to handle local sales. The Research department for the corporation is located in Los Angeles, and the Accounting department is based in London.

The example in Figure 11.6 takes another combination approach. This company is administered from a central location. The tree is organized by divisions of Accounting, Marketing, and Sales. The Marketing department works strictly from the Denver office. The other departments have an office in each location.

A more elaborate hybrid organization is shown in Figure 11.7. The first level is divided by departments: Marketing, Technical, and Accounting. The Accounting department has an office in each of two locations. The Technical department is further subdivided into Research, Service, and Support. Finally, the Research department is organized into workgroups.

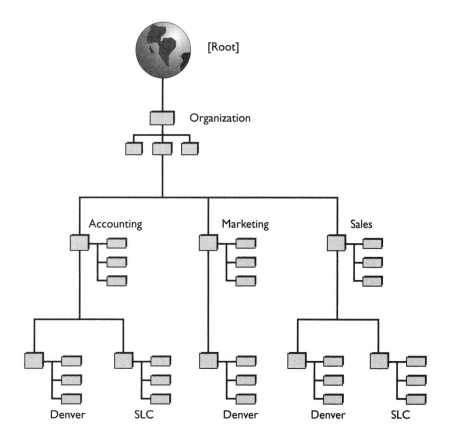

FIGURE 11.6
Another example of
hybrid organization. This
tree is organized by
department and then by
location.

Defining Naming Standards

The next step in planning your network's Directory tree is to create the standards that will be used in choosing object names and properties. Choosing standards when the network is designed is a good way to ensure that consistent names, properties, and values will be used.

Naming Objects

By using consistent naming procedures, you make network administration more efficient. For example, it will be easy to locate users, printers, servers, and other network objects that you need to maintain. Users will also benefit from consistent object names. For example, when sending e-mail, a user will have no trouble determining another user's name.

FIGURE 11.7
An example of a more
complex hybrid
Directory tree. This tree
is organized by
departments, locations,
and workgroups.

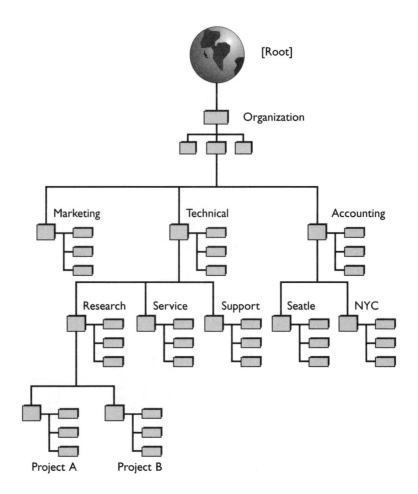

The following sections offer some guidelines for naming objects on your network.

USER LOGIN NAMES Typical standards for user login names include some combination of names and initials:

- First name, last initial, as in JOHNS. For small companies, this user naming standard might be the best solution, since employees know each other by first name. However, this combination can result in duplicate names and may cause confusion when employees are also known by nicknames.

- First initial, last name, as in JSMITH. This is another common naming method. There is slightly less chance of duplicate names, and it's easier to determine to whom the name refers.

- First initial, middle initial, last name, as in JDSMITH. More complicated schemes such as this are often needed in larger companies. There is very little chance of duplication.

It is also important to determine what you will do if two users have names that would produce the same username. For example, you might decide to add a middle initial or, as a last resort, a number. If you find that you have to do this often, you may be better off with a different naming scheme.

It is a good practice to limit user login names to 8 characters. Although NDS allows 64-character names, some e-mail systems require 8-character names. In addition, 8-character names will work better if you use an earlier version of NetWare on the network.

In some companies, it may be perfectly acceptable to have two users called JOHNS, as long as they are in different containers. However, if usernames are used for e-mail, this casual naming standard can cause problems. In addition, no two users in bindery context containers can share the same username.

GROUPS, ORGANIZATIONS, AND ORGANIZATIONAL UNITS

Since Organizations and Organizational Units usually identify divisions, locations, or workgroups in the company, you should name them after the entity they represent. Use short and concise names, since you might need to type them when referring to a user by distinguished name. For example, you might use MGMT for Management, ACCT for Accounting, AP for Accounts Payable, and NYC for New York City.

Give Group objects names that represent their function, such as DATAENTRY for the data-entry group or PROJECT1 for users working on a particular project. If the group was created to give users access to an application directory, its name might refer to that application, such as WORDPROCESSING or BACKUP.

OTHER NDS OBJECTS You should also have a standard procedure for naming other types of objects in the Directory tree. Names should be short, concise, and meaningful to the users. Here are some examples:

- Servers are often named based on their location, such as EAST1, NYC, or BLDG3. Since a user may need to type the name of a server to log in to, keep server names short. Server names must be unique, even if they are in different containers.

- Volumes are given NDS names automatically when you create them. The name combines the server name and volume name, such as EAST1_SYS.

- Printers are typically named according to the printer type and location, such as LJ4_BLDG3 or DMP_WEST.

- Print queues should be named according to their purpose or to refer to the department that uses them, as in ACCTG_QUEUE or CHECK_QUEUE.

Choosing Standard Properties

You should also determine which properties to use for each object and how to format the property values. Look carefully at the lists of properties for all of the objects—users, printers, servers, and so on—and decide which properties will be useful. Then establish a consistent format for each property value.

For example, you may decide to use the Location property to specify the building number on a college campus. Then you should choose how to format the location: Building #17 or B17 or BLDG17. When you follow a consistent format, it will be easy to perform searches, for example, to find users in a certain building.

Creating a Standards Document

In addition to planning the naming standards you will use on your network, it is important to create a *standards document*. This document should describe your company's standards for naming objects and formatting property values. If the network has multiple administrators, they should all receive a copy of the standards document.

Here is what the users portion of the standards document might look like for a typical small company:

User Names: First initial plus last name (e.g., JSMITH). Up to eight characters. If a name is a duplicate, add a middle initial.

Properties to be defined:

Given Name (first name)

Last Name (full last name)

Telephone (include area code)

Title (full title)

Location (building number in this format: BLDG XX)

Implementing NDS

In a new company, you have the opportunity to plan and create an NDS tree structure and allow it to grow with the company. For existing networks, however, it is important to plan the implementation of NDS on the network.

By choosing and planning an *implementation strategy*, you can minimize the impact on users and the network and take advantage of the features of NDS as quickly as possible. The Directory tree structure that you have chosen will determine the best implementation strategy.

Implementing NDS by Department or Division

The *departmental*, or *divisional*, implementation strategy is the most common. Each department, or division, (location, workgroup, and so on) implements NDS separately, even if the ultimate plan calls for merging them into a global organization.

This strategy uses a separate Directory tree for each division or department. These trees can eventually be merged together to provide the global benefits of NDS. (The actual merging process is described later in this chapter.)

When this implementation strategy is used, directory trees should be designed so that merging at a later date will be simple. Three divisional Directory trees created with merging in mind are shown in Figure 11.8.

You should follow these guidelines when creating Directory trees for departments or divisions:

- Each tree should include an extra Organizational Unit object at the top. This extra object makes it easy to move the division when it becomes part of a larger tree.

- Each tree must use a unique tree name (assigned during installation).

- Each tree must include a uniquely named Organization object at the top of the tree because these objects will become part of the same tree when they are merged.

FIGURE 11.8
Three Directory trees
created with the
intention of merging
them into a single
tree later.

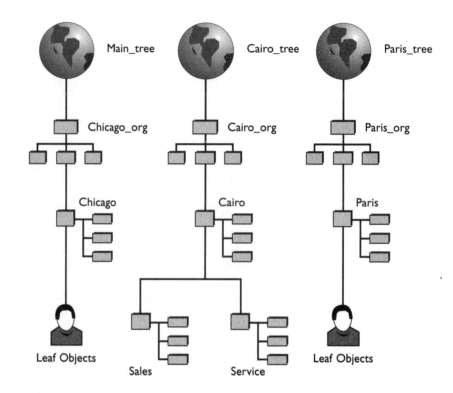

Figure 11.9 shows what the Directory trees in Figure 11.8 might look like after merging. Because we used the extra Organizational Unit object, it becomes easy to reorganize the merged tree and eliminate the unneeded Organization objects, as shown in Figure 11.10.

When separate trees have been created for divisions, you do not necessarily need to merge them. It is possible to keep separate Directory trees on the network, as long as they have different names. However, separate trees have the following disadvantages:

- It is impossible to manage all of the trees from a single login. The administrator can manage the trees from a central location but must log in separately to each tree to manage its resources.

- Users who require access to resources in different trees will need to log in to a single tree and attach to the rest through Bindery Services.

FIGURE 11.9
After merging,
the divisional Directory
trees become part of a
single tree.

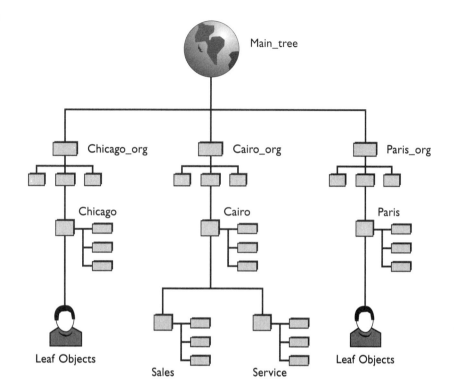

Both of these disadvantages stem from the fact that the NetWare client allows only one NDS attachment at a time. Although you lose the global advantages of NDS, multiple trees may be a practical solution for companies that have separate administrators for each location and require little communication between locations.

Implementing NDS for the Entire Organization

The *organizational* approach is the other method for implementing NDS. This method is a bit drastic—you create a tree structure for the entire organization at once. This is also referred to as the *top-down* or *all-at-once* strategy.

In an ideal world, this would be the best way to implement NDS. It immediately gives you the full benefits of a global Directory structure. However, it is rarely practical. In order to implement NDS across the entire organization, the following circumstances are required:

- There must be full connectivity between locations, via a LAN or WAN.

FIGURE 11.10
The merged tree can be
reorganized into a better
structure.

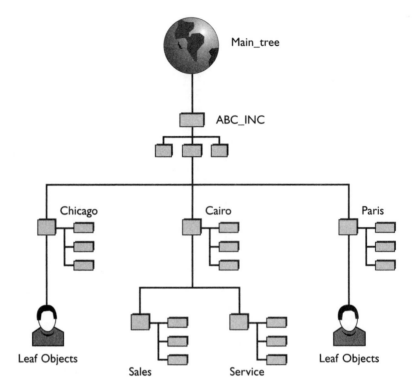

- All network administrators must be available to plan and implement the changes.

- The Directory tree structure for the entire organization must be planned at one time.

Combining Implementation Strategies

When the organizational approach is not practical, a combination of the two strategies may be the best solution. A central tree structure can be created for the entire organization, and individual departments or divisions can be created with their own trees. You can merge these trees with the central tree when they are ready. See Figure 11.11 for an example of this type of implementation strategy.

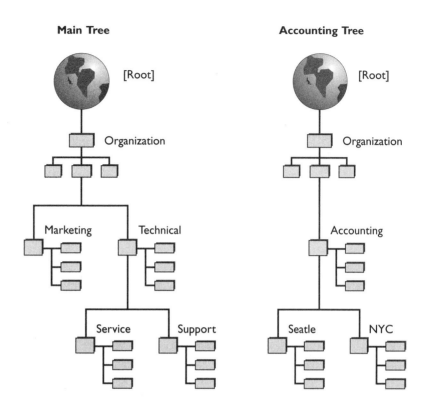

FIGURE 11.11
A department can be
given a separate tree,
which can be merged with
the central tree later.

Main Tree

Accounting Tree

Partitioning and Replicating Your Directory Tree

B ECAUSE THE DIRECTORY can grow to include a large amount of information, Novell lets you divide it into smaller units. These units,
called *partitions*, can then be *replicated* onto other servers. Because
of this ability to be divided and distributed across multiple servers, NDS is
referred to as a *distributed database*.

*Novell's choices of terminology can be confusing. Not only are there disk directories and an
NDS Directory, but there are also disk partitions and NDS partitions, which are two different things. The word partition is used exclusively for NDS partitions in this chapter.*

NDS, when distributed, appears to network users as a completely unified structure without separations. The partitions may break limbs off the Directory tree and spread them about, but to the network user, the tree still appears and functions as a single cohesive Directory.

Partitioning the Directory

In NDS, a *partition* is a branch of the Directory tree. When you install NetWare 4.1, it creates a single partition, which includes the [Root] object and all other objects, as shown in Figure 11.12.

FIGURE 11.12
The [Root] partition is created in the installation process.

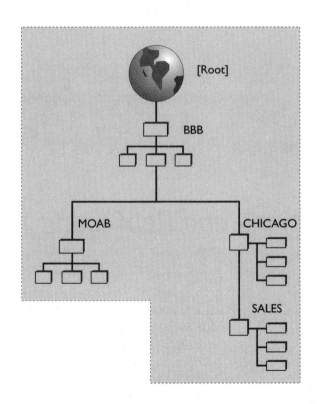

Partitions are made up of container objects, under which leaf objects are kept together as a group. Leaf objects are always kept in the same partition as the container object that holds them. The partition is named after the parent object.

Partitions are referred to as *parent* or *child* partitions, depending on their relationship to other partitions. A partition that resides above another is called the parent partition; the one below it is called the child. This relationship is illustrated in Figure 11.13.

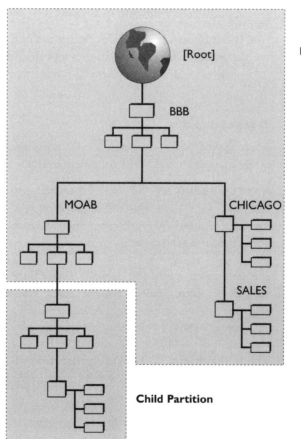

Replicating the Directory

Each partition can be copied and stored on any NetWare 4.1 server on your network. This process is called *replication* and is useful for two main reasons:

- It establishes greater fault tolerance. By storing copies of partitions on multiple servers, you can help ensure that access to your Directory will remain intact, even if a disk crashes or servers go down. Also, you will give users greater freedom to log in without being dependent on one particular server's availability to provide authentication, since a replica can fulfill this role in place of the original partition.

- It can improve network performance. If users need to use a WAN link to access Directory information, you can decrease response time and network traffic by providing a replica that they can access locally.

Types of Replicas

There are four different types of NDS replicas. Each is used for a particular purpose, as described in the following sections.

MASTER REPLICAS NetWare 4.1 creates a *master replica* when a partition is defined. This replica controls all partition operations, including creating, merging, and moving partitions. The master replica also controls replica creation, deletion, and repair.

The term replica can be a bit confusing. Even if there is only one copy of a partition, it is still called a replica. If there is only one replica, it must be a master replica.

There can be only one master replica for each partition. When objects are changed in a master replica, the same change automatically occurs on all replicas of that partition. The server that stores the master replica of a partition must be accessible before you can split the partition (create a new partition) or join it with another partition.

READ/WRITE REPLICAS Read/write replicas contain the same information as the master replica, but each partition may have multiple read/write replicas. Changes made to these replicas will also be reproduced automatically on all other replicas of the same partition. Read/write replicas, however, cannot be used when splitting or joining a partition.

If your network loses a master replica, you can change one of the read/write replicas to master replica status. Read/write replicas support the login process by providing authentication.

READ-ONLY REPLICAS Read-only replicas are used on servers where reads of the partition are necessary, but writes are to be prevented. Because read-only replicas do not support the authentication process, they have limited usefulness.

These replicas contain the same information as the master and read/write replicas but do not allow for alteration of objects. You can use them for searching and viewing objects. They can also be useful as backup replicas.

Use a master or read/write replica on servers on which users will be using Bindery Services. A read-only replica will not work because Bindery Services requires a writable replica. What's Bindery Services? Turn to Chapter 13 for the answer.

SUBORDINATE REFERENCE REPLICAS You do not create subordinate reference replicas. NDS creates these replicas automatically. Subordinate references do not contain object data; they point to a replica that does. They do not support user authentication, object management, or even object viewing.

NDS creates subordinate references on a server when a replica of a partition appears on that server without a replica of that partition's child. A subordinate reference is simply a "pointer" describing the location of the child partition or its replica.

Subordinate references provide efficient access to relevant portions of the NDS database on each server. NDS automatically removes the subordinate reference if the child partition's replica is added to the server.

Guidelines for Placing Replicas

You should consider many factors when deciding where to place the replicas on your network. These factors are discussed in the following sections.

PLACE REPLICAS STRATEGICALLY To maximize fault tolerance and access to replicas without compromising network efficiency, place replicas on servers located near the users who will be using them regularly. This will allow access to replicas without unnecessary traffic across WAN links.

Novell recommends creating three or more replicas for each partition to ensure fault tolerance. Each server used for Bindery Services must contain a master or read/write replica that contains the bindery context.

DON'T CREATE UNNECESSARY PARTITIONS To minimize problems with subordinate references, create as few partitions as possible. Avoid too many replicas of the [Root] partition because this partition tends to have many child partitions. Since a child partition or a subordinate reference must accompany its replica wherever it appears, the [Root] partition can create a lot of subordinate references, which can increase network traffic unnecessarily.

While you should avoid making too many replicas of the [Root] partition, you do need to replicate it at least once. If you fail to replicate it at all, you are taking a dangerous risk. You need the [Root] partition to access the Directory tree.

REPLICAS CAN DECREASE NETWORK PERFORMANCE The NDS database remains consistent by transmitting any change made to an object in a partition to all replicas of that partition. This process is known as *Directory synchronization*.

Directory synchronization takes place across *replica rings*. A replica ring is the group of servers that hold copies of a partition. Each partition has a Replica property. The values for any one partition's Replica property list the servers in the replica ring.

Because Directory synchronization requires that every replica be updated to reflect any changes to any object, a considerable amount of communication is required between NetWare 4.1 servers. This communication does not usually become a major consideration on LANs, because most LANs have plenty of bandwidth available. However, the extra bandwidth needed for this communication does become a concern on WAN links where bottlenecks can occur.

Be careful with subordinate references. When you change a partition that has a subordinate reference, make sure the subordinate reference is accessible before making the change. If the subordinate reference is located on the other side of an unstable connection, such as some types of WAN links, you could be creating a potential problem if the data in the subordinate reference cannot be updated to match the master.

Default Partitions and Replicas

When the first server is installed, NDS creates and stores a single partition on that server's SYS: volume. The next server installed into the existing NDS tree simply expands the partition. The third and fourth servers receive a read/write replica of the partition. Servers installed after that do not receive any replicas by default.

Replicas in Merged NDS Trees

When two or more Directory trees are merged, the *source* tree servers (servers of trees that are being merged into the [Root] of another tree) that hold replicas of their [Root] partition are given a read/write replica of the new [Root] partition unless they already hold a replica of it. They also receive subordinate references to the child partitions of the new [Root] partition.

The servers of the *target* tree (the tree whose [Root] remains as the [Root]) receive subordinate references to the uppermost level partitions in the source trees if the target tree servers currently hold replicas of the [Root] partition.

Using Time Synchronization

BECAUSE NDS IS BASED ON a database distributed across multiple servers, all the servers must keep the same time to accurately document changes to files, to order changes made to NDS objects, and for messaging applications.

NDS uses a process called *time stamping* to assign a time to each change in the Directory tree. Changes can be made to an object in the network from any server at any time. Time stamping ensures that these changes are made in the correct order and that all replicas receive the correct information.

Every activity in NDS is documented with a time stamp. Time stamps use UTC time. UTC stands for *Universal Coordinated Time* (the acronym comes from the French). This is the international standard for accurate time. UTC is the new name for *Greenwich Mean Time*, or GMT.

The UTC system is independent of time zones. Because of this, the entire network can have a standard time even if servers are located in parts of the world with different time zones. When you install a server, NetWare 4.1 asks you for a *time zone offset*. NetWare 4.1 then uses this offset to calculate the local time from the network's UTC time. For example, the time offset for Boise, Idaho, is 7:00:00 behind, or seven hours behind UTC. If the time in Boise is 2:00 a.m., UTC time is 9:00 a.m. NetWare also takes Daylight Saving Time into account.

Types of Time Servers

Unfortunately, clocks in computers tend to deviate slightly, so servers can end up with different times. To compensate for this problem, NDS's time synchronization feature uses *time servers* to keep time standardized across the network. Each of the four types of time servers has a specific purpose. The next sections examine each type of time server.

Single Reference Time Server

A *single reference time server* provides a single, authoritative source of time on the network. The first NetWare 4.1 server installed on a network defaults to this configuration.

If you use a single reference time server, you must configure all other servers as secondary time servers. Each secondary time server must receive the time from the single reference server. This configuration is the typical configuration for small networks. Figure 11.14 shows an example of a small network using a single reference time server.

Because the single reference time server never adjusts its clock, you must be sure that its time is set correctly.

Primary Time Servers

Primary time servers negotiate, or "vote," with other primary and reference servers on the network to determine the correct time. If a primary server finds itself to be out of synchronization with the network time, it gradually speeds up or slows down until it is back in synchronization. Since primary time servers work by negotiation, there must be at least one other time source—a reference server or another primary server—on the network.

Primary time servers are frequently used on WANs because they can provide a local time source for secondary time servers and workstations that would otherwise need to cross WAN links for a time source.

The negotiation process of primary time servers ensures that the servers agree on a time, but this time is not guaranteed to be accurate. In situations where accurate time is important, you should use a reference time server along with one or more primary servers. Figure 11.15 shows a typical primary time server arrangement.

FIGURE 11.14
A single reference time server is the only source of time on its network.

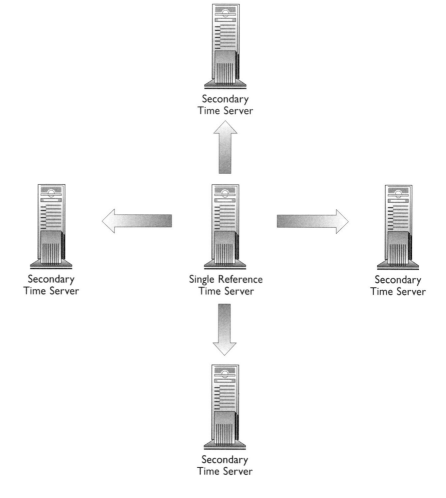

Secondary
Time Server

Secondary
Time Server

Single Reference
Time Server

Secondary
Time Server

Secondary
Time Server

Secondary Time Servers

A *secondary time server* provides the time to client workstations but not to any other servers. When you install a new server on a network that already has a NetWare 4.1 server, the new server will default to being a secondary time server.

Secondary time servers do not participate in the voting process to determine the correct time. They get time information from a primary or single reference time server. You must define at least one primary server, or a single reference server, before you can configure a server as a secondary time server.

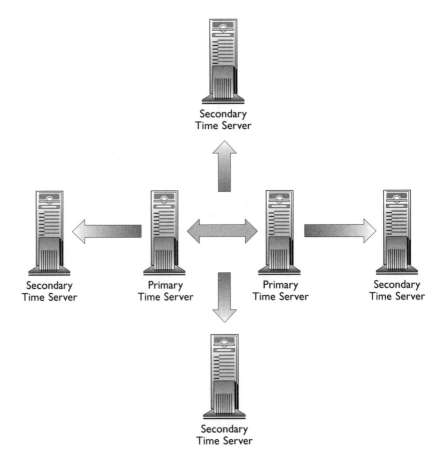

Secondary
Time Server

Secondary
Time Server

Primary
Time Server

Primary
Time Server

Secondary
Time Server

Secondary
Time Server

Reference Time Servers

A *reference time server* is the final piece of the puzzle. It is usually attached to an external time source. This could be an accurate hardware clock or a modem or radio link to a reliable time source, such as the Rugby Atomic Clock or the U.S. Naval Observatory.

Although the reference time server will adjust its time to match the external source, it does not adjust its clock in the negotiation process. When primary time servers negotiate the network time, the reference server's time is considered an accurate source; the primary servers eventually correct themselves to match that time. If you use a reference server, you must configure at least one primary time server. Figure 11.16 shows a network arrangement using primary and reference time servers.

Reference, single reference, and primary time servers are called time sources or time providers. Secondary time servers are called time consumers.

Methods of Time Synchronization

You can choose to install time synchronization in either the default configuration or a custom configuration. The default configuration will work well in most single-location networks. For larger networks and networks with multiple locations, a custom configuration will be more efficient.

FIGURE 11.16
A reference time server is usually attached to an external time source.

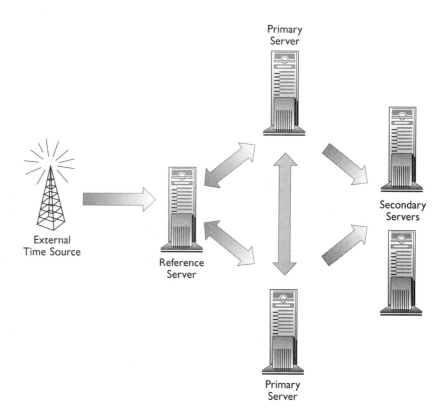

Default Configuration

The default time synchronization configuration uses one single reference time server to provide the time to all servers on the network. The first server installed will be the single reference time server. All other servers on the network are configured as secondary time servers when they are installed.

In the default configuration, the single reference server broadcasts time information using the *Service Advertising Protocol* (SAP), a standard NetWare communication protocol. SAP is an effective means of communication. However, because SAP packets are broadcast to the entire network, using SAP will increase traffic on your network, particularly over WAN links.

NetWare 4.1 provides this default method to simplify installation and to enable network administrators to set up a network without necessarily understanding the complexities of the time synchronization process. This strategy can be effective, but it has the following disadvantages:

- The single reference time server is a *single point of failure*. If this server goes down, all other servers will lose their source of synchronized time. One of the other servers can take over as the single reference server, but you must arrange this manually with a SET command at the server.

- All servers in the network will need to contact the single reference server frequently to receive the current time. This activity adds traffic to the network, particularly if servers are at opposite ends of a WAN link. Worse, if a server loses its connection to the single reference server, it will also lose time synchronization.

- Because each server is not given a specific list of time servers to receive time from, any server that claims to be a single reference time server will be used. This means that if a server is accidentally configured as a time provider, the network will end up with conflicting sources of time.

Custom Configuration

Using a custom configuration, you can optimize time synchronization on your network. You'll need to plan your custom configuration, using the right combination of primary, secondary, and reference time servers to minimize network traffic.

Don't use custom configurations unless you really need to because they require careful planning and maintenance. The default configuration is usually sufficient for a small company or department.

Custom configurations require you to create a file, TIMESYNC.CFG, at each server to specify time sources. Each time you add a new time source to the network, you will need to update each of those TIMESYNC.CFG files. NetWare does not provide a centralized method for maintaining these files.

PLANNING A CUSTOM CONFIGURATION When you are creating a plan for custom time synchronization, the main factors to consider are the physical location of servers and the speed of network connections between them. Here are some general rules to follow:

- Create primary time servers (or reference time servers, if you're using them) in major locations.

- Arrange for servers near each primary time server to receive their time from that server.

- Be sure that there are strong network links between each of the primary time servers.

- If you use a reference time server, place it near the network backbone where it can be accessed easily.

Because you use multiple primary and reference servers, or *time sources*, this strategy does not have a single point of failure. As long as network communication lines remain open, servers will have more than one available source of time. This design ensures that no server will lose time synchronization.

You should avoid using more than five primary and reference time servers on a network because the traffic generated by the voting process can slow down the network. For larger networks, you will want to use multiple time provider groups, as described in the next section.

Using Time Provider Groups

A *time provider group* usually consists of a reference time server, one or more primary time servers, and a number of secondary time servers. A simple time provider group was shown in Figure 11.16.

In a large network with many servers communicating across WAN links, single time provider groups are not practical. The voting process used by primary servers adds traffic to the WAN link and is likely to create a bottleneck. In this situation, you should use multiple time provider groups.

If you use multiple time provider groups, it is important to use some form of external time source for synchronization. If each location's reference time server communicates with the same external source (such as a radio time signal), you can keep a consistent time across all locations without adding traffic to the WAN.

An example of a network using multiple time provider groups is shown in Figure 11.17.

Implementing and Managing Time Synchronization

In order to set up and maintain time synchronization on your network, you need to adjust settings on each server. These settings determine what type of time server the server will act as and which server it will use as a time source.

Setting Time Synchronization Parameters

You can use several SET parameters to control your network's time synchronization. These SET commands all begin with SET TIMESYNC, and they are described in Table 11.1. Rather than using the SET command, these settings can be written to the server's TIMESYNC.CFG file. You should use this method unless the change is meant to be temporary.

An easy way to specify SET parameters and save them in the AUTOEXEC.NCF and TIMESYNC.CFG files is to use the SERVMAN utility. This utility is loaded at the server console with the command LOAD SERVMAN.

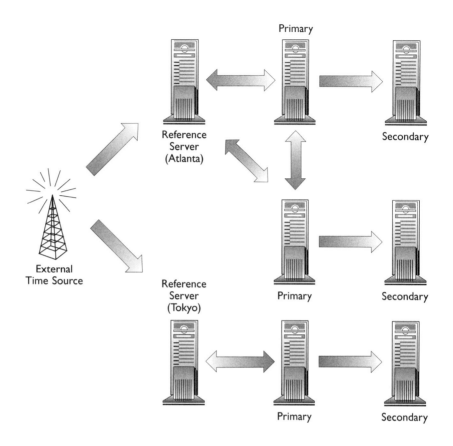

FIGURE 11.17
Multiple time provider
groups should be used on
a larger network.

Creating the TIMESYNC.CFG Files

If you are using a custom configuration, you must create a TIMESYNC.CFG file for each server. This file is located in the server's SYS:SYSTEM directory. The file consists of two parts:

- **Parameters:** These are the parameters listed in Table 11.1. When they are used in the TIMESYNC.CFG file, you do not need to include the SET TIMESYNC command.

- **Time Sources:** This is a list of time sources for a custom configuration. The first server in the list will be polled as a time source. If it is unavailable, the other servers in the list will be tried.

	SET TIMESYNC	
TABLE 11.1 NetWare 4.1 Time Synchronization SET parameters.	**PARAMETER**	**DESCRIPTION**
	Configured Sources	Controls which type of time source is used. If set to ON, you must specify a list of time sources in the TIMESYNC.CFG file. If set to OFF, the SAP protocol is used to listen for a time source.
	Directory Tree Mode	Controls whether SAP packets from other Directory trees are accepted. If set to ON, SAP packets are ignored unless they come from the server's own Directory tree. This parameter prevents time servers on different trees from creating conflicts.
	Hardware Clock	Controls whether the server's hardware clock will be used for time synchronization. This parameter should be set to OFF only if the server will use an external time source.
	Polling Count	Controls how many time packets are exchanged when servers are polled. Increasing this number can create unnecessary traffic. The default is three.
	Polling Interval	Controls how often the server polls other servers. This number defaults to 600 seconds (10 minutes). If you change this, you must use the same setting for all servers on the network.
	Service Advertising	Controls whether the SAP protocol will be used to broadcast time. If it is turned off, you must create a list of time sources in the TIMESYNC.CFG file of each server.
	Synchronization Radius	Controls the maximum amount a server's time can be adjusted and still remain in synchronization with other servers. It defaults to 2,000 milliseconds. Increasing this parameter may prevent servers from losing synchronization.
	Type	Determines the type of time server that the server is currently acting as: Reference, Primary, Secondary, or Single Reference.

Here is an example of a TIMESYNC.CFG file. This file is for the server CORP1, which is a primary time server. It negotiates with the servers CORP2 and CORP3 to determine the correct time.

```
#TIMESYNC.CFG for Server CORP1
# (lines beginning with # are comments)
Configured Sources = ON
Directory Tree Mode = ON
Hardware Clock = OFF
Polling Count = 3
Polling Interval = 600
Service Advertising = OFF
Synchronization Radius = 2000
Type = PRIMARY
# Time Sources
Time Source = CORP2
Time Source = CORP3
```

Since time synchronization operates at a lower level than NDS, you can't use NDS utilities to make changes to time synchronization. These changes must be made in the individual TIMESYNC.CFG files for each server.

Starting Synchronization

If you have configured time synchronization correctly, the servers should synchronize with each other as soon as they are brought online. You can verify synchronization by typing the **TIME** command at each server's console. Here is the typical output of the TIME command:

```
Time zone string:"MST7MDT"
DST status: ON
DST start: Sunday, April 17, 1996 2:00 am MST
DST end: Sunday, October 29, 1996 2:00 am MDT
Time synchronization is active.
Time is synchronized to the network.
Sunday, July 2, 1995 3:35:14 am UTC
Saturday, July 1, 1995 9:35:14 pm MDT
```

Check that the message "Time is synchronized to the network" is displayed on each server. If the servers are not synchronized, check the time synchronization settings.

After time synchronization is established, you should avoid changing the time on any server. If the server is a time consumer, your change will be ignored because time is received from the other servers on the network; if it is a time provider, a change will affect the network's time, which could corrupt NDS data.

Merging NDS Trees

F YOU HAVE CREATED MULTIPLE Directory trees for different departments or divisions within your network, you may want to merge them into a single tree. Then you can manage all of the objects from a single Directory. Figures 11.18 and 11.19 show an example of merged directories.

When you merge two Directory trees, objects in the [Root] of one tree (the *source* tree) are moved to the [Root] of the second (*target*) tree. The merge process must be performed at the server that contains the master replica of the source tree.

Use the DSMERGE utility to merge Directory trees. You can load this NLM at the server console.

Merging Considerations

Several conditions must exist before you can begin the merge process. Check all of the following items before you merge the trees.

- All servers that contain a replica of the [Root] partition for either tree must be up and running, and they must be accessible over the network.

- The schema for the trees must be the same. If you have used a product that extends the Directory schema on one tree, you must make the same changes on the other tree.

- The [Root] object of the source tree cannot contain any leaf or Alias objects.

- The trees must have different tree names.

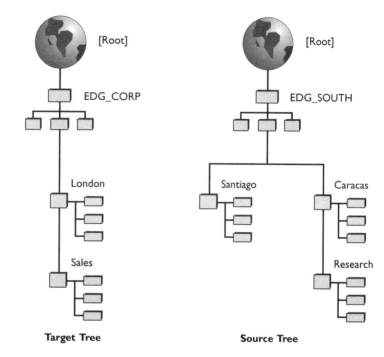

FIGURE 11.18
Two separate Directory trees before merging.

Target Tree

Source Tree

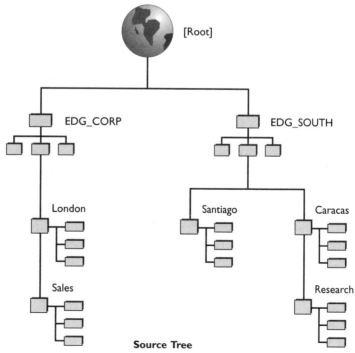

FIGURE 11.19
When directories are merged, the organizations are combined under one [Root] object.

Source Tree

- The servers containing the [Root] partitions of the trees must be running the same version of NetWare.

- You must have the password for an administrator with access to all objects in each Directory tree.

To protect your data, back up the Directory of both trees before you begin. Most NetWare backup programs include an option to back up NDS information.

Starting the Merge Process

Follow these steps to merge Directory trees:

1. Start the DSMERGE utility by typing **LOAD DSMERGE** at the server console. You must do this on the server containing the master replica of the source tree. The main DSMERGE screen is shown in Figure 11.20.

2. Select the Check time synchronization option. You will see a list of servers and their time synchronization status. The difference in times (Time Delta) must be under two seconds for all servers in both trees. You may need to change each server to use the same time source.

FIGURE 11.20
The DSMERGE utility allows you to merge Directory trees.

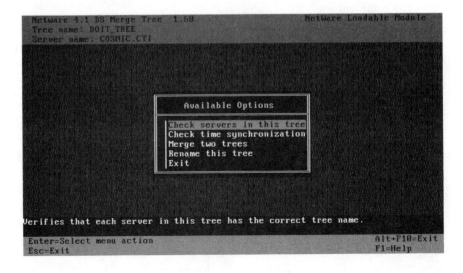

3. Select the Merge two trees option. The source tree is set to the server's tree automatically. Fill in the destination tree and provide an administrator name and password for each tree, as shown in Figure 11.21.

4. Press F10 to perform the merge. The merge process may take quite a while, depending on the number of existing replicas and the speed of your network.

If you wish to merge several trees into a single destination tree, you must merge them one at a time.

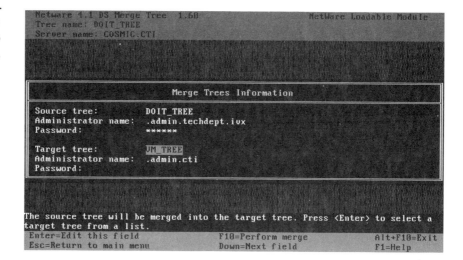

FIGURE 11.21
Enter the information to merge two trees.

Troubleshooting NDS

NDS IS THE MOST IMPORTANT new feature of NetWare 4. Not surprisingly, it is also the most common source of problems with NetWare 4.1 servers. In the following sections, you will learn how to avoid some of the most common NDS problems and how to correct them when they do happen.

In a large organization where time is critical, you may want to avoid troubleshooting yourself and go straight to Novell technical support or your local NetWare reseller or consulting company. The time you save is usually worth the expense.

Avoiding NDS Problems

There is no way to avoid all NDS problems. In fact, if you deal with a NetWare 4.1 server for any length of time, you will undoubtedly need to handle several problems. However, most common NDS problems can be avoided with a bit of planning. Here are some tips to keep NDS running smoothly:

- Always keep at least three replicas for each partition. We've mentioned this essential bit of housekeeping before, but we can't stress it enough. If a replica is lost, even if it's the master replica, it can be restored if another replica is available.

- Use your standard backup software to make frequent backups of the NDS database. The frequency depends on how often changes are made in your network, but you should perform the backup at least once a week. Many backup programs will back up NDS data automatically along with the other data.

- Use a single workstation to manage NDS partitions—when you are splitting partitions, merging partitions, or moving container objects. This plan makes it easy to keep track of the changes you have made and to avoid inconsistencies. Otherwise, conflicting messages can be received from different locations in the network, causing NDS corruption.

- Never let any server's SYS volume run out of space. The NDS database is kept in a hidden directory on the SYS volume. If the volume runs out of space, no changes can be made to NDS and the server loses synchronization with other replicas. To be safe, keep at least 50MB free at all times. If possible, keep space-consuming data, such as print queues, on a volume other than SYS.

- Use DSREPAIR (described later in this chapter) to check synchronization before performing any complicated NDS operations. This includes merging partitions, splitting partitions, and moving a container object. (It is also a good idea to make a backup copy of NDS immediately before performing any of these operations.)

Managing NDS Inconsistencies

NDS is a distributed database; each change you make to NDS begins at the replica where you make the change and is passed to each of the other servers that contains a replica. Depending on communication delays, network use, and the complexity of the change, allow anywhere from 10 seconds to an hour or two for all replicas to receive the change.

Fortunately, NDS was designed to deal with this time requirement. The NDS database is *loosely consistent*, which means that it remains functional even if replicas do not have exactly the same information. You may notice these inconsistencies, but they do not necessarily represent a problem with NDS.

The process that NDS uses to send information between replicas is called *synchronization*. Two replicas are synchronized if they contain exactly the same information. In a busy network, the synchronization process is happening constantly to update the latest changes. The exact process depends on the type of change.

Simple changes, such as adding a User object or changing a property, are synchronized quickly. All that is required is to send updates to each server that has a replica of the partition where the object is located. Creating a partition is also a relatively simple task.

Complex changes include joining partitions, moving partitions, and merging Directory trees. These changes require updates to multiple partitions, and each server with a replica of any one of the partitions must be contacted to send updates. These changes can take a long time.

Symptoms of NDS Problems

Although some inconsistencies between NDS replicas are normal, severe inconsistencies may indicate a corrupt NDS database or another problem. Here are the symptoms you should watch for:

- Changes made to an NDS object or its rights seem to disappear.

- An object or its properties change unexpectedly. For example, a user can no longer log in because the password is incorrect, but the user has not changed the password.

- Errors may be inconsistent. For example, a user may be able to log in after several attempts.

- Unknown objects, shown with a question mark, appear in the Directory tree. It is normal for these objects to show up when a server has been removed or when a partitioning operation is in progress. However, if they appear without an apparent cause, there may be a problem.

If you notice any of these symptoms or if any part of NDS seems to behave inconsistently, follow the instructions in the following sections to narrow down and correct the problem. If a corrupt Directory is left alone, it will probably become worse. Be sure to follow the troubleshooting advice below as soon as you notice any symptoms.

Checking NDS Synchronization

If the problems you are having with NDS are not severe, you should let the servers run for a few hours before attempting any repairs. NDS double-checks itself, and it may repair the problem automatically. Do not take any servers down, because doing so prevents NDS from synchronizing and correcting errors.

If the problem still occurs, you should check the synchronization of the server. You can use the DSREPAIR and DSTRACE utilities to accomplish this, as described in the following sections.

USING DSREPAIR TO CHECK SYNCHRONIZATION DSREPAIR is a versatile utility that can be used to solve many NDS problems. You can use one of the functions of DSREPAIR to check the synchronization of replicas on the network. You should do this if you suspect a problem in NDS. In addition, you should check the synchronization before performing a major operation, such as merging trees, splitting partitions, joining partitions, or moving a container object.

To use this function of DSREPAIR, follow these steps:

1. Start the DSREPAIR utility by typing **LOAD DSREPAIR** at the server console.

2. Select Replica Synchronization.

3. Enter a full distinguished name for the administrator and password. These will be used by DSREPAIR to log in to NDS. DSREPAIR will check synchronization for all replicas and display a log file, as shown in the example in Figure 11.22.

4. Examine the DSREPAIR log file. If OK appears next to each server, the server is fully synchronized.

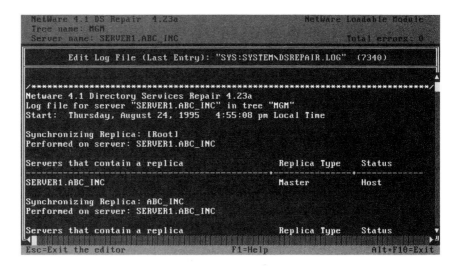

FIGURE 11.22

The DSREPAIR synchronization log displays synchronization status for all servers.

USING THE DSTRACE PARAMETER DSTRACE is a special SET parameter that can be used to monitor the activities of NDS. Information is displayed each time NDS replicas are synchronized. This information can be helpful when you are diagnosing an NDS problem. The output of DSTRACE will tell you whether synchronization is successful and if any replicas cannot be reached.

To start tracing NDS, type this command at the server console:

```
SET DSTRACE = ON
```

Press ALT+ESC at the server console to switch from the console prompt to the Directory Services Trace screen, shown in Figure 11.23.

You can leave DSTRACE running and check the screen periodically for problems. One of the most common problems will produce this message:

```
SYNC: End sync of partition name. All processed = NO.
```

If NO is displayed here and the message keeps repeating after each synchronization attempt, NDS has a serious problem. You should run the DSREPAIR utility, as described in the next section.

When you no longer need the DSTRACE screen, at the server console type:

```
SET DSTRACE = OFF
```

FIGURE 11.23
The DSTRACE screen displays information each time NDS replicas are synchronized.

```
Directory Services
(95/08/24 16:58:27)
SYNC: Start sync of partition <[Root]> state:[0] type:[0]
SYNC: End sync of partition <[Root]> All processed = YES.

(95/08/24 16:58:27)
SYNC: Start sync of partition <ABC_INC> state:[0] type:[0]
SYNC: End sync of partition <ABC_INC> All processed = YES.

(95/08/24 16:58:27)
SYNC: Start sync of partition <Western.ABC_INC> state:[0] type:[0]
SYNC: End sync of partition <Western.ABC_INC> All processed = YES.

(95/08/24 16:58:34)
SYNC: Start sync of partition <[Root]> state:[0] type:[0]
SYNC: End sync of partition <[Root]> All processed = YES.

(95/08/24 16:58:34)
SYNC: Start sync of partition <ABC_INC> state:[0] type:[0]
SYNC: End sync of partition <ABC_INC> All processed = YES.

(95/08/24 16:58:34)
SYNC: Start sync of partition <Western.ABC_INC> state:[0] type:[0]
SYNC: End sync of partition <Western.ABC_INC> All processed = YES.
```

Repairing NDS Problems

Once you have determined that there is a problem in the NDS database, you should take action to repair it. The next sections describe three ways to do this. You should try the DSREPAIR utility first. The second option, forcing replica synchronization, is a more drastic action. As a last resort, an NDS backup can be restored.

USING THE DSREPAIR UTILITY The DSREPAIR utility provides several options for repairing NDS problems. These are listed on the utility's Available Options menu, shown in Figure 11.24. The most useful of these is Unattended Full Repair. When you select this option, NetWare scans the NDS database for errors and repairs the errors if possible. The other options allow you to perform specific steps for troubleshooting, which may be useful if the Unattended Full Repair option fails or if you are troubleshooting a specific problem.

Before you run DSREPAIR, make a backup copy of NDS using your backup software. If the NDS database becomes corrupted further, you may lose information on all replicas. Since there may be errors in the database, do not overwrite an older backup if you have one.

After DSREPAIR has finished scanning the database, it displays a log file. This log lists the tasks that were performed and problems that were found and corrected. Examine the log carefully and make sure that any errors were repaired.

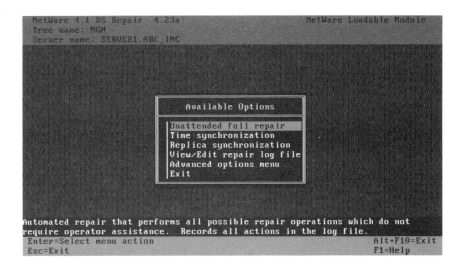

Although DSREPAIR can repair most NDS corruption, you may lose some of the information. After DSREPAIR has finished its work, use NetWare Administrator (NWADMIN) to look at the Directory tree and make sure that all its objects are intact.

FORCING SYNCHRONIZATION If DSREPAIR is unable to repair the problems you are having with NDS, you may want to try forcing synchronization. This option will send updates from the master replica to all other replicas.

If you force synchronization, you may lose changes to NDS that were made at a replica other than the master. Make a backup copy of NDS before proceeding.

Follow these steps to force synchronization using the NWADMIN utility:

1. Start the Partition Manager utility from within NWADMIN.

2. Click the Replicas button.

3. Highlight the master replica.

4. Click the Send Updates button and confirm the choice.

Updates will be sent to all other replicas. This process may take several minutes, and it will cause a lot of traffic on the network.

After the update process is completed, load DSREPAIR at the server and use the Unattended Full Repair option again. If there are still NDS errors that DSREPAIR cannot fix, you will need to restore a backup.

RESTORING AN NDS BACKUP As a last resort, you can restore NDS from a backup. Assuming the backup was performed before the NDS problems began, this process should permit a full recovery. Note the date of the backup. If you have made changes to NDS (such as creating users or changing rights) since that date, you must reenter them after restoring the backup.

To restore NDS, first use the Partition Manager or PARTMGR utility to delete all replicas for the partition. Then restore the partition data using your backup software to create a new master replica. You can then re-create the other replicas.

Be sure all users in the Directory tree are logged out of the network when you back up or restore NDS data. Do not bring down any servers, however.

Managing Server Downtime

At one time or another, your file server will go down. You might take it down to perform maintenance or reset the server, or it may go down unexpectedly because of a hardware or software problem. Because of NDS, you should be careful in these situations. The following sections discuss how to deal with planned and unplanned downtime, as well as how to remove a server permanently.

PLANNED DOWNTIME From time to time, you will need to take the server down for maintenance. This usually will not cause a problem with NDS. Once NDS notices that the server is down, other servers that need to send updates to a replica on that server will keep trying until the server comes back up. When you bring the server up, it may take several minutes to resynchronize the replicas.

If you are going to take down the server that contains the master replica for a partition, you may need to set up another master replica. If the downtime will be brief, another master should not be required. For extended periods (several hours to a day or more), you should change another replica to master status. This reassignment will allow changes to be made to NDS objects in the partition without the use of the server that is down.

If you are bringing a server down for an extended period, you should remove any replicas that are on the server first. This temporary removal will avoid the large amount of traffic resulting from other servers trying to contact the server that is down. After you bring the server back up, you can re-create the replicas.

UNPLANNED DOWNTIME A hardware or software problem can cause a server to go down unexpectedly. If this happens, diagnose the problem. If you can bring the server up within an hour or two and the hard disk containing the SYS volume is undamaged, NDS will resynchronize and there should not be any problems.

If you have lost the SYS volume on the server, you will need to reinstall NetWare 4.1 on the server. All replicas on the server will be lost. Follow these steps to restore the server:

1. Delete the Server object and Volume objects from the NDS tree. You must use the PARTMGR or Partition Manager utility to delete a Server object.

2. If the server that crashed contained the master replica, change one of the read/write replicas to master status.

3. Fix the hardware problem and reinstall NetWare 4.1 as if it were a new server. Install the server into the same Directory tree.

4. Restore a backup of the data (not NDS) onto the server.

5. Create any replicas that are needed on the server.

6. Check the synchronization of replicas before proceeding further (use DSMERGE, as described in this chapter).

7. If the server contained the master replica, reassign it as the master replica if desired. Change the status of the server that you changed in step 2 back to a read/write replica.

REMOVING A SERVER PERMANENTLY If a server is no longer needed and you wish to remove it permanently, follow these steps:

1. Remove any replicas on the server.

2. Change another server's read/write replica to master status if any master replicas were stored on the server.

3. Bring the server down.

4. Delete the Server and Volume NDS objects. To delete the Server object, you must use the PARTMGR or Partition Manager utility.

Review

THE ADVANCED FEATURES OF NDS include designing an effective tree organization, partitioning and replicating the NDS database, merging (combining) NDS trees, time synchronization, and troubleshooting NDS.

NDS Tree Design and Implementation

In order to take advantage of the features of NDS, you will need a well-designed Directory tree. Factors you should consider in your design include administration, network topology, Bindery Services, and tree depth.

There are several possible strategies for organizing your NDS tree:

- The *default organization* places all objects under a single Organization object, under the [Root].

- A *divisional* organization places divisions or departments of the company in branches of the tree.

- A *locational* organization divides the company into geographical locations.

- A *workgroup* organization groups users who perform the same tasks or projects.

- A *hybrid* organization combines two or more of the above strategies.

The next step in planning your network's Directory tree is to create the standards that will be used in choosing object names and properties:

- Choose the naming scheme for each type of object.

- Decide which properties will be defined and in what format.

- Create a *standards document* describing the plan.

Strategies for implementing NDS are related to the types of organization used:

- The *departmental* or *divisional* implementation implements NDS separately for each department, division, location, or workgroup.

- The *organizational* approach organizes and implements NDS for the entire organization at once.

- A *combined* approach combines these two options.

NDS Partitions and Replicas

The Directory can be divided into *partitions*. Each partition can be *replicated* on one or more servers. A partition consists of a container object and the objects within it. The partition is given the name of the container. The [Root] partition is the only partition in a new NDS installation.

There are four types of replicas:

- NetWare 4.1 creates a *master replica* when a partition is defined. A partition can have only one master replica.

- *Read/write replicas* contain the same data as the master replica. A partition can have multiple read/write replicas. Changes made to a read/write replica will be copied to the master replica.

- *Read-only replicas* allow access to NDS data but do not allow changes.

- NetWare automatically creates *subordinate references*. These replicas point to children of a partition that are not located on the server.

Time Synchronization

NDS's time synchronization feature uses *time servers* for keeping time standardized across the network. There are four types of time servers:

- A *single reference time server*, when used, is the only source of time. All other servers must be secondary servers.

- *Primary time servers* negotiate, or "vote," with other primary servers to determine the time.

- *Secondary time servers* receive the time from a primary or single reference time server and give the time to clients.

- *Reference time servers* are used with primary time servers and are usually attached to a hardware or remote time source.

Directory Tree Merging

When you merge two Directory trees, objects in the [Root] of one tree (the *source* tree) are moved to the [Root] of the second (*target*) tree. The merge process must be performed at the server that contains the master replica of the source tree. You use the DSMERGE utility to merge Directory trees.

Before you can begin the merge process, all servers that contain a replica of the [Root] partition for either tree must be up and accessible over the network. The schema for the trees must be the same. The trees must have different tree names. The servers containing the [Root] partitions of the trees must be running the same version of NetWare.

Troubleshooting

Most of the problems encountered in NDS deal with *synchronization*, the process of sending updates between replicas in the server. NDS can handle some loss of synchronization, but if a serious problem occurs, you must repair it. The following tools can help you determine if there is a problem:

- Check for symptoms of NDS problems, such as inconsistent behavior and unexpected changes to objects.

- Use DSREPAIR to check the synchronization of replicas.

- Use DSTRACE to display messages about NDS synchronization and detect problems as they occur.

When you have determined that there is a problem, you should act to fix it as soon as possible. You should try the following options to repair NDS corruption:

1. Use the Unattended Full Repair option of the DSREPAIR server utility to fix most problems automatically.

2. If DSREPAIR is unsuccessful, try to send updates from the master replica using the Partition Manager.

3. As a last resort, you can restore from an NDS backup.

Server downtime requires special consideration because of NDS. If you are bringing a server down for an extended period, you should first remove any replicas that are on the server. If it contains a master replica, set up another master replica on another server. If you have lost the SYS volume on a server that went down because of a hardware or software problem, you will need to reinstall NetWare 4.1 on the server.

Advanced NetWare Management

A S YOU HAVE LEARNED in the previous chapters, there is much more to networking than just accessing files and printers. In this chapter, you will learn about three NetWare management services that are important in NetWare 4.1:

- Internetworking, or connecting multiple servers and networks

- Internationalization, or configuring the server for use in multiple countries

- Messaging, which allows electronic mail to be sent within the network

Internetworking with NetWare 4.1

NTERNETWORKING REFERS TO BUILDING a wide-area network (WAN), metropolitan-area network (MAN), or simple multiserver system by interconnecting multiple local networks. NetWare 4.1 provides comprehensive support for internetworking. NetWare servers on similar networks can be connected and included in the same NDS tree for central management. In addition, the *MultiProtocol Router* (MPR) software included with NetWare 4.1 allows communication between different types of networks.

The MultiProtocol Router (MPR)

A *router* receives packets from a network and sends them to another network. The networks can use different topologies and protocols. Using a router to connect different types of networks is illustrated in Figure 12.1. A router acts as a *translator*, converting data between different topologies and protocols.

Any NetWare server that is connected to more than one network segment acts as a router, sending packets between the two. Therefore, you can construct a multiserver network without any additional hardware or software.

A NetWare server can act as an even better router with the MPR software. The MPR is an intelligent router—it does not simply resend the packets but actually determines the most efficient path and routes the packets for streamlined communication between networks. It can also filter information to avoid sending the information to segments that don't need it. For example, if your network is connected to a larger network, such as the Internet, the MPR could prevent packets intended for local machines from being sent to the other network.

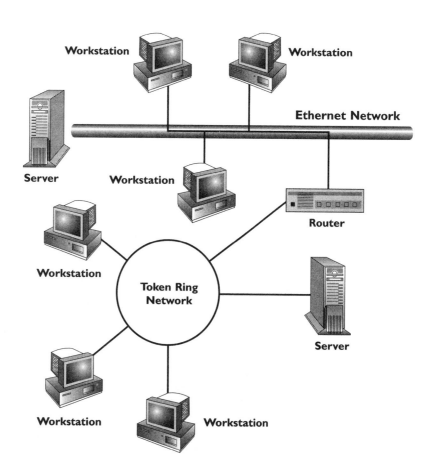

Using INETCFG to Configure MPR

Once MPR is installed, you can configure it with the INETCFG utility. This utility is loaded at the server console and provides a convenient menu for setting up network boards, protocols, and bindings. It can be used to configure protocols (such as AppleTalk or TCP/IP) on the server and to manage the MPR.

You start INETCFG with the screen shown in Figure 12.2. Answer Yes to make the modifications to the server's AUTOEXEC.NCF file that are required for routing and using INETCFG options.

The LOAD and BIND commands in the AUTOEXEC.NCF file are moved into a new file, INITSYS.NCF, which INETCFG makes changes to. This process provides a convenient separation of commands and makes the AUTOEXEC.NCF file smaller and easier to manage.

INETCFG also adds the following commands to the AUTOEXEC.NCF file:

- LOAD CONLOG allows server console messages to be logged to a file to help in debugging.

- INITSYS.NCF executes the commands in the INITSYS.NCF file.

- UNLOAD CONLOG deactivates console logging and keeps the log file from becoming too large. Also, if you don't deactivate logging, the file can be lost, since the console messages are written only when CONLOG unloads.

FIGURE 12.2
INETCFG allows you to move LOAD and BIND commands out of the AUTOEXEC.NCF file.

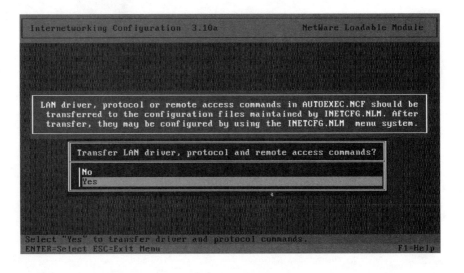

After you have moved commands to the INITSYS.NCF file using INETCFG, you should not add LOAD or BIND commands to the AUTOEXEC.NCF file or try to modify them in this file. You should make the changes using the INETCFG utility. These changes will be written to the INITSYS.NCF file automatically.

After you have accepted INETCFG's offer to modify the configuration files, you'll see the program's main menu, as shown in Figure 12.3. This menu provides the following options for server and router configuration:

- **Boards:** Allows you to configure network boards. When you configure a network board using this option, the appropriate LOAD command for the network board's driver will be added to the server's INITSYS.NCF file automatically.

- **Network Interfaces:** Allows you to configure network boards that provide multiple ports, also called WAN boards. Each port on the board can be set up to use a different protocol.

- **WAN Call Directory:** Defines remote servers that will use PPP (Point-to-Point Protocol) to communicate. This is an extension available for the MPR, which allows easy communication with dial-up networking.

- **Protocols:** Allows you to configure the communications protocols supported by the server. Protocols include IPX, TCP/IP, AppleTalk, RIP, and NLSP.

FIGURE 12.3
The INETCFG utility is used to manage network connections and routers.

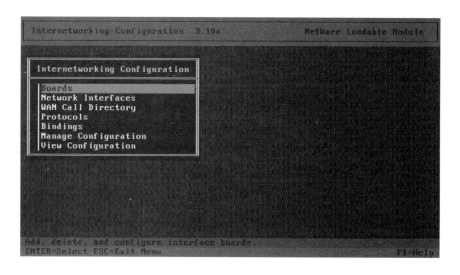

- **Bindings:** Provides the connection between protocols and network boards. This command allows you to choose the protocols that will be used for each board. The BIND commands to perform the binding will be added to the INITSYS.NCF file.

- **Manage Configuration:** Allows you to configure parameters used in routing and communication, including SNMP (Simple Network Management Protocol), remote access, and the INITSYS.NCF file parameters.

- **View Configuration:** Allows you to view the LOAD and BIND commands that are currently used in the server. You can also view error messages that might have been displayed when the server was started.

Using NetWare 4.1's Messaging Services

NETWARE PROVIDES *messaging services*, which are used to send and receive electronic-mail (e-mail) messages. These services are provided by a NetWare component called MHS *(Message Handling Services)*. MHS provides the basic services required for e-mail by storing messages in mailboxes and delivering them to mailboxes for user accounts or other objects.

Although MHS is still included in NetWare 4.1 (and in the CNE tests), Novell is currently de-emphasizing it in favor of GroupWise (formerly WordPerfect Office), a full-scale e-mail package available from Novell for an extra cost. At this writing, Novell has announced that the next release of NetWare will include a version of GroupWise instead of MHS. NetWare 4.1's MHS does not limit the number of user mailboxes you can have. However, you must have available disk storage and an available NetWare 4.1 license connection for each user on the network. The resources you need depend on a variety of factors, including the number of servers on the network and the number of users who access the system concurrently. In general, if you have sufficient network resources for your users, you can add MHS support with only a minor increase in disk space.

Installing MHS Services

MHS can be installed at any time on your NetWare 4.1 server. You can also install it as an option during the server installation process. MHS is not installed by default.

The following sections explain the hardware requirements for running MHS, the steps for installing MHS on an existing server, and the procedure for installing it during the server installation process.

Hardware Requirements

Before installing MHS, be sure that your server meets the hardware requirements for this service:

- An additional 500KB to 4MB of available RAM memory. The server should have an absolute minimum of 12MB total RAM, but most servers require more. If MHS is used heavily on your server, you will need at least 16MB.

- Approximately 2.5MB of disk storage for the MHS software. You will also need disk storage for mailboxes; 5MB per mailbox is a generous estimate. The actual number will depend on the quantity and size of messages sent and received.

- A CD-ROM drive or a network connection to a server with a CD-ROM drive. This is necessary only for installing the MHS software.

Installing MHS on an Existing Server

The process of installing MHS services on a server is actually quite simple. Although MHS is not installed on the server by default, the MHS software is provided on the NetWare 4.1 CD-ROM.

You can install messaging services on an existing NetWare 4.1 server by following these steps:

1. Start the NetWare 4.1 Installation utility by typing **LOAD INSTALL** from the server console.

2. Select Product Options and then select Choose an Item or Product Listed Above to display a list of optional services, as shown in Figure 12.4.

3. Select Install NetWare MHS Services.

4. Enter the path where the MHS software is located. You can specify a local drive or include a server name and volume name if you have mounted the NetWare 4.1 CD-ROM on another server.

5. Assign a user as *Postmaster General*. This user will be able to control all aspects of MHS. You may use ADMIN, or use another administrator, or assign a user as messaging administrator. You can also assign an Organizational Role for this purpose. You can change this assignment later.

6. Enter the password for the user you have chosen and press Enter to continue.

7. Choose the volume on which to install MHS (if you have multiple volumes on the server.) The MHS software will now be installed.

8. Exit the INSTALL utility after the process is complete.

9. Add the command LOAD MHS to the AUTOEXEC.NCF file to start MHS automatically when the server loads.

FIGURE 12.4
Select NetWare MHS from the optional services list to install MHS.

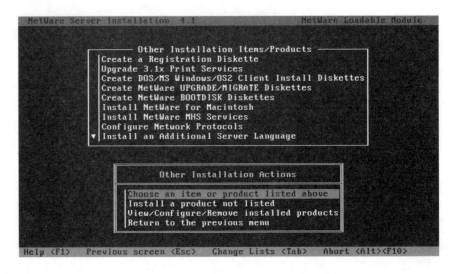

Installing MHS During Server Installation

If you know you will be using MHS on a server, you can install it during the server installation process by using the Custom installation option.

At the end of the installation process, you have a chance to install additional products. Select Choose an Item Listed Above and repeat the instructions in the previous section, starting with step 3.

Controlling MHS with NDS Utilities

Like other NetWare 4.1 services, you can easily manage MHS using NDS utilities. NDS has two types of objects that you can use to manage messaging services:

- The User, Group, Organizational Role, Organization, and Organizational Unit objects have properties related to MHS options.

- Special MHS objects include the Messaging Server, Message Routing Group, Distribution List, and External Entity objects.

Assigning and Managing Mailboxes

The first step in managing MHS is to assign mailboxes. The following objects can have a mailbox assigned to them:

- User

- Group

- Organizational Role

- Organizational Unit

- Organization

To assign a mailbox to a user using NWADMIN, select the User object, choose the Details option from the Object menu, and click the Mailbox button. This page of the Details dialog box, shown in Figure 12.5, includes the user's mail-related properties.

FIGURE 12.5
A user's Mailbox properties control MHS settings for that user.

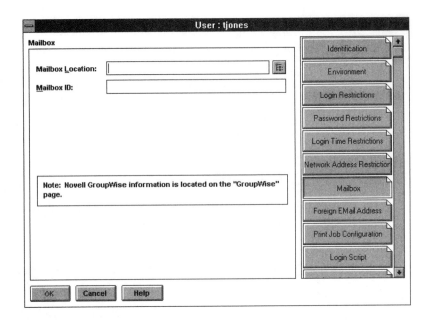

The GroupWise property is intended for use to synchronize MHS mailboxes with Novell's GroupWise. However, this property is not yet supported by GroupWise or MHS.

You can set two properties to manage the user's mailbox:

- **Mailbox Location:** This is the name of the Messaging Server object that holds the user's mailbox.

- **Mailbox ID:** This is the subdirectory on the server that stores messages for the user. If you do not set the Mailbox ID, NetWare assigns a directory based on the user's name.

Groups and Organizational Roles also have a Mailbox Location property. These objects do not have an actual mailbox. Instead, the Messaging Server you select here is used to determine the members of the Group or Organizational Role. Each member receives a copy of the message. For this to work, you will need to create mailboxes for each member of the Group or Organizational Role.

Although you can define a Mailbox Location for an Organization or Organizational Unit, these values are not supported by the current version of MHS. Future versions may use this as a method of sending messages to an entire container.

Special NDS Objects for MHS

In addition to the Mailbox properties of User and Group objects, several special-purpose objects are used for NDS organization and management. These include Messaging Server, Message Routing Group, Distribution List, and External Entity objects. Each of these objects is explained in the following sections.

MESSAGING SERVER When you install MHS services on a server, a *Messaging Server* object is automatically created in the Directory. You cannot create this type of object yourself. The properties of the Messaging Server object include the location of the directory used to store messages (usually \MHS) and the server that is used to process MHS services. This is the server on which you installed MHS.

In addition, you can use the Messaging Server object's properties to manage the users of the e-mail system. From the NWADMIN utility, select the Messaging Server object and then choose Details from the Object menu. Select the Users property category. A list of User and Group Objects with mailboxes defined is displayed. To add a user, click the Add button and select the User or Group object that you wish to create a mailbox for. To delete a User or Group object from the list, select the object and click the Delete button.

MESSAGE ROUTING GROUP When multiple MHS servers are used in the same network, you can allow messages to be transferred between them by using a *Message Routing Group*. This is simply a group of MHS engines that communicate with each other.

When you first install MHS, it creates a default Message Routing Group. If you install MHS on an additional server in the same Directory tree, it will use the same Message Routing Group. If you want existing MHS installations to communicate with each other, simply define the same name in each Message Routing Group's Name property. The properties for a Message Routing Group are shown in Figure 12.6.

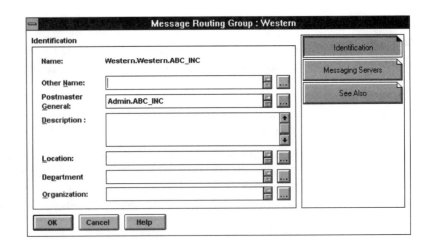

*The current version of NDS supports only one Message Routing Group per Directory tree.
You must use the same group for all messaging servers in the tree.*

DISTRIBUTION LIST You can send the same message to a list of users by using a *Distribution List* object. This object automatically sends the same message to multiple users. You can create a Distribution List object using NWADMIN by following these steps:

1. Select the container in which to store the Distribution List object and then choose Create from the Object menu.

2. Select Distribution List as the type of object to create.

3. Enter a name for the Distribution List and select the Messaging Server to use. Click on the Create button to create the object.

4. Use the Details command from the Object menu to view the Distribution List's properties.

5. Select the Members property category. This screen is shown in Figure 12.7.

6. Add members to the list with the Add button. Members of a Distribution List can be Users, Groups, or other Distribution Lists. The members of the list don't need to reside in the same container; they can be anywhere in the Directory tree.

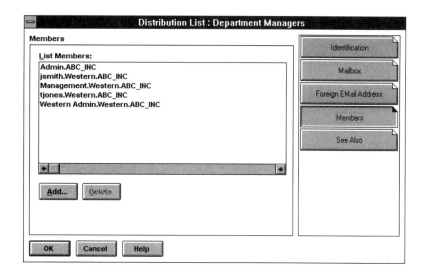

Figure 12.8 illustrates how a message is sent using a Distribution List object. Although you can also use Group objects to send the same message to multiple users, Distribution List objects have several advantages:

- Network traffic is reduced because the Distribution List has its own mailbox. A single message is sent to the Distribution List's mailbox, and the Distribution List then distributes the message to its members.

- Distribution Lists can be *nested*. For example, you could define a Distribution List called Accounting and add the Accounts Payable, Accounts Receivable, and Payroll Distribution List objects as members. Nesting allows you to create convenient groupings of users.

- You can add Group objects to a Distribution List object.

EXTERNAL ENTITY Another special object used for MHS is the *External Entity* object. This object represents an object that can receive mail messages but does not exist in the Directory.

Normally, External Entities are used with e-mail *gateway* software to transfer messages to and from a separate network (such as the Internet). You will usually not need to create these objects because the gateway software will import them for you.

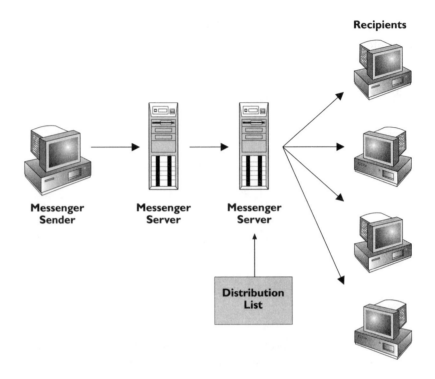

Properties for the External Entity object include information about addressing on the foreign system. These properties are shown in Figure 12.9.

For some gateways, you will need to assign a *foreign e-mail alias* to each object that will send or receive mail through the gateway. These aliases are defined using the External Entity object. The gateway documentation will explain whether you need to assign an alias.

Sending and Receiving Messages

MHS does not allow you to actually create, send, or receive e-mail. You must use an e-mail program to do this. Several MHS-compliant e-mail packages are available. Some other applications, such as word processors, include support for SMF (Simple Message Format) and can forward messages to MHS. NetWare includes a simple MHS application called FirstMail.

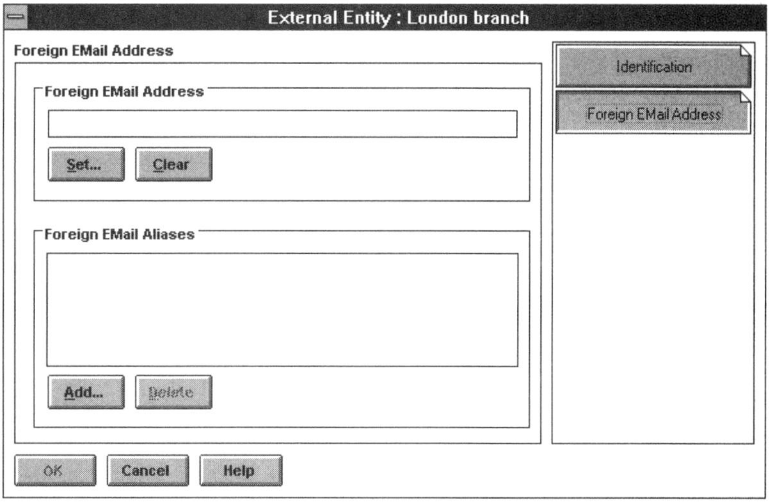

FIGURE 12.9

FIGURE 12.9
An External Entity object sends mail to users outside the Directory tree.

Netware 4.1 includes the Microsoft Windows and DOS versions of FirstMail and installs them in the SYS:PUBLIC directory of the server when you install MHS. The DOS version, shown in Figure 12.10, is MAIL.EXE. The Windows version, shown in Figure 12.11, is WMAIL.EXE.

FIGURE 12.10
The DOS version of FirstMail.

FIGURE 12.11
The Microsoft Windows
version of FirstMail.

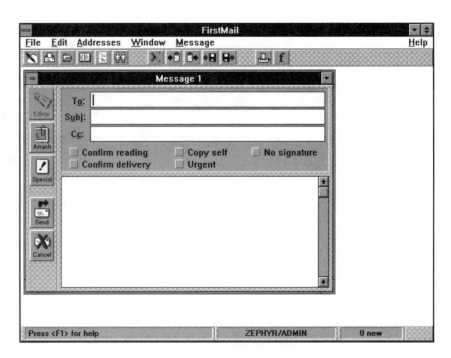

Novell also sells GroupWise, a full-scale e-mail utility as a separate product. It is more sophisticated than FirstMail and also allows complete management through NDS. GroupWise is not MHS-compliant and uses its own message-transport system.

International Features

ETWARE 4.1 PROVIDES MANY FEATURES that make it suitable for use in different countries and languages. The international features of NetWare 4.1 include the following:

- Server utilities, workstation utilities, and system status and error messages can be displayed in the chosen language.

- Numeric formats can be changed for the local country. These include the order of numbers in dates (for example, month/day/year or day/month/year) and times and whether numbers are formatted with commas or periods as thousand separators.

- Unicode support is provided. The ASCII code used for text in computers provides only 256 characters. Many languages, such as Chinese, require many more characters. Unicode is an international standard that uses two bytes per character and allows representation of all characters in these languages.

- File names can use non-English characters, and separators (such as the backslash \) can be replaced with characters that are more appropriate for the local country.

- Support is provided for keyboards other than the standard U.S. English keyboard.

Installing an Alternate Language

When you install a NetWare 4.1 server, you are prompted to choose a language for the server. You can install more than one language.

In order to select an alternate language, you must have a version of NetWare 4.1 that includes support for that language. Be sure that you purchase the international version or a version specific to your language.

You can also add languages to the server at any time using the INSTALL utility:

1. Start the installation utility by typing **LOAD INSTALL** at the server console.

2. Select Product Options.

3. Select Install an Additional Language.

4. Insert the NetWare 4.1 CD-ROM or specify a directory that contains the installation files.

5. Choose the language to install.

Changing the Server's Language

NetWare 4.1 provides complete support for alternate languages by separating messages from the programs. Text displayed by the program (menus, error messages, status reports, and other messages) resides in a separate *message file*, not in the program file (EXE or NLM) itself.

Message files include all of the messages displayed by the utility or NLM. Message files are given the same name as the utility or NLM and are designated with the MSG extension. For example, the message file for the MONITOR utility is MONITOR.MSG.

The NetWare server program itself, SERVER.EXE, has its own message file (SERVER.MSG). By replacing this file with a file for the appropriate language, you can run the server in that language. To make the change, first bring the server down. Then copy the MSG file for the chosen language into the directory where SERVER.EXE is located. The file is found on the NetWare 4.1 CD-ROM under the INSTALL directory in a subdirectory that contains the name of each language. When you bring the server back up, the new language will be in use.

Changing the Server's Keyboard Type

The NetWare 4.1 utility KEYB.NLM selects the type of keyboard used on the server. At the time of this writing, NetWare 4.1 includes keyboard support for U.S. English, French, Italian, German, and Spanish.

To use KEYB, type **LOAD KEYB** followed by the keyboard type. To see a list of valid keyboard types, type **LOAD KEYB** by itself.

Changing the Language for NLMs

You could replace the MSG file for each NLM with the version for the new language, but the task would be difficult and time consuming. Therefore, NetWare provides the LANGUAGE command that you can type at the server console at any time to select a language. Any NLM loaded after you enter the LANGUAGE command will display its messages in that language.

The LANGUAGE command uses a *language designator* to represent each possible language. These numbers range from 0 to 15:

0 French (Canada)

1 Chinese

2 Danish

3 Dutch

4 English

5 Finnish

6 French

7 German

8 Italian

9 Japanese

10 Korean

11 Norwegian

12 Portuguese

13 Russian

14 Spanish

15 Swedish

Although many languages are listed here, Novell has not yet provided support for all of them. At the time of this writing, Novell supports English, French, Italian, German, and Spanish.

Setting a Workstation's Language

Each workstation has an NWLANGUAGE environmental variable. This variable sets the appropriate language when the user at that workstation runs NetWare utilities. You can set the language in the following ways:

- Use the NetWare client software SET command for the language in the STARTNET.BAT file.

- Include a SET NWLANGUAGE = *language* command in the AUTOEXEC.BAT file or type it manually at the DOS prompt.

- Use the DOS SET command in the user, profile, or container login script.

The value of the NWLANGUAGE variable is actually the directory name that the information for that language is stored under. Typical language directory names include ENGLISH, FRENCH, ITALIAN, GERMAN, and SPANISH. For example, the following SET command sets the workstation language to English:

```
SET NWLANGUAGE=ENGLISH
```

Review

N THIS CHAPTER, you have learned about three important network management services available in NetWare 4.1: internetworking, internationalization, and messaging.

Internetworking

Internetworking refers to building a wide-area network (WAN) by interconnecting multiple local networks. A *router* receives packets from a network and sends them to another network. The router can convert the packets between different topologies and protocols.

Any NetWare server can act as a router. The *MultiProtocol Router* (MPR) software allows a server to act as a sophisticated, intelligent router with filtering capabilities. Once MPR is installed, you can configure it with the INETCFG utility. Load this utility at the server console and use it to configure protocols on the server and to manage the MPR.

Messaging

NetWare provides *messaging services*, which are used to send and receive e-mail messages. These services are provided by a NetWare component called MHS (*Message Handling Services*). MHS can be installed at any time on your

NetWare 4.1 server. You can also install it as an option during the server installation process. MHS is not installed by default.

After MHS is installed, you can manage it using NDS utilities. First, assign mailboxes to the appropriate objects (User, Group, or Organizational Role) through the object's Mailbox properties (Mailbox Location and Mailbox ID).

In addition to the Mailbox properties of User, Group, and Organizational Role objects, several special objects are used for MHS: Messaging Server, Message Routing Group, Distribution List, and External Entity objects.

Internationalization

The international features of NetWare 4.1 include the following:

- Server utilities, workstation utilities, and system status and error messages that can be displayed in the chosen language

- Numeric formats that can be changed for the local country

- Support for Unicode—an international standard that allows representation of more characters than ASCII code allows

- File names that can use non-English characters and different separators

- Support for keyboards other than the standard U.S. English keyboard

NetWare 4.1 provides complete support for alternate languages by separating messages from the programs. Text displayed by the program, such as menus and error messages, resides in a separate *message file,* not in the program file. The message files have the MSG extension.

Setting Up and Managing the Workstation

13

ARLIER IN THIS BOOK, you learned the basics of attaching work-stations to the network using the DOS client software. This chapter explains the procedures for installing the DOS client software. In addition, you will learn how to set up OS/2 and Macintosh clients for your NetWare 4.1 network. Finally, we'll explore the use of Bindery Services, which is the versatile NetWare 4.1 feature that allows NetWare 3.1*x* clients and servers to communicate with NetWare 4.1.

Setting Up DOS Workstations

OVELL PROVIDES A SIMPLE installation program for DOS clients. This program installs the DOS Requester and other network components, provides a default configuration, and can be used to install drivers for Microsoft Windows.

You can install the NetWare client software from diskettes, from the CD-ROM that NetWare 4.1 comes on, or from a directory on the network:

- **Installing from diskettes**: Place the first disk in the drive. Switch to that drive by typing **A:** or **B:**. Type **INSTALL** to start the installation.

- **Installing from CD-ROM**: Switch to the CD-ROM drive. Change directories to \CLIENT\DOSWIN. Type **INSTALL**.

- **Installing from the network**: Map a drive to the SYS: volume of a NetWare 4.1 server and then change to the \PUBLIC\CLIENT\DOSWIN directory. Type **INSTALL** to begin.

After starting the INSTALL program, you will see the screen shown in Figure 13.1. You need to work your way through six installation steps:

1. **Destination directory**: Enter the directory for the client software. This is usually C:\NWCLIENT.

2. **Modify AUTOEXEC.BAT and CONFIG.SYS**: Select Yes if you want the INSTALL program to modify your workstation's AUTOEXEC.BAT and CONFIG.SYS files.

3. **MS Windows support**: Select Yes if you want to install files for Microsoft Windows support. Be sure the correct Windows directory is selected. You can press Enter to customize settings. The customization options allow you to enable international support and to select a network installation of Windows.

4. **Configure workstation for backup**: Select Yes if you wish to enable backup support for your workstation. This option installs the DOS TSA (Target Service Agent) to allow SBACKUP (or other SMS backup software) to back up the files on your local drives.

5. **Network board driver**: Press Enter to see a list of network drivers. Select the one for your network card. If your card is not listed, select Other Drivers and select a disk or another path for the driver provided by the network card manufacturer.

6. **Start installation**: Press Enter to begin the installation process. The next screen displays the progress of the installation.

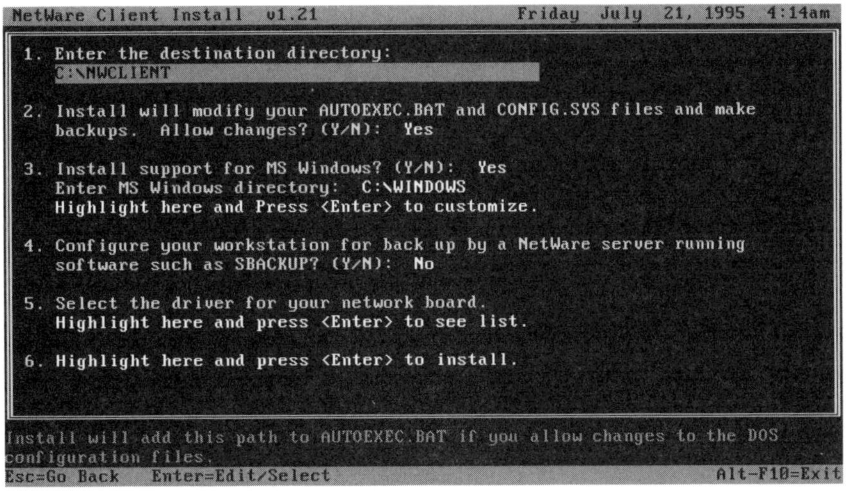

FIGURE 13.1
Installation options for the DOS client INSTALL program.

```
NetWare Client Install  v1.21                    Friday  July  21, 1995  4:14am

  1. Enter the destination directory:
     C:\NWCLIENT

  2. Install will modify your AUTOEXEC.BAT and CONFIG.SYS files and make
     backups.  Allow changes? (Y/N):  Yes

  3. Install support for MS Windows? (Y/N):  Yes
     Enter MS Windows directory:  C:\WINDOWS
     Highlight here and Press <Enter> to customize.

  4. Configure your workstation for back up by a NetWare server running
     software such as SBACKUP? (Y/N):  No

  5. Select the driver for your network board.
     Highlight here and press <Enter> to see list.

  6. Highlight here and press <Enter> to install.

Install will add this path to AUTOEXEC.BAT if you allow changes to the DOS
configuration files.
Esc=Go Back    Enter=Edit/Select                              Alt-F10=Exit
```

After completing the installation process, you need to reboot the workstation in order to load the network drivers. The installation process makes the following changes to your workstation:

- Copies the network client software, including LSL, IPXODI, VLM, and the network driver, to a directory on your workstation, usually C:\NWCLIENT.

- Creates a batch file called STARTNET.BAT in the NWCLIENT directory. This file loads the network software in the correct order.

- Modifies the AUTOEXEC.BAT file to run the STARTNET.BAT file, thus loading the network software.

- Modifies the CONFIG.SYS file to include the LASTDRIVE=Z parameter. This parameter is required for the DOS Requester.

- Copies several files to the Windows directories if you selected to install files for Windows support. These files include the NetWare User Tools program and several DLLs (Dynamic Link Libraries) for network access.

- Installs the TSA for your workstation (TSA_DOS.EXE) and adds it to the AUTOEXEC.BAT file if you opted to enable backup support.

- Creates a NET.CFG file in the workstation's NWCLIENT directory.

Customizing the DOS Client

Settings for the DOS client are provided through the use of a *configuration file* called NET.CFG. The following sections explain the changes that you can make to workstation NET.CFG files and to the STARTNET.BAT batch file. By modifying these files, you can customize your users' connections to the network.

Modifying the NET.CFG File

The NET.CFG file contains the settings for the DOS client software. This file is usually located in the C:\NWCLIENT directory on the workstation. Each workstation has its own NET.CFG file. Here are the contents of a typical file:

```
Link Driver NE2000
    Frame Ethernet_802.2
    PORT 300
    INT 5
```

```
NetWare DOS Requester
     FIRST NETWORK DRIVE = F
     SHOW DOTS = ON
     NAME CONTEXT = "OU=MKTG.O=IVR_INC"
     PREFERRED TREE = IVR_TREE
```

- The preceding file shows two typical sections of the NET.CFG file. The Link Driver section contains settings for the network card. If multiple cards are used, there can be more than one Link Driver section. These settings must match the hardware settings of your network card.

- The NetWare DOS Requester section contains settings for the DOS Requester.

Several important commands can be placed in the NetWare DOS Requester section:

```
FIRST NETWORK DRIVE
```

determines the first drive letter to be used for mapping network drives. Usually, the first drive is F:.

```
PREFERRED TREE
```

specifies the NDS tree to attach to, if more than one tree is available.

```
PREFERRED SERVER
```

can be used instead of PREFERRED TREE to specify a server to attach to. You can specify a tree or a server, but not both.

```
NAME CONTEXT
```

determines the workstation's *default context*. When a user logs in without specifying a full distinguished name, NetWare will look for the user login name in the default context.

You can place many other commands in the DOS Requester and other sections of NET.CFG files. Consult the NetWare manuals or the DynaText online documentation for details on these commands.

You can edit the NET.CFG file using any text editor, such as the EDIT program built into MS-DOS (version 5.0 or above). If you make changes to these settings, you will need to reboot the workstation to reload the network software with the new settings.

Using the INSTALL.CFG File to Modify NET.CFG Files

In a typical network, you will find yourself making the same changes to each user's NET.CFG file after installing the client software. Rather than requiring you to make these changes manually, NetWare provides an easier way. By using the INSTALL.CFG file in the installation directory, you can change all the files at one time. The INSTALL.CFG file provides settings to the INSTALL program for all aspects of installation.

The [REQUESTER] section of the INSTALL.CFG file contains settings that will be copied into the DOS Requester section of each workstation's NET.CFG file. You can load this file into a text editor and customize these items to suit your network.

Always make a backup copy of the INSTALL.CFG file before modifying it. This file controls the installation process, and making changes to some parts of the file could cause the installation process to fail.

Customizing the STARTNET.BAT

Another file called STARTNET.BAT is also created in the NWCLIENT directory. This is a DOS *batch file* (a list of commands to be executed). The commands in the STARTNET.BAT file load the network software for the workstation. A typical file looks like this:

```
SET NWLANGUAGE=ENGLISH
C:\NWCLIENT\LSL.COM
C:\NWCLIENT\NE2000.COM
C:\NWCLIENT\IPXODI.COM
C:\NWCLIENT\VLM.EXE
```

You can modify this file with any text editor. You may need to modify the file in order to load a different network driver, to change the workstation's language setting, or to provide other parameters to the network software. For example, you can add the /MC option to the VLM.EXE line to force the VLMs to be loaded in conventional memory, which may resolve some conflicts with other software.

Installing Microsoft Windows Client Software

The DOS client INSTALL program can also install the Microsoft Windows client software. The Windows client software works with the DOS Requester to provide access to all network resources. It also provides an easy way to manage network resources from the Windows environment.

NetWare Windows client software includes the following:

- Drivers for more efficient handling of mapped network drives.

- Drivers to allow printing to network printers.

- A control panel, called NetWare Settings, to customize the Windows client software.

- Pop-up message support. Messages sent from other workstations or the server (such as disk error and printer status messages) can be displayed in a pop-up window over the currently running Windows application.

- NetWare User Tools. This Windows utility allows you to change drive mappings, set printer CAPTURE settings, and specify other options.

The client software discussed here applies to Windows 3.1, 3.11, or Windows for Workgroups. It can be used with Windows 95, but will not provide full functionality. For Windows 95, follow the instructions that come with the Windows 95 client software. Windows NT also has its own NetWare client software.

Using the Windows Network Control Panel

After the Windows client software is installed, a new Network icon is created in the Control Panel. Double-click on this icon to change settings for the

Windows client. This dialog box, shown in Figure 13.2, allows you to modify Netware client settings:

- **Message Reception**: Allows you to specify whether to display messages sent from other users and warnings from the server in a pop-up window over your current application. You can enable or disable broadcasts (messages from users) and warnings (messages from the network server) separately.

- **Print Manager Display Options**: Controls how many network printing jobs the Windows Print Manager will display.

- **Permanent Connections**: Enables permanent connections to printers, servers, and drive mappings that will be restored automatically each time you start Windows. You can set up these connections using the NetWare User Tools program, described in the next section.

- **NetWare Hotkey**: Allows you to use a function key to access the NetWare User Tools program.

- **Global Drives and Paths**: Makes DOS sessions under Windows share the same drive mappings.

- **Resource Display Options**: Controls the types of resources displayed in NetWare User Tools and how these resources are sorted.

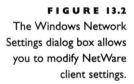

FIGURE 13.2
The Windows Network Settings dialog box allows you to modify NetWare client settings.

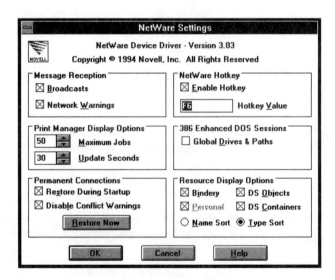

Using Windows NetWare User Tools

You can run the NetWare User Tools program from an icon in the NetWare program group or by pressing a hotkey (if you enabled this key in the Network Settings dialog box). This program allows you to perform the following functions, using a simple drag-and-drop interface:

- Change CAPTURE settings for printers

- Change drive mappings

- Attach to and detach from servers and Directory trees

- Display a list of users on the system and send messages to other users

The Help button in the NetWare User Tools window provides access to a friendly help system, which explains the specifics of the available options. Figure 13.3 shows an example of a NetWare Drive Connections screen in NetWare User Tools.

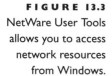

FIGURE 13.3
NetWare User Tools allows you to access network resources from Windows.

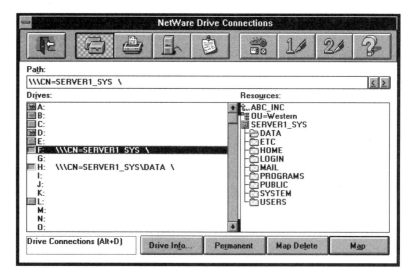

Installing Other Types of Clients

ONE OF THE BEST NEW FEATURES of NetWare 4.1 is that it can be used with a wider variety of clients—*diverse clients*, to use Novell's term. These can include OS/2, Macintosh, and UNIX workstations. The procedures for configuring OS/2 and Macintosh clients are described in the following sections. UNIX clients require additional software, and their installation is a more complicated process, which depends on the type of client and the type of connectivity involved. For details, refer to the NetWare documentation.

Configuring OS/2 Clients

NetWare provides support for the IBM OS/2 operating system. Users at OS/2 workstations can attach to the server or to the NDS tree.

Because OS/2 can work with the standard DOS file system, you can use OS/2 clients on your network without installing additional software on the file server. However, OS/2 includes the HPFS (High-Performance File System). This system allows long file names (up to 255 characters with lowercase letters) and extended attributes (other information, such as file descriptions). To take advantage of these features, you need to install the OS/2 *name space* on the server.

Installing the OS/2 Name Space

The OS/2 name space allows HPFS files to be stored on your server. You can install the name space by using the following commands at the file server console:

```
LOAD OS2
```

This loads the protocols used for the OS/2 name space. This is an NLM called OS2.NAM. After the name space is installed, this module will load automatically when you mount the volume.

```
ADD NAME SPACE OS2 TO SYS
```

This command adds the name space to the volume and allocates space to store HPFS file names. You can use any volume name in place of SYS. These changes are permanently written to the volume, so you execute this command only once.

After you have installed the name space, you will be able to use the HPFS features on your server. Note the following considerations:

- Extended OS/2 naming information will be accessible from OS/2 clients only. You will be able to access the files from DOS clients, but long file-names may be truncated. Since an OS/2 client can access DOS file names also, you can use an OS/2 client to copy the files to DOS names; however, the extended name information will be lost when you do this.

- The name space module (OS2.NAM) should load automatically when you mount the volume. If this module fails to load or is unloaded, files that use OS/2 naming will be inaccessible until the module is loaded.

Windows 95 can access OS/2 long file names; in fact, you may want to add the OS/2 name space to a volume just for the use of Windows 95. Windows NT provides a similar feature.

Installing the OS/2 Requester

The NetWare Client for OS/2 is a full-featured client software package. It includes the NetWare OS/2 Requester, which is the OS/2 equivalent of the DOS Requester and provides the same functions.

To begin the installation, run the INSTALL program using one of these methods:

- Place the NetWare 4.1 CD-ROM in a local or networked drive. Change to that drive and type **INSTALL** from the OS/2 command prompt.

- Run the MAKEDISK program from the CD-ROM or the SYS:PUBLIC\ CLIENT\OS2 directory on a server. This program allows you to create a set of installation diskettes for the OS/2 client. You can then run INSTALL from the first diskette.

The INSTALL program has several options, including built-in documentation. To install the client software, select Requester on Workstation from the Installation menu. You can choose from four different types of installations:

1. **Edit CONFIG.SYS and Copy All Files**: This option is the default. It installs all of the client software, including the LAN driver, and modifies the OS/2 CONFIG.SYS file to load the network client software.

2. **Only Edit CONFIG.SYS**: Makes changes to CONFIG.SYS only. This is useful if you have already installed the client software.

3. **Only Copy Requester Files**: Copies the OS/2 client files to your workstation but does not modify CONFIG.SYS.

4. **Only Copy ODI LAN Driver Files**: Allows you to copy optional LAN driver files from the installation directory. Drivers are provided for several common network cards. You can choose from this list or insert a disk provided by the network card manufacturer.

Choose one of the options above (usually the first one) and click the OK button to begin the installation process. Choose a LAN driver; all files are copied or modified in accordance with your selection.

After the client software has been installed, reboot the workstation. You can now use the OS/2 version of the LOGIN program to log in to the network. After logging in, you can access network drives from the OS/2 desktop.

The installation program will also install a program called NetWare Tools for OS/2. This program is similar to the Windows NetWare User Tools program described earlier in this chapter. It allows you to map network drives, set up printer capturing, and log in and out of servers and Directory trees.

Configuring Macintosh Clients

NetWare 4.1 includes support for Apple Macintosh clients. This support is provided by NetWare for Macintosh, which is a set of NLMs that run on your NetWare server.

NetWare for Macintosh supports the *AppleTalk* protocol. This is a proprietary protocol developed by Apple, and it is usually used on Macintosh networks. Since AppleTalk is a type of peer-to-peer networking, there is no dedicated server. In this system, each Macintosh workstation can act as a server by sharing files and printers with other stations.

NetWare for Macintosh provides the following functions:

- Macintosh users and other users on the network can share access to network files.

- Macintosh users can send print jobs to printers on the NetWare network.

- NetWare users can send print jobs to printers on the AppleTalk network.

Installing NetWare for Macintosh

Unlike DOS and OS/2 clients, Macintosh workstations cannot attach to the network unless NetWare for Macintosh is loaded on the file server. NetWare for Macintosh must be installed before you can install the client software. This procedure is offered as an option when you are installing the server.

You can also install NetWare for Macintosh on an existing server from an option in the INSTALL module. Follow these steps to start the installation:

1. Start the INSTALL utility by typing **LOAD INSTALL** at the server console.

2. Select Product Options.

3. Press Enter to choose an item to install.

4. Select Install NetWare for Macintosh.

5. Specify a path to the installation directory. This defaults to the directory you used for your server installation, which may be a CD-ROM or a remote network directory. NetWare for Macintosh will be installed from this directory. The directory is typically \NW410\INSTALL\ENGLISH on the NetWare 4.1 CD-ROM. If you are using a different language, substitute it for ENGLISH here.

6. Select Install NW-MAC to continue.

FINAL INSTALLATION OPTIONS The files required for NetWare for Macintosh are now copied to the server. These are placed in a directory called NW-MAC under the SYS:SYSTEM directory. When this process is complete, the Final Installation Options window appears with five options, illustrated in Figure 13.4.

FIGURE 13.4
The Final Installation
Options menu allows you
to complete tasks needed
for Macintosh
connectivity.

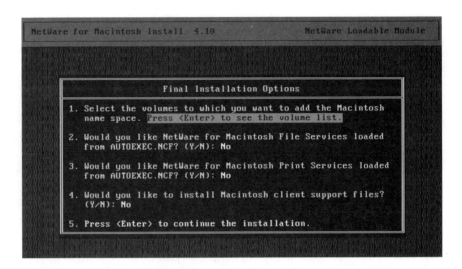

FIGURE 13.4
The Final Installation
Options menu allows you
to complete tasks needed
for Macintosh
connectivity.

1. **Volumes for Macintosh name space**: Allows you to select volumes to install the Macintosh name space, which provides compatibility with Macintosh file names. You must install the Macintosh name space on the SYS volume to run NetWare for Macintosh.

2. **Start file services**: Add the command to start Macintosh file services to the server's AUTOEXEC.NCF file. This command loads a module called AFP.NLM (AFP stands for AppleTalk Filing Protocol). You should choose this option if you wish to share files with Macintosh clients.

3. **Start print services**: Adds the command to start Macintosh print services to the AUTOEXEC.NCF file. The module that handles this task is ATPS.NLM (ATPS stands for AppleTalk Print Services). ATPS allows Macintosh clients to print to a network printer.

4. **Support files**: Lets you install support files for the Macintosh client on the server under the SYS:SYSTEM\NW-MAC directory. The next section explains how to install the software on the clients.

5. **Continue installation**: Press Enter to continue the installation.

When you continue the installation, you are asked to verify your choice. If you select Yes, the items you selected are installed on the server. Finally, the NetWare for Macintosh Configuration window appears, and you have a chance to install any options you did not already choose. In addition, four options allow you to configure NetWare for Macintosh features. These options actually run individual NLMs. You can load any of these NLMs yourself if you wish to change the configuration.

- **Configure AppleTalk Stack**: Loads INETCFG.NLM, which is used to set up the AppleTalk protocol described in the next section.

- **Configure File Services**: Loads AFPCON.NLM, which allows you to change file-sharing options.

- **Configure Print Services**: Loads ATPSCON.NLM, which allows you to control AppleTalk printing services.

- **Configure CD-ROM Services**: Loads HFSCDCON.NLM, which is used to support Macintosh CD-ROM drives.

These changes will not take effect until you restart the server. But first, install the AppleTalk protocol as described in the next section. If you need to change NetWare for Macintosh options later, you can return to the Configuration window by following these steps:

1. Start the Installation utility by typing **LOAD INSTALL** at the server console.

2. Select Product Options.

3. Select View/Configure/Remove installed products.

4. Select NW-MAC from the product list. The Configuration window will be displayed, and you can make changes as necessary.

Installing the AppleTalk Protocol

To communicate with Macintosh clients, the AppleTalk protocol must be loaded on the server. Follow these steps to install AppleTalk:

1. Load the INETCFG utility by typing **LOAD INETCFG** at the server console.

2. Select Bindings and press Enter.

3. Press Insert to add a binding to the list.

4. Select AppleTalk and press Enter to display a list of LAN cards.

5. Select the card that you will be using to connect to the AppleTalk network and press Enter.

6. Press Esc to exit and then select Yes to save your changes.

These steps added the BIND statement for AppleTalk to the AUTOEXEC.NCF file, but you need to restart the server for the new binding to take effect. Restarting the server also loads the NetWare for Macintosh modules you installed in the previous section.

Installing the Macintosh Client Software

Because the AppleTalk protocol is part of the Macintosh operating system, you can begin using NetWare for Macintosh services right away without installing additional software on the Macintosh client. However, you need to install the client software to take advantage of NDS. The Macintosh client is called MacNDS, and it provides access to NDS.

ENABLING BINDERY LOGINS Until you install the MacNDS software, Macintosh clients will attach to the server using Bindery Services (described later in this chapter). Before you can log in with Bindery Services, you must enable bindery logins for AppleTalk using the AFPCON utility as follows:

1. Type **LOAD AFPCON** at the server console.

2. Select Detailed Configuration from the Configuration Options menu.

3. Select User Access Information. These options control the types of logins that are allowed.

4. Press Enter on the Allow Clear Text Password Login option and change the option to Yes. This will allow bindery attachments.

5. Press Esc to exit and save your changes.

INSTALLING MACNDS After you have enabled bindery logins, you can install MacNDS on the Macintosh client. Follow these steps:

1. Log in to the server on the Macintosh client. Since the client files are in the PUBLIC directory, you do not need to use the ADMIN user account.

2. Click on the NetWare volume's icon and then switch to the PUBLIC/MAC directory. Inside this directory are directories for each language available.

3. Double-click on the appropriate language, such as ENGLISH.

4. Double-click on MacNDS.SEA inside the language directory. (SEA stands for Self-Extracting Archive, and it is a Macintosh standard for compressed files.)

5. Indicate where to install the files. Click OK to accept the default location or browse through the folders to select another directory.

The MacNDS client is installed in a folder called MacNDS within the folder you specify. You can open this folder to run the client software.

MacNDS relies on the features of the System 7 Macintosh operating system. If you are using an older operating system, you will need to access the network through Bindery Services.

Integrating NetWare 3.1x and NetWare 4.1

NDS, USED IN NETWARE 4.1 to store information about network resources, is a radical departure from the bindery used in previous versions of NetWare. In order to remain compatible with older systems—both previous versions of NetWare and older client software—NetWare 4.1 includes *Bindery Services*. Although the emphasis here is on NetWare 3.1x, Bindery Services also works with earlier NetWare versions.

Bindery Services uses a branch of the Directory tree to serve as a simulated bindery. All the leaf objects within a particular container object appear as a flat database to bindery-based clients. The container object that acts as a bindery is called the *bindery context*. The bindery context is set with a SET command or in the file server's AUTOEXEC.NCF file. Beginning in NetWare 4.1, you can set up to 16 different bindery contexts. All the contexts will appear as portions of the same bindery, as illustrated in Figure 13.5.

When you upgrade your server from NetWare 3.1x to NetWare 4.1, NetWare 4.1 automatically creates a bindery context. All the users, groups, and print queues from the NetWare 3.1x bindery are created as objects under a single Organization object, which is defined as the bindery context. This arrangement may not be the most efficient, but it allows the network users

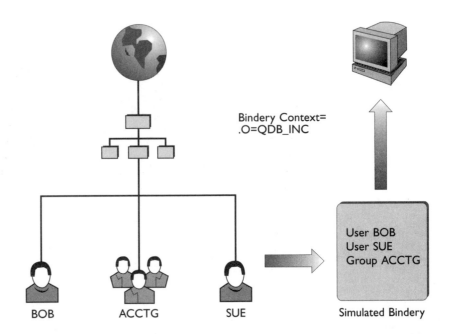

FIGURE 13.5
The contents of the
bindery context
container (.O=QDB_INC
in this example) serve as a
simulated bindery.

Bindery Context=
.O=QDB_INC

User BOB
User SUE
Group ACCTG

BOB   ACCTG   SUE   Simulated Bindery

who are still using their old NetWare setup to begin using NetWare 4.1 immediately after the upgrade.

When you install a new NetWare 4.1 server, NetWare 4.1 also creates a default bindery context. The context that contains the NetWare Server object is set up as the bindery context container.

Planning and Implementing Bindery Services

Although Bindery Services is set up automatically when you install NetWare 4.1, you need to be aware of many things when you are using Bindery Services on your server. In this section, you will learn the steps involved in planning and installing an efficient Bindery Services setup.

Planning Considerations

It is important to plan the way that Bindery Services will operate on your server. Since the bindery does not offer all the features of NDS, you must be careful to create NDS objects that will be compatible with bindery-based clients when necessary.

OBJECT NAMING The common name of an object is used as its bindery name. Suppose a user has the following distinguished name:

.CN=JIMS.OU=ACCT.O=ABCINC

Bindery Services sees this user as simply JIMS. Because the bindery is flat, you cannot address objects in their containers. This limitation invites two potential problems to occur when using Bindery Services. These problems involve bindery-compatible naming and name conflicts.

USING BINDERY-COMPATIBLE NAMES Objects that will be leaf objects in the bindery context container need to use *bindery-compatible names*. The common name of each object must follow the same rules that bindery-based objects follow in NetWare 3.1*x*:

- Spaces cannot be used in the names. If spaces are used in an object's name, they are converted to underscores for Bindery Services.

- The following special characters cannot be used in bindery names: $ (dollar sign), ? (question mark), \ (backslash), / (forward slash), " (quotation mark), [ ] (opening and closing square brackets), : (colon), | (vertical bar), < > (opening and closing angle brackets), + (plus sign), or = (equal sign).

- Names are limited to 47 characters. (NDS normally allows 64-character names.)

NAME CONFLICTS Because NDS objects with the same common name can exist in different contexts, object names can conflict with each other when you are using Bindery Services. If you have a single bindery context set on your server, this conflict cannot happen. However, because you can assign up to 16 contexts as bindery contexts, you must be careful that no identical names exist in those contexts.

Figure 13.6 shows an example of a Directory tree arrangement in which there could be name conflicts. If both .OU=SALES and .OU=SERVICE are set as bindery contexts, there will be a conflict because both contain a User object with the name FRED.

FIGURE 13.6
When using multiple
bindery contexts, you
must be careful that
name conflicts do not
exist between any
two contexts.

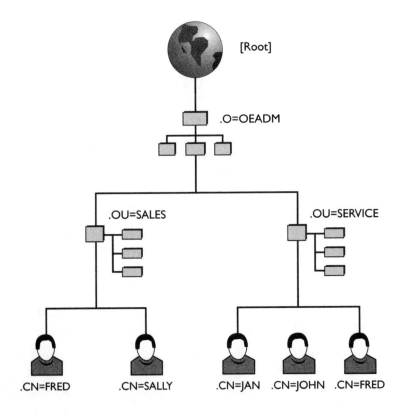

CREATING NECESSARY OBJECTS If you are using Bindery Services to ensure compatibility with a bindery-based application, you may need to create several bindery objects manually because they are not automatically created with Bindery Services.

When you install NetWare 3.1x, it creates the GUEST User object and the EVERYONE Group object. Bindery Services does not create these objects. If you upgraded your server from NetWare 3.1x, these objects should have been created as objects in the bindery context. If your NetWare 4.1 server is a new installation, you need to create the objects manually.

For example, NetWare NFS (Network File System) requires that the group EVERYONE exist in the bindery. If you are installing Bindery Services and will be using NFS, you must create the group as a leaf object in the bindery context. You will also need to add all the bindery context User objects to this group. (The current version of NFS will actually perform these steps automatically when it is installed.) If you have upgraded a NetWare 3.1x server, the EVERYONE group should have been transferred from the bindery.

Finally, NetWare creates the SUPERVISOR account when you install Bindery Services, but this is only a bindery object. Even when you upgrade a NetWare 3.1x server to NetWare 4.1, SUPERVISOR is not created in NDS and is not equivalent to the ADMIN object in NDS. The SUPERVISOR account retains Supervisor rights but only for objects within the bindery context and for the server's file system.

Limitations of the Bindery

Bindery-based clients will not be able to access all the information available through NDS. They will have access to only the information that would normally be provided by a bindery. Items not available to bindery clients include the following:

- E-mail name, phone number, and other extended addressing information

- Aliases and profiles

- Print job configurations

- NDS login scripts

Because bindery clients are logging into a server-centric bindery environment located on one server, the login script that they will access is the one in the MAIL directory on the server they log in to. This script must be maintained on the login server, and it is not replicated to other servers.

Planning Bindery Contexts

For most networks, one bindery context is sufficient. In fact early versions of NetWare 4 allowed only one bindery context. The ability to set up to 16 separate bindery contexts is new to NetWare 4.1. By taking advantage of this feature, you can have the benefits of Bindery Services without sacrificing the efficiency of a well-organized Directory tree.

In the Directory tree pictured in Figure 13.7, users in both the ACCT and CORP Organizational Units need access to Bindery Services. We can set the following as the bindery context:

.ACCT.QDC;.CORP.QDC

Leaf objects in both containers will act as objects in the simulated bindery. As you can see, this is a powerful feature for combining NetWare 4.1 with earlier versions of NetWare.

FIGURE 13.7

To give users in both the ACCT and CORP Organizational Units access to Bindery Services, use multiple bindery contexts.

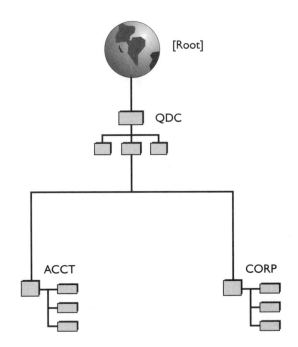

Setting Up Bindery Services

You must configure Bindery Services individually for each server that will allow bindery attachments. In addition, the server must have a master or read/write replica of the partition containing the bindery context.

Setting the Bindery Context

The bindery context for a server is configured with the SET command. You can type this command at the server console, but it is usually more practical to add the command to the server's AUTOEXEC.NCF file. An easy way to do this is by using the SERVMAN utility as follows:

1. Type **LOAD SERVMAN** at the server console.

2. Select Server Parameters from the Available Options menu.

3. Select Directory Services from the Parameter Category menu.

4. Select Bindery Context from the Directory Services Parameters menu.

5. Press Enter to edit the bindery context. When you're finished, press Esc and select Yes to save your changes.

6. Press Esc twice; you will see the Update Options menu. Select the first option, Update AUTOEXEC.NCF and STARTUP.NCF Now. Press Enter (or change the path to your AUTOEXEC.NCF file if necessary).

7. Exit SERVMAN by pressing Esc twice and then selecting Yes.

If you need to set multiple bindery contexts, use a semicolon (;) to separate the contexts in the SET command. For example, the following command sets bindery contexts for the example in Figure 13.7:

```
SET BINDERY CONTEXT = .ACCT.QDC;.CORP.QDC
```

Creating Necessary Replicas

In order to use bindery emulation on a server, you must make sure the server contains a master or read/write replica of the partition containing each of the bindery context container objects. If the server does not contain such a replica, you must create it using the Partition Manager or PARTMGR utility (described in Chapter 11 of this book).

Managing NetWare 3.1x with NDS

Netware 4.1'S BINDERY SERVICES feature allows easy integration of NetWare 4.1 with NetWare 3.1x and older clients. A final feature of Bindery Services allows even greater integration. By using the NetSync NLMs, you can use the powerful NetWare Administrator utility to manage objects on bindery-based servers as easily as NDS objects.

How NetSync Works

NetSync allows you to *synchronize* up to 12 NetWare 3.1x servers with each NetWare 4.1 server's bindery context. The NetWare 4.1 server and associated NetWare 3.1x servers are referred to as a *NetSync cluster*.

The NetSync NLM runs on both the NetWare 4.1 server and the NetWare 3.1x servers. Its purpose is to synchronize the binderies of the NetWare 3.1x servers with the bindery context of the NetWare 4.1 server. When you install NetSync, all User and Group objects in the NetWare 3.1x servers are created as objects in the NetWare 4.1 Directory's bindery context, as shown in Figure 13.8.

After the NetSync installation, the NetSync NLMs act continuously to copy all objects in the NDS bindery context to each of the NetWare 3.1x servers. Each server's bindery is replaced with a "super-bindery" containing all objects from all the bindery-based servers. Figure 13.9 shows how the binderies on two NetWare 3.1x servers might look before and after synchronization.

Limitations of NetSync

Before you install NetSync, you should be aware of some limitations and special considerations.

After the bindery is synchronized with NDS, you should not manage objects with the SYSCON utility on the NetWare 3.1x server because changes made in this way are not copied to the NDS bindery context. Instead, you will need to perform all user management using NDS utilities. The same warning applies to maintaining printing services with the PCONSOLE utility. For those changes to be copied to the NDS bindery context, you will need to use NDS utilities instead of bindery-based utilities.

FIGURE 13.8
When NetSync is installed, NetWare 3.1x objects are created as objects in the bindery context.

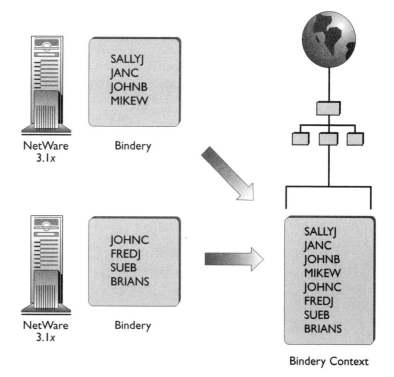

One exception to this is the accounting feature of NetWare 3.1x. Accounting information is not copied to the NDS objects, so you must use SYSCON to maintain these features. Be sure not to change any other information while using SYSCON.

Another point to consider is that trustee rights to files and directories on the NetWare 3.1x server are not copied to NDS. You still need to maintain these from the NetWare 3.1x FILER utility. You can also use the SYSCON utility, but be sure not to make other changes in SYSCON.

Similarly, you cannot use NWADMIN to maintain the NetWare 3.1x file system. You will need to do this using NetWare 3.1x utilities.

The NetWare 4.1 server's bindery context must not be changed after NetSync is installed. If it is changed, users with bindery accounts will not be able to log in and synchronization will be lost.

User login scripts will be moved to the Login Script property of the User object in Directory Services. However, the system login script from the

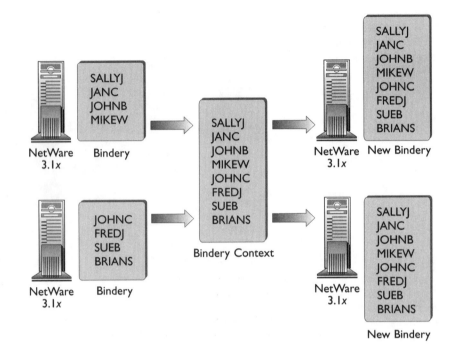

NetWare 3.1x server is not copied. If you need to execute commands from the system login script, you will need to move them to the bindery context container object's login script.

Installing NetSync

The following sections guide you through the installation of NetSync on a NetWare 4.1 server and on one or more NetWare 3.1x servers. To avoid any problems, follow all instructions carefully.

Before You Begin

You should perform the following tasks before installing NetSync:

1. Make sure the bindery context is valid and that this is where you want users from NetWare 3.1x servers to be copied.

If you have more than one bindery context set, NetSync will copy users to the first context in the list. If this is not the one you want, you will need to change the order of the contexts in the SET BINDERY CONTEXT command in the server's AUTOEXEC.NCF file.

2. Check for duplicate users and verify that no users are duplicated between the different bindery contexts of NDS and between these and any of the NetWare 3.1x servers.

The binderies of each of the NetWare 3.1x servers will be combined with any objects already in the bindery context. If any users exist in more than one of these places, only one of them will be copied. For example, if the User object FRED exists on two separate NetWare 3.1x servers, NDS will create only one FRED in the bindery context. It is best to resolve all conflicts by renaming or deleting users before beginning the synchronization process.

3. Be sure you have sufficient rights to perform the NetSync installation.

You must have full rights in the SYS:SYSTEM directory on the NetWare 4.1 server and on each of the NetWare 3.1x servers on which you wish to install NetSync. The installation program will allow you to use different login names for the NetWare 3.1x servers.

Installing NetSync on the NetWare 4.1 Server

You must perform the NetWare 4.1 portion of the NetSync installation first. The NetWare 3.1x NetSync NLM will not install properly unless it is able to communicate with NetSync on the NetWare 4.1 server. Follow these steps:

1. Load the NetSync NLM on the NetWare 4.1 server. The NetWare 4.1 version of NetSync is called NETSYNC4.NLM. Use the following command at the server console:

```
LOAD NETSYNC4
```

You will see a screen listing NetWare 3.1x servers that have been authorized for NetSync. (If this is your first installation, the list will be empty.) Press Enter to continue.

2. Authorize the NetWare 3.1x server.

3. Select the first option, Edit Server List, from the NetSync Options menu.

4. Press Insert to add a new entry to the list. Then supply the following information:

   - **3.1x File Server Name**: Enter the name of the file server that you wish to authorize for NetSync. If you are authorizing more than one server, enter the name of the first one.

   - **NetSync Password**: Enter a password to be used by the NetSync program. This is not a user or administrator password but a temporary password. This password will be used to establish communication between the NetSync modules on the NetWare 4.1 and NetWare 3.1*x* servers during installation. Remember this password. You are not required to use the same password for each NetWare 3.1*x* server, but it is easier to remember one password than many.

   - **Install NetSync Files on the 3.1x Server**: Answer Yes to copy the files needed for NetSync to the 3.1*x* server. Under most circumstances, you will want to do this, although you would choose not to copy these files if the files were already installed or if you planned to install them manually.

   - **Copy 3.1x Bindery to 4.x**: Answer Yes here to start the bindery synchronization process. Answer No only in special cases (for example, if you wish to install NetSync files but not use NetSync yet) because a negative response here would cause the servers to be out of synchronization.

5. Press Esc and then Enter. You will now be asked for a username and password for the NetWare 3.1*x* server. You need to use a username that has Read, Write, Modify, and Delete rights for the SYS:SYSTEM directory on the server. The safest way to ensure that the username has adequate rights is to use SUPERVISOR or a SUPERVISOR-equivalent user.

The password in step 5 is an actual user password and has no relation to the NetSync password that you assigned in step 4.

NetSync will now begin copying files to the NetWare 3.1*x* server. When it is finished, you should get a message stating that copying was successful. If you do not, the most likely cause is insufficient disk space on the NetWare 3.1*x* server. If copying was not successful, you should resolve the problem (such as deleting files to make room on the server) and then reload NETSYNC3.

6. Press Enter to continue. The server that you just installed should now appear in the Authorized 3.1x Servers list. You are now given the option to modify the AUTOEXEC.NCF files on the NetWare 3.1x and NetWare 4.1 servers to automatically load NetSync. (The NLM loaded on the NetWare 3.1x server is NETSYNC3.NLM.)

7. If you wish to add other NetWare 3.1x servers to the NetSync cluster, you can now repeat steps 2 through 6 for each server.

Installing NetSync on NetWare 3.1x Servers

You have now made the following changes to your NetWare 3.1x servers:

- You copied the NetSync programs to the SYS:SYSTEM\NETSYNC directory.

- You added to the AUTOEXEC.NCF file a command to load NETSYNC3.NLM.

- You installed updated versions of several system NLMs needed to run NetSync.

To finish the synchronization process, you must restart each of the NetWare 3.1x servers. Restarting them loads all the updated modules and the NETSYNC3 module. Follow these steps:

1. Make sure that all users are logged out of the NetWare 3.1x server. Type the **DOWN** command at the server console. Type **EXIT** to return to the DOS prompt and type **SERVER** to restart the server.

You can use the MONITOR utility to display users on the system and, if necessary, log them out forcefully.

2. Wait for the server to load in the usual fashion; it should automatically load the NETSYNC3 module. When NetSync starts for the first time, it will display the following prompt:

```
4.1 Server Name:
```

3. Enter the name of the NetWare 4.1 server on which you installed NetSync. You will then be asked for the NetSync password. This is the password that you assigned in step 4 of the previous section.

After you enter the password, NetSync will begin the synchronization process, which may take several minutes. NetWare will first copy all the bindery information from the NetWare 3.1x server to the bindery context. Next, it will copy objects in the bindery context back to the NetWare 3.1x server.

You have now completed the NetSync installation. Try using NetWare Administrator to edit or create some users on the NetWare 3.1x servers to make sure that the NetWare 3.1x servers are correctly synchronized with NDS.

Remember that with NetSync installed, you can no longer use SYSCON to manage users on the NetWare 3.1x server. You now must perform all administration with NDS utilities.

Using NetSync Options

The NetSync Options menu allows you to manage and fine-tune your synchronized servers. The menu becomes available in the NetWare 4.1 NETSYNC module after you have authorized at least one NetWare 3.1x server. A similar menu is available on the 3.1x server. This menu contains the following items:

- **View Active Log:** Allows you to view current events in the NetSync log file. NetSync maintains this file to keep track of operations involved in the synchronization process. This log is stored in a file called NETSYNC.LOG in the SYS:SYSTEM\NETSYNC directory. Each server maintains its own log file.

- **Log File Operations:** Allows you to maintain the log file. In the NetWare 4.1 server, an option is given to view the entire file. (In a NetWare 3.1x server, you must use a text editor to do this.) Other options allow you to control which events are shown on the log file screen, change the size of the log file, and delete the log file.

- **Edit Server List** (NETSYNC4 only): Allows you to add NetWare 3.1x servers to the NetSync cluster. You can also remove servers from the list. An additional option allows you to resynchronize a 3.1x server that is no longer synchronized, as explained in the next section.

- **Configuration Options**: Allows you to change some parameters that affect the synchronization process. For example, you can change the Watchdog Delay Interval, which is the amount of time a server waits before checking on the other servers in the cluster.

- **Move a Print Server** (NETSYNC3 only): Allows you to move the services of a NetWare 3.1*x* print server to a NetWare 4.1 print server.

- **Exit/Unload NetSync**: Terminates the NetSync NLM and returns to the server console. You should never unload the NETSYNC loadable modules in normal circumstances, but you may need to do so if you wish to discontinue using NetSync or to reconfigure the server. The server will unload NETSYNC automatically when you bring it down with the DOWN command.

Resynchronizing a NetWare 3.1x Server

If you make any changes to a NetWare 3.1*x* server using bindery-based utilities such as SYSCON, you must resynchronize the server's bindery with NetSync through the NetSync Options menu's Edit Server List item.

When you press Enter on the server name, you have the option to recopy the server's bindery. Choose this option only if you have lost synchronization. When you recopy the server's bindery, the information in the bindery will overwrite any changes you have made using NetWare 4.1 utilities.

Review

THE SUBJECTS COVERED in this chapter related to setting up NetWare workstations. You learned about installing the DOS client software, using NetWare with Macintosh and OS/2 clients, and planning and implementing Bindery Services.

DOS Client Software Installation

Novell provides a simple installation program for DOS clients. This program installs the DOS Requester and other network components and provides a default configuration. In addition, it can be used to install drivers for Microsoft Windows. The installation process makes the following changes to a workstation:

- Copies the network client software, including LSL, IPXODI, VLM, and the network driver, to a directory on your workstation, usually C:\NWCLIENT.

- Creates a batch file called STARTNET.BAT in the NWCLIENT directory. This file loads the network software in the correct order.

- Modifies the AUTOEXEC.BAT file to run the STARTNET.BAT file, thus loading the network software.

- Modifies the CONFIG.SYS file to include the LASTDRIVE=Z parameter. This parameter is required for the DOS Requester.

- Copies several files to the Windows directories if you selected to install files for Windows support. These files include the NetWare User Tools program and several DLLs (Dynamic Link Libraries) for network access.

- Installs the TSA for your workstation (TSA_DOS.EXE) and adds it to the AUTOEXEC.BAT file if you selected to enable backup support.

- Creates a NET.CFG file in the workstation's NWCLIENT directory.

OS/2 Client Installation

NetWare provides support for the IBM OS/2 operating system. Users at OS/2 workstations can attach to the server or to the Directory tree. If you wish to take advantage of OS/2's support for extended file names, you need to install the OS/2 *name space* on the server.

The NetWare Client for OS/2 software package includes the NetWare OS/2 Requester, which is the OS/2 equivalent of the DOS Requester. The installation program will also install a program called NetWare Tools for OS/2. This program allows you to map network drives, set up printer capturing, and log in and out of servers and Directory trees.

Macintosh Client Installation

NetWare 4.1's support for Apple Macintosh clients is provided by NetWare for Macintosh, which supports the AppleTalk protocol (a proprietary protocol used on Macintosh networks).

To take full advantage of the Macintosh client software, you need to install the AppleTalk protocol on the server. You do this with the INETCFG utility, and configure it using the AFPCON utility.

Bindery Services

Bindery Services is a set of NetWare 4.1 services that allow integration with NetWare 3.1*x* and older clients, servers, and applications. Bindery Services uses one or more container objects to serve as a similar object. The object that acts as a bindery is called the *bindery context*. You can set up to 16 separate bindery contexts.

Bindery Services is installed automatically when a NetWare 3.1*x* server is upgraded to NetWare 4.1. During the upgrade, a single Organization object is created and defined as the bindery context. When you install a new NetWare 4.1 server, the context that contains the server is set as the bindery context.

Because the simulated bindery does not offer all the features of NDS, you must consider several factors before using Bindery Services:

- Bindery-compatible names must be used.

- Certain objects, such as EVERYONE and GUEST, may need to be created.

- The bindery does not provide some information that NDS would normally provide, such as e-mail name, aliases, profiles, print job configurations, or NDS login scripts.

- You must configure Bindery Services for each server that will allow bindery attachments. The server must have a master or read/write replica of the partition containing the bindery context.

- You must set the bindery context with a SET command, usually located in the server's AUTOEXEC.NCF file. Multiple contexts are separated by semicolons.

Managing NetWare 3.1x through NDS

The NetSync NLMs allow you to manage bindery-based servers using NetWare 4.1 utilities. You can *synchronize* up to 12 NetWare 3.1*x* servers with each NetWare 4.1 server's bindery context. The NetWare 4.1 server and 3.1*x* servers are referred to as a *NetSync cluster*.

The NetSync NLMs are installed on the NetWare 4.1 server and the NetWare 3.1*x* servers. The names of the NLMs are NETSYNC4 and NETSYNC3. When you install NetSync, the following steps are performed:

- All user and group objects in the NetWare 3.1*x* server binderies are created as objects in the NDS bindery context.

- All objects in the bindery context are copied back to each NetWare 3.1*x* server's bindery, resulting in a "super-bindery" containing all bindery objects and equivalent to the bindery context.

Before installing NetSync, you should be aware of its limitations and some special considerations:

- NetWare 3.1*x* utilities such as PCONSOLE and SYSCON cannot be used to manage objects after NetSync is installed. (The exceptions are for managing features that are not supported by Bindery Services, such as accounting.) You must use NDS utilities to manage the objects.

- Trustee rights to files and directories in the NetWare 3.1*x* server's file system are not copied to NDS. You must continue to use NetWare 3.1*x* utilities to control these rights.

- You cannot use NDS utilities to manage the NetWare 3.1*x* file system.

- The bindery context should not be changed after NetSync is installed; this action would cause a loss of synchronization.

User login scripts are moved to the NDS User objects, but the NetWare 3.1*x* system login script is not copied. You can copy this login script to a container login script if needed.

Advanced Security and Auditing

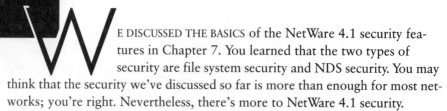

WE DISCUSSED THE BASICS of the NetWare 4.1 security features in Chapter 7. You learned that the two types of security are file system security and NDS security. You may think that the security we've discussed so far is more than enough for most networks; you're right. Nevertheless, there's more to NetWare 4.1 security.

In this chapter, we'll look at the issue of administration—assigning a central administrator for the entire Directory or separate administrators for certain parts. In addition, we'll take a look at the powerful auditing features of NetWare 4.1. With these auditing features, you can log just about everything that happens on the network. After reading this chapter you should be a true NetWare 4.1 security expert.

Before we discuss administration, here's a brief overview of the basics of NDS security.

The tools that you use to control file system and NDS security (most importantly, NWADMIN) were introduced in Chapter 7. Refer to that chapter for information on how to perform the tasks described in this chapter.

NDS Security Overview

NDS SECURITY IS USED TO control access to objects in the Directory—users, groups, printers, and entire organizations. You can control users' abilities to modify and add objects and to view or modify their properties. With an understanding of NDS security, you can assign users the rights they need in the Directory while maintaining a secure network.

Like the file system, NDS security assigns rights through the use of trustees. The trustees of an object are called *object trustees*. An object trustee is any user (or other object) who has been given rights to the object. The list of trustees for an object is called the *Access Control List*, or ACL. Each object has a property containing the ACL.

NDS security provides two categories of rights: object rights and property rights. *Object rights* are the tasks that a trustee can perform on an object. There are five types of object rights:

Object Right	Description
Supervisor	The trustee is granted all of the rights listed below. Unlike the Supervisor right in the file system, the NDS Supervisor right can be blocked by the *Inherited Rights Filter (*IRF).
Browse	The trustee can see the object in the Directory tree. If the Browse right is not granted, the object is not shown in the list.
Create	The trustee can create child objects under the object. This right is available only for container objects.
Delete	The trustee can delete the object from the Directory. In order to delete an object, the trustee must also have the Write right for All Properties of the object.
Rename	The trustee can change the name of the object.

Property rights are the tasks that a trustee can perform on the object's properties. These rights allow the trustee to read or modify the property values. There are five types of property rights, which are not the same as the types of object rights:

Property Right	Description
Supervisor	The trustee is given all of the property rights listed below. Once again, this right can be blocked by the IRF. Trustees with the Supervisor object right are automatically given Supervisor rights to All Properties of the object.
Compare	The trustee is allowed to compare the property's values to a given value. The trustee may search for a certain value but not look at the value itself.
Read	The trustee can read the values of the property. The Compare right is automatically granted to a trustee who is granted the Read property right.

Write	The trustee can modify, add, or remove values of the property.
Add Self	The trustee is allowed to add or remove itself as a value of the property. For example, a user who is granted the Add Self right for a group can add himself or herself to the group. The Write right is automatically granted to a trustee who is granted the Add Self property.

Property rights can be granted in two ways: All Properties or Selected Properties. When All Properties is granted, the same list of rights is granted to each of the properties of the object.

NDS Inheritance

NDS uses a system of inherited rights. When an object trustee is given rights to a container object, the trustee also receives the same rights for all children of the object. Inheritance affects both object rights and property rights.

Object rights are inherited in the same fashion as file system rights. When a trustee is given object rights for an object, the rights are inherited for child objects. The trustee receives rights for these objects also, unless the rights are blocked by the IRF or an explicit trustee assignment.

Property rights can be inherited in the same manner as object rights, with one exception—only rights given with the All Properties option can be inherited. If a trustee is given rights to Selected Properties of an object, those rights cannot be inherited by child objects. This restriction develops because each type of object, such as User and Organizational Unit, has a different list of properties.

When a trustee is given rights to a container object, the rights flow down the Directory tree until they are blocked. You can block inherited rights in two ways: with a new trustee assignment or with the IRF.

The IRF controls which rights can be inherited. The IRF cannot be used to grant rights; it can only block or allow rights that were given in a parent directory. The IRF is simply a list of the rights that a user or other trustee can inherit for that object from its parents. If a right is included in the IRF, it can be inherited. If you leave a right out of the IRF, no trustee can inherit that right for that object.

Security Equivalence

There are several situations in NDS in which a trustee automatically receives all of the rights given to another trustee. The two types of *security equivalence* are *implied security equivalence* and *explicit security equivalence:*

- **Implied security equivalence** means that an object receives rights given to its parent containers.

- **Explicit security equivalence** refers to rights assigned to a user with the Security Equal To property, group membership, or Organizational Role occupancy.

Effective Rights

A user's *effective rights* are the tasks the user can actually perform on the object. You can display effective rights with NWADMIN. To calculate effective rights manually, follow these steps:

1. Start with any explicit rights given to the user for the object. (Explicit rights override any inherited rights.)

2. If no explicit rights have been given to the user, calculate the inherited rights—any rights given to the user for parent objects minus those blocked by the IRF.

3. Add any rights given to the user's security equivalents for the object. These include group memberships, Organizational Roles, or members of the user's Security Equivalent To property.

Assigning NDS Administrators

N A LARGE NETWORK, it is important to determine who will administer—or control—the Directory tree and the objects within it. You can use two kinds of administration in NetWare 4.1: *centralized administration* and *distributed administration*. Both of these are made possible by NDS, and they are discussed in the following sections.

Centralized Administration

The ADMIN user account, or a group of administrators, can control the entire network. Central administration is one of the benefits of NDS, and it may be the best solution for smaller organizations. NetWare 4.1 assigns a central administrator, the ADMIN user, by default. The ADMIN user is given the Supervisor right to the [Root] object and inherits rights to all objects unless they are blocked.

Even if you choose to use distributed administration on your network, you should keep one user (such as the ADMIN account) with full rights to the entire Directory tree. This account is required to assign other administrators, move objects in the tree, merge trees, and manage time synchronization.

A central administrator can also be used in emergencies, such as when a portion of the Directory tree is left without an administrator.

WARNING

Avoid logging in with the ADMIN account unless you require the rights to administer the entire Directory tree. If the logged-in ADMIN account is left unattended, someone could cause serious damage to the network.

Distributed Administration

One of the most important advantages of NDS security is that it allows distributed administration. You can assign separate administrators to different branches of the Directory tree, as well as a separate administrator for the server's file system. The following sections describe the types of administrators that you can create.

Container Administrators

You can create an administrator who has rights to one container in the Directory tree and the objects within it. This assignment is called a *container administrator.* Since the Directory tree is divided by locations, divisions, or workgroups, this method is often the best way to distribute administrative tasks. In Figure 14.1 user BOB is a container administrator for a single Organizational Unit.

You can assign the rights for a container directly to the user who administers it. However, the Organizational Role object is a better way to create container

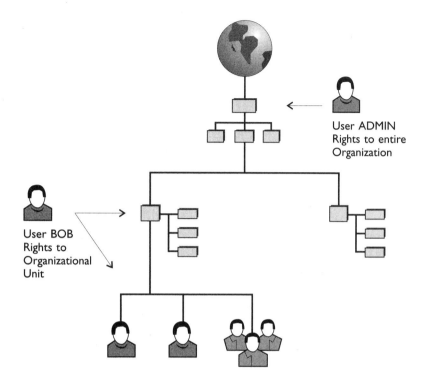

FIGURE 14.1
A container
administrator has rights
to NDS objects
in a single container.

User ADMIN
Rights to entire
Organization

User BOB
Rights to
Organizational
Unit

administrators. By using an Organizational Role as the administrator, you gain
the following benefits:

- If the job of container administrator is switched to a different user, you can
  simply make the new user the occupant of the Organizational Role object.

- If two or more users will share the job of container administration, you
  can assign multiple occupants to the Organizational Role.

- If some containers are too small to have their own administrator, you can
  assign the same user to two or more Organizational Roles.

As you can see, the Organizational Role provides a flexible, simple method
of assigning container administrators. Follow these steps to create a container
administrator:

1. Create the Organizational Role object. You should create this object inside
   the container that it will administer. See Chapter 6 for details on creating
   NDS objects.

2. Assign the Organizational Role as a trustee of the container and give it rights. The type of rights depends on your network security plans:

■ Assign the user Supervisor [S] or full rights [SBCDR] if the administrator will control the file system also. If you give the administrator the Supervisor right to the container, that account also inherits Supervisor rights to the file system of any servers in the container.

■ Assign the Browse, Create, Delete, and Rename [BCDR] rights separately if you wish to assign a separate administrator for the file system.

3. Assign any other rights you wish to give the administrator, such as file system rights (if they were not assigned in step 2).

4. Make one or more users occupants of the Organizational Role.

Exclusive Container Administrators

In a network for which security is very important, you may want to make the container administrator the only administrator for the container. You can assign an *exclusive container administrator* by blocking the rights of central administrators (such as ADMIN) with the IRF. This action allows you to maintain a highly secure network. Figure 14.2 illustrates the concept of an exclusive container administrator.

When you create an exclusive container administrator, there is no longer a central administrator. Therefore, you should take the following precautions when you set up this type of administrator:

■ If the container administrator rights are assigned to an Organizational Role object, it is best to give explicit rights for the container to a second user (or Organizational Role) also. Otherwise, if the Organizational Role object is deleted, you lose control over that branch of the Directory tree. This situation does not have an easy solution.

■ Make sure that the Organizational Role object also has the Supervisor [S] right to its own object. This allows the container administrator to add other administrators. In addition, the ADMIN user can be added to the Organizational Role temporarily if a central administrator is required.

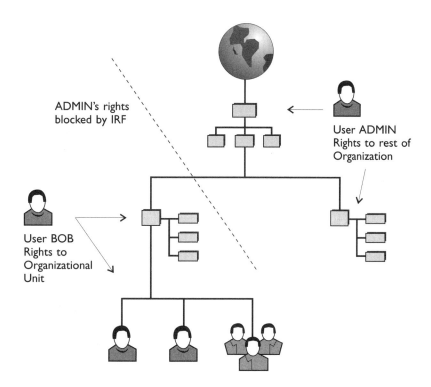

FIGURE 14.2
An exclusive container administrator is the only user with rights to a container.

ADMIN's rights blocked by IRF

User ADMIN Rights to rest of Organization

User BOB Rights to Organizational Unit

WARNING

If you do use exclusive administrators, you should coordinate with them and reestablish a central administrator before performing operations such as moving trees. You can restore a central administrator's rights. The exclusive administrator simply needs to change the IRF to allow inheritance again.

As noted earlier, if at all possible, it is best to keep a central administrator in addition to the container administrators. A central administrator will be needed when merging Directory trees or moving objects in the tree. This user provides a solution for emergencies when the container administrator is deleted or the user who occupies the role is not available.

Here are the steps required to create an exclusive container administrator:

1. Create the Organizational Role object. You should create the Organizational Role within the container that it will administer.

2. Assign one or more users as occupants of the Organizational Role. It is important to do this now. After the following steps are performed, the ADMIN user will no longer be able to add users to the role.

3. Assign the Organizational Role as a trustee of the container object. You should assign full rights [SBCDR] to ensure that an IRF of an object or container does not prevent access.

4. Give the Organizational Role the Supervisor [S] right to its own object. This step ensures that the occupant of the role can add other occupants. If a central administrator is needed (such as when merging trees), the ADMIN user can be added to this role.

5. Change the IRF of the container so that only the Browse [B] object right and the Read [R] property right are granted. This assignment allows other administrators to examine objects in this branch of the Directory tree but not to control them.

6. If ADMIN or another user has an explicit trustee assignment to the container, remove the assignment so that the container administrator will have the only control over the container.

7. If ADMIN or another user has rights to the administrator Organizational Role object, remove those rights. This action prevents other administrators from restricting the exclusive container administrator's rights or giving themselves rights. (If the administrator Organizational Role object is located in the container it will administer, the IRF will prevent other administrators from accessing it.)

WARNING

The NetWare Administrator utility does not allow you to filter the Supervisor [S] right unless you have already given this right to a container administrator. You should also assign this right to at least one other user because if the administrator Organizational Role is deleted, you lose access to that branch of the Directory tree.

File System Administrators

You can assign a separate administrator for the file system of a server. As with other types of administrators, this assignment is best accomplished with an Organizational Role object. This type of administrator is illustrated in Figure 14.3.

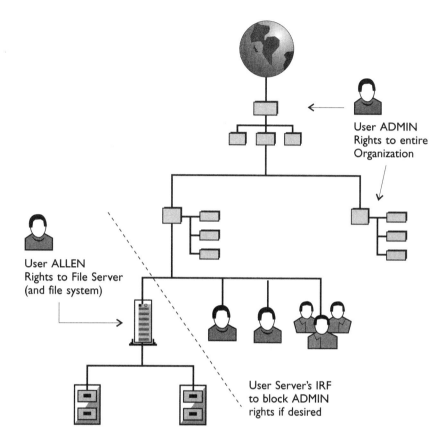

User ADMIN
Rights to entire
Organization

User ALLEN
Rights to File Server
(and file system)

User Server's IRF
to block ADMIN
rights if desired

You can create a file system administrator by following these steps:

1. Create the Organizational Role object and add one or more users to it.

2. Make the Organizational Role a trustee of the File Server object with the Supervisor [S] right. The administrator will inherit the Supervisor right for all volumes on the server. As an alternative, you can assign file system rights separately for each volume (or only one volume) on a server.

3. If you wish the administrator to be an exclusive administrator of the file system, block the rights of other administrators by removing the Supervisor [S] right from the file server's IRF.

4. Remove the current trustee assignment to create an exclusive file system administrator. (ADMIN [or another administrator] was given rights to the file system when the server was installed.)

If you create an exclusive file system administrator, be sure to assign the file system rights to at least one other user so that you will not lose access to the server.

Other Types of Administrators

In NetWare 3.1*x*, you could assign a variety of managers and operators. You can use Organizational Roles to duplicate these administrators in NetWare 4.1:

- **User account managers and workgroup managers:** These managers can be replaced with container administrators in NDS. You can use Organizational Roles to create user account managers and workgroup managers, as described in the previous sections. Unlike NetWare 3.*x*, NetWare 4.1 doesn't provide an easy way to give trustee rights to all members of a group; you can use containers to give trustee rights to all members of a group.

- **Print queue operator:** Print Queue objects in NDS have a Print Queue Operators property. You can create a print queue operator by adding a user or Organizational Role to the list of print queue operators.

- **Print server operator:** The Print Server object has a Print Server Operators property. You can add users or an Organizational Role to the Operators list to assign operators.

These are not the only types of administrators you can assign. The flexibility of NDS security allows you to create highly specialized types of administrators. You can create Organizational Roles that combine the roles described above or assign specific rights to suit the needs of your network.

Auditing the Network

NOTHER DISTINCTIVE FEATURE of NDS security is its *auditing* capabilities. By assigning an auditor on the network, you give a user the ability to monitor the activities of other users.

Auditing is another area in which the ADMIN user (or other administrator) is not always the final authority. Although the network auditor is assigned by the administrator, the auditor is the only user with access to auditing features. The administrator cannot access this information. However, the auditor can monitor changes that the administrator makes to NDS or the file system.

The auditor is able to monitor *events* (specific actions) in NDS or the file system. Events can include user actions, changes in NDS and file system security, and the usage of network resources.

Auditing provides the following benefits:

- Ensures that users and administrators are following company policies

- Monitors unauthorized access to the file server

- Determines if users are accessing the wrong objects or files

- Troubleshoots network and file server problems

Obviously, the average small company network has little use for auditing. Auditing features have the greatest benefit for large enterprisewide networks and for highly secure networks, such as those required by government agencies and government-regulated businesses.

Creating a Network Auditor

To begin an audit on your network, follow these steps:

1. Determine who will perform the audit. You can assign an existing user on the network as an auditor or create a User object for this purpose. This user is usually a member of management or an outside auditor rather than a network administrator.

2. Enable auditing for the container volume or object. This procedure is explained in the next sections.

3. Give the auditing password for the container or volume to the auditor. The remaining steps are performed by the auditor, as explained later in this chapter.

The password referred to here is an auditor's password. *This password is assigned for each container or volume to be audited and has no relation to actual user passwords.*

To enable and control auditing on the network, you use the AUDITCON utility. This program is located in the PUBLIC directory on the server. You can start it by typing **AUDITCON** at a workstation. You can use this utility to perform auditing tasks on both NDS containers and volumes. The AUDITCON main menu is shown in Figure 14.4.

FIGURE 14.4
The AUDITCON utility allows you to configure and control auditing.

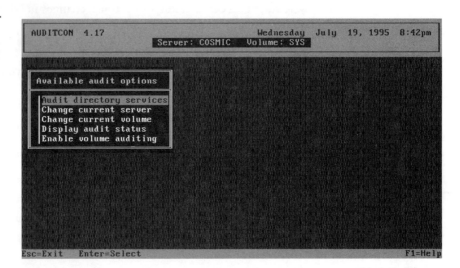

Auditing a Volume

To begin auditing a volume, follow these steps:

1. Log in as ADMIN or equivalent.

2. Type **AUDITCON** to start the utility.

3. Select Enable volume auditing from the AUDITCON main menu. If your server has more than one volume, you can choose the volume.

4. Enter the password you have chosen for the auditor at the prompt shown in Figure 14.5. (You are asked to enter it twice for verification.)

5. Give the password to the auditor. The auditor can now perform auditing tasks.

FIGURE 14.5

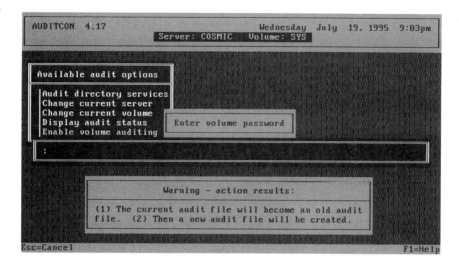

Auditing an NDS Container

You can enable auditing for any NDS container object by following these steps:

1. Log in as ADMIN or equivalent.

2. Type **AUDITCON** to start the utility.

3. Select Audit directory services from the AUDITCON main menu.

4. Use the Change Context option to select the context of the container you wish to audit from the Audit directory services menu.

5. Select Audit directory tree.

6. Highlight the container object you wish to audit in the list of container objects in the Session context, shown in Figure 14.6, and then press F10.

7. Select Enable container auditing.

8. Enter the password you have chosen for the auditor at the prompt. Enter it again for verification.

9. Give the password to the auditor. The auditor can now perform auditing tasks.

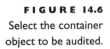

FIGURE 14.6
Select the container
object to be audited.

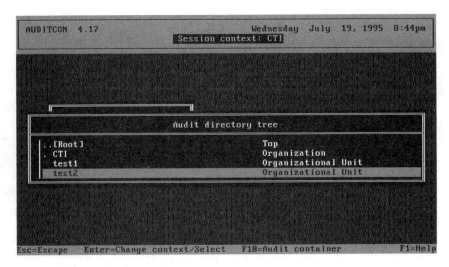

Performing Auditing Tasks

After you have enabled auditing and given the password to the auditor, the auditor can use the AUDITCON utility to monitor activities on the network. This section explains these tasks from the auditor's point of view.

First, run the AUDITCON utility. To audit a volume, select Auditor volume login and then enter the password. To audit an NDS container, follow these steps:

1. Select Audit directory services.

2. Select the correct context, if necessary.

3. Select Audit directory tree.

4. Choose the container to audit and press F10.

5. Select Auditor container login and then enter the password.

Changing the Auditor's Password

As an auditor, the first thing you should do is change the auditor's password. This ensures that the network administrator who enabled the auditing process cannot access auditing information. After the auditor's password is changed, the user with the password (the auditor) is the only user who can use the AUDITCON utility for that container or volume. The auditor performs all auditing activities, including ending the audit.

To change the password, follow these steps:

1. Run AUDITCON and log in as the auditor.

2. Select Auditing configuration from the Available audit options menu, shown in Figure 14.7.

3. Select Change audit password.

4. Enter the new password.

FIGURE 14.7
The Available audit options menu allows you to perform auditing tasks.

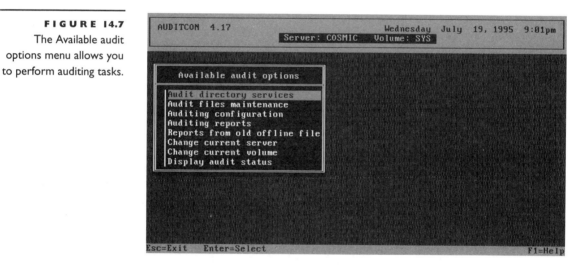

Selecting Events to Audit

When auditing is enabled, events for the container or volume are logged. As auditor, you can select which events to include in the audit. Different options are available for volumes and for NDS containers.

SELECTING VOLUME EVENTS After logging in as the volume auditor, select Auditing configuration. You are given three choices:

- **Audit by Event** allows you to monitor certain types of events.

- **Audit by File/Directory** allows you to choose directories or files to monitor.

- **Audit by User** allows you to monitor activities of certain users on the volume.

You can use any of these types of auditors or a combination of them for maximum flexibility.

SELECTING NDS CONTAINER EVENTS After logging in as the NDS container auditor, select Auditing configuration. You are given two choices:

- **Audit by Event** allows you to choose which NDS events (create, delete, and so on) are to be audited.

- **Audit by User** allows you to choose one or more users whose NDS activities you wish to monitor.

You can use either one of these options or combine them—audit certain events, regardless of the user, or audit certain users, regardless of the event.

Managing the Audit Data File

Each time an event that has been selected for auditing occurs, an entry is added to the *audit data file*. A second file, the *audit history file*, is used to log changes in the audit process. As auditor, you can view the events in these files and control how the files are used. From the Available audit options menu, select one of the following options for Audit files maintenance:

- **Close old audit file** closes the old audit file, which exists if there was a previous audit on the object or volume. This option allows all users, not just the auditor, to access the old audit file.

- **Copy old audit file** allows you to copy the old audit file to a text file in the directory you specify.

- **Delete old audit file** erases the old audit file.

- **Display audit status** displays information about the audit file, such as its size and the date it was created.

- **Reset audit data file** creates a new audit file. The current file becomes the old data file, which can be maintained with the options listed previously.

Audit files can become quite large and can use up your volume's space if you are not careful. Watch the available disk space while auditing is occurring. In addition, reset the audit file (by using the Reset audit data file option on the Audit file maintenance menu) after reports have been run and delete the old file or move it to a volume with ample space.

Creating Audit Reports

In a large network, thousands of events happen every day, and the audit data file can become quite large. Fortunately, you do not need to sort through the file yourself. The reporting features of AUDITCON allow you to create a report for very specific types of events.

To access reporting options, select Auditing reports from the Available audit options menu. The Auditing reports menu is shown in Figure 14.8. The reporting process involves two steps: creating a report filter and viewing or printing the report.

CREATING A REPORT FILTER First, you must create a *report filter* for the report. This is a set of conditions that the entries must match to be included in the report. You can create multiple filters. You can save the filters and use them to run a report regularly.

FIGURE 14.8
The Auditing reports
menu allows you to
specify reporting options
and run reports.

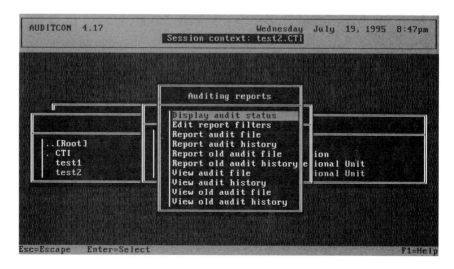

To create a report filter, follow these steps:

1. Select Edit report filters from the Auditing reports menu. A list of the existing filters is displayed. The first time you use this feature, the list is empty.

2. Press Insert to create a new filter.

3. Select the type of events to be included in the report. You can select multiple options or just a single option. The event types are

   - **Report by date/time** allows you to report events on a certain date (or list of dates and times).

   - **Report by event** presents you with a list of events from which you can select the ones to be included in the report.

   - **Report exclude paths/files** allows you to exclude certain files (in a volume) or containers (in NDS) from the report.

   - **Report exclude users** allows you to list users whose actions will not be included in the report.

   - **Report include paths/files** lets you report on certain files or NDS containers only.

   - **Report include users** allows you to report the actions of certain users.

4. Press Esc after you have made your selections. When you are asked for a name for the filter, enter it and press Enter.

VIEWING THE REPORT After you create a report filter, you can view the report on the screen. This screen preview is a simple way to browse through the report and to make sure that your report is set up correctly before you print it.

From the Auditing reports menu, select View audit file. You are then asked to select a filter. Select the filter you have created from the list and press Enter. The report is displayed on the screen. You can use the arrow keys to browse through the report.

PRINTING THE REPORT In order to print a report from a report filter, you must first create the report in a text file by following this procedure:

1. Select Report audit file from the Auditing reports menu.

2. Choose a filter from the list.

3. Enter a file name at the prompt and press Enter.

The audit report is created in the file you specified. You can then send it to a printer using a text editor or the DOS COPY command.

By default, the report file is created in the auditor's home directory. Since this is an ordinary text file, it can be read by any user who has access to that directory. To be sure that no users or administrators on the network can access the file, you can specify a floppy disk or local hard disk. Also, be sure to delete the report file after you print it.

Ending the Audit

After the auditing process is complete, you must end the audit. This step prevents the auditor from accessing any further system information and ensures that audit data files do not grow too large. The auditor should follow these steps to end the audit:

1. Select Auditing configuration from the Available audit options menu.

2. Select Disable container auditing from the Auditing configuration menu.

3. Answer Yes to Disable auditing.

4. Exit the AUDITCON utility.

Auditing can be disabled only if you have the auditor's password. Don't let the auditor leave without ending the audit or giving you the password. Without the password, the only way to end auditing is to delete the NDS container or reformat the volume and restore from a backup.

Review

THIS CHAPTER HAS COVERED two aspects of NDS security:

- Several different types of administration
- Auditing to monitor the network

Administration

Two types of administration are possible in NDS: *centralized administration* and *distributed administration*. You can also use a combination of methods. You can assign three types of administrators in the Directory:

- A **container administrator** has rights for all objects within a container.

- An **exclusive container administrator** has rights for all objects in a container; in addition, the IRF is used to prevent other administrators from having rights to the container's objects.

- A **file system administrator** has rights for a server's file system. An IRF can be used to block the rights of other administrators if desired.

By using Organizational Role objects, you can also create other types of administrators to suit the needs of your network.

Auditing

NetWare 4.1 allows you to *audit* an NDS container or a volume. An *auditor* is assigned to the task. This auditor can monitor all *events* that occur, such as the creation, deletion, and modification of files.

Auditing is managed with the AUDITCON utility. As administrator, you use AUDITCON to enable auditing for a container or volume. A password, which you give to the auditor, is assigned when auditing is enabled. This *auditor's password* is not the same as user passwords.

The auditor can perform tasks such as viewing and printing reports of events, controlling the types of events that are audited, and ending the audit process. The auditor can change the auditor's password; when the auditor's password changes, no other user (including the administrator) can control auditing or access the auditing information.

Managing Your NetWare 4.1 Server

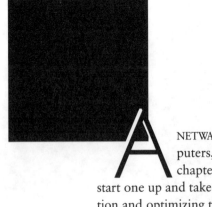

NETWARE 4.1 SERVER is completely different from typical computers, and certain techniques are required to manage it. In this chapter we'll look at the components of a server and how to start one up and take it down. We'll also cover changing the server's configuration and optimizing the server to maximize speed and performance.

Components of a Server

N CHAPTER 10 OF THIS BOOK we looked at the basic components of a server. The following sections review that information and provide additional details. The server and network are composed of hardware—the server itself, a network card, and cabling—and software, the NetWare 4.1 server software.

Hardware Components

The hardware components of a NetWare 4.1 server include the following:

- **The processor (CPU):** NetWare 4.1 requires a PC-compatible machine with a 386 or better CPU. (To run at any kind of respectable speed, you'll need at least a 486.)

- **RAM (Random Access Memory):** NetWare 4.1 requires at least 8MB of RAM.

- **Disk storage:** NetWare 4.1 uses a DOS partition for the SERVER.EXE file and a NetWare partition to hold at least one NetWare volume (SYS).

- **Network board and cabling:** Without this, the server won't do you much good. The network board allows the server to communicate with workstations and other servers.

Software Components

The main software component of a NetWare 4.1 server is the SERVER.EXE program. This program loads from DOS but takes over the operating system completely (and can even remove DOS from memory). This is the actual NetWare server software.

Other software components include disk drivers, which allow communication with disk drives in the server, and LAN drivers, which communicate with the network board. Finally, support modules add various capabilities to the server. You usually don't need to load these NLMs, as they are loaded by other NLMs that use their services.

How Servers Are Identified

NetWare 4.1 uses unique *network addresses* to identify devices on the network. The network address combines network number and Mac address (or node id). Several types of numbers are involved:

- The *internal network number* is set for each server and uniquely identifies the server.

- The *network card address* is wired into each network card. You cannot usually change it. (One exception is the ARCnet card, in which you *must* change the address to a unique value. Some Ethernet cards include the capability to change the address, but you won't usually need to do so.

- The *network number*, or *external network number*, is used by multiple servers on the same network segment. All servers on a segment use the same external network number. Each segment on the network must have a unique network number.

Starting the Server

TO START A NETWORK SERVER, you must perform the following steps. Usually these are all done from within batch files, which are discussed later in this chapter.

1. Boot DOS on the server computer.

2. Execute the SERVER.EXE program.

3. Load the disk driver. This is usually done in the STARTUP.NCF file.

4. Select the server's name and internal network number. This is usually done in the AUTOEXEC.NCF file.

5. Load the LAN driver. This is also usually done in the AUTOEXEC.NCF file.

6. Bind the LAN driver to the network.

Configuring the Server

LUCKILY, YOU USUALLY WON'T NEED to start a server manually. By specifying the correct information in the server's configuration files, you can make just about everything automatic. It is possible to bring the server up and load all needed software automatically—all you need to do is turn the machine on. Each of the configuration files is described in the following sections.

The AUTOEXEC.BAT File

This file is technically not a NetWare file, but you'll use it on almost every server. DOS uses this file to execute commands when it starts. Thus, you can use it to execute the SERVER.EXE file automatically and give control to NetWare. Here's what a typical AUTOEXEC.BAT file looks like:

```
CD \NWSERVER
SERVER
```

A two-line file is usually as complicated as it gets. Since NetWare takes over completely, you cannot use any DOS drivers or other software in this file. In fact, you should be sure that the AUTOEXEC.BAT file and CONFIG.SYS—the other configuration file used by DOS—are empty aside from these commands to ensure that all of the machine's memory is available for NetWare's use. In most cases the CONFIG.SYS file does not need to exist at all.

Both AUTOEXEC.BAT and CONFIG.SYS are located in the root directory of the server's boot drive—usually drive C: if you boot from a hard disk or A: if you boot from a floppy.

The STARTUP.NCF File

Once SERVER.EXE is run, NetWare takes over. The STARTUP.NCF file contains commands that the NetWare server processes as soon as it comes up. Only certain types of commands can be placed in this file, and they are primarily commands used for disk drivers. You can also use this file to load the DOMAIN NLM and to specify some settings for memory allocation.

The STARTUP.NCF file is located on the DOS side of the server configuration, in the same directory as the SERVER.EXE program. This placement is necessary because NetWare cannot access the NetWare volume until it loads the disk driver. If you need to load other commands, you should use the AUTOEXEC.NCF file, described in the next section.

STARTUP.NCF usually contains just one command that loads the disk driver. Here's an example of this file, which loads the IDE disk driver:

```
LOAD IDE PORT=2f8 INT=A
```

The SYS volume will be automatically mounted when the disk driver is successfully loaded. The AUTOEXEC.NCF file, described next, is located on this volume.

The **AUTOEXEC.NCF** File

This file is a handy file that you can use to execute any NetWare server command when the server starts. This file is located on the NetWare SYS volume and is read and executed after the STARTUP.NCF file and disk driver are taken care of.

The most important uses for this file are to specify the file server's name and internal network number and to load and bind the network drivers. It is also used to specify the server's time zone and time synchronization information. Here's an example of a simple AUTOEXEC.NCF file:

```
SET TIME ZONE = MST7MDT
SET DAYLIGHT SAVINGS TIME OFFSET = 1:00:00
SET START OF DAYLIGHT SAVINGS TIME = (APRIL SUNDAY
   FIRST 2:00 AM)
SET END OF DAYLIGHT SAVINGS TIME = (OCTOBER SUNDAY
   LAST 2:00 AM)
SET DEFAULT TIME SERVER TYPE = SINGLE
SET BINDERY CONTEXT = .OU=GROUP1.O=WEST
FILE SERVER NAME WEST_23
IPX INTERNAL NET 44998
LOAD NE2000 PORT=300 INT=5 FRAME=ETHERNET_802.2
BIND IPX TO NE2000 NET=99
```

You can edit this file, along with STARTUP.NCF, using an option in the INSTALL NLM.

If you use INETCFG to install internetworking features, as described in Chapter 12, the LOAD and BIND commands for network drivers will be moved to a separate file, INITSYS.NCF. You must edit this file if you wish to modify the commands. You can use the EDIT NLM to edit the file from the server console: LOAD EDIT INITSYS.NCF

Server Batch Files

AUTOEXEC.NCF and STARTUP.NCF aren't the only batch files NetWare 4.1 uses. You can create your own files to execute common commands. Use the NCF (*NetWare Command File*) extension when you create server batch files. Any command you can type at the server can be used in a command file.

Optimizing the Server and the Network

NETWARE 4.1 IS STABLE ENOUGH to run for months at a time without a problem. However, it is important to monitor network and server performance so that you can correct problems before they become severe. You can also use various settings to optimize and streamline your network for maximum performance.

Optimizing Memory and CPU Performance

The server's memory is used to store the NetWare 4.1 operating system, device drivers, NLMs, and buffers for disk and network communication. Because many different types of memory storage are required, NetWare 4.1 uses sophisticated *memory management* techniques. By understanding how NetWare manages memory and how memory management affects network performance, you can keep your network running smoothly.

Memory Allocation

Memory allocation is the process that NetWare uses to assign memory needed by the system or applications. NetWare 4.1 assigns memory in 4KB blocks, or *pages*. The memory manager assigns, or *allocates*, pages of memory needed by the application. The pages can be located in several different areas of memory, but they appear as a single block of memory to the application.

NLMs or system programs are assigned an *allocation pool* when they start. The allocation pool is based on an estimate of the memory that the application requires. As the application requests memory pages, NetWare assigns them from this pool, and when the application frees the memory, it is returned to the pool. Memory is assigned efficiently because each application uses its own memory pool.

MEMORY DEALLOCATION When an NLM no longer needs memory, it turns the memory over to the system. This process is called *deallocation*. When memory is deallocated, it is simply marked as unused. However, the memory is not available to other applications yet.

GARBAGE COLLECTION *Garbage collection* is a process that runs periodically (every 15 minutes by default) on the server. This process finds areas of memory that have been deallocated and returns them to the main memory pool so that they can be used by other applications. You can use SET commands to control how often garbage collection is performed and improve its efficiency.

Monitoring Memory Usage

The Memory Utilization option in the MONITOR utility allows you to view the server's total allocated memory. In addition, you can press Enter when the name of a system module is highlighted to view detailed memory information about that module. The Memory Utilization screen is shown in Figure 15.1.

FIGURE 15.1
MONITOR's Memory
Utilization screen displays
information about
memory use.

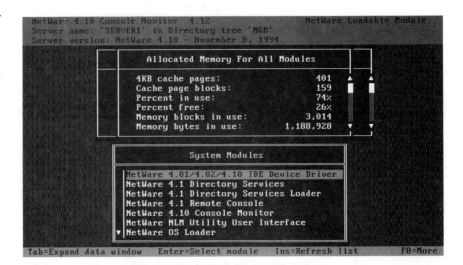

Protecting the Server's Memory

In previous versions of NetWare, the operating system memory was *unprotected*. Nothing could stop an NLM or driver from writing to the wrong area of memory. When an NLM or driver writes to the wrong area of memory, it can become corrupted, which can result in the loss or corruption of data or in a server *abend* (crash).

The *memory protection* features of NetWare 4.1 provide protection against many of the problems that result from memory corruption. Memory protection in NetWare 4.1 is a flexible system that allows NLMs to run without risk of corrupting the operating system or data. When a crash occurs, the basic operating system processes can often continue.

MEMORY DOMAINS Memory protection uses a system of *domains* to manage areas of memory. Server memory contains two domains. The *OS domain* is used for trusted programs, such as parts of the NetWare operating system. You can use the *OS_Protected (*or OSP*) domain* to run NLMs that may cause corruption.

The NetWare 4.1 memory domains use a system of *rings,* which are illustrated in Figure 15.2. The OS domain runs in ring 0. The OSP domain runs in ring 3. Processes in an outer ring are prevented from accessing the memory in inner rings. Each ring has a different level of protection. Some system NLMs use rings 1 and 2, but NetWare generally uses rings 0 and 3 exclusively.

FIGURE 15.2
NetWare secures
memory through
the use of rings.

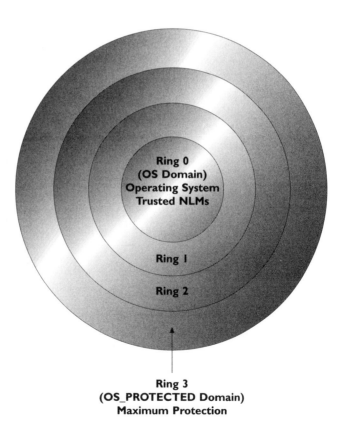

Ring 0
(OS Domain)
Operating System
Trusted NLMs

Ring 1

Ring 2

Ring 3
(OS_PROTECTED Domain)
Maximum Protection

The OS domain, ring 0, provides the lowest level of protection. Programs in this domain can access all server memory. Because no validation is performed when these applications access memory, you can gain the fastest performance by running NLMs in this domain.

All NLMs included with NetWare are safe to run in the OS Domain. Most certified "NetWare Tested and Approved" NLMs are also safe. If an NLM is new or noncertified, you may want to run it in the OS_Protected domain until it has proven itself safe.

USING MEMORY PROTECTION By default, all NLMs run in the OS domain (ring 0). In order to separate some NLMs into the OSP domain, you must load the DOMAIN NLM. This module controls memory protection and provides commands so that you can determine which domain each NLM is loaded in.

You should use the OSP domain only as a temporary measure. Running an NLM in this domain can seriously degrade the performance of your system.

DOMAIN must be loaded before all other NLMs on your server. To do this, place the LOAD DOMAIN command in the server's STARTUP.NCF file. Because STARTUP.NCF loads programs from the server's DOS partition, you must copy DOMAIN NLM to the DOS partition. You must also copy files that DOMAIN uses: NWTIL.NLM, NWTILR.NLM, and DOMAIN.MSG. These are loaded automatically when DOMAIN is loaded.

After the DOMAIN NLM is loaded, you can use the DOMAIN command at the server console to control the use of domains. You can also place this command in the AUTOEXEC.NCF or STARTUP.NCF files to control the domains used by NLMs loaded in these files. The following are the valid DOMAIN commands:

- **DOMAIN OS** makes the OS domain the current domain. NLMs loaded after this command are placed in the OS domain.

- **DOMAIN OS_PROTECTED** changes the default domain to the OSP domain. NLMs you load after this command are placed in the OSP domain.

- **DOMAIN** (with no parameters) displays the current domain name and lists the NLMs that have been loaded into that domain.

- **DOMAIN HELP** displays help information about the DOMAIN NLM and its commands.

Not all NLMs can be run in different domains. Consult the documentation for a particular NLM to determine which domain it can be run in.

SET Commands for Memory Management

You can use several SET commands to control the allocation and use of memory. You can also control whether several types of memory protection errors display messages on the console or abend the server. Type these commands at the server console followed by the equal sign (=) and the desired value for the parameter. You can also place these commands in the server's STARTUP.NCF file. Here's an example of a SET command that shows the correct syntax (capitalization is optional):

```
SET GARBAGE COLLECTION INTERVAL = 25
```

Most servers can run efficiently with no change to these parameters. Be sure that you understand what the settings mean before changing them. If a setting does not solve your problem or improve speed, change it back to the default.

- **SET Garbage Collection Interval** controls how often the garbage collection process is performed. This value is in minutes and can range from 1 to 60. The default is every 15 minutes.

- **SET Number of Frees for Garbage Collection** allows garbage collection to be performed automatically when an NLM completes a certain number of *free* calls to deallocate memory. The default is 5,000. This value can range from 100 to 100,000.

- **SET Minimum Free Memory for Garbage Collection** sets the number of bytes that must be in the system memory pool for successful garbage collection. This value ranges from 1,000 to 1,000,000 and defaults to 8,000.

- **SET Allow Invalid Pointers** can be either OFF or ON. This parameter allows an application to define a pointer to an invalid area of memory. The default is OFF. With this parameter ON, the system displays a warning at the console rather than an abend.

- **SET Read Fault Emulation** defaults to OFF. When an application attempts to read memory in a nonexistent page, a *read fault* usually occurs and the server abends. If this parameter is set to ON, it causes an error message at the console but does not bring down the server. NetWare *emulates* the read request and returns a value to the application so that it won't crash.

- **SET Read Fault Notification** can be set to ON or OFF and defaults to ON. This controls whether read faults that are emulated will cause a message to be displayed on the server console and in the error log.

- **SET Write Fault Emulation** controls whether *write faults* (attempts to write to invalid areas of memory) are emulated.

- **SET Write Fault Notification** controls whether write fault messages are logged to the server console and the error log.

- **SET Alloc Memory Check Flag** can be set to ON if you wish the server to constantly check for memory corruption. This process slows system performance but can be useful for tracking down ill-behaved NLMs.

Although many of these SET parameters can prevent an abend, they are usually not a permanent solution. You should determine which NLM is causing the problem. Then you can avoid loading that NLM, upgrade to a newer version, or use the DOMAIN commands described earlier in this chapter to run the suspect NLM in a protected area of memory.

The following two SET commands cannot be typed at the console but must be in the STARTUP.NCF file.

- **SET Auto Register Memory Above 16 Megabytes** defaults to ON. This allows EISA computers to automatically use memory above 16MB if available. You may need to set this to OFF to provide compatibility with the disk controller.

- **SET Reserved Buffers Below 16 Megabytes** reserves buffer space in the lower 16MB of memory for device drivers that are limited to that area. You can set this value between 8 and 300; it defaults to 16.

Most of these SET commands, and the others we'll introduce in this chapter, can also be modified with the SERVMAN utility, described in Chapter 10.

Checking CPU Performance

The type and speed of the server's CPU can dramatically affect system performance. If your server is running slowly, you can use the SPEED command and the MONITOR utility to determine the cause of the problem.

First, type **SPEED** at the server console to verify that your CPU is running at its normal speed. SPEED calculates a number based on CPU performance; speed should be approximately 90 for a 386; 900 for a 486; and 3,000 or more for a Pentium-based machine. If your server displays an unusually low number, check the Turbo or Speed switch on the server and be sure it is set to the highest speed.

Next, you should check to see if an application is using a high percentage of the CPU's resources. Select Scheduling Information in the MONITOR utility to display the percentage of the CPU's time being used by each NLM. Figure 15.3 shows the Scheduling Information screen. Most NLMs use between 2 and 10 percent of the CPU time. If an NLM is using a higher percentage, unload it or configure it differently. Of course, if you are running an intense application such as a backup or database, you can expect its utilization to be high.

FIGURE 15.3
The Scheduling Information screen can be used to detect NLMs that are overworking the CPU.

```
NetWare 4.10 Console Monitor  4.12              NetWare Loadable Module
Server name: 'SERVER1' in Directory tree 'MGM'
Server version: NetWare 4.10 - November 8, 1994

  Process Name           Sch Delay        Time     Count       Load

  Console Command              0            0         0        0.00%  ▲
  MakeThread                   0            0         0        0.00%
  Media Manager                0            0         0        0.00%
  MONITOR main                 0            0         0        0.00%
  Remirror                     0            0         0        0.00%
  Remote                       0       51,994       148        1.47%
  RSPX                         0            0         0        0.00%
  Sync Clock Event             0            0         0        0.00%
  TimeSyncMain                 0          102         3        0.00%

  Interrupts                            3,867        56        0.10%
  Idle Loop                         3,471,434        54       98.29%
  Work                                  4,301       189        0.12%

  Total sample time:                3,538,962
  Histogram overhead time:              7,362   ( 0.20%)
  Adjusted sample time:             3,531,600

 +=Increase delay   -=Decrease delay   Esc=Previous list          F8=More
```

Note that the Idle Loop included in the scheduling information probably displays a high percentage. The Idle Loop amount is the percentage of CPU time that is free for use by other NLMs. If this number is below 50, your server may be overworked.

Optimizing Disk Performance

The speed of disk access on NetWare volumes also affects the speed of the server and the network. NetWare 4.1 provides sophisticated *cache* mechanisms that move frequently accessed information from the disk to the server's RAM for faster access. You can optimize these mechanisms to streamline performance. In addition, the *file compression* and *block suballocation* features allow the server to store more information on available disk space.

Monitoring Cache Buffers

A NetWare server always sets aside a certain amount of RAM for *cache buffers*. When blocks are read from the disk, they are first transferred into the cache. If the same information is needed again, it can be read from RAM rather than by accessing the disk drive. Blocks written to the disk are also written to the cache, and blocks in the same area are written all at once. Cache buffers provide a dramatic improvement in disk speed.

You can view cache statistics by using the Cache Utilization option in the MONITOR utility. This screen, shown in Figure 15.4, provides several pieces of information about the performance of the cache, much of which concerns *cache hits*. A cache hit occurs when the information required is found in the cache and the disk does not need to be accessed.

If the network is running smoothly, the short-term and long-term cache hit percentages should be 90 percent or higher. When these numbers are low, the server runs slowly. Applications that read many files with little repetition, such as backups, can cause a low cache hit percentage; this is nothing to worry about.

Optimizing Cache Buffers

The simplest solution to cache problems is to add more RAM to the server. You can also use the following SET commands to optimize the cache process:

- **SET Dirty Disk Cache Delay Time** specifies how long the server waits after a write request before it is written to the disk. This value can range

FIGURE 15.4
The Cache Utilization Statistics screen provides information about the disk cache.

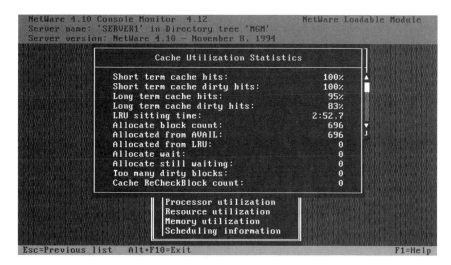

from .1 second to 10 seconds and defaults to 3.3 seconds. You can set the delay time to a higher value if users frequently write to the disk. This change may improve access speed.

- **SET Maximum Concurrent Disk Cache Writes** specifies the number of write requests the server waits for before beginning to write them to the disk.

- **SET Minimum File Cache Buffers** controls the minimum number of cache buffers that are available. When NLMs are loaded, they take memory away from cache buffers. You can set this parameter to make sure some buffers are always available. This value defaults to 20 and can be set as high as 1,000.

- **SET Minimum File Cache Report Threshold** sets a threshold for warnings about low cache buffers. It can be set between 0 and 1,000 and defaults to 20. When the number of available cache buffers decreases below the set number, a warning is displayed on the server console.

- **SET Read Ahead Enabled** can be set to ON or OFF. This parameter controls whether the server reads ahead, or reads extra blocks into the cache, when reading from the disk. Read Ahead assumes that the extra blocks will be requested next and in most cases improves disk access speed. The default is ON.

▪ **SET Read Ahead LRU Sitting Time Threshold** controls the read ahead process. Reading ahead writes over the least recently used (LRU) areas of the cache. These areas must be sitting, or unused, for the set number of seconds before they are overwritten. The sitting time can range from 0 seconds to 1 hour and defaults to 10 seconds.

Block Suballocation

The *suballocation* feature of NetWare 4.1 was introduced in Chapter 2. This feature divides the blocks used for disk storage into portions as small as 512 bytes, allowing more efficient use of disk space. Block suballocation eliminates the space wasted by very small files and by files that use a fractional block.

HOW SUBALLOCATION WORKS Block suballocation uses two types of blocks on the volume: normal blocks and suballocated blocks. A file always begins at the boundary between two blocks. Whole blocks are used for as much of the file as possible. If a partial block is left at the end of the file, the block is suballocated. The remaining suballocation units (512-byte fragments) of the block can be used for suballocated portions of other files. Normal blocks and suballocated blocks are illustrated in Figure 15.5.

ENABLING BLOCK SUBALLOCATION You can enable block suballocation for a volume when the volume is created. You can also enable it later with the INSTALL utility. Once enabled, you cannot disable it without reformatting the volume. Follow these steps to enable suballocation on a new volume:

1. Start the INSTALL module by typing **LOAD INSTALL** at the server console.

2. Select Volume Options.

3. Press Enter when the volume name is highlighted. The status of the volume is shown.

4. Move the highlight to Block Suballocation and press Enter.

5. Press Enter to toggle the suballocation from OFF to ON.

6. Press ESC to exit and save the changes.

CONTROLLING SUBALLOCATION WITH FILE ATTRIBUTES To use some files efficiently, you should avoid using suballocation. Files that are added to frequently, such as database files, should not be suballocated. You can

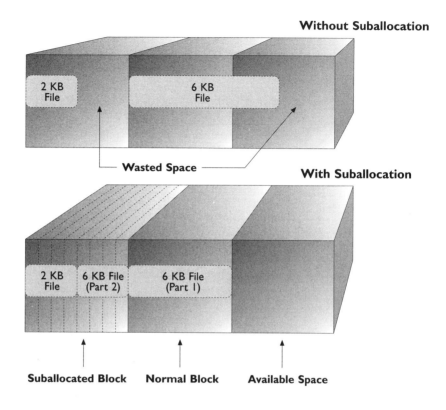

FIGURE 15.5
Block suballocation uses
normal blocks and
suballocated blocks to
optimize disk storage.

turn off suballocation for a file using the Ds (Don't Suballocate) file attribute. To set this attribute, use the FLAG command:

```
FLAG filename DS
```

File Compression

The NetWare 4.1 *file compression* feature, introduced in Chapter 2, allows files that are not currently in use to be compressed. This feature can dramatically improve the amount of disk storage available on your server and yet keeps the files available for easy access.

NetWare checks for files that have not been accessed for several days. When such a file is found, it is compressed into a temporary file. If the compression process is successful and the compressed file is significantly smaller, the original file is deleted and the compressed file is put in its place.

You can use file attributes to disable compression for specific files or directories and to determine whether a file is compressed. Information about these attributes is given in Chapter 7.

ACTIVATING FILE COMPRESSION   NetWare 4.1 enables file compression by default; however, if you have upgraded to NetWare 4.1 from a previous version of NetWare, you must activate the feature manually. Once activated, you cannot disable file compression without re-creating the volume; however, you can disable compression for directories and files. You can also use a SET command to disable compression on the server. Follow these steps to enable file compression:

1. Start the INSTALL utility by typing **LOAD INSTALL** at the server console.

2. Select Volume Options.

3. Press Enter when the desired volume is highlighted.

4. Change the File Compression option to ON.

5. Press ESC to exit and save the changes.

DISADVANTAGES OF FILE COMPRESSION   Although NetWare's file compression eliminates the problems of most compressed file systems, this feature has some disadvantages. You should take these disadvantages into account when deciding whether to activate file compression on your server.

- **Speed of access:** When a user requests a file that has been compressed, a delay occurs as the server uncompresses the file. In most networks this won't happen very often, but if your users need to access a compressed file—for example, a large database that is updated monthly—the network may slow to a creeping halt. Depending on the file size and the server speed, decompression can take from 30 seconds to as long as 10 minutes. You can avoid this delay by turning off compression on these files. Using a SET parameter, you can also change the time that NetWare waits before compressing the files.

- **Backups:** Files backed up from a compressed volume should be restored onto a volume that also has compression enabled, to ensure that space is available. In addition, unless the backup system supports compression, files are restored in an uncompressed state and NetWare compresses them after seven days. Thus, restoring an entire volume could require a much greater amount of disk space than the original volume.

- **Compression is enabled permanently:** Once you enable compression on a volume, you cannot turn it off and uncompress the files without re-creating the volume (which erases all data on the volume!). You can, however, disable compression for individual files and directories. You can also disable compression with a SET command, described in the next section.

- **Server Performance:** In a heavily used server, compression and decompression can happen constantly, which can slow your server. However, this slowing is minimal and well worth the increase in available storage.

CONTROLLING FILE COMPRESSION WITH SET COMMANDS You can optimize the file compression process with a variety of SET parameters, which allow you to enable or disable compression, control how often compression is performed, and fine-tune the compression process. The SET commands listed below can be typed at the server console, or you can add them to the server's STARTUP.NCF or AUTOEXEC.NCF file to set the parameter permanently.

- **SET Compression Daily Check Stop Hour** specifies an hour in military time when the server stops checking for files that are ready to compress. You can use this setting, along with the Check Starting Hour setting described below, to ensure that the compression process happens at a time when few users are on the network. The default is 6 (6:00 a.m.).

- **SET Compression Daily Check Starting Hour** sets the time that the server begins checking for files to compress. The default is 0 (12:00 midnight).

- **SET Minimum Compression Percentage Gain** controls the level of compression that is required in order to keep the file compressed. For example, if this value is 10 percent, the file must be at least 10 percent smaller; otherwise, the original, uncompressed version of the file is kept.

- **SET Enable File Compression** can be ON or OFF and controls whether the compression process will occur. The default is ON. If you set this to OFF, there may still be compressed files on the server, but no additional files will be compressed.

- **SET Maximum Concurrent Compressions** specifies the number of volumes that can be compressing files at the same time. This defaults to 2. Larger values may slow the server considerably.

- **SET Convert Compressed to Uncompressed Option** can be set to 0, 1, or 2 and controls what happens to a file after it is accessed and subsequently uncompressed. Option 0 keeps the file compressed, 1 keeps it compressed after the first access only, and option 2 leaves the file uncompressed. The default is 1.

- **SET Uncompress Percent Disk Space Free to Allow Commit** specifies the percentage of the volume's space that must be available before a file is uncompressed. This parameter is quite possibly the longest SET parameter available, but its purpose is simple: It prevents uncompressed files from filling up the volume.

- **SET Uncompress Free Space Warning Interval** controls how often a warning is displayed when there is not enough free space to uncompress a file. This parameter can be set to a value in minutes or to 0 to disable the warnings.

- **SET Deleted File Compression Option** controls whether compression is performed on deleted files. (The files are still available for salvage using the FILER or NWADMIN utilities.) The setting can be 0, 1, or 2. Option 0 never compresses deleted files, option 1 compresses them one day after deletion, and option 2 compresses files immediately when deleted.

- **SET Days Untouched Before Compression** controls how many days a file must remain untouched before it is compressed. The default is seven days.

FILE ATTRIBUTES FOR FILE COMPRESSION Several of the new NetWare 4.1 file attributes are related to file compression. File attributes are explained in detail in Chapter 7.

- Ic (Immediate Compress) can be used to specify that a file (or directory of files) should be compressed immediately each time it is written to. This compression happens regardless of the time of day and may slow the server.

- Dc (Don't Compress) can be used to prevent files or directories from being compressed. This attribute can be used on a file that needs to be accessed quickly or one that must be updated frequently.

- Cc (Can't Compress) is set automatically by the server. This attribute indicates that the file has been left uncompressed because the savings in disk space would be insufficient if it were compressed.

Disk Controller Considerations

The speed of disk access on the server depends heavily on the type of drive and controller used. The main types of disk drives are IDE (Integrated Drive Electronics) and SCSI (Small Computer Systems Interface). While IDE drives are most commonly used in PCs, SCSI devices are better suited for NetWare servers. SCSI is a reliable, intelligent protocol and allows multiple drives—up to 16 with the latest SCSI-2 devices.

High-end SCSI controllers include such features as a built-in cache, bus mastering, and PCI or VESA local bus interfaces. By taking advantage of these devices, you can streamline disk performance on your network.

Using Turbo FAT Indexing

The *File Allocation Table* (FAT) keeps track of each file on the volume and lists the blocks that the file occupies. Randomly accessed files that are added to frequently can be spread across many different blocks on the disk, which can slow access.

To alleviate this slowdown, NetWare includes turbo FAT indexing. When a file is randomly accessed and has more than 64 FAT entries, a turbo FAT is created for the file. This index points to the location of blocks for that one file only. Because the file has its own index, it can be quickly accessed.

The turbo FAT is loaded into memory when the file is accessed. A single SET parameter, SET Turbo FAT Re-Use Wait Time, controls how long the turbo FAT remains in memory, in case the file is accessed again. This value defaults to about five minutes.

Optimizing Network Communication

The final category of settings that affects server performance is network communication. You can use packet and buffer settings and the new Packet Burst Protocol to streamline communication between the server and clients. NetWare 4.1 also supports Large Internet Packets, which can improve communication between multiple servers in an enterprise network.

Packets and Buffers

All communication between the server and clients is divided into *packets*. A packet is a set number of bytes that are transmitted at the same time. The packet includes a header that identifies the destination and source of the packet and the data itself. Figure 15.6 illustrates packet transmission. The size of packets and the buffers used to transfer them can be changed to improve performance.

CHANGING PACKET SIZE The size of packets depends on the software and hardware used and on the topology of the network. Default packet sizes are 1,514 bytes for Ethernet and 4,202 bytes for ARCnet and Token Ring.

You can modify the packet size used with the Maximum Physical Receive Packet Size parameter but not with the SET command at the server console. Instead, use SERVMAN or change the STARTUP.NCF file manually. The change takes effect when the server is restarted.

You can use different packet sizes only if your network interface cards and drivers support them; consult their documentation for more information. If your network uses a router, you must consider the packet size that it supports; see the section Using Large Internet Packets later in this chapter for more details.

PACKET RECEIVE BUFFERS NetWare reserves an area of memory for *packet receive buffers*. These buffers are used as an intermediate area to hold each packet as it is transferred between the server and other servers or clients. To ensure efficient communication, make sure that sufficient packet receive buffers are available.

The main screen of the MONITOR utility displays the current number of available packet receive buffers. NetWare allocates additional packet receive buffers when needed. You can control the minimum and maximum number with SET commands. Here are the SET commands used for packet receive buffers:

- **SET Maximum Packet Receive Buffers** sets the maximum number of buffers that can be allocated. This parameter defaults to 100. You can set this value

FIGURE 15.6
Data sent over the network is divided into packets.

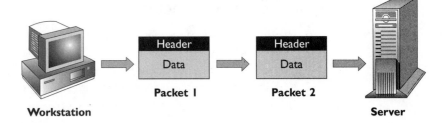

between 50 and 4,000. If the MONITOR statistics show that the maximum number of buffers are being used, you should increase this number.

- **SET Minimum Packet Receive Buffers** sets the minimum number of buffers. Although NetWare will gradually allocate more buffers if needed, the minimum setting allows users to access the server at optimal speeds immediately. The number can range from 10 to 2,000 and defaults to 50. If the server is slow after you start it, you can increase this number.

- **SET Maximum Service Processes** allows you to control the number of communications that can be processed at the same time. This command may reduce the need for additional packet receive buffers.

- **SET New Packet Receive Buffer Wait Time** is the time that NetWare waits before it allocates additional buffers. This delay prevents the number of buffers from being increased by a brief period of high usage. This period of time ranges from .1 second to 20 seconds and defaults to the minimum .1 second.

Monitoring Network Interface Cards

You can use MONITOR to display statistics for the Network Interface Cards (NICs) in the server. You can access this information through the LAN/WAN Information option. The type of statistics provided depends on the NIC and driver software used on the server. The statistics include packets sent and received, errors, and other information. This screen is shown in Figure 15.7.

Along with global statistics, such as packets sent and received, this screen also lists custom statistics for the network card type. For example, the EnqueuedSendsCount statistic (provided for NE2000 cards) lists the number of times that the card was busy when a packet was ready to be sent. This statistic can indicate that communication between the server and NIC is too slow. You can improve performance in this situation by switching to a 32-bit (VESA or PCI) NIC or a high-performance card.

Using Packet Burst Protocol

In normal communication, packets are sent one at a time, and an acknowledgment is sent after each packet. This method requires two-way communication for each packet. Two-way communication can be particularly

FIGURE 15.7
Network Interface Card
statistics provide details
about communication
through the board.

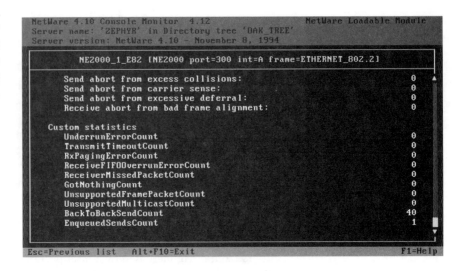

slow when a WAN link is involved because each acknowledgment must be sent across the WAN before the next packet can be sent.

Using Packet Burst Protocol, multiple packets can be sent without individual acknowledgments. This protocol allows much faster transfers of large files. Up to 64KB can be sent in a single *burst*, or group of packets. Packet burst can improve performance across the network between 10 and 300 percent, depending on the server and the way it is used. Packet Burst Protocol is illustrated in Figure 15.8.

How Packet Burst Works

The client (using the NetWare DOS Requester) and the server negotiate to determine the size of the packet bursts, also called the *window size*. The server may also use a delay, called the *burst gap time*, to ensure that packets are sent slowly enough for the client to keep up. These parameters are set automatically.

Once Packet Burst Protocol is enabled, the client sends a single request and receives an entire burst of packets. After the packets are received, it sends an acknowledgment. The acknowledgment specifies which packets were received correctly. If any packets were not received, they are resent individually; there is no need to resend the entire packet burst. This error-correction process is illustrated in Figure 15.9.

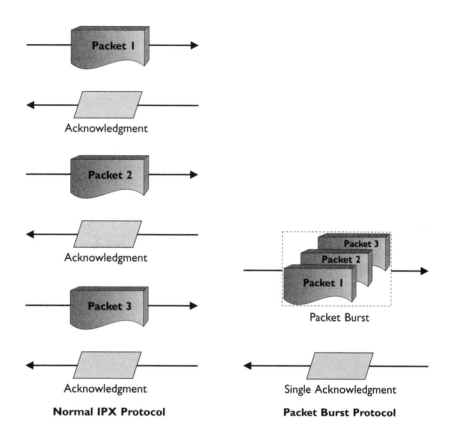

FIGURE 15.8
Packet Burst Protocol
improves the speed of
network communication.

Enabling and Optimizing Packet Burst

Packet burst is automatically enabled on the NetWare 4.1 server. It is also enabled automatically on the client by the NetWare DOS Requester provided with NetWare 4.1. If clients are still using the NetWare shell, you must upgrade them in order to take advantage of Packet Burst Protocol, which requires the NetWare DOS Requester.

When a workstation establishes a connection with a server, the client and server negotiate to determine whether packet burst can be used. If a client is used that does not support packet burst, the normal NetWare protocols are used instead. The DOS Requester also supports servers that do not use packet burst;

FIGURE 15.9
Packet Burst Protocol
resends packets that
were received incorrectly.

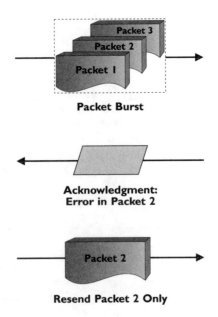

in fact, a client connected to two servers might use packet burst with one and not the other.

To disable packet burst for individual clients, set the PB BUFFERS parameter in the DOS Requester section of the NET.CFG file. This value can range from 0 to 10. The zero setting disables packet burst entirely. Higher values enable packet burst and allow the DOS Requester to set the actual number of buffers to be used.

Using Large Internet Packets

The *Large Internet Packet* (LIP) feature is another method of improving the speed of communication on the network. As described in a previous section, packet sizes can be changed to improve communication. The client and server negotiate to determine the packet size. Ethernet and Token Ring topologies allow larger packet sizes to be used.

When a NetWare server is used as a router, however, the packet size of routed packets is limited to 512 bytes. This size restricts all communication through the router to smaller packets. The Large Internet Packet feature avoids this limitation and allows full-size packets to be routed. The use of routers with and without Large Internet Packets is shown in Figure 15.10.

LIP can be used in conjunction with Packet Burst Protocol for maximum performance. This combination allows several large packets to be sent across the network with a single acknowledgment and eliminates the bottlenecks associated with normal network communication.

ENABLING LIP Large Internet Packets are enabled by default at the NetWare 4.1 server and the client using the NetWare DOS Requester. You must also ensure that the correct packet size is set for the router.

The SET Maximum Physical Receive Packet Size parameter can change the allowable packet size on each server that acts as a router. This parameter can range from 618 to 24,682. The default value, 4,202, is sufficient to allow LIP for Ethernet or Token Ring protocols. Because the largest packet size for Ethernet networks is 1,518 bytes, you can save server RAM by reducing this setting.

FIGURE 15.10
Large Internet Packets
allow more efficient use
of a router.

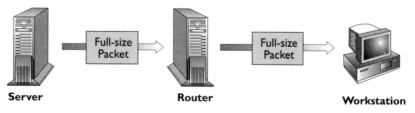

Review

Server Components

The hardware components of a NetWare 4.1 server include the following:

- **The processor (CPU):** NetWare 4.1 requires a PC-compatible machine with a 386 or better CPU. (To run at any kind of respectable speed, you'll need at least a 486.)

- **RAM (Random Access Memory):** NetWare 4.1 requires at least 8MB of RAM.

- **Disk storage:** NetWare 4.1 uses a DOS partition for the SERVER.EXE file and a NetWare partition to hold at least one NetWare volume (SYS).

- **Network board and cabling:** Without this, the server won't do you much good. The network board allows the server to communicate with workstations and other servers.

The main software component of a NetWare 4.1 server is the SERVER.EXE program. This program loads from DOS but takes over the operating system completely (and can even remove DOS from memory). This is the actual NetWare server software.

Other software components include disk drivers, which allow communication with disk drives in the server, and LAN drivers, which allow communication with the network board.

NetWare 4.1 uses *network numbers* to identify devices on the network:

- The *internal network number* is set for each server and uniquely identifies the server.

- The *network card address* is wired into each network card. You cannot usually change it.

- The *network number*, or *external network number*, is used by multiple servers on the same network. All servers use the same number.

Configuration of the Server

You can configure the server using several special files:

- AUTOEXEC.BAT runs under DOS and is a list of commands needed to execute the SERVER.EXE program.

- STARTUP.NCF is a list of NetWare commands that are executed when the server starts. It is used to load disk drivers.

- AUTOEXEC.NCF executes next and is used to set parameters and load network drivers.

- You can create your own batch file with the NCF extension to execute a set of commands.

Optimizing the Network

If you monitor server and network performance, you can detect problems before they become severe. You can also optimize and streamline your network using SET commands and other settings. The major areas that affect performance are memory and CPU, disk access, and network communication.

Memory and CPU Performance

NetWare 4.1 uses sophisticated *memory management* techniques. Memory is divided into 4KB blocks called *pages*. These pages are *allocated*, or made available, for each NLM or other application that requires memory. These pages may not be located in a single area of memory, but the application sees them as one block.

NLMs or system programs are assigned an *allocation pool* when they start. The allocation pool is based on an estimate of the memory that the application requires. As the application requests memory pages, NetWare assigns them from this pool, and when the application frees the memory, it is returned to the pool. Memory is assigned efficiently because each application uses its own memory pool. When an application no longer needs an area of memory, it returns the memory to the system, or *deallocates* it. A periodic *garbage collection* process finds these areas of memory and returns them to the main memory pool, allowing them to be used by other applications.

MEMORY PROTECTION The *memory protection* features of NetWare 4.1 allow you to control the behavior of NLMs in the server's memory. Normally, NLMs are given access to the entire memory of the server and can access memory belonging to other applications.

Memory protection uses a system of *domains* to manage the server's memory. The *OS Domain* is used for trusted programs, such as the NetWare operating system. The *OS_Protected* (or OSP) domain is available for untrusted NLMs, which may cause memory corruption.

Domains are organized into *rings*. The inner ring, ring 0, has the lowest level of protection and is used for the OS domain. The outer ring, ring 3, has the most protection and is used for the OSP domain.

To use memory protection, load the DOMAIN NLM in the server's STARTUP.NCF file. Then use the DOMAIN command to control the use of domains. This command can be used to display the current domain or to set the domain for NLMs you load subsequently.

CPU PERFORMANCE The CPU speed and type of the server can also affect system performance. You can use the SPEED command to determine whether your server is operating at the optimum speed. In addition, the Scheduling Information screen in the MONITOR utility shows you if a particular NLM is using a large part of the CPU's resources.

Disk Performance

The speed of disk access on NetWare volumes also affects the speed of the server and the network. Areas relating to disk access include cache buffers, disk controllers, turbo FAT indexing, file compression, and block suballocation.

NetWare sets aside a certain amount of RAM as *cache buffers*, which optimize performance because they are used to hold information from the disk drive and limit use of the disk. You can view statistics relating to cache buffers in MONITOR; several SET commands allow you to optimize their use.

SUBALLOCATION AND COMPRESSION The *suballocation* feature of NetWare 4.1 divides the blocks used for disk storage into portions as small as 512 bytes, allowing for more efficient use of disk space. This eliminates the space wasted by very small files and by files that use a fractional block. Block suballocation is enabled individually for each volume and can be changed only when the volume is created. It can also be controlled for individual files and directories using file attributes.

The *compression* feature allows files that are not currently in use to be compressed. When a file has not been accessed for several days, it is compressed into a temporary file. If the file is significantly smaller, it replaces the original file.

File compression is enabled by default for each volume. You cannot change the setting without re-creating the volume. You can use file attributes to disable compression for individual files and directories or to specify files or directories that will be immediately compressed each time they are written to. You can also use a SET command to prevent any files from being compressed.

OTHER FACTORS The disk controller and drive type affect disk performance. IDE drives are commonly used, but SCSI drives are more suited to a NetWare server. High-end 32-bit (PCI or VESA local bus) disk controllers should be used whenever possible for optimum performance.

The *turbo FAT indexing* feature provides an extra index for files that use more than 64 different areas of the disk. This index makes access to the file more efficient. The turbo FAT is kept in the server's RAM while the file is being accessed. Only randomly accessed files can be indexed with the turbo FAT.

Network Communication

The final category of settings that affect server performance is network communication. You can monitor and optimize several factors in order to improve communication:

- The **packet size** is negotiated between the client and server; larger packets can improve performance.

- The number of **packet receive buffers** is controlled by SET commands, which control the amount of RAM used to hold packets. You can use MONITOR to determine the correct settings.

- MONITOR allows you to check statistics for the server's NIC (Network Interface Card). These statistics provide information about the amount of use, errors that have occurred, and performance limitations.

- The **Packet Burst Protocol** allows several packets to be sent with a single acknowledgment and improves communication speeds, especially over WAN links. Packet burst is enabled by default.

A NetWare server used as a router is typically limited to 512-byte packets. The Large Internet Packet (LIP) feature allows packets to be passed through the router without limiting their size. LIP improves speed through the router and can be used in combination with Packet Burst Protocol for maximum efficiency. LIP is enabled by default.

Career Choices
for CNAs

PART

4

The Current State of Networking

CONGRATULATIONS! IF YOU'VE BEEN READING this book in order, you have covered a lot of territory. There's quite a bit of information to learn and remember, so before going in for the CNA exam, we suggest that you review the appropriate chapters and complete the practice questions at the end of each chapter as well as the questions on the CD-ROM that comes with this book.

To conclude this book, we're going to take a closer look at network use in the real world. The information we've gathered should give you some idea of what to expect if you're hired to work on a network. What kinds of hardware are you likely to find on the networks you will work on? What are the differences among NetWare versions? Finally, what are the best sources of help for when you are troubleshooting?

In the next chapter, we take a look at your jobs prospects as a CNA. We'll also consider the trends and technologies that will shape the future of networking so that you have a better idea of what's in your future as a network professional.

All of the information in this chapter is current as of the date of this writing. However, because computer and networking technology changes very quickly, we highly recommend that you subscribe to a few PC and network magazines to keep up with current conditions and constant changes. InfoWorld, Network World, and LAN Times are a few of the better journals. You may be a network expert now, but if you ignore the changes in technology and in the industry, you'll quickly find yourself out of date (and, quite possibly, out of a job).

Network Statistics

NETWORKS RANGE FROM LANs to MANs to WANs and use a vast array of technologies, topologies, and network operating systems. In the past several years, networks have grown from a budding innovation to a multibillion-dollar industry. There are an estimated 1,500,000 networks in use in the United States, and this number is constantly growing. It is becoming cheaper and easier to set up a network, and most companies with five or more PCs now connect them with some sort of network. A wide variety of network operating systems—in addition to NetWare 4.1—are in use.

An important point to keep in mind is that not everyone is using the latest technology. Many corporations have tight budgets, and both users and administrators often avoid change—If it works, why fix it? You can expect to find many networks still running NetWare 3.1x and even earlier versions of NetWare. In some cases, your job will be to upgrade these networks to NetWare 4.1. On the other hand, many companies prefer to keep that old network running as long as it will last, and your job will be to maintain it.

Network Topologies

Ethernet is the clear winner among the types of network topologies (the wiring and protocols used for network communication) in use. Other topologies include ARCnet, Token Ring and FDDI, or Fiber Distributed Data Interface. These topologies were introduced in Chapter 1 of this book, but we'll take a real-world look at each one in the following sections.

Ethernet

The Ethernet standard was developed by Xerox, Intel, and Digital Equipment Corporation. The first version was produced in the 1960s, and the current standard, Ethernet 2.0, was developed in 1982. It is the most common network topology and is used on from 60 to 90 percent of all networks. At least 1,000,000 Ethernet nodes are in place around the world. (They're not all hooked together, of course.)

Ethernet is most commonly used with RG-58 coaxial cable (thinnet) or unshielded twisted pair (UTP) cable. Ethernet can also be used with thick coax cable (thicknet) and fiber optic cable. Older networks typically use thin coax, or 10Base2. These networks can be fun to troubleshoot because coaxial cabling works like old-fashioned Christmas tree lights: If one node is disconnected, the entire network can go down. The newer standard, 10BaseT, uses independent connections between each workstation and a hub. If a workstation is disconnected, it has no effect on the other stations.

The maximum bandwidth for Ethernet is 10 Mbps (megabits per second). The real world speed is usually slower, though, because of network cards, PC processing power, header information, and delays as data are transmitted through the hub. Nevertheless, Ethernet provides a definite advantage over ARCnet, which is typically limited to 2.5 Mbps. A standard for *fast Ethernet* is emerging; it allows speeds of up to 100 Mbps using category 5 twisted pair cable. You'll learn more about that in the next chapter.

In terms of usability and reliability, there's a big difference between the types of wiring used with Ethernet. 10Base2 (thinnet) can be unreliable and difficult to troubleshoot. In contrast, the 10BaseT standard is probably the easiest network type to troubleshoot. Unfortunately, most Ethernet networks use the older thinnet wiring. If you get to make a choice, stick to 10BaseT.

ARCnet

ARCnet (Attached Resources Computer Network) was developed by Datapoint Corporation in the late 1970s. It was a very popular topology for some time, but never as popular as Ethernet.

Although ARCnet has few advantages for new networks, it is still in wide use. ARCnet, like Ethernet, can use a variety of cabling standards. It typically uses coaxial cable, but it can be used with twisted pair if the equipment supports it. Because most of the existing ARCnet networks are old, coax cable is very common.

ARCnet operates at a maximum speed of 2.5 Mbps, and in practical terms 50 to 60 percent of that speed is typical. Thus, it pales by comparison to Ethernet. However, the speed is largely dependent on the number of nodes; for smaller networks, ARCnet runs reasonably fast. However, there are high-speed alternatives for ARCnet: ARCnet Plus, which operates at 20 Mbps, and TCNS, a proprietary standard from Thomas Conrad Corp. (now part of Compaq) that allows speeds up to 100 Mbps over standard ARCnet coaxial cable or fiber optic cable.

ARCnet networks are a bit more difficult to configure and troubleshoot than Ethernet 10BaseT networks, chiefly because each workstation must be given a unique node number that is usually set by a DIP switch in the network card. However, 10BaseT is easier to troubleshoot than 10Base2.

ARCnet is not very practical for new networks largely because of its high cost and lack of support. But for the next few years at least, you shouldn't be surprised to find yourself supporting an ARCnet network.

Token Ring

The Token Ring standard was developed by the IEEE, but didn't become popular until IBM introduced a revised version of the standard. Token Ring works well for high-traffic networks and is widely used in systems that need to link NetWare networks with IBM mainframes. Although Token Ring is not as common as Ethernet, many companies do use it.

The original Token Ring specification allowed speeds of 1 to 4 Mbps. IBM's version allows speeds up to 16 Mbps. IBM standards define the cable types, which include shielded twisted pair (STP), UTP, and fiber optic cable. Multistation Access Units (MAUs) are used as hubs to connect nodes to the Token Ring network.

Token Ring networks are highly reliable because the nodes are constantly checking on each other. When a node goes down, you should be able to isolate the failure without difficulty. Also, although the name is "ring," Token Ring uses a star topology; therefore, one node's problems can't affect any other nodes. There are some considerations specific to token ring—configuration can be difficult and much of the equipment is proprietary—but in general it's easy to work with.

FDDI

The FDDI standard is designed around fiber optic cable and high-speed connections. It has some amazing capabilities: The network can operate at speeds of up to 100 Mbps; can accommodate up to 1,000 nodes; and can work with connections as far as 62 miles (100 kilometers) apart.

These capabilities don't come without a price. FDDI network cards and hubs are expensive, and fiber optic cable costs as much as 10 times more than good quality twisted pair cable. Thus FDDI is only used when it's required—in networks that require high speeds, a large number of nodes, or long distances between nodes.

Because of its high cost and the fact that FDDI is a relatively new standard, this is not a common network configuration. You will usually see it only in large corporations and in high-tech areas such as CAD and data acquisition. In addition, FDDI is often used as a network backbone, connecting multiple networks and multiple buildings.

FDDI is extremely reliable and can survive in situations where other networks would easily fail. However, you may find it hard to work with because the fiber optic cable is expensive and requires special tools for installation. A new standard, called CDDI (copper distributed data interface) provides an alternative, supporting similar speeds using category 5 twisted pair cable.

NetWare Versions

With all of the advantages of NetWare 4.1 you've been reading about, you would expect everyone to use it—but at the moment, that's not the case. NetWare 3.1*x* is still more widely used. Here are the versions of NetWare you can expect to see in the real world.

NetWare 3.1*x*

NetWare's current popularity was gained as a result of NetWare version 3.11. This version introduced several enhancements to the NetWare operating system, including optimization for the 386 (or better) processor and support for many more users, more memory, and more disk storage. NetWare 3.12, introduced to correct some of the deficiencies and bugs in NetWare 3.11, includes several features created for NetWare 4, for example, the DOS Requester and the new menu system.

While NetWare 4.1 has grown to comprise over 10 percent of existing networks, NetWare 3.1*x* is still much more common, running on between 50 and 60 percent of all networks worldwide.

Although Novell is still selling NetWare 3.12, it is now encouraging the use of NetWare 4.1, as it costs the same as (or recently even less than) NetWare 3.1*x* and includes all the features you've read about in this book—NDS, auditing, and so on. Many people in the industry expect Novell to stop selling and supporting NetWare 3.1*x* some time in the next year or two.

NetWare 2.*x* and Earlier Versions

NetWare 2.*x* was, at one time, the most popular network operating system worldwide. Quite a few companies still haven't upgraded, so don't be surprised if you run into a NetWare 2.*x* server here and there. Although much of the functionality is the same, NetWare 2.*x*, at least in the base configuration, does not include all of the features of 3.11—not to mention 4.1. It does not include MHS, full ODI support, or disk duplexing, among other things. It also has much lower limits on the amount of disk storage and the amount of memory, meaning that fewer users can be supported.

The cost of upgrading from NetWare 2.*x* may be too high for the budgets of some companies. NetWare 2.*x* was capable of running on a 286 machine, so upgrading to Netware 3 or 4 also entails purchasing a new computer. However, the number of 2.*x* users is decreasing steadily. There is one very compelling reason to upgrade—Novell no longer sells or supports NetWare 2.*x*. Consequently, many companies are forced to upgrade when they experience a major network problem.

NetWare 4.0, 4.01, and 4.02

Before NetWare 4.1, Novell positioned NetWare 4 as an enterprise networking system—specifically designed for large, multi-location networks, with features such as NDS. NetWare 4.0 was the first version of this system, and many network administrators did not trust it—and for good reason. It had many bugs and was difficult to work with. These problems were gradually corrected in NetWare 4.01 and NetWare 4.02, which Novell gave away as free upgrades to those who had purchased NetWare 4.0.

With NetWare 4.1, Novell resolved most of the problems associated with NetWare 4.02. For example, NetWare 4.02 had no way to move or delete an entire container object and its contents; this procedure can now be done from PARTMAN or the Partition Manager utility in NetWare Administrator as discussed in Chapter 11. NetWare 4.1 is now practical (and affordable) for all networks, large and small.

If you run into a NetWare 4.0, 4.01, or 4.02 network, recommend an upgrade to NetWare 4.1 as soon as possible to eliminate the many bugs that can cause serious problems.

Running earlier versions of NetWare 4 in the same Directory tree as NetWare 4.1 can cause corruption of NDS data. In this situation, it's best to upgrade all servers to NetWare 4.1 at the same time.

NetWare 4.1

This brings us back to NetWare 4.1, which Novell considers to be a multi-purpose network environment for practically everybody. Novell expects the popularity of Netware 4.1 to grow and NetWare 3.1*x* use to decline. The main competition for NetWare 4.1 is from Windows NT Server.

Other Network Operating Systems

Other popular network operating systems were introduced in Chapter 1. One to watch out for in particular is Windows NT—it includes many of the features of NetWare 4.1 and is gaining in the market. Some industry watchers have predicted that Windows NT will overtake NetWare 4.1 in the next five years. Of course, Novell will probably release a new version of NetWare by then.

Helpful Reference Sources for Troubleshooting

RUNNING A NETWORK often involves troubleshooting new and difficult problems. Fortunately, you aren't left alone in the troubleshooting battle. Several reference sources can help you solve the problems on your network or server. The following tools can provide valuable data about hardware and software problems:

- The **Network Support Encyclopedia** is a CD-ROM available from Novell. It is produced monthly and contains information about all versions of NetWare, including common problems and technical notes.

- The **Microhouse Technical Library** is available from Microhouse Corporation. It is a CD-ROM database of network cards, motherboards, hard drives, and other hardware.

- **NetWire** is Novell's support area on CompuServe. It allows access to much the same information as the Network Support Encyclopedia, but NetWire information is updated continuously. In addition, you can post questions and receive answers from other NetWare users.

Each of these is discussed in detail in the following sections.

The Network Support Encyclopedia

Novell's Network Support Encyclopedia, Professional Edition, or NSEPro, is a huge database of information about NetWare and networking. It contains more than 170MB of text, graphics, and downloadable files (some with fixes and patches for NetWare versions).

Novell sells the NSEPro on a subscription basis, and it is quite expensive—about $1,000 per year. However, the company gives a single copy of the latest version to candidates who complete the CNE certification. You may also be able to purchase a single copy from a NetWare reseller.

Installing the NSEPro

Installing the NSEPro is easy but does require a decision or two. You'll need a CD-ROM drive to install it (and probably to run it). There is an installation program and NSEPro viewer for both DOS and Microsoft Windows.

To install the Windows version, insert the CD-ROM into the drive and start Windows. From the Windows Program Manager, select Run from the File menu. In the Run dialog box, enter the path to the SETUP program, as in D:\SETUP (use the letter of your CD-ROM drive; D is typical). The setup dialog box, shown in Figure 16.1, asks you to choose one of the following installation options:

- **Setup:** Use this option if you have very little disk space. It will run all programs from the CD-ROM and use no space on your hard drive. You can also use this option if the NSEPro files have been installed in a network directory.

- **Install:** This option copies the program files for the NSEPro, but not the database, to your hard drive. This will use only about 2.5MB of disk space and will speed things up considerably.

- **Stand Alone:** This option installs all of the files to a network drive or your hard drive. This installaton requires a whopping 200MB of disk space, but it is much faster than running from a slow CD-ROM drive.

Typically, you'll choose the Install option. This saves you disk space but still allows the NSEPro to run at a reasonable speed.

After you choose an installation option, specify the location to install to and then click OK. The files will be installed, and the NSEPro program group will be created.

If you wish to run the DOS version of the NSEPro, you can use the installation program, but there's an easier way. Just insert the CD-ROM, change to

FIGURE 16.1
The NSEPro installation
program has three
separate setup options.

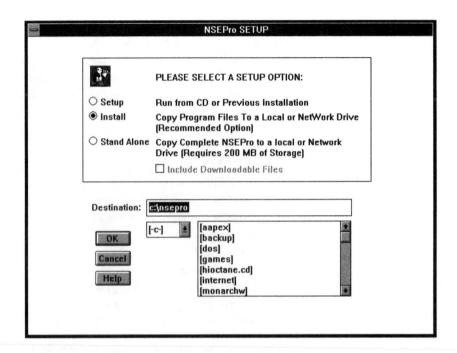

its drive letter, and type NSEPro. However, be warned: The DOS version of
the program is not as simple to use as the Windows version.

NSEPro Features

In Windows, click on the NSEPro icon to start the NSEPro. The main screen
resembles a shelf with eight books on it, as shown in Figure 16.2.

These books represent the main options available from the NSEPro. To
access one of these options, double-click on the corresponding book. Here's a
summary of each option:

- **What's New:** Provides a quick summary of the new material in this
  edition of the NSEPro. You can click on items in this list to skip directly to
  them. An example of a What's New screen is shown in Figure 16.3.

- **Service and Support:** Provides options that are related to servicing and supporting a network, as shown in Figure 16.4. Again, you can click on each
  option to view a submenu or text on a subject. From a troubleshooting

FIGURE 16.2
The NSEPro main screen
includes eight options,
cleverly disguised
as books.

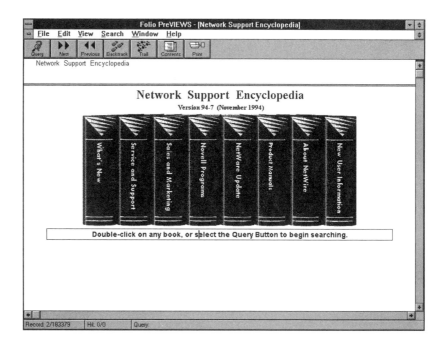

FIGURE 16.2
The NSEPro main screen
includes eight options,
cleverly disguised
as books.

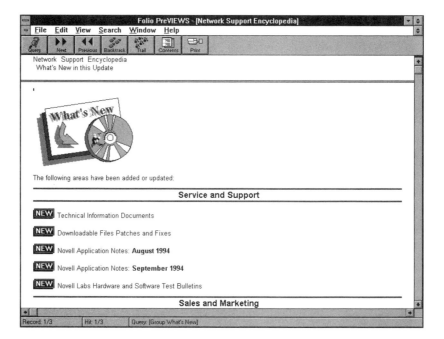

FIGURE 16.3
The What's New option
provides links to the
newest NSEPro additions.

FIGURE 16.4
The Service and
Support menu offers
information useful for
servicing networks.

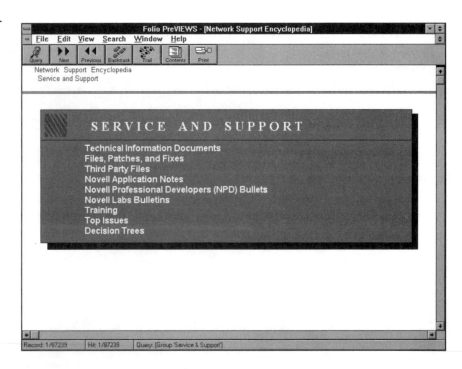

FIGURE 16.4
The Service and
Support menu offers
information useful for
servicing networks.

perspective, this is probably the most useful option (aside from the Query option, described later).

- **Sales and Marketing:** Includes press releases, marketing information, and other material you might use if you're selling NetWare. It's also useful if you want to find out which Novell products include which features.

- **Novell Programs:** Supplies information about Novell's sales and training programs, such as the CNE program and Novell Authorized Reseller and Education Center programs.

- **NetWare Update:** Allows you to access files, patches, and fixes for NetWare. Needless to say, you'll need the most up-to-date NSEPro to be sure you have the most current files. You can copy the files to your hard disk and install them.

- **Product Manuals:** Displays a list of manuals for NetWare products, as shown in Figure 16.5. The complete text of each manual is included. The DynaText manuals, described in Chapter 2, provide this same information,

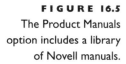

FIGURE 16.5

The Product Manuals option includes a library of Novell manuals.

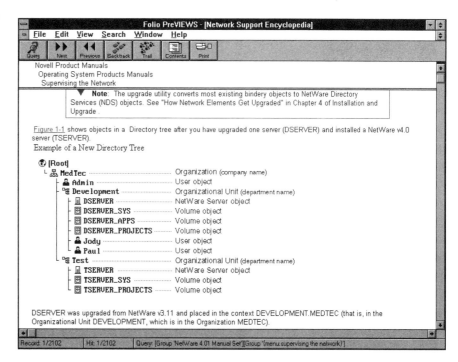

and in a better format. But the NSEPro includes older manuals, all the way back to NetWare 2.15. This is a great resource when you are supporting older versions.

- **About NetWire:** Provides information about NetWire, Novell's forum on CompuServe. NetWire is covered in the next section.

- **New User Information:** Provides information about using the NSEPro and where to obtain a more recent version. (This book should be the first one on the shelf!)

Searching the Database

Each NSEPro book includes a list of options of its own, often divided into sub-menus. Worse, the same information appears in different menus. You might spend hours moving from menu to menu before you find an answer to your specific problem. Luckily, there's a better way to get answers.

The Query option allows you to find any information you need in the entire NSEPro 200MB database, and the search is amazingly fast. The results of a query include links to each of the documents so you can quickly search through them.

To perform a query, click the Query button (the one with a picture of a magnifying glass) on the toolbar. The Query dialog box is shown in Figure 16.6.

Here are the components of the Query dialog box and their uses:

- **Scope:** This list shows the range of the query, which can be the entire database or a more limited search area.

- **Words:** This list box supplies all the words indexed in the NSEPro. You can scroll through this index to find a topic, but it's easier to use the Query For option.

- **Records With Hits:** This box shows the current results of the search.

- **Query For:** This is where you can type the words to search for. The search will be performed as you type.

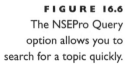

FIGURE 16.6
The NSEPro Query option allows you to search for a topic quickly.

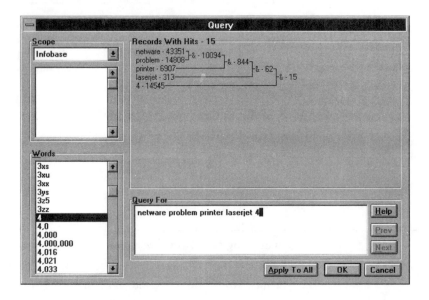

As you make a query, the NSEPro searches for each word. If you type more than one word, the program will find sections that contain all the words. For example, suppose that you are having problems with a LaserJet 4 printer on a NetWare network. Obviously, searching for the word *NetWare* won't help (there are 43,351 NetWare matches in the database!). However, you can add terms to make the search more specific. By adding *problem*, *printer*, *laserjet*, and *4*, as in Figure 16.6, you can make the search more specific. The result is 15 documents that match the query words.

After you're satisfied with the number of matches, choose OK. The documents that match the query words are listed, and you can click on each one to display it. The list of entries matching our sample query about LaserJet 4 printing is shown in Figure 16.7.

FIGURE 16.7
After you enter a query, you get a list of relevant documents.

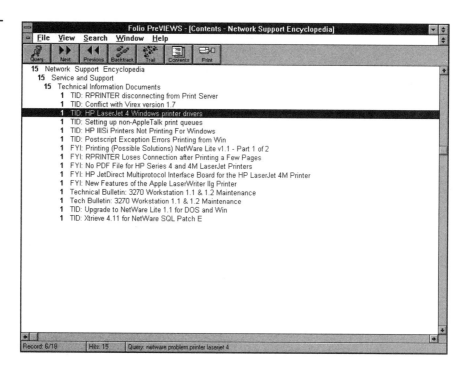

NetWire on CompuServe

Another service provided by Novell is NetWire. NetWire can be accessed on the Internet at

```
http://netwire.novell.com
```

NetWire can also be accessed as a forum on CompuServe. NetWire does not have an additional cost beyond CompuServe's fee. It includes much the same information and features as the NSEPro but in a constantly updated form, and it's actually cheaper than an NSEPro subscription—especially if you have a low-cost Internet connection. NetWire also allows you to post questions, receive answers from other NetWare users, or answer questions others have posted.

To access NetWire on CompuServe, use WinCIM, the CompuServe Information Manager. Novell has its own version of WinCIM called NOVCIM. The only difference is that the NetWire options are on the main menu in NOVCIM; if you are using WinCIM, you can simply go to the keyword NETWIRE. You can access NetWire equally well with either program. WinCIM is available for Microsoft Windows and will run in OS/2 Warp or Windows 95.

WinCIM isn't the only way to access CompuServe. It is possible to access CompuServe from any operating system, although the interface may be just a simple text-based command line.

NetWire Options

Figure 16.8 shows the main NetWire screen. This screen includes several options as starting points, which are similar to the options in the NSEPro (but they don't look like books).

These NetWire options work as follows:

- **What's New:** Displays recent Novell news and changes that have been made to the NetWire service.

- **Technical Services:** Displays a menu that allows you to access technical information. It includes a search option to help you find articles that match a specific topic (although it isn't as versatile as the NSEPro's Query option).

FIGURE 16.8
The main NetWire menu
offers six options for
NetWare-related
information.

- **File Updates:** Allows you to access the latest files, patches, and fixes for Novell products. This option is similar to the NetWare Update option in the NSEPro, but the files on NetWire are always up-to-date.

- **Sales & Marketing:** Allows you to access sales and marketing information, similar to the NSEPro.

- **Novell Programs:** Allows you to view information about Novell's programs, similar to the NSEPro.

- **New User Information:** Provides basic instructions for using NetWire and an option to download the latest version of NOVCIM.

The Microhouse Technical Library

The Microhouse Technical Library, or MTL, is the ultimate reference for hardware. It includes more than 500MB of data on a CD-ROM. The MTL has four main components:

- **Encyclopedia of Hard Drives:** Provides information about hard drives, such as jumper settings and BIOS parameters.

- **Encyclopedia of Main Boards:** Provides information about all aspects of PC operation and motherboards.

- **Encyclopedia of Network Cards:** Provides configuration information about network interface cards. It also includes driver software for a wide variety of cards.

- **Encyclopedia of I/O Cards:** Supplies information about other cards you might install in a PC, such as video cards, printer cards, modems, and disk controllers.

These encyclopedias don't just give you technical information about how things work. The database includes complete details for thousands of cards and hard drives, including jumper settings, configuration information, and even diagrams of their actual appearance.

At this writing, the retail price for the MTL CD (a single copy) is $395. New updates are released regularly, and you can subscribe to receive the latest versions. If you would like to try out the MTL without spending $395, you're in luck—a demo version of the MTL is included on the CD-ROM that comes with this book. Obviously, it doesn't include all the features of the real version, but it does include the entire encyclopedia of I/O cards. For details, see the inside front cover of this book.

Using the MTL

The main MTL screen is shown in Figure 16.9. To use any section of the MTL, click on the corresponding button on the main screen. The options are described in the following sections.

The Encyclopedia of Hard Drives

Figure 16.10 shows the table of contents of this encyclopedia:

- **Chapter 1: Interface Types and Installation:** Describes the types of hard drive interfaces and provides the information needed to install and use them.

- **Chapter 2: Directory of Manufacturers:** Provides contact information for all of the common hard drive manufacturers.

FIGURE 16.9
The MTL includes four
main options.

FIGURE 16.10
The MTL Encyclopedia of
Hard Drives supplies
information about hard
drive interfaces,
manufacturers, and
specifications,

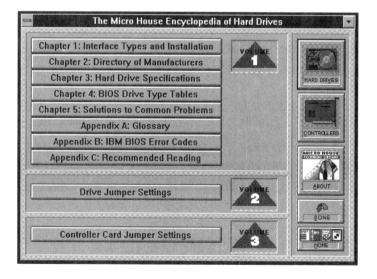

- **Chapter 3: Hard Drive Specifications:** Lists specifications for hard drives. This includes the settings you must enter into your computer's BIOS to use the drive.

- **Chapter 4: BIOS Drive Type Tables:** Lists common BIOS drive type codes, which may be used instead of entering each parameter individually.

- **Chapter 5: Solutions to Common Problems:** Lists common problems with hard drives.

- **Appendix A: Glossary:** Provides definitions for many hard drive related terms.

- **Appendix B: IBM BIOS Error Codes:** Lists the codes the IBM BIOS displays for errors. This is useful if you are diagnosing hardware and have access to a diagnostic card.

- **Appendix C: Recommended Reading:** Lists books that explain some of the concepts in more detail.

Volume 2 of the Encyclopedia of Hard Drives includes jumper settings for hundreds of different hard drives, including diagrams of the jumper locations. Volume 3 contains jumper setting information for hard drive controller cards.

The Encyclopedia of Main Boards

The Encyclopedia of Main Boards includes several options relating to the motherboard in your PC. The menu for the Main Boards option is shown in Figure 16.11.

The sections of this encyclopedia offer information about all aspects of the board's operation. You can also search for boards by manufacturer or other specifications.

The Encyclopedia of Network Cards

The Encyclopedia of Network Cards includes two main options: the Network Interface Technical Guide, which includes information about the technical aspects of network cards and their operation, and the Network Cards listing, which includes specifications for hundreds of network cards. The main screen for the Technical Guide is shown in Figure 16.12.

FIGURE 16.11
The Encyclopedia of Main Boards gives information about PC motherboards.

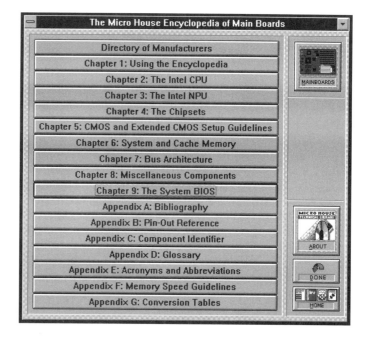

FIGURE 16.12
The Encyclopedia of Network Cards provides information about LAN cards.

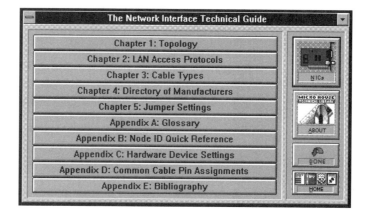

The Encyclopedia of I/O Cards

The Encyclopedia of I/O Cards is the most recent addition to the MTL. It includes information about cards that are not hard drive or network cards.

This category includes video cards, serial and parallel cards, and so on. The main screen for this encyclopedia is shown in Figure 16.13.

This screen may appear a bit overwhelming with all of its options. It lists all of the possible criteria for I/O cards. You can select a manufacturer, a type of card, and many other options. After you have selected options, click the Search button to list the cards that match your criteria.

FIGURE 16.13
The Encyclopedia of I/O Cards offers an abundance of options.

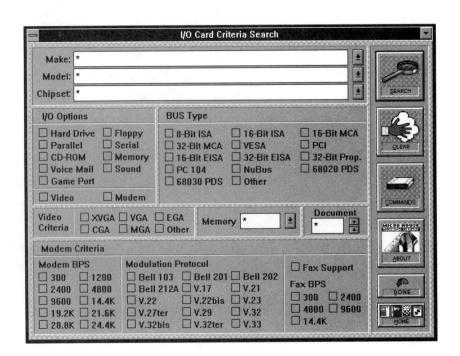

Review

THIS CHAPTER HAS CONSIDERED some of the real-world issues about networking. We have also looked at several reference sources available to network administrators.

In the past several years, networks have grown from a novelty to a multi-million-dollar industry. There are an estimated 1,500,000 networks in use in the United States, and this number is constantly growing. It is becoming cheaper and simpler to set up a network, and most companies with five or more PCs now connect them with some sort of network.

There are many network topologies:

- Ethernet, used by about 60 percent of networks

- ARCnet, an older standard that is still widely used

- Token Ring, a reliable but more expensive alternative

- FDDI, an extremely high-speed system using fiber optic cable

Helpful Reference Sources

We introduced the following valuable reference sources:

- The Network Support Encyclopedia (NSEPro)

- The Microhouse Technical Library (MTL)

- NetWire, Novell's online support forum

The Future of Networking

CHAPTER

17

A S A FINAL CONSIDERATION, let's take a look at the network job situation and what you can expect in the near future. This industry changes overnight, so staying on top of new developments is crucial for most network administrators.

Some of the technologies introduced in this chapter are already in use—or will be, by the time you read this book. However, we'll still consider them the future, since they are not yet in widespread use or standardized.

The CNA Job Market

A S A CNA, you have a large number of job options. Many jobs in the network industry require Novell experience—and often Novell certification. Of course, a CNA won't help you unless you really understand the information and can apply the knowledge in real life. Make sure you practice and understand the information covered in this book, rather than simply memorizing it. It's helpful to set up your own network to practice on, or use the one at your job. Don't do anything that can take the network down, of course. Most job scenarios also require a wide variety of other skills. General PC and DOS knowledge is helpful. Any specialized networking or computing knowledge will give you an advantage in the workplace.

Novell's current figures show that more than 70,000 people are Novell-certified CNAs and CNEs. The job market varies widely depending on your location and the type of work you want to do. A network administrator job that requires a CNA typically pays between $20,000 and $50,000 annual salary, with an average near $40,000.

With about 40,000,000 NetWare nodes in use, knowledgeable network administrators are in great demand. Nearly all major corporations have a department that employs network administrators.

There are also approximately 30,000 authorized Novell resellers throughout the United States and other countries. These sales organizations often employ CNAs. A job with a reseller will give you a wide variety of experience with many different networks and will also be an excellent introduction to the real world of networking. Working for a reseller can also be a good job choice if you are preparing to go on for your CNE certification because the company will often pay for training and the tests.

New Networking Hardware and Topologies

ALTHOUGH SOME COMPANIES are happy (or at least stubborn) with their vintage 1982 ARCnet networks, manufacturers continue to introduce new innovations in network standards, connections, hardware, and protocols. Here we'll look at the new, fast Ethernet standards as well as two truly revolutionary standards—ISDN and ATM.

100 Mbps Ethernet

The popular Ethernet standard, with a maximum transmission speed of 10 Mbps, is beginning to show its age. The first entry in the race to replace it with a faster standard was FastEthernet, developed by MicroAccess Corp. Fast-Ethernet allows speeds up to 100 MBPS. Although it is not yet an accepted standard, it is available now and may be a solution where high speed is needed.

There are additional costs to consider when talking about FastEthernet. Although FastEthernet uses the same type of cabling as Ethernet 10baseT (unshielded twisted pair, category 5), it requires six pairs of wires, rather than the two pairs required by normal Ethernet. Thus cabling may be more expensive. In addition, hubs and NICs that support FastEthernet are currently proprietary and expensive.

Alternatives include 100VG, which has been approved by the IEEE as a standard for 100 Mbps Ethernet. An alternative standard is 100baseT, which has not yet been approved. Once it is approved, you can expect to see many more 100 Mbps networking products. Support for both standards is available in some products already. Most of the cards and hubs that support these protocols also support conventional Ethernet, allowing you to upgrade a network one segment at a time.

ISDN (Integrated Services Digital Network)

ISDN replaces conventional analog phone lines with digital lines. In its basic form, it can support speeds of up to 2 Mbps—nothing amazing for a network but revolutionary for a phone-system link.

Although ISDN is over 10 years old, it hasn't quite caught on in the United States because of the lack of support from local phone companies. However, ISDN is gradually growing in popularity, and some major U.S. cities are already wired for ISDN service as an alternative for phone connections in homes and businesses.

The advantage of ISDN over conventional phone systems is that it is digital and supports *multiplexing*—meaning that several conversations can be carried at once or that a combination of voice, computer data, fax, and even video can be sent at once.

Once ISDN becomes an accepted standard, you can expect it to revolutionize wide-area networking. International businesses could connect their branches with inexpensive ISDN service provided by the phone company.

The latest ISDN rage is *broadband ISDN*, which transmits multiple digital signals at once and can achieve speeds of up to 300 Mbps. Although you won't see that speed in your local phone system anytime soon, you may see it in your company's network.

ATM (Asynchronous Transfer Mode)

ATM is a high-speed network architecture based on broadband ISDN and is expected to revolutionize network communications and become a standard in the next few years. It is already in use in some cutting-edge corporate networks.

The current ATM standard offers an effective throughput of 155.52 Mbps—over 15 times the speed of Ethernet. Future versions are expected to increase this to 622 Mbps, and even further. Speeds up to 2.4 Gbps (gigabits per second) have been tested and will undoubtedly become available in the next few years.

ATM currently requires fiber optic cabling but even that may change. The ATM working group, an organization of companies that are working to develop standards, is investigating methods for using the ATM standard on ordinary category 3 or category 5 unshielded twisted pair wire.

In addition to the expense of fiber optic or category 5 cabling, the devices needed to implement ATM on a network—switches and hubs—are currently quite expensive. Over the next few years, however, ATM should become affordable even for small companies.

New Network Operating Systems

NETWARE 4.1 IS A FINE NOS, but there are alternatives— as you learned in Chapter 1 of this book. In this section we'll look at alternatives that Novell and other companies are planning for the future. The good news is that NetWare 4.*x* will probably continue to be the latest version of NetWare at least through 1996.

Novell—32 Bits and Beyond

Of course, Novell plans to continue to upgrade NetWare 4.1. Here are a few of the improvements in store:

- A new, 32-bit client software for DOS, Windows, and Windows 95 replaces the DOS Requester and offers improved memory management and automatic reconnection to a server that has been down. Currently referred to as Client32, it also uses NIOS (NetWare Input/Output Services), which replaces IPXODI and allows a tighter integration with PCs and greater expandability.

- The long-awaited SMP (Symmetric MultiProcessing) upgrade for NetWare 4 has been announced and is beginning to ship at this writing. Because of the difference in multiprocessor systems, Novell has formed partnerships with a number of hardware vendors to distribute this upgrade as a package with the actual server hardware.

- Upgrades to the NetWare 4 file system will allow files and directories to be managed as part of NDS; in other words, there will no longer be a distinction between NDS security and file-system security.

- Novell will no longer offer UnixWare, the UNIX clone Novell purchased from AT&T. Novell sold UnixWare to SCO in the fall of 1995.

- Novell plans an update to NetWare 4.1 in 1996, code named "Green River." This release will include increased security and will allow integration with Windows NT; Windows NT servers can be managed through NDS. It will also include a new API, NET2000, that allows easy creation of NLMs. This API will even allow applications to be run on non-NetWare operating systems.

- The next releases of NetWare—code named "Moab" and "Park City"—will include full memory protection (NLMs will have their own memory areas, rather than sharing "rings"), 64-bit communication with peripherals (assuming hardware supports it), and distributed parallel processing—the ability to run a NetWare server on several machines, each handling part of the load.

- Novell has announced plans to sell its application products (Word Perfect, Quattro Pro, and PerfectOffice). Its intention is to focus on network computing. Groupwise and the other groupware applications will remain in Novell's product line. At this writing, Corel Corporation was the leading candidate for the purchase of the Novell Applications Group.

Of course, don't expect all of these predictions to come true. Novell has changed strategies before, and you can expect it to continue to change and adapt to market conditions.

Microsoft—Destination Cairo

As you've probably heard, the big news from Microsoft is code named "Cairo." Cairo, the next major release of Windows NT Server, is scheduled for release in 1997. It is expected to include the following features:

- More compatibility with Windows 95; in fact, Cairo may replace Windows 95 as well as NT.

- Integration of NDS with Windows NT.

- A directory service, similar to NDS.

Microsoft has already released Windows NT 3.51, which can use a new module to give it a user interface similar to Windows 95. Microsoft's most recent announcements involve the integration of NetWare—the ability to manage a NetWare 4.1 network from within Windows NT and for the Windows NT server to emulate a NetWare server in some ways. Considering the money Microsoft spends on marketing, expect these products to receive a lot of attention in the months and years ahead. Use of Windows NT Server is expected to increase dramatically over the next year; it may eventually eclipse NetWare 4.1.

New PC Hardware

NEXT, WE'LL TAKE A LOOK AT the future of hardware. Many of these improvements won't help much with a server, but will greatly improve workstation performance. Let's look at the latest innovations in PC systems, Macintosh clients, and the peripherals they use.

Microprocessors

The biggest news in microprocessors at the moment is Intel's sequel to the Pentium—the P6, or as Intel calls it, the Pentium Pro. (Never mind the fact that the "Pent" prefix means five.)

The P6 performs roughly twice as fast as a Pentium processor of the same clock speed. However, it is optimized for 32-bit applications. This means that you'll need to run a 32-bit operating system, such as Windows 95, and 32-bit applications to really benefit from the P6 power. In fact, since Windows 95 is not fully 32-bit, Windows machines won't receive the full benefits of the P6 until a future version. Because NetWare is a fully 32-bit OS, the P6 should run well as a NetWare server, although it may be overkill for most networks.

Intel's competition includes the AMD AM5x86 and the Cyrix 6X86. Both of these processors are expected to run faster than a Pentium and may even surpass the P6, at least for 16-bit applications.

For Macintosh and compatible computers, the latest version of Motorola's PowerPC chips will give new machines a processor that compares to the P6.

Motherboards

Intel has announced the ATX motherboard, which uses a completely different layout than current motherboards. The ATX runs cooler and will fit into a smaller case without sacrificing any ISA and PCI slots. These boards also cost less to manufacture and provide easier access to slots, cables, and other connections.

Although not quite so new, the plug and play standard is also revolutionizing motherboards. This standard allows you to install drive controllers, LAN cards, and other peripherals without hassling with jumpers, DIP switches, memory addresses, or IRQ settings.

Don't forget everything you learned about setting up network cards just yet—although most of the new motherboards now support the plug and play standard, very few network cards and other controllers do. In addition, the operating system needs to support the standard. Currently only Windows 95 supports the standard. With luck, a future version of NetWare will include plug and play support. (It would sure make the Network Technologies CNE test easier to pass.)

Disk Storage

Hard drive technology hasn't changed much recently, and no major changes have been announced at this time. However, one change is always occurring: price decreases. The price for 1GB IDE drives has already dropped below $300 and will probably be under $200 by the end of 1996. SCSI drives are typically a bit more expensive but not too far behind.

Optical storage devices are also decreasing in price. Recordable CD-ROM drives (CD-R) are now available for under $1,000, and that price should drop below $800 by the end of 1996. Other devices are less standard, but allow even more storage. For example, two new optical CD formats allow up to 10MB per disk.

Finally, floppy disks as we know them may disappear—although it won't happen overnight. Economical, high-capacity alternatives are emerging. These include the very popular ZIP drive from Iomega, which stores 100MB on a disk slightly larger than a 3.5-inch floppy. The disks cost about $10 apiece. Syquest is marketing the EZDrive as an alternative to the ZIP, with a slightly larger capacity and higher speed. Finally, Compaq has announced a drive that will use optically indexed floppies to store up to 120MB; this drive can also read conventional floppies. The drive may ship in Compaq PCs by the end of 1996.

Monitors

Although they won't do your server much good, innovations continue in the area of monitors. Monitors as large as 21 inches are becoming available at reasonable cost. In addition, desktop LCD monitors are coming into the market. These nearly flat devices display sharp, flicker-free images, similar to the better notebook computer displays. The catch? They're a bit expensive at the moment. One entry from Sceptre technologies starts at $1,595. The price will undoubtedly decrease, and these monitors may eventually replace conventional CRT monitors.

New Network Concepts

I N ADDITION TO CONSTANT IMPROVEMENTS in every area of networking technology, entirely new technologies are emerging. Sometimes it's hard to keep up with all of the new ideas and proposals, but here are a few of the hot topics that are making the rounds. One or more of them may concern a network you will work on in the future.

Embedded Systems

Imagine the latest NetWare client running on your television—or even your toaster. Although it sounds strange, these devices may reach the network through a technology called *embedded systems*. (Your toaster will probably be the last to experience this particular revolution.) Embedded systems are dedicated hardware, not PCs, that offer network services. Novell is planning to produce embedded

NetWare systems, which can be built into just about any product and enable it to establish connectivity with the NetWare server.

Novell's embedded system will be called NEST (Novell Embedded Systems Technology). Novell has also announced plans for a Smart Energy Network that will use the NEST system to allow networking over ordinary power lines. This connection will make it easy to form small, wireless networks in offices and even in homes.

NEST will allow the network to control intelligent devices—TVs, VCRs, even coffee machines and toasters. Of course, the devices will have to be built with embedded NetWare technology. For a more practical solution, imagine controlling and monitoring your home security system through your home computer.

More serious uses for systems like this include factory control systems and manufacturing systems. The NetWare server could manage and control these systems—for example, increasing production in response to a decrease in inventory—and they could be managed within NDS. This technology would bring the auditing and management features of NetWare 4.1 to entirely new application areas.

Computer Telephony

One of the latest trends, both for network and single-PC applications, is the integration of telephone functions into the computer, otherwise know as *computer telephony*. Imagine answering the phone by clicking a button on your workstation or receiving voice-mail messages in the same in-box as you receive e-mail messages. Computer telephony is made possible by a *voice card*, which interfaces between a PC (either a server or workstation) and the phone system. Using these systems, a PC can act as a telephone, a voice-mail system, a fax-on-demand system, or even a multiline phone system.

Two standards are competing for the telephony market right now. Not surprisingly, these systems are produced by Novell and Microsoft. Novell's standard, TSAPI, provides a standard interface for NetWare NLMs and client software to access voice functions. Microsoft's entry is called TAPI and provides the same function for Windows 95 and Windows NT. Which one becomes a standard in the future will depend on the application software that becomes available. Several telephony applications are available currently, but none have yet become popular.

While TAPI focuses on workstation operating systems, TSAPI is based on a NetWare server and telephone switch. This means that TSAPI may be more practical for large-scale corporate use, but a TAPI application may find its way to your home PC (in fact, Microsoft has included one with Windows 95).

Application Servers

While a file server allows printer and file sharing, another type of server is being used more and more frequently in modern networks: the application server. This type of server is used to run a "back end" for applications, such as accounting software, and greatly reduces the processing power required at the client workstation.

Popular application servers at this time include NetWare 4.1, UNIX, and Windows NT. Many networks are beginning to use Windows NT as an application server on NetWare 4.1 networks. Novell's preferred application server solution was UnixWare, but Novell is now discontinuing that product. Instead, Novell will focus on enhancing NetWare 4.1's features as an application server.

Internet Connectivity

You've probably heard a lot about the Internet recently. Although it's been around for over 10 years, the Internet has experienced a dramatic gain in popularity in the last few years. As the importance of the Internet increases, the process of providing a connection between your network and the Internet will become more and more important.

Right now, the most widely used feature of the Internet is e-mail. Using MHS, Groupwise, or almost any other e-mail system and a piece of software and hardware called a *gateway*, you can send messages to and receive messages from other people connected to the Internet. Since UNIX is still the most common operating system for Internet nodes, gateways typically operate using TCP/IP.

The World Wide Web (WWW) is the most popular Internet area, as well as the fastest growing. WWW servers can make hypertext information—similar to the Windows help system or Novell's DynaText documentation—available to people in every corner of the world. Anyone with an Internet connection and a web browser—software that allows web access—can view your documents, called *web pages*.

Novell has made the DynaText online documentation for NetWare 4.1 available as a web document. It provides searching, linking, and graphics, similar to the DynaText viewer. If you have a web browser, you can find DynaText at this address: http://www.netware.com/.

Traditionally, web pages are provided by placing them on a UNIX machine that has an Internet connection and acts as a web server (technically, an HTTP, or HyperText Transfer Protocol, server). However, NetWare 4.1's simplified TCP/IP support makes it easy to attach a NetWare server directly to the Internet, and software is available that allows it to act as a web server. Over the next several years, a good portion of the UNIX web servers will be gradually replaced by NetWare and Windows NT (which also has a number of web servers available, as do Windows 3.*x*, Windows 95, and Macintosh systems).

Novell has also introduced the NetWare Web Server, a full-scale web server for NetWare 4.1 systems. It allows you to quickly distribute documents to an entire company, or the entire Internet.

Videoconferencing

If you've dreamed of the day when you could look at your bosses on your computer screen and have a conversation with them in real time, you're in luck—videoconferencing isn't science fiction anymore. You may never have to leave your desk again—unless you're the one who has to maintain the video-conferencing system.

AT&T actually introduced a videoconferencing system that would work over ordinary phone lines in the 1970s, but it was clumsy and produced extremely poor quality pictures. The videoconferencing systems of today are getting close to the reality of a picture that looks as good as your TV. Connections can be made over normal phone lines. In addition, new network standards like ATM make it possible to send digital video over the LAN, and ISDN may eventually improve the quality of pictures going over phone lines.

Recently, AT&T and other vendors, such as Intel, established a standard for videoconferencing systems. This means that systems from different vendors will actually be able to communicate with one another. Thanks to this standard and the improving quality of PC processing and video, videoconferencing is starting to become downright practical. Just wait—you'll see the day when the CEO can appear in a window on your computer, look at your desk, and criticize you for not working hard.

Certification and the Job Market

I NNOVATIONS IN THE WORLD OF NETWORKING are not limited to strictly technological aspects of the field. In fact, Novell recently changed its CNE program in response to complaints that it emphasized memorization rather than practical knowledge. Nevertheless, just being a CNE won't qualify you for most jobs anymore—you'll need to be experienced with NetWare and possibly with other NOSs.

A variety of other training and certification programs are also available. Microsoft, for example, offers a certification program for Windows NT.

Regardless of the certifications that you have, one thing is certain: The network market is growing steadily. New networks are being installed daily, and there will always be a need for professionals to maintain them.

To keep yourself ready to enter the job market, be sure to keep up with the latest network developments. Network administration is one area where you can't just pass a certification exam and then expect to work comfortably for 10 years.

Further Education

For many network professionals, the CNA is just a stepping stone toward the CNE. The CNA, in fact, counts toward one of the seven requirements for CNE certification. A CNA can help you get your foot in the door in the network industry. The CNE can then be a further career advancement. In case you are interested in pursuing CNE, the following section gives an overview of the CNE program.

How Does the New Novell CNE Program Work?

On September 30, 1995, Novell's new CNE program went into effect. The features and requirements of the new program differ significantly from the old one.

The old program defined two types of CNE certification:

- Certified Novell Engineer (CNE)

- Enterprise Certified Novell Engineer (ECNE)

To attain the CNE credential, you needed to complete at least seven tests, including a test covering basic DOS and microcomputer concepts, as well as at least one elective test drawn from a wide variety of networking subjects. The ECNE certification simply meant that you had completed further electives.

If you have taken, and passed, the DOS/MicroComputer Concepts test, you may still qualify to complete your CNE certification under the old program requirements. Contact Novell's education department for more information.

The new CNE program, which has been designed to completely supersede the previous program, has more specific credentials. There are now five types of CNE certification:

- **CNE-4:** Designates specialization in Novell NetWare 4

- **CNE-3:** Designates specialization in Novell NetWare 3

- **CNE-GW:** Designates specialization in Groupware (Groupwise, etc.)

- **CNE-U:** Designates specialization in Novell UnixWare

- **Master CNE:** Designates advanced specialization beyond the CNE-4, CNE-3, CNE-U, or CNE-GW level. A Master CNE continues on one of the CNE paths and takes tests covering more advanced topics.

Each of these certifications has specific requirements and a limited field of electives from which the elective requirement may be chosen. Many of the tests are the same as the tests administered under the old program, but for any given certification, there are fewer from which you may chose.

Because NetWare 4 is Novell's flagship product, the CNE-4 is quickly becoming the most sought Novell certification. While the other certifications are for individuals who wish to focus on some of Novell's older products, Novell is stressing NetWare 4 to the extent that all CNEs are now required to complete a test on NetWare 4 by June 30, 1996, or lose their certification. In an April 10, 1995, news bulletin Novell's education department stated that "Novell intends to expand the network computing industry significantly before the turn of the century. Central to this effort is NetWare Directory Services—a key feature inherent in NetWare 4."

For the reasons stated above, we recommend that you choose the CNE-4 certification. To attain this certification you must complete six required tests plus one elective. The six tests are

- 50-152: NetWare 4.1 Administration

- 50-161: NetWare 4.1 Advanced Administration

- 50-163: NetWare 4.1 Installation and Configuration

- 50-601: NetWare 4.1 Design and Implementation

- 50-153: Service and Support

- 50-147: Networking Technologies

Fifteen electives are currently available. The two that we recommend, which also happen to be the most popular, are

- 50-86: NetWare TCP/IP Transport

- 50-137: Printing with NetWare

If you are interested in the CNE program, we recommend you pick up a copy of our book The CNE-4 Study Guide, *also published by Network Press. The book covers all six core exams, as well as the NetWare TCP/IP Transport elective.*

Review

THIS CHAPTER HAS EXPLAINED some of the latest innovations in networking—both those that are available now and those that have been announced for the near future. We've done our best to be accurate, but the future is never completely predictable; be sure to read industry magazines to keep up with current developments.

Here's a quick recap of what we've covered in this chapter:

- *Improvements to network topologies* include several competing standards for fast Ethernet, ISDN (Integrated Services Digital Network), and ATM (Asynchronous Transfer Mode).

- *New network operating systems* from Novell and Microsoft will include more features and provide increased compatibility with competing products.

- *New concepts in networking* include embedded systems, computer telephony, application servers, Internet connectivity, and videoconferencing.

- *CNE certification*—and certification for other systems—will continue to be an important part of qualifying for a job in the network industry.

Well, you've reached the end of this book. But as you've read in this chapter, you are nowhere near the end of learning about computing or networking. Things change almost daily, and it may be hard to keep up—but it's worth the effort. Networks will become more and more important to companies in the future, and with this knowledge you can be a part of that future.

Answers to CNA Practice Test Questions

HIS APPENDIX CONTAINS the answers to the CNA practice test questions that appear in Chapters 5 through 10.

Chapter 5

1. NetWare Directory Services (NDS)
    A. Stores information for each network resource
    B. Uses a treelike structure
    C. Refers to each resource as an object
    D. All of the above

    Answer: D

2. Which of the following is *not* a benefit of NDS?
    A. Better organization of resources
    B. Fault tolerance
    C. An efficient file system
    D. Increased security

    Answer: C

3. The type of organization NDS uses is
    A. Server-centric
    B. Network-centric
    C. Noncentralized
    D. Resource-centric

    Answer: B

4. The three basic types of NDS objects are
    A. Container, Leaf, [Root]
    B. Properties, Values, Objects

    C. Organization, Organizational Unit, Country

    D. Typeless, typeful, distinguished

  Answer: A

5. The [Root] object

    A. Can be located anywhere in the Directory

    B. Contains all objects in the Directory

    C. Can be deleted when it is no longer needed

    D. All of the above

  Answer: B

6. Container objects include

    A. Country, Group, Organization

    B. Organization, [Root], Group

    C. Country, Organization, Organizational Unit

    D. Organization and Group

  Answer: C

7. Leaf objects include

    A. User, Group, Organization

    B. User, Printer, Resource

    C. User, Group, Printer

    D. All container objects plus User

  Answer: C

8. NDS properties

    A. Are the same for all objects

    B. Are used by container objects only

    C. Are all optional

    D. Can be assigned values

  Answer: D

9. An object's name in its context is

    A. Its distinguished name

    B. The relative distinguished name

    C. Its common name

    D. Its context name

  Answer: A

10. An object's context is

    A. Any object in the same container

    B. The container object it resides in

    C. Its common name
    D. The name of the Directory tree

Answer: B

11. A relative distinguished name (RDN)
    A. Begins at the [Root] object
    B. Begins at the current context
    C. Begins with the first Organization object
    D. Uses the default system context (DSC)

Answer: B

12. Which is an example of a *typeless* name?
    A. .CN=FRED.OU=ACCT.O=ORION
    B. CN=FRED
    C. .FRED.ACCT.ORION
    D. .CN=FRED.ACCT.O=ORION

Answer: C

13. The protocol usually used with NetWare is
    A. VLM
    B. IPXODI
    C. IPX
    D. TCP/IP

Answer: C

14. Which is the correct order for loading network drivers?
    A. LSL, LAN driver, VLM, IPXODI
    B. IPXODI, LAN driver, VLM, LSL
    C. IPX, ODI, LAN driver, VLM
    D. LSL, LAN driver, IPXODI, VLM

Answer: D

15. Which program represents the NetWare DOS Requester?
    A. LOGIN.EXE
    B. VLM.EXE
    C. IPXODI.COM
    D. NETX.COM

Answer: B

16. Until you log in, the only files you can access are
    A. LOGIN.EXE and client software
    B. All files in the PUBLIC directory

C. All files in the LOGIN directory

D. All files on the SYS: volume

Answer: C

17. Which is the correct order of NetWare file system organization?

A. Directory, file, volume

B. Volume, directory, file

C. File, volume, directory

D. File, directory, NDS

Answer: B

18. The NDIR utility

A. Must be used in place of the DOS DIR command

B. Lists files in the current directory

C. Lists information about NDS objects

D. All of the above

Answer: B

19. The NLIST utility

A. Can be used to list volumes or other NDS objects

B. Displays a list of files in the current directory

C. Is another name for NDIR

D. Was used in NetWare 3.1x

Answer: A

20. Which is the correct syntax to map drive F: to the SYS:PUBLIC directory?

A. MAP F: SYS\PUBLIC

B. MAP SYS:PUBLIC /D=F

C. MAP SYS:PUBLIC=F:

D. MAP F:=SYS:PUBLIC

Answer: D

Chapter 6

1. The two utilities used to manage NDS objects are
   - **A.** NetWare Administrator and NWADMIN
   - **B.** NETADMIN and NetWare Administrator
   - **C.** SYSCON and NETADMIN
   - **D.** NDSADMIN and NWMANAGE

   Answer: B

2. The Create function in NWADMIN is found under
   - **A.** The File menu
   - **B.** The Function menu
   - **C.** The Actions menu
   - **D.** The Object menu

   Answer: D

3. The required properties when creating a User object are
   - **A.** Login name and address
   - **B.** First name and last name
   - **C.** Login name and last name
   - **D.** Network address and first name

   Answer: C

4. The User Template object
   - **A.** Is created for each user
   - **B.** Specifies defaults for new User objects
   - **C.** Lets you change all User objects at once
   - **D.** Lets you control access rights

   Answer: B

5. The menu item used to display property values is
   - **A.** Properties
   - **B.** Values
   - **C.** Attributes
   - **D.** Details

   Answer: D

6. The move option can move which types of objects?
   - **A.** User, Server, Printer
   - **B.** Container objects only
   - **C.** Leaf objects only
   - **D.** User objects only

   Answer: C

7. NETADMIN can be used to manage

    A. User objects only

    B. Only the basic NDS objects

    C. All NDS objects

    D. Bindery objects

    Answer: C

8. The Group object can group users

    A. In the same container only

    B. In different containers only

    C. In the same or different containers

    D. In the [Root] container only

    Answer: C

9. To assign a user to an Organizational Role, you use the

    A. User's Role property

    B. Organizational Role's Member property

    C. User's Profile property

    D. Organizational Role's Occupant property

    Answer: D

10. The NetWare Server object

    A. Can be created when you wish to install a new server

    B. Is created automatically when the server is installed

    C. Is deleted automatically when the server is removed

    D. Can be used to add logins to the server

    Answer: B

11. The Alias object

    A. Represents, or points to, another object

    B. Is created whenever an object is deleted

    C. Can be used instead of the User object

    D. All of the above

    Answer: A

12. Which is the correct MAP command for the Directory Map DATA?

    A. MAP F:=DATA:

    B. MAP F:=DATA.MAP

    C. MAP F:=DATA

    D. MAP F: DATA /DM

    Answer: C

Chapter 7

1. The two types of NetWare 4.1 security are
   A. File system security and NDS security
   B. File system security and object rights
   C. Trustee rights and object rights
   D. All properties and selected properties

   Answer: A

2. Which of the following can NOT be a trustee?
   A. Organization
   B. User
   C. Organizational Role
   D. File

   Answer: D

3. The File Scan right
   A. Allows you to copy files
   B. Allows you to list files in a directory
   C. Allows you to read the contents of files
   D. Allows you to search for a file

   Answer: B

4. The IRF affects
   A. Security equivalence
   B. Inherited rights
   C. Explicit assignments
   D. All of the above

   Answer: B

5. File attributes
   A. Are always set by NetWare itself
   B. Are always set by the user
   C. Cannot be changed
   D. Give a file certain behaviors

   Answer: D

6. You can manage file system security with
   A. NetWare Administrator
   B. NETADMIN

    C. SYSCON
    D. SECURE

  Answer: A

7. The IRF lists
    A. Rights to be blocked
    B. Rights to be granted
    C. Rights allowed to be inherited
    D. Rights that cannot be inherited

  Answer: C

8. The list of trustees for an object is stored in
    A. The Trustee property
    B. The ACL
    C. The Trustee database
    D. The Trustee file

  Answer: B

9. The two types of rights in NDS are
    A. Object rights and file rights
    B. Object rights and property rights
    C. All Properties and Selected Properties
    D. Object rights and the IRF

  Answer: B

10. Inherited rights can be blocked with
    A. The IRF
    B. An explicit assignment
    C. Both A and B
    D. None of the above

  Answer: C

11. Explicit security equivalences can be granted with
    A. Container occupancy
    B. Group, Organizational Role, Security Equal
    C. Group, container occupancy
    D. All of the above

  Answer: B

12. Which of the following does NOT affect effective NDS rights?
    A. Explicit rights
    B. Inherited rights

    C. Rights given to child objects

    D. Rights given to parent objects

    Answer: C

13. The [Public] Trustee

    A. Assigns rights to all users when logged in

    B. Assigns rights to anyone attached to the network

    C. Assigns rights to ADMIN only

    D. Assigns rights to the file system only

    Answer: B

Chapter 8

1. Which is the correct order for login script execution?

    A. User, container, default, profile

    B. Container, user, profile, default

    C. Container, profile, user, default

    D. Container, default, user, profile

    Answer: C

2. The container login script is executed

    A. For each container the user is in

    B. For the user's parent container

    C. For the profile container only

    D. For the [Root] container only

    Answer: B

3. Which is a correct MAP command in a login script?

    A. MAP F:=SYS:APPS

    B. #MAP F:=SYS:APPS

    C. MAP NEXT SYS:APPS

    D. MAP F:=SYS

    Answer: A

4. The INCLUDE command

    A. Exits the login script and starts another

    B. Executes another script and then returns

    C. Adds commands to a login script

    D. Adds a login script to the Profile object

    Answer: B

5. Which of the following is NOT a valid comment?

    A. REM Do not change this script

    B. ***Do not change this script***

    C. # Do not change this script

    D. ;Do not change this script

    Answer: C

6. To use a DOS command in a login script

    A. Include the name of the command only

    B. Include # and the name of the command

    C. Include ; and the name of the command

    D. Place the command in an INCLUDE file

    Answer: B

7. Which is a valid EXIT command?

    A. EXIT "NMENU MYMENU.DAT"

    B. EXIT NMENU /N=MYMENU

    C. EXIT "NMENU MYMENU"

    D. EXIT TO MENU MYMENU.DAT

    Answer: C

8. Which is a valid MENU command?

    A. MENU #1: The Main Menu

    B. MENU Main Menu, 01

    C. MENU "The Main Menu"

    D. MENU 01, The Main Menu

    Answer: D

9. Which is the correct menu command to exit the menu?

    A. EXIT

    B. EXIT "MENU.DAT"

    C. EXEC EXIT

    D. EXEC "EXIT"

    Answer: C

10. The LOAD menu command

    A. Runs a submenu from the same file

    B. Runs a submenu from a different file

    C. Includes a menu within the current menu

    D. Exits to a different menu

    Answer: B

11. Menus are compiled with the _____ command.
    A. MENUCON
    B. COMPILE
    C. MENUCNVT
    D. MENUMAKE

    Answer: D

12. Which of the following MENU commands is optional?
    A. MENU
    B. ITEM
    C. EXEC
    D. GETR

    Answer: D

Chapter 9

1. The NDS objects used for printing are
    A. Print server, print queue, port driver
    B. Print server, print queue, printer
    C. Printer, print server, port driver
    D. CAPTURE, printer, print server

    Answer: B

2. The number of printers controlled by a NetWare 4.1 print server
    A. Is limited only by the server's memory
    B. Is limited to 16 printers
    C. Is limited to 256 printers
    D. Is limited to three parallel printers and two serial printers

    Answer: C

3. The three basic types of network printer are
    A. Workstation, server, queue
    B. Workstation, server, directly connected
    C. NDS, bindery, workstation
    D. Dot matrix, laser, daisy wheel

    Answer: B

4. Which is the correct CAPTURE command to capture the LPT2 port to the CHECKS queue?

  A. CAPTURE J=2 P=CHECKS
  B. CAPTURE L=1 B=2 Q=CHECKS
  C. CAPTURE LPT2 P=CHECK_PRINTER
  D. CAPTURE LPT2 Q=CHECKS

  Answer: D

5. The Print Server object

  A. Is not used in NetWare 4.1
  B. Moves jobs from the print queue to the printer
  C. Moves jobs from the print queue to the port driver
  D. Stores a list of jobs to be printed

  Answer: C

6. To configure a workstation printer, you use the _____ program.

  A. RPRINTER
  B. REMOTE
  C. WPRINTER
  D. NPRINTER

  Answer: D

7. Which is the correct order of components when a print job is processed?

  A. CAPTURE, print queue, printer
  B. CAPTURE, print queue, print server, port driver, printer
  C. CAPTURE, port driver, print server, print queue, printer
  D. port driver, CAPTURE, print queue, print server, printer

  Answer: B

8. CAPTURE can use which LPT ports?

  A. LPT1-3
  B. LPT1-5
  C. Only those you have the hardware for
  D. LPT1-9

  Answer: D

9. The Print Server object

  A. Is created automatically when the printer is installed
  B. Needs to be created for each printer
  C. Can handle up to 256 printers
  D. Is not needed for most printers

  Answer: C

10. You can stop and continue a print job with which NWADMIN functions?

    A. Pause and play

    B. Pause and resume

    C. Hold and resume

    D. Hold and unhold

    Answer: C

11. The number of printers on the network is limited by

    A. The print server

    B. The number of ports on the server

    C. The number of queues

    D. Disk storage available

    Answer: A

12. You can CAPTURE to

    A. A printer or a print server

    B. A printer only

    C. A printer or a queue

    D. A printer or NPRINTER

    Answer: C

Chapter 10

1. Commands that you can use at the server console include

    A. DOS commands

    B. NLMs and console commands

    C. NLMs only

    D. DOS or NLM commands

    Answer: B

2. The NetWare core operating system does NOT include

    A. File sharing

    B. NDS

    C. Network management

    D. Printer sharing

    Answer: C

3. NLMs come from

   A. Novell

   B. Third parties

   C. Both of the above

   D. None of the above

   Answer: C

4. The two parts of a NPA disk driver are

   A. NPA and CDA

   B. HAM and CAM

   C. HAM and CDM

   D. NPA and HDM

   Answer: C

5. LAN Driver modules have the extension

   A. NLM

   B. DRV

   C. LAN

   D. MOD

   Answer: C

6. The command to display configuration information is

   A. DISPLAY CONFIG

   B. MODULES

   C. CONFIG

   D. VERSION

   Answer: C

7. The command used to prevent logins is

   A. SET LOGIN = NO

   B. DISABLE LOGIN

   C. LOGIN OFF

   D. SECURE CONSOLE

   Answer: B

8. The two commands needed to bring down the server are

   A. DOWN and QUIT

   B. DOWN and RESET

   C. DOWN and CLS

   D. DOWN and EXIT

   Answer: D

9. The key used to switch screens in RCONSOLE is
   A. F3 or F4
   B. ALT+ESC
   C. CTRL+ESC
   D. ALT+F3 and ALT+F4

   Answer: D

10. The two modules you must load to enable remote access are
    A. REMOTE and MONITOR
    B. REMOTE and ACCESS
    C. RSPX and REMOTE
    D. RSPX and RCONSOLE

    Answer: C

NetWare
Commands
Quick Reference

HIS APPENDIX IS intended as a handy reference to the various Net-Ware 4.1 commands. It is organized into four sections based on the types of commands used in NetWare:

- **Workstation commands** are executed from a DOS workstation and accept parameters on the command line.

- **Menu and Windows utilities** provide a full user interface in DOS or Windows to allow access to available functions.

- **Console commands** can be typed directly at the file server console.

- **Console utilities** (NLMs) can be loaded at the file server with the LOAD command.

This appendix lists only the most common commands that you are likely to use or encounter frequently when managing a NetWare 4.1 network. For a complete reference, see the Novell Utilities manual.

Workstation Commands

CAPTURE

Redirects a printer port on the workstation to a print queue or printer on the NetWare 4.1 server. The following example redirects the LPT1 port to the CHECKS print queue:

    CAPTURE L=1 Q=CHECKS

CX

Use this command to change your current NDS context—the NDS container object that will be used by default when searching for objects. For example, this command sets the current context to .O=ADMIN:

```
CX .O=ADMIN
```

FLAG

Allows you to manage file attributes or to display the attributes for an existing file. The FLAG command is followed by a path or filename as well as options to specify attributes to be added or removed. FLAG by itself displays the attributes of all files in the current directory. Here are some examples of the FLAG command:

```
FLAG SYS:ETC\DATA +H
```

adds the Hidden attribute to the SYS:ETC\DATA directory.

```
FLAG *.* N
```

sets all files in the current directory to Normal (read/write).

```
FLAG SYS:PUBLIC\FILER.EXE +RO
```

gives the FILER.EXE file the Read Only attribute.

LOGIN

Logs you in to a NetWare 4.1 server or NDS tree. If not specified, LOGIN uses the default server or tree in the workstation's NET.CFG file. The /NS switch can be added to attach to a server without logging out of the current server or tree. The following command logs in the user TED on the tree OAK_TREE:

```
LOGIN OAK_TREE/TED
```

LOGOUT

Ends your current login session and allows another user to log in. By default, you are logged out of all servers. However, you can also log out of just one server, keeping your connection to the others, by specifying the server name:

```
LOGOUT SERVER1
```

MAP

Use this command to map a drive letter, or network drive, to a volume and directory on the server. This command can also be used with Directory Map objects.

```
MAP J:=SYS:APPS\PROGRAM
```

maps the network drive J: to the APPS\PROGRAM directory on the SYS volume.

```
MAP S3:=SYS:PUBLIC
```

maps the third search drive to the PUBLIC directory.

```
MAP K:=WP
```

maps network drive K: to the volume and directory specified by the Directory Map object WP.

NCOPY

Copies files from one directory to another. This command can be used with both local and network directories and can copy entire directory structures.

```
NCOPY C:\DOS\*.* F:\PUBLIC\DOS
```

copies all files in the DOS directory on local drive C: to the PUBLIC\DOS directory on network drive F:.

```
NCOPY C:\*.* /S
```

copies all files on drive C:, including subdirectories, to the current directory.

```
NCOPY F:\BACKUP\*.* C:\ /S/E/V
```

copies all of the files from the BACKUP directory, including subdirectories and empty directories, to drive C: and verifies each file.

NDIR

Lists the files in a directory. This command is similar to the DIR command in DOS but also displays NetWare file attributes and ownership information. NDIR has a wide variety of options that enable you to search for files or list specific types of information. Here are some examples:

```
NDIR
```

lists all files in the current directory, using the default format.

```
NDIR * /R
```

displays a list of rights for each file in the current directory.

```
NDIR F:\*.TMP /SUB
```

lists all files with a TMP extension on drive F:, including those in subdirectories.

```
NDIR F:\* /SUB /OW EQ SUE.ACCT.STECH
```

lists all files owned by the user SUE on the network drive F:. If the user is in the current context, the full distinguished name is not necessary.

```
NDIR F:\PUBLIC\* /CR BEF 03-22-97
```

lists all files in the PUBLIC directory created before March 22, 1997.

NLIST

A general-purpose utility for listing NDS objects. Can be used to list users, servers, or any other type of NDS object or to look for objects with a certain property. Here are several examples:

    NLIST USER /A

lists all users in the current context.

    NLIST SERVER /B

lists all bindery servers.

    NLIST USER WHERE "GROUP MEMBERSHIP" = ACCTG

lists all users who are members of the ACCTG group.

    NLIST USER SHOW "TELEPHONE NUMBER"

lists all user names and their telephone numbers (if defined).

    NLIST GROUP /S

lists all groups defined in the Directory tree.

    NLIST *

lists all objects in the current context.

NPRINT

Allows you to send a text file to a network print queue. For example, the following command sends all files with the TXT extension in the current directory to the LASER1 print queue:

    NPRINT *.TXT Q=LASER1

NPRINTER

Starts the driver for a workstation printer or a remote printer. This program remains in memory to drive the printer until you unload the driver. The following command sets up the LASER1 printer attached to the current workstation:

```
NPRINTER LASER1
```

NVER

Displays NetWare version information, such as the server you are attached to and the revision of client software.

PURGE

Purges deleted files from the current directory, preventing them from being salvaged with the FILER or NWADMIN utilities. The /A switch can be added to purge all files on the server.

```
PURGE *.*
```

purges all deleted files in the current directory.

```
PURGE \*.* /A
```

purges all deleted files on the volume.

RENDIR

Renames a directory. This command can be used on local directories or on the NetWare server. The following command renames the BACKUP directory on the SYS volume and gives it the new name TEMP:

```
RENDIR SYS:BACKUP TEMP
```

RIGHTS

Displays your current rights in a directory of the file system. This command also allows you to grant or revoke rights to a user or to maintain the IRF. Here are a few examples of the RIGHTS command:

```
RIGHTS VOL1:USERS R W C F /NAME=KRISTEN
```

gives the user KRISTEN the Read, Write, Create, and File scan rights for the VOL1:USERS directory.

```
RIGHTS SYS:DATA REM /NAME=JohnS
```

removes all rights that user JohnS had in the SYS:DATA directory.

```
RIGHTS SYS:APPS\WP /T
```

lists all trustees of the SYS:APPS\WP directory.

```
RIGHTS . R F /F
```

sets the IRF for the current directory (referred to with a single period) to Read and File scan only.

SEND

Sends a message to a user or group. This is similar to the BROADCAST console command.

```
SEND "Please log out immediately" BOB, SVEN
```

asks users BOB and SVEN to log out.

```
SEND "System going down at 3:00" EVERYONE
```

sends a message to the EVERYONE group.

```
SEND /A=C
```

sets your workstation to receive messages only from the console or the system.

WHOAMI

Displays information about your current login session and the server or servers you are attached to.

Menu and Windows Utilities

FILER

A general-purpose utility for managing files and directories in the NetWare file system. Can be used to copy, rename, or delete files; to manage rights to files and directories; to control file attributes; and to salvage deleted files.

NETADMIN

A DOS utility for managing users and other NDS objects on the network. Can be used to create, rename, or delete objects; grant trustee rights; and manage property values.

NETUSER

Allows you to map drives, capture printers, and send messages to users on the network from a simple menu-based interface.

NWADMIN

A Windows utility for managing NDS objects. Can be used to create, rename, or delete objects; manage rights to other objects; and control property values. This utility can also manage files and directories in the file system and control NDS partitioning and replication. Chapter 6 is a guide to using the NWADMIN utility.

NMENU

Allows you to create user-friendly menus with specific commands for a user or department. Chapter 8 explains the menu system.

PARTMGR

Allows you to manage partitions and replicas in NDS. This utility is explained fully in Chapter 11.

PCONSOLE

This utility provides a Print Console from which you can create printers, print queues and other NDS printing objects, and control all aspects of printing. It also includes a quick setup feature for setting up printers and queues.

PRINTCON

Allows you to manage print job configurations—specific sets of parameters that can be referenced with a quick CAPTURE command.

PRINTDEF

Allows you to define printer commands and forms, which can be used to send special codes to the printer to control print modes.

RCONSOLE

Allows you to establish a connection to the server and access the server console from a DOS workstation. While RCONSOLE is attached to a server, you can use the following key commands:

- **Alt+F1** activates the RCONSOLE Available Options menu. This menu allows you to navigate between screens, view files and directories on the server, and transfer files to the server.

- **Alt+F2** exits the RCONSOLE utility. You will be asked to confirm your selection.

- **ALT+F3** moves to the next server screen, similar to ALT+ESC at the server console.

- **ALT+F4** moves to the previous server screen.

- **ALT+F5** shows the network address of your workstation.

Console Commands

BIND

Connects a network protocol, such as IPX, to a network adapter driver that you have loaded. For example, to bind the IPX protocol to the NE2000 driver:

```
BIND IPX TO NE2000 NET=1
```

BROADCAST

Sends a message to all users on the system or to a specific user or group. Similar to the SEND workstation utility.

DISABLE LOGIN

Prevents users from logging into the network. Does not affect those who are already logged in.

DISMOUNT

Dismounts a NetWare volume. This command is necessary if you are removing the volume, changing its parameters, or maintaining it with the VREPAIR utility. For example, to dismount the SYS volume:

```
DISMOUNT SYS
```

DOWN

Brings the server down. This can be followed by the EXIT command to return to DOS or by the RESTART SERVER command to restart the server.

ENABLE LOGIN

Allows login to the server after the DISABLE LOGIN command has been used. Also resets accounts that have been locked by the intruder detection feature.

EXIT

Exits the server and returns to DOS. This can be used only after the DOWN command.

LOAD

Loads a NetWare Loadable Module (NLM) into the server's memory. NLMs serve as device drivers, add additional functions to the system, or allow you to manage the server. For example, this command starts the MONITOR utility:

```
LOAD MONITOR
```

MODULES

Displays a list of the currently loaded modules (NLMs).

MOUNT

Mounts a volume so that it can be used. For example, this command mounts the VOL1 volume:

```
MOUNT VOL1
```

SET

Sets a parameter for server performance. Typing SET by itself lists the available commands. The SERVMAN utility manages these parameters in a more user-friendly way.

UNLOAD

Removes an NLM from memory. For example, to unload the MONITOR utility:

```
UNLOAD MONITOR
```

VERSION

Displays information about the version of NetWare that is running and about the network drivers that are loaded.

Console Utilities (NLMs)

CDROM

Allows a CD-ROM disk in the server to be mounted as a NetWare volume.

DOMAIN

Allows you to manage memory domains and use the memory protection features. If used, this NLM must be loaded in the STARTUP.NCF file.

DSMERGE

A utility to merge NDS Directory trees; can also be used to check synchronization.

DSREPAIR

A general-purpose utility for repairing problems with the NDS Directory. DSREPAIR will diagnose and advise you of problems—and fix them if possible.

EDIT

Allows you to edit a file on a NetWare volume. Useful for editing AUTO-EXEC.NCF, TIMESYNC.CFG, and other server configuration files. For example, to edit the AUTOEXEC.NCF file:

```
LOAD EDIT SYS:SYSTEM\AUTOEXEC.NCF
```

INSTALL

Allows you to install additional Netware features or manage the server's configuration.

MONITOR

Displays information about the server's memory, processor, disks, and many other components. Useful for fine-tuning the server's performance.

NETSYNC

Allows you to manage a NetWare 3.1*x* server from NetWare 4.1 NDS utilities. NETSYNC is actually two NLMs: NETSYNC4, loaded on the NetWare 4.1 server, and NETSYNC3, which you can load on up to 12 NetWare 3.1*x* servers.

NPRINTER

Loads the port driver for a server-attached printer. PSERVER will usually load NPRINTER automatically.

PSERVER

Starts a print server, corresponding to a Print Server object in NDS. Can be used to control printing in progress and change settings. The following command starts the PS1 print server:

```
LOAD PSERVER PS1
```

REMOTE

Allows users to attach to the server using RCONSOLE. The RSPX NLM must also be loaded for this function.

SERVMAN

Provides a user-friendly system for changing server parameters. The SET command can also be used.

SBACKUP

Provides a basic backup system for files in NetWare volumes and for the NDS database.

VREPAIR

Analyzes and repairs problems in a disk volume. The volume must be dismounted before VREPAIR is used. If only one volume is currently dismounted, VREPAIR will automatically repair that volume; otherwise, you will be asked which volume to repair.

Glossary
of Terms

GLOSSARY

Abend

Short for abnormal end. This is NetWare's term for a server crash. An abend is usually caused by an application (NLM) writing to an area of memory that belongs to the operating system.

Access Control List (ACL)

The property of an NDS object that contains the list of *trustees* or other objects that have rights to the object.

Across-the-Wire Migration

One of the two possible migration strategies from NetWare 3.1x to NetWare 4.1. In the across-the-wire strategy, a new NetWare 4.1 server is connected to the same network as the NetWare 3.1x server, and data is copied over the network.

Additive Licensing

NetWare 4.1's licensing system, which allows you to add licenses when your network needs to allow more user logins. For example, you can add a 5-user license to a 25-user license for a total of 30 possible users.

Alias Object

An object used to represent, or point to, another object in the NDS tree. Alias objects can be created to make a resource in a different context available in the local context. Netware can create Aliases automatically when an object or container is moved.

Aliased Object

The object that an Alias object refers to. Also called the *source* object.

Allocation Pool

The area of memory that NetWare 4.1 sets aside for each server application (NLM). When the NLM requests additional memory, it is taken from this pool.

AppleTalk

A networking system developed by Apple for use with Macintosh computers. The software for AppleTalk connectivity is built into the Macintosh operating system (MacOS or System 7). NetWare for Macintosh allows connectivity between AppleTalk and NetWare networks.

Attributes

File attributes are stored for each file and directory on a server's file system. Attributes are used for security and for status information for the file. For example, the Read-Only attribute prevents a file from being written to or erased, and the Can't Compress attribute indicates that NetWare was unable to compress the file.

Auditing

A NetWare 4.1 service that allows a user, or auditor, to monitor activities on the network. The auditor can monitor the file system or an NDS container. Auditing is done through the AUDITCON menu utility.

Auditor's Password

A password that is set when you begin an audit on a volume or NDS container. The auditor should change this password when the audit begins. The password is required for all auditing activities, including ending the audit.

Authentication

Part of the login process, in which NDS verifies that the user's password, access rights, and other settings are correct. Authentication is handled by the nearest read/write or master replica.

Backup Engine

Part of the NetWare Storage Management System (SMS). The backup engine is the front end, or user interface, to the backup software. Novell's SBACKUP is a backup engine that can be run on the server or on a DOS or Microsoft Windows workstation.

Base Schema

The NDS base schema defines the structure of NDS—which objects are possible, which properties an object can have, and so forth. The NDS base schema is written to the server when NDS is installed. Third-party applications can extend, or add to, this schema using the NetWare API (Application Program Interface).

Batch File

A file containing a list of commands to be executed. DOS batch files have the extension BAT. Examples include AUTOEXEC.BAT, which executes when the workstation is booted, and STARTNET.BAT, which is used to attach to the network. NetWare also provides batch file capability for the server in the form of NCF (NetWare Command Files).

Bindery

The database used to store information about users, printers, and other network objects in NetWare 3.1x and earlier versions. The bindery is a simple, flat database, which is stored separately on each server. NetWare 4.1 replaces the bindery with NetWare Directory Services (NDS).

Bindery Context

The context that will be provided as a simulated bindery by Bindery Services. You can set up to 16 separate contexts to serve as bindery contexts. These will be combined into a "bindery" that bindery-based clients can access.

Bindery Services

NetWare 4.1's service that allows the simulation of a bindery. By using the Bindery Services feature, clients using older client software, such as the NetWare DOS shell, can access the network. A branch of the NDS tree, the bindery context, is used as a simulated bindery.

Block

One of the divisions of a hard disk. NetWare stores files on the volume in terms of blocks. In NetWare 3.1*x* and earlier, entire blocks are always used. Block sizes are typically 4K for NetWare 3.1*x* and variable for NetWare 4.1.

Block Suballocation

A NetWare 4.1 feature that allows smaller portions of disk blocks to be used. Each block is divided into 512-byte units, which can be used instead of entire blocks. This feature allows more efficient use of disk space.

Cache

A technique used by NetWare servers to increase disk performance. Data read from the disk drive is stored in a block of memory, or *cache*. When clients request this data, it can be read directly from the cache, avoiding the use of the disk. NetWare provides both read and write caching.

Cache Buffer

NetWare sets aside a portion of the server's memory as cache buffers. These buffers hold information for the file system. The number of cache buffers depends on the amount of available memory.

Cache Hit

A statistical term used when data is successfully read from the disk cache. A high percentage of cache hits indicates that the number of cache buffers is sufficient for the application and that the server is running smoothly.

Centralized Administration

One of the two types of administration in NetWare 4.1. In centralized administration, a single (central) administrator has rights to manage the entire NDS tree. The other type of administration is *distributed* administration.

Child Object

In NDS, an object that is under a container object. The container object is referred to as the *parent object*.

Client

Any device that attaches to the network server. A workstation is the most common type of client. Clients run *client software* to provide network access.

Common Name

In NDS, a name associated with a leaf object. This is the name given to the object when it is created. The common name designator is abbreviated CN in typeful naming.

Compile

In the menu system, the process of converting a *menu source file* into a *menu data file* that can be used by the NMENU program. The MENUMAKE program is used to compile menus.

Container Administrator

An administrator that is given rights to a container object and all of the objects under it. A container administrator can be *exclusive,* meaning that no other administrator has access to the container.

Container Object

In NDS, an object that contains other objects. Container objects include Organization, Organizational Unit, and Country objects. The [Root] object is also a specialized kind of container object. Objects within a container can be other container objects or *leaf objects*, which represent network resources.

Container Security Equivalence

See *Implied Security Equivalence.*

Context

In NDS, an object's position within the Directory tree. The context is the full path to the container object in which the object resides.

Current Context

The current position in the Directory tree maintained for a workstation connection. By default, objects are assumed to be in this context, unless you specify the full *distinguished name*. The current context is also called the *default context*.

Custom Device Module (CDM)

Part of the NPA (NetWare Peripheral Architecture) system of device drivers. The CDM provides an interface between the device and the Host Adapter Module (HAM).

Custom Installation

One of the two installation options for NetWare 4.1. The Custom installation option allows you to specify all parameters for the server during the installation process.

Data Migration

A system where less frequently used data is moved to a high-capacity storage device, such as a *jukebox*. The HCSS (High-Capacity Storage System) is the NetWare 4.1 service that handles data migration.

Deallocation

In NetWare 4.1 memory management, the process of returning memory to an allocation pool when it is no longer needed, thus making it available for other applications.

Dedicated Server

A server that serves no other purpose; it cannot be used as a workstation. All NetWare 3.1*x* servers and most NetWare 4.1 servers are dedicated. NetWare 4.1 provides a nondedicated server option through NetWare Server for OS/2.

Default Context

See *Current Context*.

Demigrate

The process of moving data back from a high-capacity storage system that it was migrated to. This is done when a user attempts to access the file that was migrated.

Departmental Implementation

One of the methods of implementing NDS. In this method, departments or other divisions of the company are moved to NDS one at a time, each with its own Directory tree. The trees can be merged later.

Device Driver

Software that allows a workstation or server to communicate with a hardware device. For example, disk drivers are used to control disk drives, and network drivers are used to communicate with network boards.

Directly Connected Network Printer

One type of network printer allowed by NetWare 4.1. This type of printer is attached to the network rather than to a workstation or server. Directly connected printers can operate in either *remote mode* or *queue server mode*.

Directory

In NDS, the database that contains information about each of the objects on the network. The Directory is organized into a treelike structure, the *Directory tree*, with a *[Root] object* on top and *leaf objects* at the bottom. To distinguish it from disk directories, the NDS Directory is written with a capital *D*.

Directory Map

A special NDS object that is used to map directories in the file system. The MAP command can specify the name of the Directory Map object rather than the exact directory name. The directory name is contained in a property of the Directory Map object.

Directory Tree

See *Directory.*

Distinguished Name

In NDS, the full name of an NDS object. This includes the object's *common name* and its *context*, or location in the Directory tree. Also referred to as the *full distinguished name.*

Distributed Administration

One type of administration allowed by NetWare 4.1. (The other option is *centralized administration.*) In distributed administration, separate administrators are assigned for different portions of the Directory tree and file system.

Distributed Database

A database that is contained in multiple locations. NDS is a distributed database that is contained on multiple NetWare 4.1 servers.

Distribution List

A special NDS object that is used to send e-mail messages to multiple users. This object is part of the Message Handling Service (MHS) in NetWare 4.1.

Divisional Implementation

One method of implementing NDS in a network. Each division is moved to NDS separately and has its own Directory tree. This method is similar to the *departmental* implementation.

Divisional Organization

A type of NDS organization that divides the Directory tree into branches for each division or department within an organization. This is often a practical way to organize, since members of a department or division may require access to the same set of resources.

Domain

In NetWare 4.1 memory management, the domain system is used as a *memory protection* feature. Domains include the OS domain, which is the default, and the OS_PROTECTED domain, which provides memory protection.

DOS Shell

The client software used for DOS workstations in NetWare 3.1x and earlier versions. The executable program for the DOS Shell is NETX.COM. The DOS Shell does not provide access to NDS but can be used with NetWare 4.1 via Bindery Services.

DynaText

The online documentation system included with NetWare 4.1. This is provided on CD-ROM, and it can be used from the CD-ROM or installed on the network or on a workstation. DynaText replaces *ElectroText* used by NetWare 3.1x and earlier versions.

Effective Rights

The rights that a user (or other trustee) has in a file system directory or NDS object after all factors are considered. Factors include explicit rights, inherited rights, the IRF (Inherited Rights Filter), and security equivalences.

ElectroText

An online documentation system provided with earlier versions of NetWare. This has been replaced by *DynaText* in NetWare 4.1.

Enterprise Networking

The type of networking required to connect an entire enterprise, or a large corporation. This usually means a WAN (wide-area network). NetWare 4.0 was intended as an enterprise networking system, but NetWare 4.1 is suitable for networks of any size.

Events

In NetWare 4.1 auditing, the types of activities that can be monitored by the auditor for a volume or NDS object.

Exclusive Container Administrator

A special type of *container administrator* that is given rights to a container and the objects within it. The IRF (Inherited Rights Filter) is used to prevent other administrators from having rights in the container.

Explicit Rights

In NDS or the file system, any rights that are given directly to a user for a directory or NDS object. Explicit rights override inherited rights.

Explicit Security Equivalence

In NDS, a method of giving a trustee the same rights as another trustee. Explicit security equivalence can be assigned with Group object membership, an Organizational Role, or the trustee's Security Equal To property.

External Entity

A special NDS object that is used by MHS (Message Handling Services) to represent outside objects that can receive mail.

File Attributes

See *Attributes*.

File Compression

A NetWare 4.1 feature that automatically compresses files that are not in use. A compressed file can take as little as 33 percent of the space of the original file. Compressed files are uncompressed automatically when a user accesses them.

Full Distinguished Name

See *Distinguished Name*.

Garbage Collection

In NetWare 4.1 memory management, the process of returning memory that has been deallocated to the main memory pool so that it can be used by other applications.

Gateway

A system used to send and receive e-mail from a different e-mail system, such as a mainframe or the Internet. Gateways are supported by MHS (Message Handling Services).

Greenwich Mean Time (GMT)

See *Universal Coordinated Time (UTC)*.

Group Rights

NDS or file system rights that a user receives because of membership in a Group object. This is an example of *explicit security equivalence*.

Handshaking

In network communication, a process used to verify that data is sent correctly. After each packet is sent, an acknowledgment is sent back to indicate that the packet was received properly.

High-Capacity Storage System (HCSS)

The NetWare 4.1 service that allows data to be migrated to high-capacity storage. See *Data Migration.*

Host Adapter

A hardware device that allows communication with a peripheral, such as a disk drive or tape drive. The host adapter, also called a *controller*, is usually a card that is inserted into a slot on the server's motherboard.

Host Adapter Module (HAM)

One of the components of the NPA (NetWare Peripheral Architecture) device driver standard. The HAM provides communication with the *host adapter.*

Hybrid Organization

An NDS organization strategy that combines two or more of the other methods: locational, divisional, or workgroup. Hybrid organizations are the most useful for larger companies.

Implementation Strategy

The method used for implementing, or moving to, NDS on a network. Strategies include the departmental (or divisional) implementation and the organizational implementation.

Implied Security Equivalence

In NDS, an object is security equivalent to (receives the rights of) the object's parent object and its parents, leading up to the [Root] object. This is also called *container security equivalence.* The IRF (Inherited Rights Filter) does not affect this process.

Inherited Rights

In NDS or the file system, inherited rights are rights that a trustee receives for an object because of rights to the object's parent (a directory in the file system or a parent object in NDS). Inherited rights can be blocked by an explicit assignment or by the IRF (Inherited Rights Filter).

Inherited Rights Filter (IRF)

In the file system, the IRF is the list of rights that a user can inherit for a directory from directories above it. An IRF also exists for each NDS object, and it lists the rights that a trustee can inherit from the object's parents. In NetWare 3.1x, the IRF was called the IRM (Inherited Rights Mask) and applied only to the file system.

In-Place Migration

One of the methods for migrating (upgrading) a server from NetWare 3.1x to NetWare 4.1. In this method, the server is upgraded directly to the new NOS (network operating system), leaving data files on the server intact. The alternative method is *across-the-wire migration*.

Internetworking

The process of connecting multiple local-area networks (LANs) to form a wide-area network (WAN). Internetworking between different types of networks is handled by a *router*.

IPX External Network Number

A number that is used to represent an entire network. All servers on the network must use the same external network number.

IPX Internal Network Number

A number that uniquely identifies a server to the network. Each server must have a different internal network number.

Jukebox

A device that provides high-capacity storage to optical media. Jukeboxes are supported by NetWare 4.1's High-Capacity Storage System (HCSS).

Large Internet Packet (LIP)

A system that NetWare 4.1 provides to increase the speed of network communications. Packets sent through a router are kept at their maximum possible size, rather than reducing them to 512K as in older versions of NetWare.

Leaf Object

An object that cannot contain other objects and represents a network resource. Leaf objects include User, Group, Printer, Server, and Volume.

License Diskette

A diskette that contains licensing information and is included in the NetWare 4.1 package. This diskette controls the number of users that can log in to the network at one time. Multiple licenses can be used thanks to the *additive licensing* feature.

Local-Area Network (LAN)

A network that is restricted to a local area, such as a single building, a group of buildings, or even a single room. Most LANs have only one server, but they can have more.

Locational Organization

A method of organizing the Directory tree that divides it into Organizational Units for each geographical location of the organization. This strategy is often the best for network communication.

Logical Ports

Ports used by the CAPTURE command to redirect a workstation printer port to a network print queue. The logical port has no relation to the port the printer is actually attached to, or the *physical port*.

Login Script

A set of commands called *login script commands,* that are automatically executed when a user logs in. NetWare 4.1 includes Container, Profile, User, and Default login scripts. Up to three of these can be executed for each user.

Login Security

The most basic form of network security. A user name and password are required in order to log in to the network and access resources.

Master Replica

The main replica for a partition. The master replica must be available when major changes, such as partition merging and splitting, are performed. Another replica can be assigned as master if the master replica is lost.

Memory Allocation

The system NetWare 4.1 uses to provide memory for use by applications (NLMs) on the server. Memory is allocated from an *allocation pool*.

Memory Protection

NetWare 4.1's system for protecting the server's memory from NLMs that do not behave properly. NLMs can be run in *domains*. The OS domain is the default, and the OS_PROTECTED domain allows memory protection. NLMs in this domain are not allowed any access to the OS domain's memory.

Menu Data File

A file used to run a menu using the NMENU program. The data file is the result of *compiling* the menu source file using the MENUMAKE utility. Menu data files have the DAT extension.

Menu Source File

The file that you write, using *menu commands*, to create a user menu. This file must be compiled into a *menu data file* using the MENUMAKE utility before it can be used. Source files typically have an SRC extension.

Menu Utilities

A type of NetWare utility that presents a menu of options when it executes. Menu utilities have a consistent interface. FILER and NETADMIN are two examples.

Merging Directory Trees

The process of combining two Directory trees into a single tree. The objects in the *source* tree are combined into the *destination*, or *target*, tree. The DSMERGE utility is used to merge trees.

Merging Partitions

The process of combining an NDS partition with its parent partition, resulting in a single partition. The master replica of the partition must be available for this process.

Message File

A file used to store prompts and messages for a NetWare workstation or server utility. Message files are provided for each supported language (English, French, Italian, German, and Spanish).

Message Handling Service (MHS)

The NetWare 4.1 service that provides electronic mail (e-mail) facilities. All aspects of MHS are managed through NDS. MHS must be installed on the server before it can be used.

Message Routing Group

A special NDS object that groups together messaging servers and allows mail to be sent between them. This is a component of NetWare's MHS (Message Handling Service).

Messaging Server

An NDS object used to manage MHS (Message Handling Service). Each Directory tree where MHS is used should have a Messaging Server object. This object is created when you install MHS on the server.

Multiprotocol Router (MPR)

The software that provides *routing* capabilities for a NetWare 4.1 server. MPR enables communication between different types of networks.

Multivalued Property

In NDS, a property that can have multiple values. For example, a User object's Telephone Number property can store multiple telephone numbers.

Name Conflict

A situation where names conflict with each other. This typically happens in Bindery Services or when using NetSync. All users in the bindery context must have unique common names.

Name Space

A service that you can install on a NetWare 4.1 server volume to allow different types of file names to be used. Name spaces are available for OS/2 and Macintosh naming.

NetSync

The software that allows NetWare 3.1*x* servers to be managed through NDS utilities. This is accomplished using the NETSYNC3 NLM at the NetWare 3.1*x* servers and the NETSYNC4 NLM at the NetWare 4.1 server.

NetSync Cluster

A NetWare 4.1 server and a group of NetWare 3.1*x* servers that it can manage using NetSync. Each NetWare 4.1 server can manage up to 16 NetWare 3.1*x* servers.

NetWare Directory Services (NDS)

The system NetWare 4.1 uses to catalog objects, such as users, printers, and volumes, on the network. NDS uses a *Directory tree* to store this information. All of the NetWare 4.1 network's resources can be managed through NDS.

NetWare DOS Requester

The client software that is used on a DOS workstation to access the NetWare 4.1 network and NDS. The DOS Requester replaces the *DOS Shell* in previous NetWare versions. The VLM.EXE program is used to load the DOS Requester.

NetWare Loadable Module (NLM)

An application or program that executes on the NetWare server. NLMs are used for device drivers, LAN drivers, and applications such as backup software. Netware 4.1 includes a variety of utility NLMs, and others are available from third parties.

NetWare OS/2 Requester

The client software used to access a NetWare 4.1 server and NDS from an OS/2 workstation. The OS/2 Requester provides the same benefits as the DOS Requester.

NetWare Peripheral Architecture (NPA)

A new system that NetWare 4.1 allows for *device drivers*. The driver is divided into two modules: a Host Adapter Module (HAM) and a Custom Device Module (CDM) for each device attached to the host adapter. Older device drivers use a single program with a DSK extension. These can still be used in NetWare 4.1.

Network Address

A unique address that identifies each node, or device, on the network. The network address is generally hard coded into the network card on both the workstation and server. Some network cards allow you to change this address, but there is seldom a reason to do so.

Network-Centric

The architecture used in a NetWare 4.1 network. Objects are created for the entire network, rather than for a single server. This feature is one of the benefits of NDS.

Network Operating System (NOS)

The software that runs on a file server. NetWare 4.1 is a NOS. Other examples include NetWare 3.1*x*, Banyan VINES, and IBM LAN Server.

Nondedicated Server

A server that can also act as a workstation. NetWare 2.2 provided this capability, and NetWare 4.1 provides it through NetWare Server for OS/2. NetWare 3.1*x* does not permit nondedicated servers.

Object

In NDS, any resource on the network. Users, printers, and groups are examples of *leaf objects*. *Container objects*, such as Organizations and Organizational Units, are used to organize other objects.

Object Trustee

See *Trustee*.

Occupant

A user who has been assigned to an Organizational Role object. Each Organizational Role can have multiple occupants, stored in the Occupants property of the object.

Organization Object

Usually the highest level container object used. Organizations are created under the [Root] object (or Country object if it is used). This object usually represents an entire organization or company. Multiple Organization objects can be used in the same Directory tree.

Organizational Implementation

One of the methods of implementing NDS. (The *divisional* and *departmental* implementations are the alternatives.) In this method, the entire Organization is moved at once. This is also called the *top-down* approach. This method is rarely practical.

Organizational Role Object

An object that is used to represent a role—an administrator or other specialized user who requires access to certain NDS objects or files. This type of object is often used for container administrators. The user assigned to the Organizational Role is called the *occupant* of the role.

Organizational Unit Object

The lowest level container object. Organizational Units can be used to divide locations, divisions, workgroups, or smaller portions of the Directory tree. Organizational Units can be subdivided further with additional Organizational Units.

OS Domain

One of the domains used to protect memory. See *Memory Protection*.

OS_PROTECTED (OSP) Domain

One of the domains used to protect memory. See *Memory Protection*.

Packet

The basic division of data sent over a network. Each packet contains a set amount of data along with a header, containing information about the type of packet and the network address it is being sent to. The size and format of packets depends on the *protocol* used.

Packet Burst Protocol

A streamlined protocol available in NetWare 4.1. In this protocol, several packets (a *burst*) are sent, and a single acknowledgment is sent back. If there is an error, only the packets that were not received correctly need to be resent. This protocol eliminates most of the *handshaking* process.

Packet Receive Buffers

Areas of memory that NetWare sets aside for receiving packets over the network. Packets are stored in the buffers until the server is able to process them.

Paging

A technique possible on the Pentium processor, and to a lesser extent on 386 and 486 processors, that allows memory to be handled in 4K blocks, or *pages*. NetWare 4.1 supports this feature for increased speed.

Parent Object

In NDS, an object that *contains* another object—a container object. This is a relative term; a parent object also has parent objects of its own and is considered a child object from that perspective.

Partition (Disk)

NetWare uses disk partitions to divide a hard disk. A disk typically contains a single NetWare partition, which is used to hold one or more NetWare volumes. In addition, a disk can have a DOS partition to boot the server and to hold the SERVER.EXE program.

Partition (NDS)

A branch of the NDS tree that can be replicated onto multiple servers. The partition includes a container object and the objects under it, and it is named according to the name of that object. By default, a single partition—the [Root] partition—exists.

Physical Port

In NetWare 4.1 printing, the port a printer is actually attached to. This differs from the *logical ports* used in the CAPTURE command for printer redirection.

Port Driver

A component of NetWare 4.1 printing. The port driver accepts data from the print server and sends it to the printer. The port driver can be NPRINTER.EXE on a workstation, NPRINTER.NLM on a server, or a hardware device.

Postmaster General

The user who has the rights to control MHS (Message Handling Services). This user is assigned when MHS is installed on a server; the default Postmaster General is ADMIN.

Primary Time Server

One of the four types of time servers. A primary server communicates with other primary servers and reference servers and negotiates, or "votes," to determine the correct time.

Print Job

A file that has been sent by a client for printing. Print jobs are stored in a *print queue* until they can be serviced by the print server.

Print Job Configuration

A set of parameters for network printing. These are similar to the parameters in the CAPTURE command. Print job configurations can be set for user and container objects.

Print Queue

The area used to hold the list of print jobs that are waiting to print. The print queue is managed through the Print Queue object in NDS. Print jobs are sent from the print queue to the print server one at a time.

Print Server

A device that is used to manage printing. The NDS Print Server object is used to manage printing. The print server itself can run on a NetWare 4.1 server (PSERVER.NLM) or in a hardware device. NetWare 3.1*x* includes PSERVER.EXE, which can run on a DOS workstation; NetWare 4.1 does not support PSERVER.EXE.

Printer Redirection

The process of mapping a logical printer port in the workstation to a network printer. The user can then print to the port as if it were an actual printer, and the print job will be sent to the print queue. The CAPTURE utility is used to start redirection.

Profile Object

A special NDS object that is used to assign the same login script to a group of users. The Profile login script is executed after the Container login script and before the User login script.

Properties

In NDS, all of the possible information that can be entered for an object. The properties of a User object include Login Name, Full Name, and Telephone Number. The information in a property is the *value* of the property.

Protocol

A method of communicating between NetWare servers and clients. The protocol is the "language" used for sending data. Data is divided into packets specified by the protocol. IPX is the typical protocol for NetWare networks.

[Public] Trustee

A special NDS trustee that can be used to assign rights to all users in the network, including those that are not logged in. This trustee is used to allow users to browse the Directory tree before logging in. You should avoid assigning rights to this trustee.

Reference Time Server

One of the four types of time servers. The reference server provides an authoritative source of time. It is often attached to an external clock, a modem, or a radio link to a time source. One or more primary time servers must be used.

Relative Distinguished Name (RDN)

A shortened version of an object's full distinguished name that specifies the path to the object from the current context. RDNs do not begin with a period. Periods can be used at the end of the RDN to move up the Directory tree.

Remote Printer

See *Workstation Printer.*

Replica Ring

A group of replicas that are synchronized. This includes a master replica and one or more other replicas.

Replication

The process of keeping copies of the NDS information on separate servers. Each *partition* in NDS has a set of replicas. These include the master replica—the original partition—and optional read/write and read-only replicas.

Ring

An alternate term used for the domains in NetWare 4.1's *memory protection* scheme. Ring 0 is the OS domain, and ring 3 is the OS_PROTECTED domain.

[Root] Object

The ultimate NDS container object. The [Root] object is created when NDS is installed, and this object contains all other objects. [Root] cannot be deleted, renamed, or moved.

Router

See *Internetworking.*

Scalability

A feature of NetWare 4.1 services, including NPA (NetWare Peripheral Architecture) and the DOS Requester. This means that features can be used as they are needed, providing benefits for both small-scale and large-scale systems.

Secondary Time Server

One of the four types of time servers. Secondary time servers are strictly time consumers; they do not provide time to any servers. They receive time from a primary or single reference server and provide the time to clients.

Security Equivalence

In NDS, any situation where an object, or *trustee*, receives the same rights given to another object. There are two types of security equivalence: *implied* and *explicit*.

Server-Centric

The type of network organization used on NetWare 3.1*x* networks. In this organization, each server keeps its own catalog of users and other resources (the *bindery*). A user who requires access to more than one server must be added to the bindery of each one. NetWare 4.1 provides a *network-centric* alternative.

Server Printer

A common method of attaching a printer to the network. The printer is attached to a printer port on the NetWare server. The port driver, NPRINTER.NLM, is used to drive the printer.

Service Advertising Protocol (SAP)

The protocol used for various NetWare 4.1 services. Single reference time servers use this protocol to broadcast time information to the entire network at once.

Simple Installation

One of the two options in the NetWare 4.1 installation. The Simple installation assumes default answers to installation questions. To specify information for all of the questions, use the Custom installation option.

Single Reference Time Server

One of the four types of time servers. If it's used, the single reference server is the only time provider on the network. All other servers must be configured as secondary time servers. This is the default configuration when NetWare 4.1 servers are installed.

Splitting Partitions

The process of creating a new partition. A container object within a current partition is specified, and that object and all objects under it are moved (split) to a new partition.

Standards Document

A document that describes the naming standards, properties, and values to be used for a network. A standards document is a vital part of NDS planning.

Storage Management Services (SMS)

The NetWare 4.1 service that allows for backup services. SMS consists of several components, ranging from the device driver that handles access to the backup device to the front end, or *backup engine*.

Synchronization

The process used by NDS to ensure that all replicas of a partition contain the same data. Synchronization is handled through *replica rings*.

Target Service Agent (TSA)

One of the components of the NetWare 4.1 Storage Management System (SMS). The TSA provides an interface to the device that will be backed up. Devices include servers, workstations, and the NDS database. A separate TSA is used for each one.

Time Consumer

A machine that receives time information but does not send time information to any other server. Secondary time servers are time consumers, as are network workstations.

Time Provider

A type of time server that provides the time to other time servers. These include single reference, reference, and primary time servers.

Time Provider Group

A group of time servers, usually including a reference server and one or more primary servers. In a wide-area network (WAN), separate time provider groups can be used for each location.

Time Server

A server that is used for time synchronization. All NetWare 4.1 servers are time servers of one type or another. The types of time servers include primary, reference, single reference, and secondary.

Time Source

See *Time Provider.*

Time Synchronization

The process by which NetWare 4.1 ensures that all servers are provided with the correct time. Time synchronization is managed through *time servers.*

Trustee

Any object that has been given rights to an NDS object or file. Trustee rights can include explicit, inherited, and effective rights.

Turbo FAT Indexing

A NetWare 4.1 service that increases disk access for large files by keeping an index, or turbo FAT (file allocation table), of the disk blocks in use by the file. NetWare uses this system automatically for larger files.

Typeful Naming

The formal method of naming NDS objects, including name types for each portion of the name. For example, .CN=Terry.OU=Mktg.O=QAZ_CO.

Typeless Naming

The more common method of NDS object naming, which does not include name types. For example, .Terry.Mktg.QAZ.CO. Typeless naming is adequate for most uses within NDS utilities.

Universal Coordinated Time (UTC)

The standard time system supported by NetWare 4.1. The abbreviation is from the French. UTC was formerly known as GMT (Greenwich Mean Time). The time zone for a NetWare server is defined in terms of difference from UTC; for example, the Mountain time zone is UTC plus seven hours.

User Template

In NDS, a special User object that assigns defaults when a new user is created. A user template can be created for each NDS container, and you can change the property values of this object to provide defaults for new users in the container. The user template does not affect existing users.

Values

The data that is stored in the *properties* of an NDS object. Properties can have one or more values. Some are required, and others are optional.

VINES (Virtual Networking System)

A network system developed by Banyan Corporation. VINES includes StreetTalk, a Directory Service similar to NDS. VINES is intended for enterprise networks.

Virtual Loadable Module (VLM)

One of the components of the *DOS Requester*. The VLM.EXE program loads various VLMs, each for a certain purpose. For example, PRINT.VLM allows redirection of printers. VLMs that are not needed can be unloaded to increase available memory.

Wide-Area Network (WAN)

A network that extends across multiple locations. Each location typically has a local-area network (LAN), and the LANs are connected together in a WAN. WANs can be used for *enterprise networking*.

Workgroup Organization

One of the methods of organizing the NDS tree. In this method, users who perform similar functions or are participating in the same project—workgroups—are used to divide the Directory tree. This method is best used in a hybrid, or combined, organization.

Workstation Printer

A printer that is attached to a workstation on the network. NetWare 3.1*x* referred to these printers as *remote printers* and controlled them with the RPRINTER.EXE program. In NetWare 4.1, the NPRINTER.EXE program handles workstation printers.

Index

Micro House Technical Library, Novell Education Sampler, and Complete 801 Self Test

To install the Micro House Technical Library demo, the Micro House Technical Library Encyclopedia of I/O Cards, the Novell Education Certification Sampler, and the Complete 801 Self Test, run INSTALL.EXE, which you'll find in the root directory of the CD-ROM. You can do this in several ways:

- Display the Run dialog box (in Windows 95, choose Start ➤ Run; in Windows 3.1*x*, choose File ➤ Run from Program Manager). Enter *cd_drive*:**install**, where *cd_drive* is the drive letter assigned to your CD-ROM drive (for example, d:install or e:install), and choose OK.

- In Windows 95, open an Explorer or My Computer window for your CD-ROM drive and double-click on INSTALL.EXE.

- In Windows 3.1*x* File Manager, display the contents of your CD-ROM drive and double-click on INSTALL.EXE.

In the first MTL Book Bundle dialog box, choose the Next button to continue with the installation.

In the second MTL Book Bundle dialog box, choose between Express Setup and Full Setup, then choose the Next button.

- Express Setup installs the programs so that they run from the CD-ROM as much as possible. This option takes up less than 1 MB of disk space on your hard drive, but the programs will run more slowly than with Full Setup.

- Full Setup copies the database files to a hard drive, which makes searching much faster. This takes 24 MB of disk space.

In the third MTL Book Bundle dialog box, you'll see a summary of the installation you're about to perform. If this looks okay, choose the Next button; otherwise, choose the Back button to return to the previous dialog box.

In the fourth MTL Book Bundle dialog box, choose options for how the dialog boxes should appear on screen, then choose the Next button. The Install program will install the programs with the options you chose and (for Windows 3.1*x*) will create a program group and icons for the programs:

- Certification Sampler
- Complete 801 Self Test
- MTL Help
- MTL
- MTL Demo
- MTL Setup

For Windows 95, the Install program will create a Start menu listing for the programs.